GRESLEY AND HIS LOCOMOTIVES

In memory of my late uncle, Ronald Hillier, who made this book possible. (The author and his uncle in 1957 when, in between learning the finer points of cricket and a trip to the Oval, we visited King's Cross many times to marvel at and photograph Gresley's Pacifics.)

CONTENTS

	Acknowledgements	6
	Prologue	7
Chapter 1	No One Man	13
Chapter 2	Time, Place, Influences and Opportunities (1876–1911)	34
Chapter 3	Gresley's New World (1912–22)	69
Chapter 4	A Time of Politics and An Age of Science (1922–28)	99
Chapter 5	A Necessary Distraction (1929–31)	144
Chapter 6	A Master at Work (1932–34)	168
Chapter 7	Speed, Competition, Art Deco, Aerodynamics and the Science of Publicity (1935)	197
Chapter 8	Fete and Fated (1936–41)	230
	Epilogue	275
	Sources	289
	Photo Credits	291
	Index	292

ACKNOWLEDGEMENTS

My late uncle, Ronald Hillier, made this book possible. His research over nearly three decades proved crucial. He marshalled information from many sources – publications, eye-witness accounts, personal observations, photographs, documents and much more – and from this produced an outline history for me to follow. So to him must go great credit, but more than this, he imbued me with an interest in Britain's railway history and a desire to finish the work he began in 1946. Judging by his scrapbooks and photograph albums, he was also a witness to many significant events at King's Cross; the launch of the first P2 and then *Silver Link's* press run in September 1934 amongst them. Such a personal connection is deeply affecting and it is one for which I will always be grateful.

In Britain, we are lucky to have many institutions that meticulously preserve material for all to see and research. Much was destroyed by BR in the 1960s, when steam locomotives were being scrapped en masse. More by luck than judgement, a great deal was saved by concerned individuals and now exists in public and private collections. There are significant gaps and where these exist, many people have committed time and energy to seek out information and publish the results of their work wherever possible. By this diverse means an important part of our social and engineering history has been preserved to illuminate our understanding of the past.

In writing this book, I drew heavily on many of these sources. First and foremost, there is Search Engine at the National Railway Museum and 'Discovery' at the National Archives. The staff who manage these collections do so with great skill and always proved friendly and co-operative when answering my many questions, despite their busy schedules. The same can be said of library staff at the Institution of Mechanical Engineers HQ in London. To all of them, I say a big thank you.

Through my uncle's work, I was privileged to have access to a number of personal archives. These people clearly gave freely of their time and allowed him to copy items they held. Foremost amongst them are Bert Spencer and his wife Elsie; Oliver Bulleid and his son Henry; Frederick Johansen; Ernest Cox; O.S. Nock; Alfred Ewer; Tom Coleman and Robert Riddles. But there were many more.

A number of official documents are cited in this book. My thanks to the NRM and NA for permission to include this material. I have also quoted sections from various publications and where appropriate permission to do so was given by the authors, their descendants or the publishers.

It was my uncle's wish that the material he collected should eventually find its way to the NRM. Some has already done so, and the rest will follow in due course, so that future generations can make use of these items.

PROLOGUE

Having been commissioned by Pen and Sword to write a trilogy of books about the LNER I visited King's Cross to view Gresley's statue. It is a fine piece of work, the 'missing' duck notwithstanding, and provokes many thoughts about the nature of the man and his achievements. My father, who was a Design Engineer, always spoke of the many multi-million pound projects he led with great passion and instilled in me a profound respect for the leaders in his field, but he always said that no one man could have succeeded in such a complex field without a good team around them.

When looking at Gresley's statue his words came back to me. The leader takes responsibility for all that happens on their watch and copes with the many stresses and strains that come with these heavy obligations, but how much do they actually contribute to the creative process for which they are ultimately given credit? Amongst the seemingly faceless team around them there must be those who contributed the ideas, both large

Two of Gresley's A1 Class locomotives ready for duty. 2544, *Lemberg* is at the front. In 1927, this three-year-old engine was rebuilt as an A3. The number of the second engine is unclear, but a note attached to the negative suggests it is No. 4480, *Enterprise*, which became an A3 four months before 2544.

and small, that made each project a success. In truth, any statue commemorates the leader, but not the realities of the achievement. All well and good, but with the passing of time, these symbols become the only way later generations see history, and the complexities of great endeavour become camouflaged by simple explanations or titles. Clearly, those such as Gresley, Stanier and Churchward led teams containing people of immense talent and creativity, who rarely if ever received credit for their achievements.

As Ernest Cox, a noted design engineer himself, wrote:

'To such men as Gresley, Maunsell, Stanier, George Ivatt and Riddles, the historian must rightly accord the direction and authority, which made this work possible. To the lesser names of Tom Coleman, Bert Spencer, James Clayton and Sam Ell, among the unsung heroes, goes the credit for the original thought and application which assured its success.'

Behind Gresley, there were many clever individuals all happy to work for the collective good, some of whom now sit as unannounced ghosts around their leader's statue. Three of them, Thompson and Peppercorn and Oliver Bulleid, became CMEs themselves and are remembered for that reason, though none of them equalled their late leader's achievements. Others, such as Robert Thom, Bert Spencer, Arthur Stamer and Tom Street remain shadowy figures, with little acknowledgement of their immense contributions to the LNER legend.

Luck plays a part in all lives. To be present at a particular moment in time and be equipped with an open mind and the right skills to exploit possibilities, can make a huge difference to our progress as human beings. It is the same when researching the history of a person or an event. I was very lucky to inherit my uncle's collection, but over the years, chance, and auctions, gave me the opportunity to acquire other items to help complete this picture. An antique shop in Bedale, North Yorkshire, produced Robert Thom's personal journal in which he recorded all the locomotives he had worked on before joining the LNER. Then, by chance, three more volumes appeared on eBay, from sellers in Yorkshire, taking his career up to the late 1930s, when he retired. How these books and albums survived is a mystery. Thom died in 1955 and they may have passed on to descendants who themselves then passed away. I shall never know, but their value to this book is immense.

Gresley's B17 No. 2805 about to be re-named the *Lincolnshire Regiment* at Lincoln in 1938. When built in 1928, she was called *Burnham Thorpe*. The engine was condemned in 1958.

Then there were the papers – loco record cards, reports and general correspondence – that were salvaged in the 1960s by concerned individuals observing its wanton destruction by BR. Much of this was presented to public archives, but a lot remained in private hands and, in the last decade or two, some of this has found its way to auction houses for sale to the historian or the collector.

Amongst these appeared a substantial collection of papers describing all aspects of life at the LNER sheds at Immingham from the 1920s to the end of steam. These had been saved by a retired engine driver shortly before it was due to be destroyed. His death in Grimsby a few years ago, led to a house clearance and his family releasing all these items to auctioneers for sale. In due course, I purchased a great deal of this unique collection and found that if stacked vertically it would have reached 8 or 9 feet in height; though this isn't a suitable way of describing items of historic importance. Once sorted and preserved, the collection was donated to the National Railway Museum (NRM), where others may now make use of it through Search Engine, and so, in this random way, more gaps in history are filled but one wonders how much more there may still be lurking in attics and boxes to take these stories still further?

Perhaps of greater significance to this story are the largely unpublished cache of papers collected by Bert Spencer. He became Gresley's technical assistant in the 1920s and was in the enviable position of working by his side during the most dynamic period of his career and experienced all the key events with him. Then, when his chief died suddenly in 1941, he was able to observe his successors from close quarters as well. Once they had gone, he worked for many years with the Eastern Region of British Rail and witnessed all the locomotives he had help create reach the end of their operational lives.

His papers were found in many locations, both private and public, and many do not seem to have aroused the interest of other researchers or were simply not available to them. When reading these documents, and his correspondence from his home in Devon, it soon became apparent that he was a man steeped in all elements of engineering and possessed a keen and agile mind. He also had the ability to observe, analyse and produce effective and sometimes novel ideas and solutions himself. He also knew and greatly respected Herbert Nigel Gresley as a man and engineer and sought to emulate all he did in his own life. There are even traces of hero-worship in his words, such was his depth of feeling for the CME but at no stage did he seek the limelight or try to minimize

P2, *Cock o' the North*, is launched at King's Cross on 1 June 1934.

Gresley's achievements in any way, in an effort to play up his own role as some may have done. He also supported and observed Thompson, Peppercorn and his new BR masters in the same way.

Modesty, privacy, hard work and loyalty seem to have been the guiding principles of his life and so, the memories he recorded are of the most valuable kind. He doesn't criticise or denigrate and there is no sense of self-importance or self-promotion but there is a most profound understanding of events, people and the engineering possibilities those days contained.

So these books are principally about Gresley's achievements as a locomotive engineer and leader, but with an appreciation of the men he commanded with great skill and understanding and of those who succeeded him. He was a generous and perceptive man, like Spencer, and I am sure he would have wished that his dedicated team could have shared in the honour he so richly deserved. They'll have no statues on main line stations or be feted by a history which has always been polarised by single names defining major events or achievements, but that is often the fate of team members.

The CME's premature death in 1941 opened the door for Edward Thompson and then Arthur Peppercorn to push their and his ideas forward, but whatever they did, their achievements would always be measured against Gresley's. One wonders, if granted a few more years, where his fertile imagination and drive might have taken the LNER and then BR. It was a question Bert Spencer contemplated when asked in 1947 to present a paper to the Institution of Locomotive Engineers on the eve of nationalisation. Having been Gresley's close associate for many years and a designer of great merit himself, he was thought best placed to review the work of his late CME from 1923 to 1941. He was greatly encouraged in this by Peppercorn, recently appointed CME in succession to Thompson. In some preliminary notes Spencer wrote:

'This was a very important period in which Gresley was given free rein to test and evaluate many ideas. Some of these were simply experiments with the aim of extracting the last few ounces of performance from steam locomotives, but others looked more broadly at other forms of tractive power. The war curtailed much of this activity, but he, even when very ill and increasingly confused, saw this

Although the railway companies were often in competition with each other the world of locomotive engineers allowed many close bonds to exist that overrode commercial considerations. They were in many ways a 'Band of Brothers' where greater openness and sharing of ideas was possible. Crewe Works had, over the years, become a rallying point for many young apprentices who went on to great things and it was a link they valued greatly. Periodically this connection would be celebrated by formal dinners and reunions. In the 1920, and '30s they met regularly and this photograph was taken on one of these occasions. Here we have, in the front row left to right, Richard Maunsell, the Southern Railway's (SR) CME and Hewitt Beames, who rose to become the London and North Western Railway's (LNWR) CME and just missed out on becoming the LMS's CME. Monsieur Lacoin, CME of the Paris-Orleans Railway, is the next in line and, finally, we have Gresley, then at the height of his powers.

Night time seemed to capture the allure of steam best. Here A4 4496, *'Golden Shuttle* (to be renamed *Dwight D. Eisenhower* in 1945) is caught in the flash of an anonymous photographer's camera as it thunders through an anonymous station

as a temporary matter and used the pause to think more deeply about the future. To him steam was not the be all and end all of locomotive development and he foresaw its demise.'

And towards the end of his life he added:

'I think Gresley would have been a far better man to have shaped BR when it was formed in 1948 if blessed with good health. Although in his early 70s by then he would have grasped the need to develop electric and diesel alternatives and not simply have built more and more steam locomotives as Riddles did. He was a practical man and a pragmatist who took change in his stride and would have fought for more efficient and effective solutions.'

We shall never know if Britain's railways would have been better served by a man of his undoubted skill and vision once the war was over. For most of his life, steam was the only practical option – coal was cheap and plentiful and fuelled the economy let alone locomotives, but he doesn't seem to have been

4469, 'Gadwall', at rest and barely attracting a passing glance. This engine was re-named 'Sir Ralph Wedgwood' in June 1939 and was destroyed during a bombing raid on York in April 1942.

Gresley in his prime.

wedded to this ageing technology, as his seminal work on electric alternatives would prove.

Oliver Bulleid probably best described his late CME's accomplishments when he wrote in 1945:

'He was more than the Locomotive Engineer of one company. His constant search for improvements, his awareness of developments in all locomotive engineering, and his interest in all advances in engineering practice in fields, however remotely related to railway work, were reflected in the adaption to his locomotives of the work of other engineers.'

And in 1967 he added a supplementary note:

'The locomotives were the major part of his work, but one tends to forget the giant strides he made in carriage design as well and the particular interest he took in this aspect of railway life. He foresaw by many years the way customers, in a growing economy, would demand better facilities. He saw more than the locomotives; he saw the entire train.'

Gresley was in many ways a polymath who thought broadly and anticipated change in a railway world populated by many who were hidebound traditionalists. So it is important to remember his life and work, but also the many individuals without whom he would have struggled to meet very challenging goals.

Chapter 1
NO ONE MAN

In 1945, Paul S. Baker, a leading scientist and test pilot with Vought-Sikorsky, was asked to identify who in the company was most responsible for the creation of a particular aircraft. Without a pause he replied, 'the day of one-man engineering of major projects is long gone. You might as well print the organisation table of the engineering department.' This very talented man was a leader of unparalleled skill and one who understood the complexities of design in the modern age and believed wholeheartedly in the dynamics and democracy of team working. He was speaking at a time now long distant, when steam locomotives still dominated the world's railways and not 20 or 30 years later when science had taken a quantum leap forward and space travel and supersonic flight were commonplace. He was describing a scientific and management ideal that many engineers in the first part of the twentieth century had come to recognise and those in the new millennia would do so too.

The drama captured so well by Leslie Howard in his film *First of the Few*, of R.J. Mitchell struggling by himself to develop the Spitfire, though moving, was a poor perception of design reality. One person might lead, but it took a unified team of specialists to truly develop and advance ideas to the point of delivery in any chosen field. This was nowhere more apparent than in the railway world, where steam locomotives, though not their successors for some reason, still received the misnomer

On 26 November 1937 engine No. 4498, the 100th Pacific built by the LNER, was named after the company's talented CME. For the occasion a number of Gresley's team, past and present, gathered together to witness the event and pose for this extremely rare photograph. Left to right – W. Massey, formerly Chief Clerk to the CME, H. Harper, the Chief Clerk, B. Spencer, Chief Technical Assistant to the CME, G. Musgrave, Loco Running Shed Supt, Scotland, W. Brown, Carriage Works Manager, York, A. Stamer, formerly Mechanical Engineer Darlington and Assistant CME, D.R. Edge, Personal Assistant to the CME, A.H. Peppercorn, Locomotive Running Supt, Southern Area, F. Wintour, formerly Works Manager Doncaster, Sir Nigel Gresley, R. Thom, formerly Mechanical Engineer, Doncaster, O.V.S. Bulleid, CME Southern Railway, H. Broughton, formerly Chief Draughtsman, F. Eggleshaw, the Works Manager at Doncaster, E. Thompson, Mechanical Engineer, Darlington, T. Street, Chief Draughtsman.

of a leader's name – Churchward's Stars, Stanier's Coronations, Bulleid's Pacifics, Gresley's A4s and more. Sadly, this still holds good today in our view of history, as though we can only appreciate effort and skill, or even assign blame or guilt, if ascribed to just one person, no matter how involved that person might have been or not.

To truly understand the nature of invention and leadership, we have to look much deeper than the appellation of a leader's name and dissect all the elements that come together to achieve success in any field let alone engineering. At the top of any list must be an effective design philosophy, where understanding the need and possibilities and then translating a broad specification into an advanced product exists. But the range of skills has to be much more varied than this if success is to be achieved. Good leadership, a variety of up to date scientific and engineering skills, a strong sense of the economics of big business, effective day to day management of all aspects of any project and a clear understanding of how a myriad number of demands fit together are all essential. A safety first principle has to be applied, because loss has to be avoided and shareholders have to be appeased, but gambling on an emerging technology and developing new ideas can often achieve a higher return in the long term. So the ability to take calculated risks becomes an essential part of good business philosophy too and quizzical, educated minds will always seek to push back boundaries anyway, not simply regurgitate old ideas as though they are stamped with the embargo of an unchanging religion.

Gresley was aware of all this and much more and seems to have wholeheartedly adopted the business mantra 'on time, on cost and always adding value' as a

A scene typical of Gresley's first years as Locomotive Engineer then CME of the Great Northern Railway (GNR). A small boilered Ivatt Atlantic with a mixed rake of coaches defining the company's gradual evolution in his hands.

matter of course but he contributed much more than this and always sought to stretch what was possible within the limits imposed by good business principles and practice. In addition, he learnt how to manage constraint and expectations with a master's touch, leading and being supported by many talented people of equally sound judgement and skills along the way.

Leading any business is a juggling act that seeks to balance many factors, but some of these are less obvious than others and here Gresley also proved his worth. Politics, both positive and negative, will inevitably come into play as different, sometimes conflicting views are expressed or driven home with some venom. The chairman may seek a traditional solution with quick returns, but little long-term potential. Politicians, as they often do, may try to inflict their creed on any business, especially one as large as the railways, but underlying these interventions, whether good or bad, lies the sentiment contained in the 1950s aphorism that 'a horse designed by a committee is a camel'. Therein lies a significant danger that has to be managed if true and lasting progress is to be achieved. Gresley seems to have been a master of this balancing act, working through direct persuasion and argument or by marshalling his many contacts, to achieve success.

His rise to pre-eminence coincided with many significant changes in society taking place. Personal expectation and improved employment rights were beginning their inexorable rise, ensuring that disputes were becoming more commonplace if improvements weren't

The twentieth century heralded improved rights for workers but with labour cheap and plentiful, the railways didn't need to automate such things as carriage cleaning to get the work done. Most tasks, for men and women, consisted of hard graft in the open air with few comforts.

Life in the GNR/LNER's unheated workshops was little better.

The growing power of PR and advertising.

docile society yet to find its full voice of protest. In the background lay the gradual spread of reforms to industry, with much tighter controls on working practices and conditions being slowly applied. The spreading influence of the press, increasing newspaper circulation and higher rates of literacy played an essential part in this process, offering, as it did, a forum for sublimating and encouraging change. But it was more than this. Wider circulation and a growing readership meant that businesses, but particularly the railways, also had the opportunity to exploit this medium with carefully placed news items and adverts. This set in motion the concept of Public Relations and publicity departments and the world of propaganda and spin we see everywhere today.

All in all, there was much to consider when Gresley reached the pinnacle of his profession. His primary responsibility was for the design, development and maintenance of all locomotives and rolling stock, but there was much more to manage. These included a mass of machinery supporting many other functions, such as docks, workshops, gas, electricity and water supplies and more. He also bore responsibility for the huge number of people working in these departments. 'Pay and rations', as it was called, could be a daunting task for even the most astute and often provided an unwanted distraction when other requirements became more pressing. He also took on an active apprenticeship programme, retaining the right to tutor a small number of young men who, like himself, had chosen,

forthcoming. These were issues that his predecessors didn't have to manage to any great extent, with deeply rooted, well established patterns of subservience ensuring unquestioning compliance in a

and had the funds, to become premium apprentices.

When trying to establish who supported Gresley during his 30 years as Locomotive Engineer, and later as CME, the historian faces one significant problem. His life has been described in some detail, though not necessarily his way of working, but the people and structures beneath him have avoided the writer's gaze almost entirely and, in most cases, these men and women didn't feel moved to record their memories in books or letters either. This leaves only the dryness of official documents to suggest what they may have thought or felt and led to some conjecture by writers not party to the events themselves. So it is little wonder that individual leaders such as Churchward, Gresley and Stanier have been feted as though existing in an unaccompanied bubble. Nevertheless, some accounts and information have surfaced to take the story a little deeper and reveal a wider picture of those who led and those who served.

When Gresley was appointed Locomotive Engineer within the GNR in 1911 – a post later to be re-titled Chief Mechanical Engineer – Francis Wintour was Works Manager at Doncaster. Under Ivatt, he had been successful in this post and might have expected to be considered for the top job, but this wasn't to be and though described by Bert Spencer, Gresley's trusted assistant, as a 'very skilful engineer, but a forthright and strong individual who tended to call a spade a spade', he served the CME very effectively until his retirement in 1927. His knowledge of locomotive design and construction methods appears to have been good and his influence on the N1 and N2

Romantic images of rail travel were a far cry from the hard reality of the life of many workers on the railway, particularly the footplate crew and those in the workshops.

Mr. F. Wintour,

designs has long been suggested. However, his pivotal role as Works Manager, and the heavy demands this placed upon him, precluded greater involvement in design work. Nevertheless, he had a degree of oversight of this work through the drawing office that sat beside him at Doncaster. In time, he would be appointed Assistant Mechanical Engineer, such was the faith Gresley placed in him.

The Chief Draughtsman's post is a key position in any engineering organisation and today would attract a title more fitting of its central role and function; which is to turn a broad specification into an effective, possibly cutting-edge, product that will last for a considerable time. Tom Coleman, the LMS's talented CD, later referred to these posts as Chief Designers, and this seems a far more accurate description of the work they and their teams did. There are four men who can be identified as being CDs at different times during Gresley's reign.

The first of these was William Elwess, who was born near Doncaster Works in 1867, where he appears to have served his apprenticeship before becoming a fitter. A move to the drawing office followed and he rose to become CD, relinquishing the post, possibly on retirement, in 1927, being replaced by Sydney 'Harry' Broughton, a school master's son born at Monks Coppenhall in Cheshire on 23 April 1870. He chose to become an apprentice under Francis Webb at Crewe in the late 1880s and became a fitter when qualified. Being a near contemporary of Gresley on the LNWR may have influenced the CME in selecting Broughton to be CD. Broughton remained in post until 1935 and was superseded by Tom Street, who hailed from Lancaster and served his apprenticeship at Horwich, where he emerged as a millwright before training to become a draughtsman. He moved to Doncaster in 1911, when he was 28. During his career with the GNR and then the LNER, he served Gresley in a variety of posts before being appointed CD in early 1935, where he remained until the CME's death in 1941. He was followed by Edward Windle, Street's principal assistant, who would stay with the LNER until 1948, when it passed into the 'ownership' of British Rail as nationalisation took effect.

Windle was born during 1893 in Doncaster; his father, John, a railway clerk, died in the West Yorkshire Asylum in March 1903, leaving a widow, a daughter and three sons. In straitened circumstances, employment became essential for the boys and each joined the GNR Works at Doncaster when their time came. In the 1911 Census, Edward is listed as being a fitter's apprentice and, according to Spencer, 'quickly showed his worth, caught Gresley's eye and made rapid progress, becoming essential to the CME in the process'.

A key need of any senior manager is to have an 'outer office' populated by people with the skill to guard their leader, not simply be secretarial in nature. To ensure this happens, there is a need to interrogate those seeking access and filter the amount of information reaching the person in charge and providing detailed briefs where necessary. If this didn't happen, that person would be plagued by all manner of distractions, become swamped by work they didn't necessarily need to see, with time to manage their key duties becoming seriously disrupted. It was a difficult role to undertake at times, especially when the leader was someone with the skills and status of Gresley, who seems to have preferred a hands on, even autocratic style of management at times. But the world was changing rapidly and with it came many more pressures than his Victorian counterparts could ever have countenanced.

Today, accountability for one's actions, on many levels, has become commonplace and in the early years of the twentieth century, this process was in its infancy. Even so, Gresley was too strong a character to be corralled and he displayed a penchant for personal intervention where he thought necessary. In the few files that remain, there are many examples that show him writing memos or minutes on all manner of subjects to his staff in each department. Some of these are important but many are not, and quite often he personally directed junior staff to produce an item of work for him, seemingly without their seniors being aware of what was happening. Although this technique may seem to undermine the authority of middle managers, it did have some benefits. It allowed him to check progress being made by up and coming engineers, to gauge their readiness for promotion. In addition, it had the dual benefit of reminding his managers that he was on the ball, prepared to intervene if he thought performance was slipping in some way.

In Gresley's case the 'outer office' had another function. With technical assistants numbered amongst his personal staff, he could use them as sounding boards to discuss new proposals and produce outline drawings. They could also be his eyes and ears around the organisation and progress chase particular tasks on his behalf. No leader can be omnipresent and by this method, his influence could be assured. In this role, he was lucky enough to have two very gifted engineers – Oliver Bulleid in 1912 and Bert Spencer from the early 1920s – and each served him in different, but sometimes complementary ways.

Bulleid, born in 1882 in New Zealand to British émigré parents, returned to Britain following the death of his father in 1889. From an early age, engineering and science had fascinated him and he attended Accrington's Municipal Technical School for four years before becoming an apprentice under Ivatt at Doncaster in January 1901. But he became more than a pupil and would in time marry Ivatt's youngest daughter, Marjorie. Whilst an apprentice, he attended local evening classes and then followed more advanced courses at Sheffield and Leeds Universities. It was a practice he continued, eventually recording in his application to join the Institution of Mechanical Engineers in 1910, 'achieved matric at London University'. Clearly imbued with great ambition and talent, he quickly rose through the ranks. In 1906, he was appointed to be Assistant to F. Webster, the Loco Running Superintendent at Doncaster, and took charge of 'experiments with petrol motor driven coaches'. This was quickly followed by Assistant to the Works Manager (Wintour) where he managed 'Shop Costs'.

As time passed, he decided to broaden his horizons and seek work beyond the confines of the GNR and took a post in Paris with the French Westinghouse Company as a test engineer. This was quickly followed, in 1910, by a period as Mechanical Engineer for exhibitions with the Board of Trade in London. However, this job came to a premature end

Oliver Bulleid and his soon to be wife, Henry Ivatt's youngest daughter Marjorie, in 1908.

Oliver Bulleid with his parents-in-law and two of his children in 1920.

Bert Spencer in the 1940s.

imagination second to none, but it came at a cost as E.S. Cox described in his book *Locomotive Panorama*:

> 'An individualist of the deepest dye, he had no sympathy at all with the painstaking improvement of the breed, but wished with brilliant and dramatic improvisations to solve the remaining problems of steam by quite other means. To him novelty was everything. If it would not work then this could not be the fault of the idea itself, but only of the incapacity of those who tried to carry out or use it. The cross he had to bear was that his developments with conventional practice were successful, sometimes brilliant, whereas his exercises in the bizarre often failed.'

Bert Spencer was a man of a very different hue and, arguably, a more accomplished design engineer than Bulleid or Gresley, but with neither the dynamism or driving ambition the other two shared. He was born on 6 May 1898 at 148 Catherine Street, Doncaster, the fifth child and fourth son of Abel Spencer, a 'journeyman' cabinet maker who became a carriage fitter with the GNR. Bert's mother Frances was Abel's second wife, the first having died many years earlier. He proved to be a gifted child and successfully passed through Doncaster's Grammar School, then the Mechanical Engineering faculty of the town's Technical College before beginning an apprentice at the railway works in July 1914. He seems to have been an exemplary student who gained a number of awards and certificates. In his 1918

a year later and he had to find alternative employment quickly, especially with the responsibility for a wife and child hanging over his head. One wonders if it was impetuosity that led him down this path, or a genuine attempt to build a career away from the railways. If so, the GNR would prove to be his salvation. His father-in-law, whether as an act of nepotism or through the desire to recruit someone with outstanding abilities, was instrumental in re-employing him at Doncaster before he retired. In early 1912, Bulleid was appointed Personal Assistant to the newly promoted Gresley. As the years unfolded, the younger man displayed a dynamism and

application for membership of the Institution of Mechanical Engineers, he listed his placements whilst under training and his pursuit of a higher education qualification: 'Course comprising 8 months in Elec. Car Repair Shops, 8 months Loco Shed, 8 months power station, finish at Horwich Works. Hope to obtain Engineering Degree at Liverpool.'

Undoubtedly, he was a gifted student and one who shone throughout his time at school and during his apprenticeship. Whilst at Doncaster, he came to the notice of Gresley, John Ralph Bazin, the Assistant Works Manager at Doncaster, and Bulleid. With their backing, he spent the last year of his training at Horwich in the drawing office. Whilst there, he came under the direct control of the Lancashire & Yorkshire Railway's (L&YR) talented Chief Draughtsman, John Billington, with George Hughes as CME having oversight of what he did. There is some evidence to suggest that he became involved in the design work on 0-8-0 tender engines and a single battery powered electric locomotive whilst at Horwich.

Bazin seems to have played a central role in Spencer's career, before transferring to the Great Southern & Western Railway (GS&WR) as Works Manager in 1919 and then CME at Inchinore two years later but it was Gresley, in the post-war rush to restore the GNR to peacetime running conditions, who was instrumental in developing this talented young man still further. In 1919, he was posted to the GNR's drawing office where he remained for several years. During this period, he was given the occasional 'special project by the CME', as he later called them. It seems that these might have been linked to his continuing work for an engineering degree, but it also helped cement a growing relationship between the two men. Having been nurtured by Aspinall and Ivatt, Gresley was keenly aware of the need to bring on the next generation of engineers and leaders and saw in Spencer someone to be encouraged. Gradually, as his experience and knowledge increased, he worked ever more closely with the CME, becoming a Technical Assistant alongside Bulleid in the early 1920s when Gresley was relocated from Doncaster to the LNER's HQ at King's Cross. Here he would remain serving Gresley until the CME's death in 1941, at all times providing wise counsel and content to play a supporting role.

Very late in his life, Spencer recalled the period when he and Bulleid acted as Gresley's scouts and advisors and touched on the way ideas were developed by the CME:

'Gresley and Bulleid were like chalk and cheese. Each of them was very skilled in their own way, but without the CME's careful handling his assistant could have wasted much time on work that probably wouldn't have led anywhere. His was a lively mind and was always engaged by some new idea, many of which served us well, but Gresley often had to rein him in before he became too distracted by an idea which was likely to lead to a dead end. There were disagreements and lively discussions, as you would expect from two such forceful men who held many strong opinions and could produce fresh ideas with little apparent effort. I think Gresley used me as a foil or filter to keep Bulleid's ideas in check and found that keeping him busy greatly reduced his ability to stray.

'Gresley was not an accomplished draughtsman, but would develop ideas based on his wide knowledge of engineering, then sketch them out very roughly. These he passed to me to produce slightly more detailed drawings and a brief for the Chief Draughtsman and his team to consider. This became a much more regular process when we began developing the W1, the P2 Mikado and then the streamliners. I kept many of his sketches and remember well him calling to me in his slightly gruff way, 'Spencer, here's something I want you to look at, get me out some drawings will you!' and then being handed several sheets of paper, some lined, covered with rough sketches. A few days later we would pore over these plans and gradually his ideas would take shape at which point he would call in the Chief Draughtsman and Bulleid to get their point of view. More often than not he wouldn't give them any forewarning of what he would lay before them, believing that first reactions were always more revealing.'

It was an interesting technique, because even the ablest managers will resort to sycophancy when

One of the Institution of Locomotive Engineer's formal dinners at the Trocadero in London, attended by both Gresley (near the centre of the main table in the background) and Spencer.

faced with the thoughts and demands of a strong leader. Better to observe first impressions and see these as truer reactions to his ideas than wait until a diplomatic gloss had been given to any response. Gresley was an astute man and allowed his team to use their skills and continue developing an idea until all seemed satisfied with the result. But as Spencer again recalled, 'the CME had the last word and made the final decision having gathered these opinions.'

Another area of work Spencer described concerned Gresley's ideas on staff development:

'He believed that learning didn't have a limit and should be pursued as a matter of course through education and the study of other people's work in many fields of research. We were encouraged to join relevant bodies such as the IMechE and ILocoE, participate in their work and keep up to date by reading their journals as well as the *Engineer*, *Gazette* and other magazines, but also follow the course of various patents, files of which we retained many. I was also encouraged, early in my career, by Gresley and Bazin to submit and present papers, which I did on three occasions [at meetings of the ILocoE in 1924 – numbers 158,166 and 171] and comment on others. We were also encouraged to attend institution annual dinners where contacts could be made and renewed.'

This then was the core of staff who sat in the centre around Gresley. Over the years, they came and went in a largely unrecorded pattern and more joined as the GNR and all its contemporaries were absorbed by amalgamation in 1923. But around

the whole organisation there were many others who made all that Gresley achieved possible.

Francis Wintour played a crucial role in his position as Works Manager at Doncaster, but when he retired in 1927 it left a huge gap which the company might have found difficult to fill. However, a highly effective replacement was available in the form of Robert Absalom Thom, who was born in Old Machar in Aberdeenshire on 14 June 1873. After attending the Causewayend School, he began an apprenticeship in 1888 with the Great North of Scotland Railway (GNSR), qualifying five years later. At the same time, he studied for an Advanced Certificate at Robert Gordons College in Aberdeen, which included many disciplines, amongst them mathematics, machine construction, mechanical drawing, applied mechanics and steam engines. Having obtained this qualification, he moved on to take a City and Guilds first class certificate in Mechanical Engineering, completing this course successfully in 1896.

Until 1898 he remained with the company 'gaining varied experience', as he related years later and then applied to be Works Foreman for the Metropolitan Railway Company at Neasden in North-West London. There seems little doubt that he was an ambitious man and pursued promotion whenever he could. During 1902, this resulted in his appointment as the Locomotive, Carriage and Wagon Superintendent of the Lancashire, Derbyshire and East Coast Railway (LD&ECR) and here he remained until this company was taken over by the Great Central (GCR) in 1906, when he became Deputy Locomotive Works Manager at Gorton in Manchester during December of that year. This appointment lasted until amalgamation in 1923, during which time he rose to become Assistant to the CME, John Robinson, serving him with great skill and determination. In the absence of clear evidence, it is hard to say how his work and ideas may have influenced the multi-talented Robinson.

Thom held two key posts as the GCR developed many 4-4-2, 4-6-0 and 2-8-0 class locomotives, plus an 0-8-4 hump shunting engine. Of all the locomotives produced during this period, the 8K 2-8-0s probably made the greatest impact. The GCR built 126 of these two cylinder engines for use on coal trains and during the Great War they become, in slightly modified form, the main class of heavy freight engine used by the War Office. 521 of this class were ordered and built by a number of companies, including North British, Robert Stephenson and Kitsons. Post-war, these were purchased by railway companies all over the world and when the LNER was formed, they acquired 421, which proved highly successful and evolved into the 04 and 05 classes. Some lasted, in BR's service, until 1966 and were likely to have influenced Gresley when designing his own classes of 2-8-0s.

Whilst with Robinson, Thom would also have been aware of the CME's work in developing a superheater system. Between 1912 and 1919, he produced 18 patents on the subject and his superheater design achieved widespread use within the GCR and in the world beyond. He also experimented with the concept of pulverised coal during the war when the quality of fuel available dropped away and more. Thom would also have observed the symmetry of Robinson's designs and appreciated

Robert Thom in the early 1920s.

By all accounts, Gresley (middle) and Thom (right) enjoyed a good professional and personal relationship and, according to Bert Spencer, shared a similar sense of humour. Here they are photographed with William Whitelaw, the LNER's Chairman, enjoying a sporting day at Doncaster.

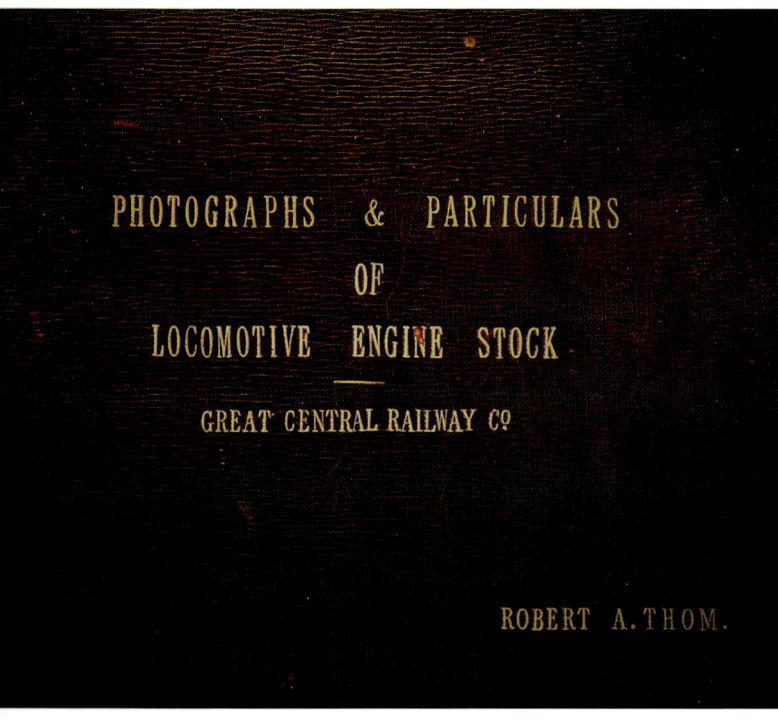

Examples of personal records kept by Thom.

with Gresley, which he did in 1923 when becoming District Mechanical Engineer at Gorton. A move to Cowlairs Works near Glasgow as Scottish Area Mechanical Engineer followed, before becoming Mechanical Engineer and Works Manager at Doncaster in 1927. It was here that his career reached its peak and he became a pivotal figure in the Gresley revolution, as Spencer later called it. Of Thom he wrote:

'He was a very astute man, with exceptional engineering skills and a strong sense of authority…. He was always polite and had a canny way of remembering a face and the details of a person's life. With his clear Highland accent, he could command a room and express himself effectively on many topics…. He had an encyclopaedic knowledge of locomotive design, construction and performances, as well as all the functions of the workshops under his control and could work many of the machines as well as their operators did if it came to it…. In his office at Doncaster he kept many records. In particular, there were a number of volumes, with his name embossed on the front covers, detailing each locomotive and item of rolling stock he'd worked with, adding many hand written notes to keep the records up to date….. He and the CME worked well together and Thom seemed able to predict many things Gresley wanted and quickly turn ideas into working products….. He was his own man, as they used to say, and without him it is likely that all we achieved would not have been possible. No one man makes an organisation and it helps considerably if there is a hard-core of men with the experience and skill of Gresley and Thom who can lead.'

Whilst Wintour then Thom dominated the workshops for most of Gresley's tenure as CME, and the likes of Bulleid and Spencer provided more direct technical support to him, there were others who would also contribute a great deal. Amongst them was Arthur Cowie Stamer, now largely forgotten, but in his day an engineer of note, who, conceivably might have become the LNER's CME instead of Gresley.

Born during 1869 in Staffordshire, he was the fifth child of Sir Lovelace Stamer, Baronet and Rector of Stoke on Trent, and his wife Ellen. Educated at Rugby School, he became an engineering pupil at the Manchester Works of Beyer, Peacock. Whilst there he was tutored by Herrmann Lange, then a director of the company and a locomotive designer, and worked alongside Carl Schobelt in the drawing office. In his application for membership of IMechE in 1899 he recorded that he 'served time in various departments of the Shops from September 1887 to July 1891 and was then a year in the North Eastern Railway's Shops at York, and on the footplate. Since 1892 I have been Assistant Shed Foreman and have taken charge of various sheds for short periods and was then, for 4½ years, Outside Inspector in the Loco Dept at York.

their aesthetic strengths; form and function coming together in balance no matter what the role of the locomotive. It was certainly an active and stimulating period in his career and one that prepared him well for working

In May 1895 I became Supt of the Southern Division of the [North Eastern Railway] NER.'

Like Gresley, he made his mark in a very short time and rose swiftly through the ranks and by 26 was in a senior position, although hadn't been directly involved in locomotive design to any great extent. Nevertheless, he caught the eye of the NER's CME, Vincent Raven, and became his Assistant Mechanical Engineer in 1910 then assistant CME at Darlington. The coming of war in 1914 saw Raven detached from the NER and made Superintendent of the Royal Arsenal at Woolwich, where he used his vast engineering skill and experience to enhance munitions production. In his absence, Stamer was made acting CME until early 1919 and then reverted to his old job.

When amalgamation became a reality in 1923, and the NER became part of the LNER, he was chosen to be Gresley's assistant CME and maintained his office at Darlington. It seems, but cannot be confirmed, that the well-connected Stamer was in the running for the top job after Raven chose to retire rather than compete for the LNER's new CME post himself. This may be conjecture of course but does provide an interesting exercise in 'what might have been', especially as Stamer had his own distinctive ideas on motive power development and was a strong advocate of electrification.

Arthur Stamer in the late 1920s.

The NER under Raven were keen to develop ideas on electrification. Before the Great War this resulted in the two schemes portrayed here. Below - one of the two ES1 Bo Bo locomotives built in 1905 to run on the Newcastle Quayside Branch line.

The second scheme, between Shildon and Newport Yard, opened in 1915 and operated the EF1 Bo Bo Class of which there were ten, the first, No. 3, being pictured here. Numbers 1 and 2 were assigned to the ES1s (Darlington's Chief Draughtsman, R.J. Robson, is fourth from the left).

During his years with the NER, Stamer played a key role in many projects boosting his design credentials in the process. These included the continuation of the company's electrification programme, begun by the previous CME, Wilson Worsdell, in projects around Newcastle. The second phase, under Raven, saw a line opened between Shildon and Newport in 1915 and the construction of ten centre cab electric locomotives to provide motive power. A York to Newcastle line was also planned but this scheme was eventually abandoned in 1923. Alongside this work, the NER had a full and active steam locomotive programme in which Stamer played a leading role. Raven and he favoured three cylinder designs, with the locomotive driving on the leading coupled axle. Consequently they produced five principle designs using this concept – the S Class 4-6-0, Y Class 4-6-2T (designed under Worsdell's leadership but not built before he retired), D Class 4-4-2T, Z Class 4-4-2 Atlantic and the Pacific Class (later designated A2 by the LNER); it is the last of these that drew the greatest attention when the first two appeared in 1922.

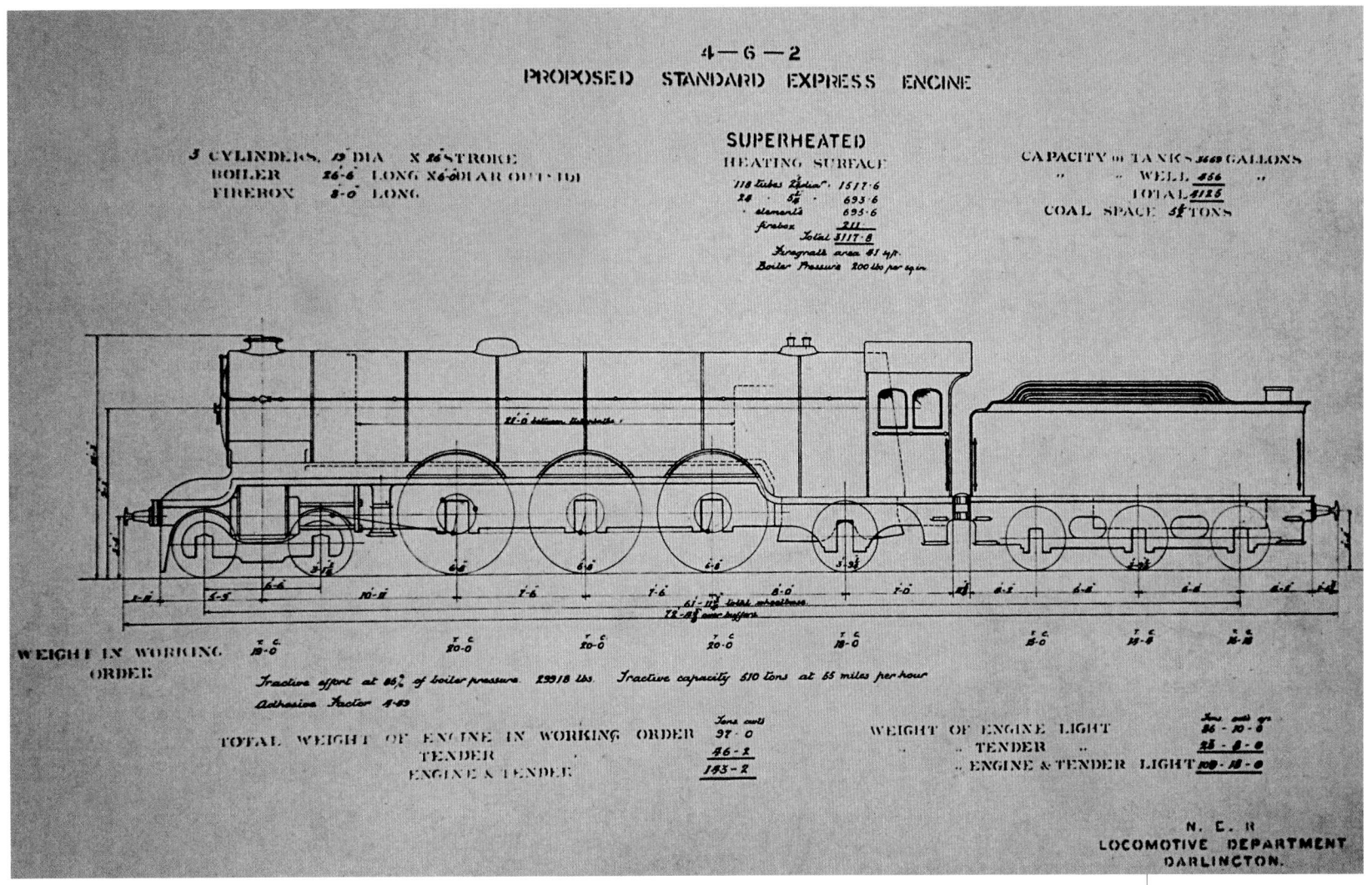

So by the time the LNER was formed, and Stamer became Gresley's assistant CME, the Darlington man had developed an enviable reputation in the design and construction of locomotives. He had a great deal to offer the new CME, and Gresley appears to have cultivated him with some vigour in the years that followed. Stamer was also a very well-connected man, who could wield great influence if he wished and would become President of the ILocoE as well as a leading light in the IMechE, so great was his reputation. Until he retired in December 1933, to be succeeded by Edward Thompson, he supported Gresley effectively; if he hadn't, the CME would undoubtedly have moved him on very quickly. In his role at Darlington he would lead in many key development projects, particularly the construction of many LNER engines at the works there. The most noteworthy of these were the K3 2-6-0s from 1924, the J38 and J39 0-6-0 Classes from 1926, the D49 4-4-0 in 1927, the B17 4-6-0s from 1928 and the experimental 4-6-4 W1 in 1929. Although no more Pacifics were built at Darlington, during his time there, Stamer would still have been party to this programme and would have had a voice in their development.

Two other people of great significance in the LNER's history,

The Raven/Stamer A2 Class Pacific which appeared in 1922 in competition with the first of Gresley's A1 Class Pacifics. Five A2s were built and all were scrapped by 1937.

Thompson (left) and Peppercorn.

who in time would become the LNER's CMEs, were Edward Thompson and Arthur Peppercorn. Under Gresley, they cut their teeth, although their role in his locomotive programme was more to support than to direct for most of the time. Throughout this period, they found themselves in a variety of posts and roles, gradually gaining ground and establishing their careers. However, each had found their way to the railway world by different routes.

Thompson was born on 25 June 1881 and grew up in Marlborough, his father, Francis, being an assistant master at the public school there. In fact, his and Gresley's paths probably crossed between 1890 and 93, when Herbert was a pupil there and possibly under Thompson senior's care. At the time, Edward was at a prep school in Surrey and wouldn't attend the college itself until 1895, the year his father retired, though he remained a governor until his death in 1916. Unusually for the time, Thompson, though fascinated by engineering, didn't follow the apprenticeship route into this profession, but read Mechanical Sciences at Pembroke College Cambridge instead. He was awarded a BA in 1902 and then became a premium pupil with Beyer, Peacock to learn more practical elements of engineering. Soon afterwards he found employment with the Running Department of the Midland Railway as an 'Improver'.

Ever conscious of the need to gain experience, he left Derby in 1905 to become a supervisor at the Royal Ordnance Factory at Woolwich. And so his climb upwards began and, in due course, he joined the NER with postings to Hull, Darlington and Gateshead following in quick succession. During this time, he worked closely with Raven and Stamer, cementing his relationship with the CME when marrying his second daughter, Gwendolene, in 1913. However, shortly before this happened he decided to take up an appointment with the GNR at Doncaster, recruited by Gresley to be his Carriage and Wagon Superintendent. Here he remained until war broke out, in which he served with the Royal Engineers with distinction, rising to the rank of lieutenant colonel in the process.

The years after such a terrible, deeply unsettling war would inevitably be difficult for many people and Thompson found it so. He returned to the GNR in 1919, but soon sought a return to Raven and the NER. He recorded no reason for this change, which may have been for personal or professional reasons, but some believe that he and Gresley may not have seen eye to eye on some issues and this was a diplomatic way of avoiding any deeper disagreements. Either way, he moved to York and took the post of Works Manager in the Carriage and Wagon Department there. Amalgamation three years later forced a return to Darlington, where he became Area Carriage and Wagon Works Manager under Gresley once more and here he stayed for four years, deepening his experience of rolling stock design and construction, but having little or no involvement in the design and construction of locomotives.

All this would change in 1927 when he was posted to Stratford, in East London, as Assistant Mechanical Engineer, and again in 1933 when he was chosen to replace Stamer at Darlington. Here he remained until 1938, managing the continuing production of the B17s, J39s and the second batch of V2 2-6-2 tender engines then being introduced into service. There appears to have been little scope to develop new ideas and he focussed instead on ways in which existing designs might be modified and improved, expressing reservations about some of Gresley's ideas along the way.

In 1938, Robert Thom announced his intention of retiring and Thompson was offered, and accepted, the Works Manager and Mechanical Engineer post at Doncaster. His appointment was due to take effect in July but first he had to cope with a profound personal tragedy. In May, his wife died suddenly and this cast a terrible cloud over his life, making the transition a difficult one. However, the move to Doncaster did at least provide a distraction from this personal misfortune and there was plenty of work for him to immerse himself in. Yet in many ways, the premier status of this works were beginning to fade. The glamorous days of the Pacific construction programme were over, and the work Thompson inherited focussed on maintenance tasks and the construction of the V3 2-6-2T and the V2. This left him little scope to push forward his own ideas on design or any possible modifications to existing classes, which was often his favoured option. This was the situation he found himself in when Gresley died suddenly in 1941 and he was thrust into the limelight as CME.

Arthur Peppercorn was cast in a very different mould and shared a very close relationship with Gresley, Bulleid, Thom and Spencer, something that Thompson never seemed able to achieve. He was born on 29 January 1889 to Alfred, a clergyman serving at St Luke's Church in Stoke Prior, and his wife Agnes, from Queensland, and became the tenth of their fourteen children. He is recorded as receiving private education before attending Hereford Cathedral School between 1901 and 1905. As often seems to be the case with budding engineers, he displayed an interest in machines, the railways and construction from an early age, but rather than go down the university route favoured by Thompson and his family, Peppercorn elected to seek a premium apprenticeship at Doncaster under Henry Ivatt. Alfred Peppercorn may have had other ideas, of course, especially being an alumnus of Jesus College Cambridge, but if so, he didn't deflect Arthur from his goal.

In 1912, when applying for membership of the IMechE Peppercorn simply recorded that his five years of study saw him '…passing through the machine, erecting shops, &c., also drawing office.' In addition, he described attending Doncaster Technical School between 1906 and 08 where he undertook evening classes in Machinery Drawing, Mathematics, Applied Mechanics and more to round of his education. By now this was fairly traditional fare for the budding engineer and his work and dedication clearly drew the attention of Gresley, in particular, who seems to have taken the young man under his wing. He also became, and remained, a firm friend of Bulleid and his family, with many photographs taken over the years underpinning the depth of this relationship. It is difficult to say how much this boosted his career, but at least it must have given him great encouragement so far away from his family and friends, especially when his father died suddenly in February 1908.

Each phase in his career after that become a step upwards. Firstly, he was assigned to Colwick Loco Depot in Nottingham where he did a variety of duties, including assisting the foreman, shed fitting and loco firing for nearly 2½ years. This proved to be an excellent grounding and prepared him for his next post of any importance, Assistant to the District Locomotive Supt at Ardsley, then at Peterborough from 1914. However, the Great War intervened and his undoubted skills and willingness to volunteer saw him commissioned into the Royal Engineers. In France, he was posted as a lieutenant to the CME for the Directorate of Transport, where he became his technical assistant, rising to acting captain by the end of the war.

In the post-war years, his career continued to blossom under Gresley's guiding hand, with moves to Retford as District Locomotive Superintendent, then Doncaster before becoming the Carriage and Wagon Works Manager at York, where he remained for six years. Two senior appointments followed, the first to Stratford, as Loco Running Supt, then Darlington, as Mechanical Engineer but everything changed when Gresley died and he returned to Doncaster to be both Assistant CME to Thompson and Mechanical Engineer in charge of the works. It would be a testing and often frustrating time for him but, as Bert Spencer recorded, he was an 'affable, intelligent and accommodating man, at ease with all he met, with a very quick mind

Part of the backroom team. A photograph of Doncaster's Locomotive Drawing Office team in 1945, with Teddy Windle, the Chief Draughtsman, front and centre. No names seem to have been recorded and we are left to ponder who in this picture may have contributed, in any small but crucial way, to the design of any of Gresley's masterpieces. It seems that Edward Thompson was instrumental in setting up this and many other group photos to commemorate the contribution of so many people.

and an ability to command men and women from all backgrounds. This allowed him to support both Gresley and Thompson effectively and, on occasions, lead them to better solutions.'

So, these are some of the main characters involved in Gresley's locomotive development programme. There are many others, probably numbered in their hundreds, but the passing of time, coupled with a lack of documents and memoirs, means that most of them will never be identified or recognised. Who is to say whether even the lowliest member of staff, in workshops or drawing offices, didn't suggest something that made a new locomotive the great work of engineering it became? The simplicity of Paul S. Baker's suggestion, recorded in the opening paragraph of this chapter, is deliberately challenging but who is to say if it is true or not? The only certainty is that there were

The anonymous heroes of this story? A tiny part of the work force, which numbered in thousands, directed by Gresley, in this case at Doncaster.

many voices pitching many ideas that filled out the broad concepts that Gresley and his senior team pursued with such vigour. A single person wrestling with new ideas, struggling alone against all odds to create a masterpiece, belongs to Hollywood, not Doncaster, Derby, Crewe or any other centre of the railway engineering centres.

Yet more would have been known if the growing world of PR, so adeptly used by the LNER to promote its glamorous locomotives and streamlined services, had been targeted at the people who created these engines and made them run. The LMS had a very different approach and believed strongly in the benefit of advertising all that it did, not simply the premier services. Some of this was for training purposes and to show their own employees the size of the task the company faced, but it went further and looked in fine detail at the people at work. This often found its way into films that were distributed widely and shown in cinemas around the country,

30 June 1938 Stevenage – the 50th anniversary of the *Flying Scotsman* service. It was a ceremony that reflected the span of Gresley's career and the advances made in locomotive design during his time – Patrick Stirling's classic 4-2-2 Single No.1 built for the GNR that first appeared in 1870 and the A4 which first appeared in 1935. Gresley is in the group by the Stirling's tender with his shadow, Bert Spencer, as ever close by.

or in photo montage articles appearing in national journals or simply the railway press. Years later, this means that we can still see this material and understand how projects were developed and not simply see an end result. No such archive appears to exist for the LNER, though there is plenty of material showing new Pacifics leaving King's Cross.

Another huge gap is in the lack of documents that describe the management structures that existed across the LNER. Who did what and when is a crucial starting point when trying to understand the process of design and construction. Once again, the LMS was luckier. Amongst others, it had Robert Riddles, Roland Bond, Ernest Cox and Eric Langridge to observe and record in great detail all that happened at senior and middle management levels. Their efforts were supported by a number of autobiographies written by staff at a more junior level, so giving the modern reader a deeper insight into the lives and achievements of a large number of those who were there. There is no depth of archive of material or personal reminiscences to illuminate the LNER's role, though the company's magazine, published monthly, does provides some broad background. However, this journal is dominated by a variety of articles on sport, charitable work, retirements, obituaries and more, with little focus on structures or the complexity of design.

The GNR, being a smaller company than the monolith that became the LNER in 1923, is probably easier to fathom than the LNER. Being based in Doncaster, individual roles and responsibilities were more clear-cut and easier to understand, but when the LNER was formed, it inherited a clutter of often competing companies each with their own history, ideas and structures, which many tried to perpetuate in the new order. It took the LMS, their principal rival, more than a decade to sort these issues out, and even then, tribal tendrils kept reaching out to cause conflict even under the gifted Stanier. The LNER was no different, with the main constituent company centres of Doncaster, Darlington, Cowlairs and Stratford remaining difficult to manage centrally, with their variety of histories, customs and design preferences. So, perhaps, it is little wonder that no serious attempt has been made to unravel the intertwined stories and provide a broader picture of who actually did what and who truly contributed in the design and construction of locomotives.

So, in trying to describe the individual contributions in the design and construction of Gresley's P2, A4, W1, V2 and many more locomotives, we only have hints and conjecture, which by any standards is an imprecise science. However, sufficient is available to present a rather more detailed picture of Gresley and his team at work. Does an appraisal of this sort diminish Gresley's contribution in any way? Of course not, because without his inspiring leadership, driving ambition, inquiring mind and deep understanding of science, the LNER would have achieved far, far, less in another man's hands. It was a team he created, led brilliantly and constantly nurtured from the time he succeeded Henry Ivatt to the end of his life. They will always be his locomotives, but he needed a lot of help in designing and building them.

But first we need to go back to Gresley's birth and see how his life evolved and the many influences that came to play on him in these formative years.

Chapter 2
TIME, PLACE, INFLUENCES AND OPPORTUNITIES (1876–1911)

When Joanna Gresley gave birth to her youngest child, Herbert Nigel, in June 1876 during a visit to Edinburgh, Britain was at the height of Empire and much of the world was dominated by its presence – for good or bad. The Industrial Revolution continued to change society and Britain's landscape, vast tracts of land becoming polluted wastelands in the process. Tiny, insanitary cottages and houses, built by the hundreds of thousands, to provide a basic level of subsistence for workers migrating from a rural existence, sprang up and sat hunched around pitheads, factories and towns. Farming, for centuries Britain's biggest industry, had slipped into recession, helping to feed the passage of workers and their families to cities, where the prospects, if not the reality, seemed much better. The footprint of these conurbations continued to spread ever wider, each marked and shaped by the ever-growing rail networks threading their way through the countryside, seeming to expand in an uncoordinated way as speculators sought to exploit its possibilities before the bubble burst and boom turned to bust.

Yet for many, it was hard to believe that such change had been wrought in so short a time. Only 60 years earlier, the threat Napoleon posed still cast a heavy shadow and youngsters in the 1870s and '80s would still have been surrounded by the signs and attitudes imposed by these wars and there was still a constant reminder of the conflict – a fading number of 'survivors' ever present in society providing a living link to those times, for whom the nickname 'Boney' still conjured up fears of invasion and subjugation. But since then, the British Empire had continued expanding, with war becoming its common denominator; to acquire and subdue, until the spread of the German Empire provided a much sterner test and decline became inevitable. Yet, while it lasted, this period of growth stimulated great developments and provided opportunities for those with the skills and the perception to exploit them. Inevitably, much depended on one's position in society and access to good education. Social democracy and social mobility were still a very long way in the future and birth-right and

Herbert Nigel Gresley, known as Tim to his family, in the early years of the twentieth century.

position were still all. Gresley was blessed with both in a time when most lived their lives in abject poverty with a high mortality rate, their chance of advancement muted.

The development of science, engineering and invention, the availability of new materials and ready money were the keys to much that happened. Without them, the Industrial Revolution might have been long delayed and Britain's place in the world harder to sustain. But once in motion, the cycle of progress grew ever more intense as new discoveries brought more change and gave industry new mechanised tools to play with.

By 1876, the Revolution was well into its second, more intense phase across Europe and in the United States, after decades of comparative slumber. However, this time greater emphasis was placed on more advanced technology, supported by steam and gas power and with this, industry marshalled its resources and introduced new manufacturing techniques. These significantly enhanced production, creating and feeding new markets and providing, along the way, the impetus for an arms race, then conflict on an industrial scale. First there had been the Crimean War of the 1850s, followed by the American Civil War a decade later, then came the Franco-Prussian War of 1870–71 – and the future held much worse.

The advance of industry and science also drove social change, though this was often resisted by the majority of owners eager to maximise profits, condemning their workers to lives of great deprivation in the process. But change was in the wind and social reformers, battling within the limits of a restricted democracy, were beginning to bring about a transformation in living and working standards that continues to this day. Better health and education, followed by greater equality, became the central themes of this parallel revolution. As general standards improved, so did the level of expectation. Victorian Britain may be remembered for its focus on Empire, the acquisition of wealth and power and the suppression of dissent, but it was forced to become much more in an effort to appease a population growing in ambition for better lives. In 1876, when young Herbert Gresley entered the world, this struggle between old and new was just beginning and would become the cornerstone of his life. Victorian power and certainty was giving way to greater democracy and better existences for those prepared to work hard.

Undoubtedly our lives are shaped by our nature, the environment in which we live and the opportunities that come our way. The wise, whether privileged or deprived, will use these elements as a launching pad to a successful life and one of achievement and Gresley's life best personifies this philosophy. Born to upper middle-class parents, with a link to nobility, he grew up in a seemingly sheltered and privileged world as far removed from the modern world of engineering as it was

St Peter's Church in Netherseal in the late 1890s, from the wall in front of the Rectory.

The Old Rectory in Netherseal where the Gresley family lived until the death of the Reverend Nigel Gresley in 1897.

possible to get. His father, Nigel, was the rector of Netherseal in Leicestershire and was able to raise five children, a daughter and four sons, in reasonable comfort. This was something not always possible for a clergyman at that time, their existence being described as one of 'genteel poverty' in many books of the period.

The Rector seems to have been a strong advocate of education, having attended Rossall School in Lancashire and then Trinity College Cambridge himself. In fact, Rossall had been established in 1844 with the specific aim of 'providing, at moderate cost, for the sons of clergymen and others, a classical, mathematical and general education'. A year earlier, Marlborough College had been set up with the same aim and, in time, would receive the youngest Gresley child, though none of his siblings. But first, he attended Barham House Preparatory School in St Leonards-on-Sea, Sussex, only arriving at the Wiltshire school aged 14 during September 1890.

One central issue in any biography is the need to explore and understand cause and effect and the individual factors involved in mapping the course of a life – personality, influences and opportunities, but this path can be a tricky one to navigate. Two and two do not always make four when analysing humanity, because of so many variables present in determining why a person follows one course and not another. And quite often the path followed may simply be a result of a single incident or some difficulty in a personal relationship, for example, between a parent and child where both are strong willed and determined to have their own way. Although filial obedience was a

Barham House School, in Dane Road, as it appears today.

St Leonards on Sea and Hastings at the time Gresley attended school there.

key part of life in Victorian Britain, it seems that within the Gresley family it was practised more in the breach than the observance, Herbert's parents seemingly possessing reserves of tolerance and perception of their children's needs and personalities.

So, what may have influenced the young Gresley as he made his way through life? His relationship with his father seems to have been a beneficial one, the Rector being a kindly man with some understanding of human nature and the ambitions that drive us all; he certainly supported them and provided opportunities not open to many at that time. His eldest son, George, studied at Selwyn College Cambridge then followed his father into the church, serving in Darlaston, Tamworth and then, having converted to Catholicism, Shenfield in Essex. Beatrice, as many daughters did, remained at home, never married and helped her parents until their deaths.

Arthur joined the Liverpool-based corn brokers, Gresley and Utermarck and died of tuberculosis in 1903. Meanwhile the third son, Nigel, went into banking and eventually emigrated to Vancouver where he worked for the Bank of Canada, but illness intervened and he returned home, dying in Doncaster on 9 June 1915.

As one would expect, coming from their background, the Gresley boys seem to have chosen careers that reflected their talents and their aspirations after a good education, by the standards of the age. None seem to have expressed any interest in science or engineering or sought to enter this world, all that is except Herbert. So there is a slight conundrum to unravel. His time at prep school would have seen him focus on French and Latin, the three 'Rs', some natural sciences such as geography, which required little in the way of equipment so necessary for deeper scientific education, and religious teachings. Anything more was unlikely even in private education, though occasionally something from the classics may have slipped into a curriculum. Science only seems to have come into play if a child was able to stay in school beyond the age of 14, when there was an expectation that they might move on to higher education. So Herbert's interest in engineering is unlikely to have been stirred by his time at prep school, but such a passion usually has its roots in something more tangible and stem from a fascination borne of some experience or influence at a young age. At Barham House, he was living very close to the London, Brighton and South Coast Railway, that ran from Victoria Station to Brighton then St Leonards, with an engine shed close by. Here he would have seen William Stroudley's golden ochre painted locomotives and probably travelled on the line regularly, especially at the beginning and end of each term. This may have stimulated or helped develop an existing interest.

In his excellent biography of the engineer, Geoffrey Hughes relates that Gresley recalled later in life expressing a 'wish to become an engine driver when only four years old' and this seems more than likely. It was and is a common refrain amongst many young children spellbound by some passing exposure to locomotives, but for most soon passes when the next toy appears. In the 1870s the railways were still a novelty and attracted great attention because of it. Living in Leicestershire he would have had ready access to many lines, with the Midland Railway's HQ and workshops at Derby a particular place of interest and within easy reach of his home. As he grew so the opportunity to ride on trains for school or family outings became a part of his life and increased his exposure to this stirring form of transport.

His father may also have fostered his interest in science, there being a suggestion that he was, himself, a keen amateur researcher and may have written scientific papers, though on what seems unclear. Perhaps it was simply the higher standard of education he sought for himself and his sons that fed a sense of wonder and encouraged academic curiosity leading them into a world of study and knowledge. From this, Herbert discovered the world of engineering and found a calling that fascinated him. If so, the Victorian world was full of the work of many eminent engineers to catch his eye – Brunel, George and Robert Stephenson amongst them and books describing their lives and achievements were readily available in the late nineteenth century to feed an enquiring mind eager for knowledge.

So a childhood interest, probably encouraged by his family, the world around him and fed by books, continued to grow, but it needed something else to become more than a passing fancy and it was here that Marlborough College undoubtedly played an important part in his development and choice of career. Sitting 12 or so miles south of the Great Western Railway's (GWR) works in Swindon and served by two railway stations itself, the town and college were well placed for a young man starting out in the world with an interest in engineering. Gresley was also known to visit Clifton in Bristol by train regularly during his holidays and stay with his widowed aunt, Emily Douglas and her son, a theology student. They lived in Canynge Square, bordering Clifton College, within easy reach of Brunel's Suspension Bridge and other centres of the great man's work. By this stage, Brunel's GWR was gradually coming under the influence of its most enigmatic and dynamic engineer, George Jackson Churchward. And before him Daniel Gooch, Joseph Armstrong and William Dean had also effectively developed its motive power. All this would have been evident to Gresley in the early 1890s, as would the final stages of the GWR's conversion from broad to standard gauge, the yard at Swindon being full of withdrawn engines. For someone with a love of steam locomotives, the sight of this would have had a magnetic attraction. A sense of how important the GWR was in this phase of his life can be gauged by his attendance at Churchward's funeral in 1933 and a statement he

Marlborough College in the late nineteenth century.

made shortly afterwards, when elected President of the Institution of Locomotive Engineers:

'He (George Churchward) was without doubt one of the most eminent railway engineers of recent times, and we see evidence of his influence in the designs of the most up-to-date engines of each of the great railways of this country.'

The closeness of his relationship with Churchward is hinted at a month later in the record of proceedings:

'This practice (the stretching of ordinary boiler tubes) has been introduced by the Great Western Railway and has been a very good one indeed. I myself have copied it, as I have copied many Great Western Railway practices. I remember an occasion when I went down to see the works at Swindon and got Mr Churchward to lend me the drawings so that I could make a stretching bench for myself.'

So chance, an educated open personality and a growing appreciation of science seemingly brought him to engineering and

The Reverend Nigel Gresley late in life when blind and barely mobile, relied on this small cart to carry him from home to church and around the village. The donkey is recorded as being Susan and the Spaniel as Bob.

in the railways, he found a ready outlet for his enquiring mind and may have seen a future in this world beckoning. However, the unrefined intellect of a teenager needs to be guided and encouraged if it is to blossom and Marlborough College facilitated this metamorphosis, opening doors and creating new opportunities that his prep school couldn't hope to fulfil. One wonders whether he discussed his ideas and aspirations with his father and family before deciding what to do. As a 'varsity' man his father may have wished that his youngest son might follow suit and benefit from the academic qualifications and status that went with these institutions. By the 1890s engineering and science courses had been established in many schools of learning and were quickly gaining ground and any one of these could have offered Gresley a place to study, research and learn.

So he went to Marlborough in September 1890, then under the leadership of the Rev George Bell, a graduate of Oxford, who had become head in the year Gresley was born. Here he would have found a college well equipped to teach the sciences and populated by some able masters. He would also have discovered an extensive library containing an array of books that defined the progress made in many areas of science and engineering, including the *Engineer* magazine, which had become a widely read source of information since its launch in 1856. Through these he would have been exposed to the work of such bodies as the Institutions of Civil Engineers, Mechanical Engineers and Electrical

Shortly before Gresley's arrival at Marlborough the teaching staff posed for this photograph. The Headmaster, Reverend Bell, is standing centrally looking to his right. It is no longer possible to identify who amongst them taught the new student and little could they know how greatly they were contributing to railway history when taking this young man under their collective wing. In the group (back row head highest) is Francis Thompson whose son, Edward, would succeed Gresley as the LNER's CME in 1941.

Engineers, formed in 1818, 1847 and 1871 respectively, and their regularly published journals. In time, Gresley would join all three bodies, reflecting his wide interests in all elements of science and engineering.

It seems that Herbert was proficient in both practical and academic subjects. He was, by all accounts, an able carpenter, who was good at languages, the sciences and had some ability as a draughtsman. Towards the end of his time at Marlborough, he was awarded a science prize in recognition of his work in that college year. By any standards, he was educationally sound and had a well-balanced set of skills that would have suited university life. Yet despite this he chose a quite different route instead, possibly led by his interest in the railways, but also his father's failing health. By the time Gresley left Marlborough in July 1893, the Rector was blind and disabled and could barely undertake his duties as his health continued to fail dramatically. The future would have seemed uncertain and the costly business of attendance at university would have been a significant drain on family resources. So Herbert chose to enter into the tough, uncompromising world of engineering apprenticeships instead, where he could seek to earn his 'own keep' and find a worthwhile career.

It is in the choice he made that we can see many elements of Gresley's personality emerge. It takes a strong and perceptive person when offered two routes in life to take the harder one but it also demonstrates a strong sense of responsibility remarkable

Early in his time at Marlborough Gresley is recorded as having been particularly fascinated by Patrick Stirling's locomotives and skilfully traced a copy of this illustration which appeared in the early 1890s.

for one so young. Here we have someone able to see clearly, weigh all factors and come up with the best solution even in the most difficult circumstances. Armed with these skills, it is little wonder that he succeeded in his chosen field. One is left to ponder what this talented man might have achieved in the world of science if he had attended university instead.

As it was, his father died in 1897, when only 62, and left an estate of £5,200 (worth approximately £560k today according to the measuringworth website) to support his wife and daughter. Although not an inconsiderable sum, it would have reduced quickly without a pension or other income, particularly if his dependants lived a long time, which they did.

One wonders if his parents counselled him to think again about the university option. Heavy industry was a rough, no-nonsense world with an appalling record for killing and injuring huge numbers each year. No parent would let their greatly loved child enter such an environment without serious misgivings and concerns and it does seem an unusual choice for a child from a family with no links to the railways or industry. Herbert was determined to continue, however and seems to have had no qualms about doing so, with the only remaining issue being the choice of apprenticeship and location. Here he was faced with a number of options, so numerous were the companies, both large and small, offering training schemes. But, as always, choice is affected by many issues – the companies' reputations, the quality of teaching, opportunities beyond the apprenticeship, living and working conditions, proximity of family and more. A careful balance has to be struck and Gresley's parents, being intelligent, concerned individuals, would undoubtedly have looked at the options available and advised their son accordingly. Of course, Herbert would have had his own views on the subject and was clearly astute enough at 17 to judge these issues for himself.

When choosing a place of further education, it remains a simple rule to pursue the best available, no matter the level of ability that a young person has shown and this led Gresley to seek an apprenticeship with the London and North Western Railway's Locomotive Department at Crewe. It was then under the control of the 57-year-old Francis William Webb, who had been appointed Locomotive Superintendent in 1870 (a post that was re-titled Chief Mechanical Engineer shortly afterwards, or so it seems). Born in Staffordshire in 1836, he became an articled clerk at Crewe when only 15 and then spent the rest of his working life there, except for a 5-year period with the Bolton Iron and Steel Company. During this time, he held the posts of Chief Draughtsman, Works Manager and Chief Assistant before rising to the top job. In a long and active career, he frequently demonstrated his skill as a locomotive engineer and had a string of designs to his credit by the time Gresley joined the company in October 1893 as a premium apprentice. Although regarded as an autocratic and dogmatic person, he provided an interesting example for fledgling engineers to follow, but he could offer much more than this. He was also an educationalist and teacher of great skill, able to guide his students through their formative years in a balanced and educated

Crewe Works at the time Gresley served his apprenticeship there.

Francis Webb, CME of the LNWR from 1871 to 1903.

way. It was an ability recognised in the 1870s when he was elected to be President of the Crewe Mechanics Institute, where for many years he had been a tutor and with his skills becoming widely known, many young men sought places on the company's apprenticeship schemes, often turning down courses closer to their homes.

The most noteworthy of these, other than Gresley himself, were two of his contemporaries, both from the West Country, Hewitt Beames and Frederick Arnold Lemon. Beames would rise to become the LNWR's CME and then the LMS's Deputy CME, whilst Lemon would hold the crucial position of Works Superintendent at Crewe from the 1920s until 1941, when the race between the LMS and LNER was at its height. In fact, the three men maintained a friendship and a close professional association, even though working for these competitors in later years. In each case, Gresley would either encourage or sponsor the other two when applying to join the Institution of Mechanical Engineers, so close was the bond formed at Crewe when they were trainees together.

The nature of apprenticeships was undergoing radical change when Gresley arrived at Crewe. For centuries, the practice had been widespread and valued, especially for those living in poverty. Although at times they could resemble bonded slavery, with only a pitiful standard of living thrown in to soften the blow, they did offer the prospect of secure long-term employment and an escape from the work house or worse. Trades were valued and apprentices, if they worked hard and survived, could improve their lives significantly but this came at a price. Most were unregulated and involved inherent dangers that were taken as a part of the business. As the nineteenth century passed, so the many schemes run by bigger companies came under scrutiny and their conduct began being governed by Act of Parliament. It was a slow process but marked the first steps in a path to the Health and Safety legislation we accept as the norm today. By 1893, the statutory need

Crewe Mechanics Institute late in the nineteenth century. It played a key role in Gresley's education during his apprenticeship.

for such things as age limitations, conditioned hours, remuneration, general education and welfare were gradually being recognised and implemented. So, as time passed, the concept of indentured servitude began to disappear to be replaced by a more balanced system, where life and individual development had greater value. Gresley's father, with sufficient funds to sponsor his child, was able to pay a fee enabling his son to achieve 'premium' status, which was only open to a few selected students each year. This meant that he would periodically receive personal tutoring from Webb, Henry Earl, the Works Manager, or other senior officers to supplement the harder graft entailed in working on the shop floor. It was a feature of an apprenticeship that was greatly valued. In Webb, he found a leader of some authority, whose professional standing and influence could enhance an individual's career exponentially if nurtured carefully. And here we see another element of Gresley's personality gradually emerging – the ability to work maturely with senior and junior staff, to understand

An everyday scene in No 8 Locomotive Erecting Shop for Crewe's young apprentices.

Webb, second from the right, entertains a group of directors from the Caledonian Railway.

the politics of relationships and the way to negotiate and exploit opportunities that arose with balance and common-sense. In other words, a sound business sense and an awareness of the many diverse issues that senior professionals have to address and manage if they are to be successful.

As a premium apprentice, Gresley was expected to attend evening classes at the Institute to study the theoretical side of engineering and develop such things as technical drawing skills. In the five years of his apprenticeship, this became a regular part of his life, but, sadly, he seems to have left no description of the work he did at college or, for that matter, experience gained whilst under training at Crewe Works, However, there seems little doubt that he would have spent time in a number of workshops acquiring a range of skills and in his last year he worked as a fitter – confirmed by his application, in 1907, for membership of the Institution of Mechanical Engineers.

Alfred Hill, who became the Great Eastern Railway's CME and a leading advocate of these training schemes, set out the basic aims of mechanical engineering apprenticeships:

'He should spend a minimum of three years (out of five) in the workshops. The sub-division of this time must vary, but should include:

A year in the Machine Shop on machines and lathes.
A year in the Fitting Shop on bench work, three months of which on a tool bench.
A year in the Erecting Shop divided between new and repair work.

'If the opportunity occurs, a few weeks might be spent in the Smiths' Shop, and also in the Boiler Shop, and in the case of a locomotive engineer some time with the Running Shed fitters should prove useful. Of course, some knowledge of other shops, such as the Pattern Shop and Foundry, etc, is advantageous, but in most cases it is impossible to give apprentices experience of this sort.

'The workshop training should fill a double purpose. Becoming proficient, to some extent, in the use of tools and of acquiring an understanding of the method by which the work is done, and obtaining a general knowledge of the organisation.

'The premium apprentices are obliged, under the terms of their indenture, to attend such evening science classes at the Company's Institute as the

Locomotive Superintendent may consider necessary. Promotion to the Drawing Office (an essential part of these apprenticeships) is conditional upon satisfactory progress at these classes. At the end of these classes the apprentices should have a fair knowledge of mathematics, machine construction, drawing, applied mechanics, theoretical mechanics and physics, and practical geometry and graphics.'

The mix of practical and theoretical work would have appealed to someone of Gresley's nature, but they were a tough five years, requiring considerable effort and commitment to succeed. Some of his contemporaries did take the university route, which essentially was a theoretical programme, and then undertook an abbreviated apprenticeship to hone more practical skills. But did they enjoy greater benefits having taken the higher education route? In the railway industry probably not, essentially being a low-tech business. Some graduates did rise to senior positions, but the majority of the CMEs in the twentieth century seem to have been apprentices – Gresley, Stanier and Bulleid amongst them. So Herbert's decision to become Webb's pupil doesn't seem to have damaged his prospects in any way.

But there was another factor to consider in all of this. There was a huge benefit in working alongside Webb and seeing his locomotive development programme immerge. To observe all the processes involved and the techniques of design and construction in operation gave Gresley a rare insight into the business that he never forgot. Webb was a highly creative man, although at times he was thought to have courted controversy with his advocacy of certain design principles. He also possessed a dynamic personality that could soothe or bite in an unpredictable way. Fred Lemon later described him as possessing 'great charm, understanding and patience one minute, then became a martinet almost impossible to deal with the next. But he did treat all his apprentices sympathetically and made every effort to ensure we were taught well and understood what was expected of us. I'm glad I came under his guiding hand and didn't regret my choice, even though Swindon would have been much closer to my home in Somerset'.

Webb's 32 years as CME saw many locomotives developed and he experimented with many ideas as the LNWR's fleet gradually expanded. He also sought a degree of standardisation in types and some commonality of parts for ease of maintenance and economy. The railways had grown in such a way that they contained a myriad number of designs and the benefit of such policies wasn't lost on Webb. There was also the issue of performance; the demands of industry and a growing number of passengers meant that bigger and faster locomotives were needed if the business was to continue growing. So the company built for the future and Webb drove forward an active research and development programme that sought to draw the maximum output from the technology available. Over the years, new classes made their appearance, with an active programme continuing throughout Gresley's time as an apprentice at Crewe. He recalled, in 1919 at a Crewe Apprentices re-union dinner, the impression this made upon him:

'It is just 25 years since I started at Crewe Works in an atmosphere of compounding in the locomotive engineering profession. When the 2-2-2-2 type 'Greater Britain' was built it was thought that the limit of size and power of the locomotive had been reached, and when, in an excess of loyal zeal she was painted crimson, and another engine of the class, "Queen Elizabeth" was painted white at the same time as the Queen's Diamond Jubilee, surely the limits of artistic resource of the locomotive engineer were attained. How long they ran in their splendour I do not recollect, but I remember Greater Britain was re-christened by the men the "Scarlet Runner" and the delicate hue of the Queen Empress began to darken like a well-behaved Meerschaum pipe. But there was no lack of enterprise in those days at Crewe; a triple expansion engine was tried, a figure-eight firebox with a water space underneath at the sides of the ashpan were built…..'

The construction programme continued with him witnessing the arrival of the 2-4-0 improved Precedents Class and the Whitworths, an ever growing number of 0-8-0 coupled tender engines, a 2-2-2-2 three-cylinder

Webb's three-cylinder compound Experiment Class were a common sight to Gresley throughout his time at Crewe, having been constructed in the early to mid-1880s. The 30 built were Webb's first experiment with a class of compound express locomotives.

class compound, plus a 4-cylinder Jubilee Class 4-4-0, which began appearing in 1897. It was a very mixed bag that reflected his desire to experiment and push back engineering boundaries. But although most of his engines didn't adopt the compound principle, he was later judged, some would say harshly, on his work developing this concept. Even in death, his critics made hay, as though he had been guilty of some cardinal sin in pursuing this course or that – a not uncommon reaction amongst some elements of the railway fraternity who take these things far too seriously and fail to see the bigger picture. But he does seem to have been a man who polarised opinion, intentionally or otherwise.

Opinions of his work and career can best be summed up by an obituary that appeared shortly after his death in 1906:

'From time to time we have had to chronicle some of his designs or inventions. His ingenuity was by no means confined to the actual design of locomotives alone.

'A distinguished feature in his character was intense faith in himself, very largely justified by the successes which he not infrequently secured….It is, however, as the persistent advocate of the compound locomotive that Mr Webb will be best remembered in the future. For more than 20 years he built nothing but compound locomotives for his fast passenger service. The first of them 'The Experiment' was put to work in 1882. These locomotives were quite original in principle, and have never been used, save experimentally, off the London and North Western system. Two outside cylinders fitted with Joy's valve

gear drove the trailing pairs of four driving wheels. The leading pair had a single-crank axle which was worked by one very large low pressure cylinder between the frames…. The wheels were not coupled, nor was there any separate starting valve. The two pairs of driving wheels acted on the 'go as you please system'.

'The great defect of these engines were, first, that they could not run fast downhill because of the great back pressure on the huge inside cylinder, which was in the larger engines 30in in diameter. Again they were bad starters. The two small outside cylinders could not start a heavy train but they could slip the small pair of driving wheels and so put steam into the low pressure chest. An engine might be seen at a station, with the trailing drivers revolving on the rails until the back pressure in the receiver became too great, and they stopped; then the low pressure engine would start. In all cases the train began to move with a more or less violent surging action and of this the passengers complained. It has always been impossible to obtain any accurate data as to the consumption of fuel in regular work….We have spoken of them in the past tense because the type is dead. Even Mr Webb gave up building them in 1897, when he brought out a very fine four-cylinder compound engine which has done excellent work, and is doing better since Mr Whale fitted it with separate expansion screws for the high and low pressure cylinders.

'Mr Webb's temperament was peculiar, and he was not fortunate enough to make many friends.'

Such was the man who led Gresley and so many other engineers in their formative

October 1897 and No 50, one of Webb's three-cylinder compound 0-8-0 Class A engines, built four years earlier, was posed in front of the materials used in its construction for publicity. With the spreading influence of PR and advertising, companies began exploiting this new medium ever more proficiently. Gresley learnt this lesson very early and proved excellent at manipulating its possibilities.

Webb's compound Jubilee Class gained a reputation for unreliability and his successor, George Whale, took the opportunity of re-building these, and Webb's Alfred the Great Class, into a new class of 2 cylinder simple engines called Renowns. Ex-Jubilee No 1913 *Canopus* is seen approaching Broad Street just before the Great War. Some accounts suggest that the rebuilds performed much better than the originals.

years who would later rise to prominence in their industry. Undoubtedly, they learnt a lot from Webb and don't seem to have shared the same cutting and dismissive views expressed in this caustic obituary. But what lasting effect did his leadership have on Gresley in particular?

To survive working with someone of Webb's temperament, you would have to be tough and diplomatic in equal measures. Inevitably you would also have to be sure of your ground and be well prepared to debate and justify your ideas, because everything you did would be scrutinised closely. Woe betide the person who sought to cut corners or waffle. Hard work, a keen understanding of your trade, original thought and extensive preparation would be key to your survival and development; these were disciplines essential to success at all levels, as Gresley would soon discover.

He would also have learnt a valuable lesson that was perhaps unintended by the CME. Webb worked frantically on many issues not simply those related to locomotive development. He was, by all accounts, an inveterate inventor, registering more than 80 patents during his lifetime. In addition, he was very active in local politics and contributed substantially to charitable causes. He was a man with many sides and a level of energy that men half his age would have envied. But there was a downside to this. His level of involvement could easily stifle creativity in others, especially as he seems to have disliked alternative ideas or anything that he might consider a criticism. Dynamism is a form of mania that can be very difficult to live with and may account for the suggestion that he had few friends. Gresley, who was also a man of great energy and intelligence, rarely, if ever, made this mistake, perhaps having seen Webb at work. He would choose a route that encouraged discussion, alternative views and team working, though ultimately, he took responsibility and expected loyalty, if not obedience, from those around him.

As his apprenticeship came to an end in 1898, Gresley could look back on an interesting period of education in a vibrant, uncompromising environment. He came away with good qualifications, although his final assessment fell short of the 'very good' rating most sought, being described simply as of 'good character and good ability'. But as Fred Lemon later recalled, 'Webb was grudging in his praise and rarely, if ever, waxed lyrical about any apprentice. A better measure of his opinion was the offer of a job when qualified and few premium apprentices managed this.'

So Gresley's time as an apprentice came to an end and he left with a broad array of engineering skills and knowledge, but also a deep understanding of the problems of design, construction and operation, to which was added a valuable lesson in how a senior manager could and should operate. He also took with him first-hand knowledge of the many concepts that Webb had espoused, whether it be the number of cylinders, the benefits of compounding and more and would himself toy with many of these ideas in due course.

Finding work after completing training, whether a premium apprentice or not, could prove difficult and in the aftermath of his father's death, and the dislocation this caused to his mother, sister and his life, the pull of many conflicting emotions added another degree of difficulty. The process could be more testing if that person was ambitious and looking for a post that would actively enhance their career. In Gresley's case, his answer was to seek, then settle for a period of 'pupillage' under another of Webb's ex-apprentices, John Aspinall, by then CME of the Lancashire and Yorkshire Railway,

John Audley Frederick Aspinall in 1899.

based at Horwich. It is uncertain how long this would last, but a year or two is suggested by a letter his mother wrote to Aspinall in early 1899.

Clearly concerned about her son's future, she sought some assurance that Herbert might be taken on permanently when his 'pupillage' came to an end. In response, he gave no promises but did hold out the possibility of future employment, adding (as Geoffrey Hughes relates), 'I shall be willing to consider that question if your son sees me personally on the subject.' His words contain a mild rebuke, suggesting it might have been better if Gresley had spoken to him directly, rather than through his mother, but he took the point and in due course considered a permanent position for the 22-year-old. In fact, it is quite revealing that Joanna Gresley, now living with her daughter in Turnditch,

In 1912 current and former L&YR senior managers gathered together for a re-union. In the seated front row were (left to right) Gresley, Aspinall, Hughes, Winder, Tatlow, Fowler and O'Brien. Also present were A C Stamer who would become Gresley's deputy within the LNER and John Billington (4th left middle row), Hughes's noted and some thought brilliant Chief Draughtsman who, but for his early death in 1925, might have risen to high rank within the LMS.

Derbyshire, became involved in her son's career in this way. One can only think that he was sufficiently worried about the future to express his concerns to her and as a good parent will she 'went into bat for him'. Within a month or so their joint effort bore fruit; Gresley being offered the post of Test Assistant in the materials testing laboratory at Horwich. But his stay there was to be a short one and he was posted to Blackpool in 1900 to become its running shed foreman for a summer season.

Meanwhile, Britain had been drawn into conflict in South Africa and many young men, Hewitt Beames amongst them, volunteered for service overseas. It seemed, as 1900 approached, that many more would follow and but for his blossoming career and meeting, then marrying Ethel Fullager, a solicitor's daughter, in 1901, Gresley may have gone to war as well. Instead he settled into married life and found his career quickly going from strength to strength as his IMechE application again bears witness:

1900 – Loco Shed Foreman, Blackpool.
1900–1901 – Outdoor Assistant, Carriage and Wagon Department, L&YR.
1901–1902 – Assistant Works Manager, Newton Heath, L&YR.
1902–1904 – Works Manager, Newton Heath, L&YR.
1904–1905 – Assistant Superintendent, Newton Heath, L&YR.

His rise was, by any standards, meteoric, but only one of these posts within the L&YR seems to have had any direct involvement in the business of locomotive design. For someone with his ambitions and aspirations, this was unusual. In fact, he doesn't seem to have spent much time, if any, in a locomotive drawing office or working on their design up to then, usually an essential part of an engineer's education, giving, as it did, time to learn, consider and set out practical design solutions. He would still have learnt a great deal about locomotive construction and performance in the wings, so to speak, plus the more practical problems associated with running a railway, but no direct involvement in design was a significant ommission. With Aspinall's elevation from CME to General Manager in 1899, with Henry Hoy promoted into the vacant seat, greater exposure to this sort of work was unlikely in the foreseeable future.

Hoy was, primarily, an electrical engineer, who had studied for a degree at Liverpool University before becoming a Webb apprentice in 1872. But he resigned in 1904 to become Beyer, Peacock and Co's General Manager, leaving the way open for the 39-year-old George Hughes, also a Webb apprentice, to take his place. It was a post he would occupy in one guise or another

at Horwich until retirement in 1925. For a rising star like Gresley, this presented an insuperable obstacle, because becoming a CME was an essential part of his climb upwards and now this route was likely to be blocked for a considerable time. So he was encouraged to look elsewhere and in 1905 successfully applied to become the Great Northern Railway's Carriage and Wagon Superintendent at Doncaster, a town soon to be the scene of his greatest triumphs.

Although only spending a comparatively short time with Aspinall, Gresley seems to have regarded this period of his life as a particularly important one, probably because it helped establish his name and career. The older man, it seems, quickly recognised the depth of Gresley's talents and felt sufficiently confident in his assessment to sanction such rapid promotion, then nurture and shape his burgeoning career as a leader and a close friend. During this pivotal period, Gresley would also have seen and been influenced by Aspinall's management style and his locomotive development programme, although largely curtailed by his promotion to General Manager, with three designs in particular being of note. These engines began appearing in the last year of Aspinall's tenure as CME, so best reflect the direction in which his thoughts had been moving since taking on the Locomotive Superintendent post in 1882. It was a comparatively short period but a highly productive one.

As always, it seems to be the case that express locomotives attract most attention, even though their impact on a company's profitability may be significantly less than a goods engine; his Class 7 4-4-2 two inside cylinder engines fell into this category. Once in service, their height, which was set by a large Belpaire firebox and 7ft 3in driving wheels, soon attracted the nickname 'High Flyers' and they quickly proved themselves to be strong, fast machines, considered capable of reaching 100mph, which it is said to have been achieved on at least one occasion. Forty were built in two

Aspinall was a locomotive designer of great standing and his 4-4-2 Atlantic Class passenger engine was a particular success. All 40 appeared between 1899 and 1902.

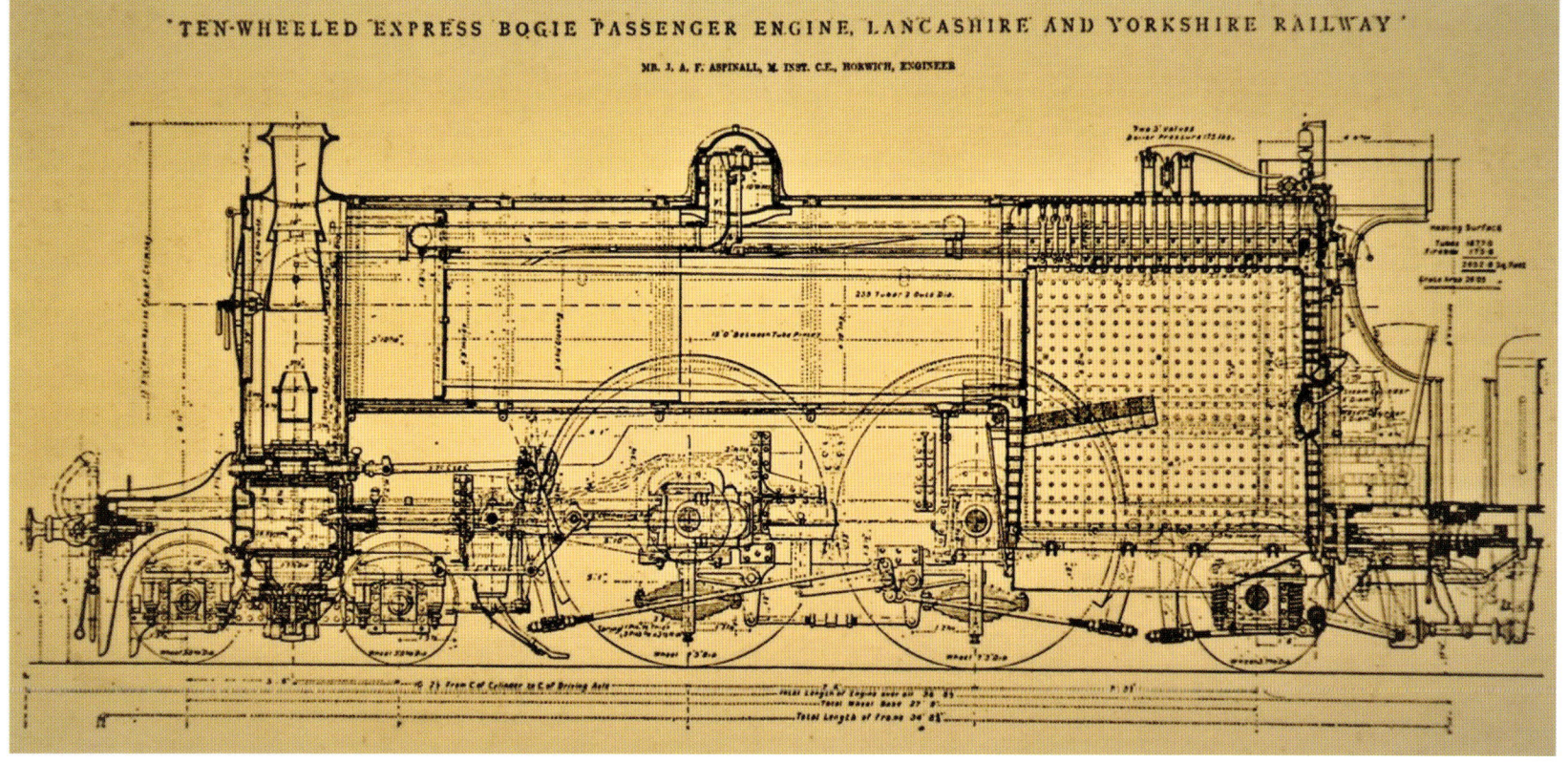

Aspinall's 2-4-2T engines under construction at Horwich. The photo also demonstrates the production line methods used by the L&YR at that time. Aspinall, as his IlocoE obituary recalled, was 'responsible for laying out the new works at Horwich'. In so doing he demonstrated the wider duties of a Loco Supt/CME, a lesson which Gresley was quick to recognise and practice.

batches, some seeing service well into the 1930s.

In terms of innovation, Aspinall decided to fit an experimental low heat superheater to a first batch engine, number 737. In this he was undoubtedly influenced by pioneering development work being undertaken in Germany by Wilhelm Schmidt. For a decade he had been working on this concept and by 1898 had advanced sufficiently to fit a Prussian Railways S4 4-4-0 locomotive with a unit with some success. Aspinall's model, within a 3ft 6in long drum fitted into the smokebox, was found to produce a level of superheat barely higher than normal steam temperatures, so, with heat dissipation quickly removing any advantage that might be gained, any benefits were minimal. But the trials continued and five batch two engines were fitted with a similar apparatus in 1902. However, despite mediocre results, these six engines kept their superheaters until 1917 when they were all removed. Schmidt and Aspinall's pioneering proved to be valuable and during the twentieth century was greatly refined and became hugely successful and achieved wider application, especially in Gresley's hands.

The second class which defined Aspinall's career seems to have been his Class 5 2-4-2 tank engines, which appeared between 1888 and 1911, 270 being constructed. Under Hughes, forty more were added, this time fitted with superheaters and a new Belpaire type firebox. He went on to adapt the design still further in 1911 by developing the Class 6, building twenty, and rebuilding 26 of Aspinall's originals and eighteen of his own, into this form.

In many ways, the design of this class provides an interesting demonstration of the way engineering projects evolve, then and now. Original thought there may be, but for the most part it is an amalgam of established ideas fused together to produce something new and, hopefully, better. Tom Coleman, later to be the LMS's Chief Draughtsman, called it 'cherry picking'. Maybe an over simplification, but coming from a man of such skill and experience, contains a strong element of truth and the 2-4-2T was just such a mixture – driving wheels from the William Barton Wright designed 0-4-4T, David Joy designed valves, Webb's axleboxes for leading and trailing axles, boiler from the Beyer, Peacock 4-4-0, Aspinall's vacuum operated reversible water scoop, round topped boilers replaced on many engines with the Belpaire firebox and much more. It was a mix and match arrangement which seemed to suit the industry, but there was also the occasional scientific leap forward that

embraced and developed a new concept, which then revolutionised design and construction. It was a lesson not lost on new engineers as they viewed the world around them, amongst them Gresley.

Aspinall's Class 30 0-8-0, introduced between 1900 and 1908, was a good example of the sort of unglamorous utility engines that were the backbone of any railway. In this case, the locomotives were designed specifically for the lucrative coal trade and were capable of pulling loads of 1,000 tons or more. The 60 engines in this class epitomised many of the ideas that Aspinall espoused during his career, particularly standardisation, simplicity of design, economy and strength. They incorporated, amongst other things, Joy valves, two inside cylinders, the Belpaire firebox, in this case a shallower version of those attached to the 'High Flyers', Richardson balanced side valves, steam reversing gear and built up crank axles. Although he didn't experiment with the 0-8-0 configuration himself, Gresley obviously understood the design concepts Aspinall pursued and would adopt the same practical, forward thinking approach to design when his time came.

Another area in which Aspinall influenced Gresley was in his advocacy of learned institutions, which he encouraged the younger man to join. He was himself a member of IMechE and the Institution of Civil Engineers, plus various Engineering Societies, and regarded this as an essential move for anyone wishing to further their career, explore their science and develop a wide range of contacts. So in 1907 he sponsored Gresley's membership of the IMechE and, earlier, the Liverpool Engineering Society. It was here that Gresley began to establish his credentials as a forward-thinking engineer and demonstrate his growing interest in the carriage and wagon side of the railway industry; an aspect of his career which would underpin much of his work when CME of the LNER in the years ahead.

In 1901, during a Society meeting in Liverpool, Oliver Winder, the Works Manager at Newton Heath, delivered a paper entitled 'The Design of Underframes and Bogies'. Gresley was quick to analyse its value and astutely found its weaknesses adding that:

'I would say, therefore, that the design submitted by the author would be hardly suitable for wagons in England. Of course, if a form of automatic coupler with a central draw and buffer arrangement is eventually used, the design for the underframes suggested by the author, could be adopted with advantage, but then the present wagons would be unsuitable to stand the shock of being buffered through the centre of the headstock. I should be much interested to know if the author could give any information as to the cost of

Aspinall's ultimate locomotive design – the Class 30. The last of these locomotives were retired in 1950.

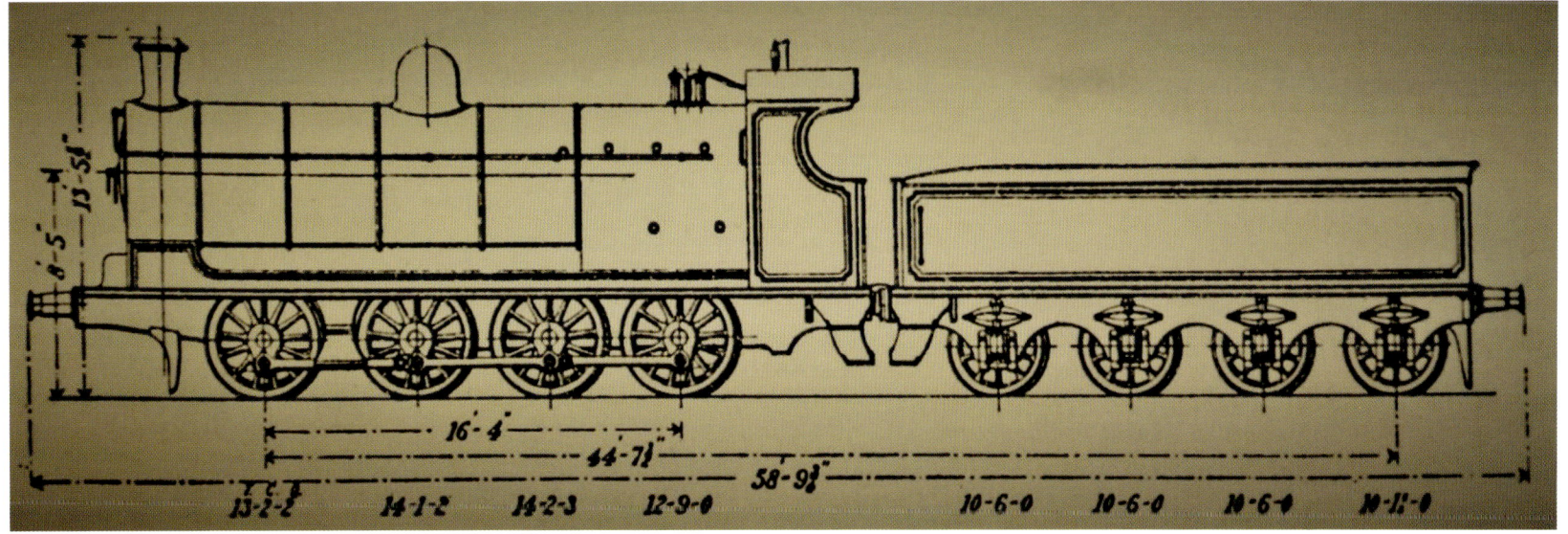

Henry Alfred Ivatt.

altering the underframe of the present form of wagon, so as to make it suitable for central, instead of side buffers.'

With such an incisive summary and apparent knowledge of the subject, it is perhaps not surprising that Gresley was promoted to become Works Manager at Newton Heath in 1902, replacing Winder in the process. Two years later he was promoted again, this time to Assistant Superintendent. From premium apprentice to such a high position in just six years is remarkable by any standard and in each case, he appears to have discharged his responsibilities with great skill and determination, proving that his elevation wasn't a case of benign patronage on Aspinalls' part. However, even allowing for such rapid progression an ambitious person will often cast about for other opportunities to exploit. This led Gresley to the Great Northern Railway where a new Carriage and Wagon Superintendent was being sought in late 1904, the current incumbent, Frank Howden, having decided to retire.

Henry Ivatt, the GNR's Locomotive Superintendent, had arranged for the post to be advertised, but none of the six candidates were found to be suitable and this led Ivatt, possibly with Aspinall's agreement, even at his suggestion, to approach Gresley. A private interview followed and from this Ivatt felt sufficiently confident to offer him the post and a start date of 20 February 1905 was agreed. With this, the final stage of his progression to the coveted post of Chief Locomotive Superintendent at Doncaster began, though by now the title of Chief Mechanical Engineer was becoming the norm in many companies.

It was here that Gresley renewed his working relationship with Francis Wintour. They had both been employed by the L&YR, but Wintour had preceded Gresley to the GNR, becoming the District Locomotive Superintendent at King's Cross in 1901. Born in Lincolnshire in 1862, the son of the rector of High Hoyland, he served his apprenticeship with Manning, Wardle and Co in Leeds, before moving to the L&YR then holding various Loco Superintendent posts with the company across Lancashire. He was one of the six unsuccessful candidates for the C&W Superintendent post eventually offered to Gresley. Although falling at this hurdle, he did impress the GNR's directors sufficiently to be offered the equally prestigious position of Works Manager at Doncaster and, until retiring in 1927, he forged a strong and productive working relationship with Gresley though, apparently, he wasn't Ivatt's choice. He wished to appoint Richard Maunsell but, for reasons which aren't clear, was overruled in this by the GNR's Management Board. Maunsell, then Works Manager at Inchinore near Dublin, went on to become the Great Southern and Western Railway of Ireland's Locomotive Superintendent and would eventually rise to become the Southern Railway's first CME, when the company was formed in 1923. It is an interesting thought that he might, if selected by the GNR, have been a natural successor to Ivatt. This could have changed the course of Gresley's career quite significantly and, in turn, the locomotive policy adopted by the LNER; conceivably no Pacifics or Mikados, but a preponderance of 4-6-0 designs, as befell the SR under his leadership.

When Gresley arrived at Doncaster, Ivatt was at the height of his powers having been appointed to the GNR ten years earlier, supported in his application by Aspinall and Webb, two of his fellow Crewe apprentices. Like Gresley and Wintour, he was the son of a clergyman, the Rector of Coveny-cum-Manea, born at Wentworth in Cambridgeshire during 1851. Unusually for an apprentice, he also trained as a fireman and worked on the footplate for six months with the LNWR before becoming Assistant Foreman at Stafford, then head of the loco departments at Holyhead and Chester. Ever eager for advancement, he applied and was selected, in 1882, to be

Continuous education was a theme practiced by the GNR as demonstrated here by a ceremony attended by Ivatt and Gresley, and many other senior officers, in 1910, to mark the opening of new classrooms and training facilities at King's Cross.

the Locomotive Engineer with the GS&WR at Inchinore, where Maunsell was his apprentice.

As his career progressed, he displayed an enquiring inventive mind, which he used to good effect. Like Webb, he experimented with compounding, the number of cylinders to be employed and much more, but he also looked broadly across the railway world for new ideas to consider, championing such things as wide fireboxes and Walschaerts valve gear. With the GNR, he had great scope to develop new locomotives and rolling stock with standardisation as one of a number of his aims. He also tackled the way the business was managed, including the workshops, which he re-organised along modern lines. Following his death in 1923, a widely circulated obituary neatly summed up his career and contribution to railway history:

'At this period [1885/1886] large increases in traffic were experienced, and more powerful engines were called for. His first engine differed from the practice of his predecessor – Sir Patrick Stirling – being a four coupled engine with a leading bogie, and a steam dome. He was the first to introduce into this country the 'Atlantic' type of engine, which at that time was the largest and heaviest in the kingdom.

'In 1901 he introduced a very powerful mineral locomotive which successfully hauled from Peterborough to London a train of 52 fully loaded 10 ton trucks, which, with a 20 ton brake, represented some 750 tons. Mr Ivatt believed in having plenty of boiler power on his engines, and was the first to adopt the Walschaert valve gear in this country. He was also the first to adopt superheating on both passenger and goods engines, and took out several patents in connection with locomotives and carriages – including the water scoop, built up crank axle and a sprung flap for vertically opening carriage windows.'

To this could be added a study of locomotive development in both France and the USA, which he regarded as being ahead of practice in Britain in many cases, plus a close interest in developing better, more modern rolling stock. In some ways, all he espoused could equally be applied to Gresley, As Bert Spencer recalled:

'They had much in common in their approach to locomotive and rolling stock design. When reading the copy of Ivatt's obituary that I kept it seemed to me that it could have applied equally to Sir Nigel. Although he must have learnt a great deal from Ivatt, he did not follow his ideas religiously but did adopt his working practices and way of thinking. They probably influenced each other in many ways and together must have made a dynamic impact on the GNR.'

It is probably the development of 4-4-2 tender engines for which Ivatt will be best remembered. It was a programme he began in the early 1890s when searching for a more powerful express locomotive to equip the GNR. Until then, the 4-2-2 class introduced in 1870 by his predecessor, Patrick Stirling, held sway. Ivatt believed that they were no longer capable of meeting the company's expanding needs and a replacement was required. His solution was to design a new class of engine based on the 4-4-2 Atlantic configuration, the first of which, No.990, appeared in 1898 to be tested and evaluated. It proved

Ivatt's first, experimental, Atlantic Class locomotive, number 990, which appeared in 1898 and were trialled rigorously before more of the type were built. They were later fitted with superheaters.

sufficiently successful to warrant production and twenty-two would eventually see service, the first of these in 1900. But it was a design he continued to develop and improve, leading to a version with a larger boiler.

The first decade of the twentieth century proved to be a dynamic period for the GNR with many new engines appearing in addition to the Atlantics. Although Gresley would be focussing on rolling stock designs, following recruitment in 1905, he would undoubtedly have been aware of these other developments and studied them closely. He was close to Ivatt and one wonders whether the younger man was drawn into discussions about locomotive policy or was able to advise his leader in any way. Someone with Gresley's strength of character and clarity of thought on many railway related matters would have made an excellent sounding board as projects developed, but this must remain conjecture, because neither man recorded their thoughts or memories of this period to any great extent.

Ivatt's development programme, which was driven by his perception of what the railway needed, based on statements of requirement from his Board of Directors, produced many new locomotives, not only the Atlantics, which pushed back the boundaries of what was possible. But this imposed a heavy burden on the works at Doncaster and it was necessary to 'sub-contract' some construction to other manufacturers. However, capacity across Britain appeared to be stretched at that time and the GNR, at the same time as the Midland and Great Central Railways, approached the Baldwin Locomotive Works in Philadelphia with a proposal for new engines, giving them a broad specification which allowed them a certain amount of freedom in their design. They produced a 2-6-0, with outside cylinders and six coupled 5ft 1 1/2 in driving wheels. Twenty were delivered to the GNR in 1900, but they appear to have been mediocre performers, their chief claim to fame being that they introduced the 2-6-0 concept to British designers who would take the concept forward, including Gresley with his GNR Class H2, then the LNER K series.

Also in 1900, a two-cylinder heavy duty 0-8-0 class of locomotive for the mineral trade appeared, with construction running on until 1909. This was followed by one more C1 Atlantic, No. 271, which was an experimental high pressure four-cylinder version of the originals, which, in 1904, was fitted with Walschaerts valve gear. Following tests, Ivatt concluded that any improvement over the original Atlantics was marginal. Consequently he looked at other means of enhancing their performance and in 1902 produced the first of his large Atlantics, the key difference being the size of the boiler. The first of these, No 251, appeared in December 1902 to great acclaim and led to further refinements, including the addition

One of the GNR's twenty imported Baldwin built 2-6-0 engines designated the H1. Apparently nineteen were assembled at Ardsley and one in France. They had short lives, all being scrapped by August 1915.

Ivatt's two cylinder 0-8-0 that appeared in 1900. The first of the class, No. 401 as designed and portrayed in publicity material. The reality with No.429, working hard in service. Ivatt's 0-8-0s became known as 'Long Toms'. Officially they were designated K1s by the GNR and later became Q1/Q2/Q3s under the LNER banner. Fifty-five were built and some lasted into the late 1930s.

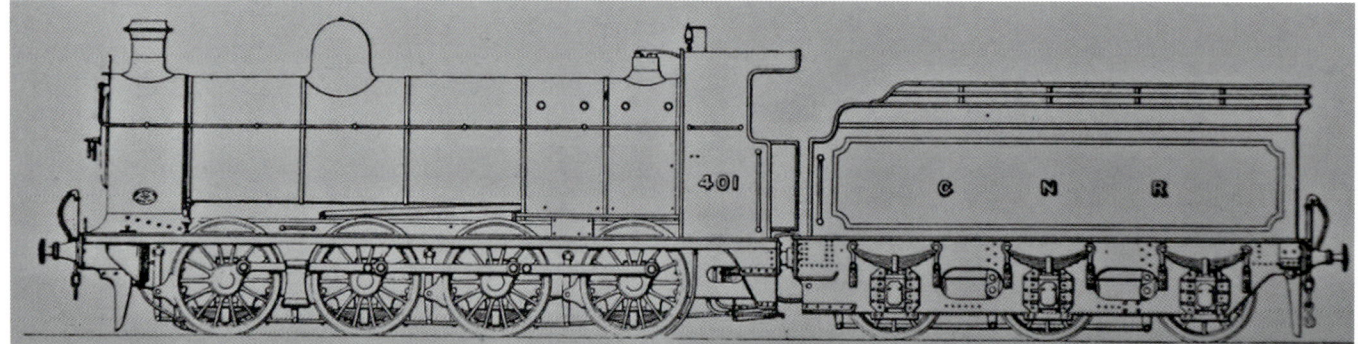

of a compound high pressure four-cylinder version, No 292, which was constructed in 1905 for comparative purposes. It was a project that underlined Ivatt's belief in trials and tests to prove a design and seek improvements. It was a mantra that Gresley adopted and relished, and one that became a cornerstone of all he did as a CME.

Amongst the remainder of Ivatt's locomotives there are two

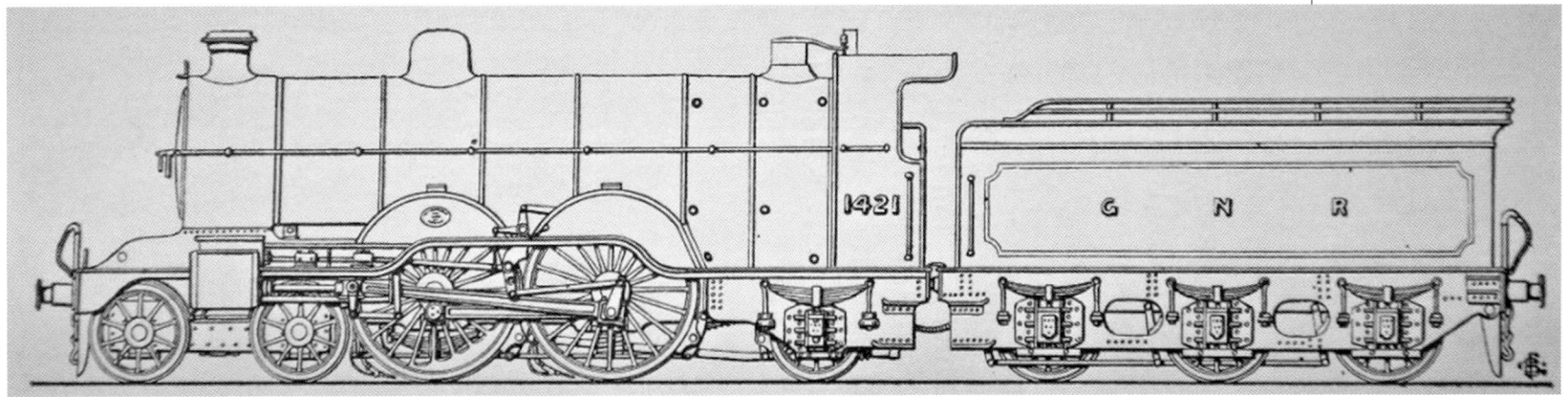

In 1907 Ivatt added another four-cylinder compound Atlantic to the GNR's fleet (No. 1421). Although having the general dimensions of engine No. 251 (below) it adopted some principles applied to the compound high pressure version of this class, No. 292. But in this case had all Walschaerts valve gear fitted instead of two being Stephenson's link motion based. The leading coupled axle was of the Ivatt built up, balanced type, and the boiler was also modified, the smokebox was set in advance of the chimney rather than extended backwards. It continued the compounding experiments with some success, but any gain in performance over the originals was deemed marginal and insufficient to justify the added costs of construction. It was modified in 1914 with the addition of a Robinson 22 element superheater, then completely rebuilt as a standard C1.

One of Ivatt's later C1 Atlantics, with larger boiler, at King's Cross in 1908.

that stand out. First came his N1 0-6-2 tank in 1907, followed a year later by the J21 0-6-0 six coupled goods tender engines. These both proved to be ubiquitous designs, often seen, but rarely given the attention or credit they deserved, but their influence on locomotive design in the GNR and then the LNER was significant. In the days before electrification, city commuter lines relied upon N1 engines and their like for motive power. In this role, and as general-purpose tank engines, they would see service until the late 1950s, so effective was their design. Yet it only came about when 0-8-2 tank engines designed and built to work on the GNR's suburban lines in London proved too heavy for this task, even when their weight was reduced.

The first N1, with its two inside cylinders, had the same problem and this led to their weight being redistributed. This was achieved by lengthening the rear frames

The N1 as designed and modified by Ivatt when its weight proved to be a problem (left) and then in service with the LNER (below).

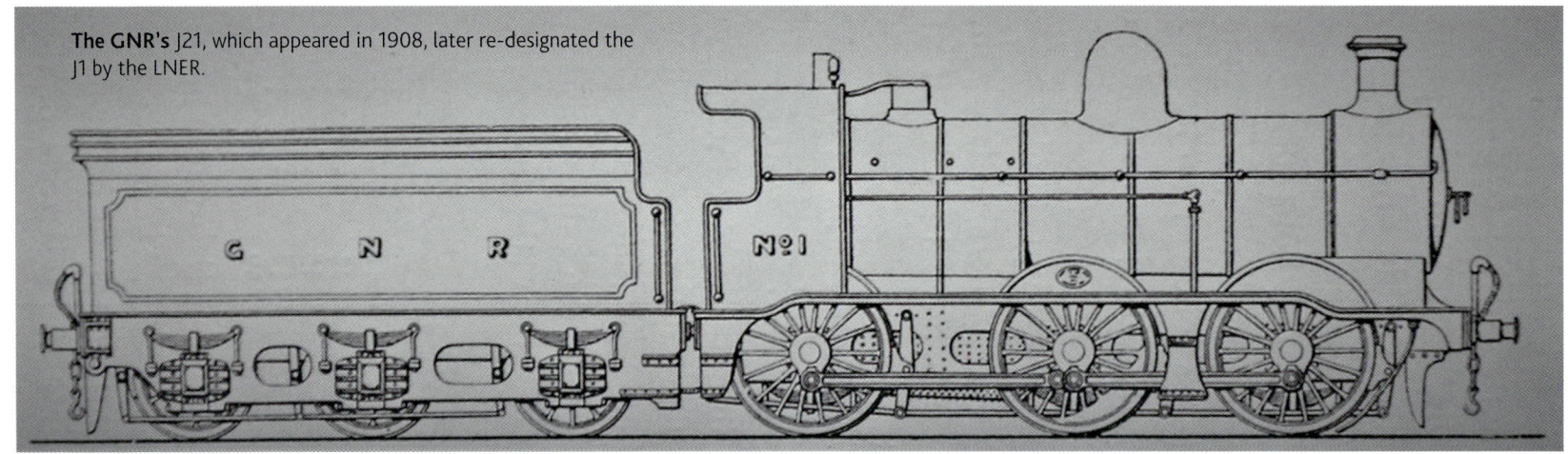

The GNR's J21, which appeared in 1908, later re-designated the J1 by the LNER.

A day to day scene on the GNR under Ivatt's management.

which allowed the radial wheels to be moved backwards. In addition, the side water tanks were shortened and a larger rear bunker was constructed. Fifty-two of the fifty-six built were also fitted with condensing gear to allow them to work on the Metropolitan's underground lines and in time eleven would be superheated with Schmidt or Robinson units. These modified boilers performed so well that they became a standard fit on other classes, including the D1, D2 and N2.

Ivatt, ever conscious of the need to achieve some commonality of parts and spares, would use the boiler, cylinders, motion and wheels when designing the J21s. With their two inside cylinders, six 5ft 8in coupled driving wheels, a total heating surface of 1250sqft and a grate area of 19sqft, they proved successful in pulling fast goods and could also be pressed into service on passenger duties when necessary. Only 15 were built, but their mixed traffic ability made them a valuable addition to sheds at New England, King's Cross, Ardsley and Colwick. It was a type that seemed to impress Gresley and, as the LNER's CME, he would take the concept further and build the J38 and J39 classes, producing 35 and 289 of these respectively.

While Ivatt was designing and constructing locomotives, many of which would carry on being developed long after he retired, Gresley's main focus remained on the carriage and wagon side of business. In many ways it was a sideshow, especially for someone who aspired to be a CME and pursue the more complex, but higher profile field of locomotive development. Nevertheless, his post did, at least, allow him to cut his teeth on the design of rolling stock and bring it up to a standard better able to meet the ever-increasing demands of industry and passengers. It proved to be an essential part of his education as an engineer, but also helped his development as a senior manager, where so much more has to be considered and accomplished.

During his six-year tenure, he led on developing an experimental 35 ton goods wagon with rotating bogies, then took the concept

During 1905, within months of Gresley's appointment as Carriage and Wagon Supt, two steam rail motor-cars appeared from the works at Doncaster. They combined a tiny 0-4-0 locomotive on the same frames as carriages with elliptically shaped roofs for use on the Louth to Grimsby line. The design of the carriages, but not the loco, is often credited to Gresley and they do clearly show some hallmarks of his work. It was a small project, but an interesting beginning to a long career as a designer.

forward with carriage design. The GNR had built up a large stock of fixed wheelbase coaches and need dictated the development of longer carriages. However, the heavy investment in older style units made it impractical to simply abandon them and the GNR developed the idea of joining two together permanently, with three bogies, the middle one shared by both carriages. This idea, which became known as articulation, was adopted and gained Gresley much credit in the process, though, as Geoffrey Hughes pointed out in his biography, it seems to have had its origins in the USA during the 1860s. By 1911, 100 fixed wheelbase carriages had been converted and new construction had also adopted this principle. Gresley, in due course, patented the idea and would use it again when creating a set of carriages to accompany his high profile streamlined locomotives in the 1930s.

An Ivatt Atlantic. No 984, with a rake of teak sided clerestory carriages, passes by in the early years of the twentieth century. This style of carriage would give way to Gresley's more modern designs.

The result of the GNR's experiments with articulation, a concept pursued by Gresley with his Silver Jubilee set in the 1930s.

A typical example of Gresley's early ideas on carriage design, in this case a dining car that appeared in 1906. The six-wheeled bogies soon gave way to the 4 wheeled type. One constant complaint centred on the square corners of windows and panels, which were poor at letting water run away. As a result, rot set in quite quickly.

The GNR's senior managers in late 1911 on the eve of Ivatt's departure. Lord Allerton, the Chairman, and Oliver Bury, the General Manager, are not included.

A formal portrait of Gresley issued by the GNR in early 1912.

It is fair to say that Gresley involved himself fully in the development of rolling stock and was prepared to investigate and use novel ideas whenever necessary. But the bulk of his work was more traditional in nature and focussed on providing carriages with greater capacity and other refinements when necessary, such as corridors and dining facilities. He built these to the full width and height allowed by the loading gauge, sometimes with two six-wheeled bogies, but he didn't ignore other needs and led in producing such things as non-corridor types with 4-wheeled bogies for the less important routes.

Although his time as Carriage and Wagon Superintendent would have been active and rewarding, promotion to CME would have been his undoubted goal. In 1911 an opportunity arose for this to happen when Ivatt announced his intention to retire in September on his 60th birthday. It seems that Gresley, now an engineer with an emerging profile and a mature father of four (Nigel, born in 1903, Violet in 1904, Roger in 1906 and Marjorie in 1908), was thought to be his natural successor and was groomed for the role by Ivatt and the Great Northern's 70-year-old chairman, William Jackson, 1st Baron Allerton. But their plans nearly came unstuck when Gresley received a leg wound from a blackthorn spike, which caused sepsis and superficial phlebitis to set in. Today, anti-inflammatory and antibiotic drugs, with sterilized dressings, would be standard treatment. In their absence, Gresley's health quickly deteriorated to the point at which amputation and severe disablement seemed likely, with death a possibility too. To halt the decline, leeches were applied to draw out the poison. This cure, recommended and administered by a Harley Street specialist brought in by Jackson, took some time to restore Gresley to health and left him with a weakness in the infected leg.

It appears that the chairman had few, if any, doubts about Gresley's ability to do the job, though would clearly have harboured concerns about his health, allayed, somewhat, by his eventual return to work in October 1911. He may also have looked around the railway industry for other likely candidates just in case he didn't recover, but without advertisement, application or interview the matter was resolved in Gresley's favour. Ivatt postponed his departure until December, allowing a smooth transition to take place. As the new year dawned the new man at the helm could look back on his professional life with some satisfaction. He was lucky to have been blessed with great skills and even luckier to have been nurtured and trained by so many able people, who seem, for the most part, to have identified his potential and help draw it out. But even the most optimistic of them may not have realised how much higher he could fly and the impact he would have as a leader and an engineer.

Chapter 3
GRESLEY'S NEW WORLD (1912–22)

No matter how talented and trusted a deputy is, that person cannot experience the true rigours of leadership until in the seat themselves. There is so much more to consider and balance, with unknown and unsuspected levels of politics, economics and social pressures brought to bear. A deputy may have some insight into this complicated world but will have little or no experience of dealing with these problems first hand. There is no substitute for experience and those thrust into the limelight may soon be exposed and found wanting. In the commercial world, this can quickly lead to disaster, as the GNR's directors knew only too well. So in selecting Gresley, the in-house candidate, Lord Allerton played for safety and hoped this course of action would succeed and avoid too many pitfalls along the way. But it was still a huge gamble, especially when selecting a man to follow a leader of such skill and quality as Ivatt. In these situations, comparisons will be drawn, unfairly or otherwise, and criticism follow if the expected high standard of work isn't maintained. In truth, it is probably better to succeed someone who has performed badly where the bar has been set far lower. Gresley didn't have this luxury, but he was astute enough to ease himself into the role, with guile and common sense. With Ivatt's work on locomotives and rolling stock, in which he had actively participated, now well founded, there was a comparative period of calm in which to play himself in.

Behind him he had an established and experienced team to provide support. For the next two years they worked effectively on plans initiated by Ivatt to meet the company's developing needs. However, few could have guessed what lay ahead when in 1914 a European war became a reality. Peacetime plans were put on hold and the world descended into a conflict of unimagined horror and ferocity.

So Gresley's time as the GNR's Locomotive Engineer had three distinct phases – before, during and after the war, with each being

Gresley in 1916.

driven by different priorities and needs. And each would present a stern test for this most vigorous and motivated of men. Although his work was driven by external needs and economic pressures, there was still room for him to experiment and look beyond established ideas to consider novel or unusual solutions. Whilst Gresley's career up to then centred primarily on rolling stock, he had

At the 1909 Imperial International Exhibition the GNR displayed two of their locomotives to show how far they as a company had developed their designs. Ivatt's Atlantic No 1442 dwarfs Stirling's 8ft Single No 1. Gresley would continue this locomotive development programme to great effect.

always shown great interest in all facets of railway engineering and locomotive design in particular. He looked broadly and kept abreast of all new concepts being explored and this approach became a cornerstone of all he did.

To supplement all the knowledge he was acquiring, Gresley became a member of the IMechE in 1907, sponsored by Ivatt and Aspinall, then the Institution of Civil Engineers and, during 1911, the Association of Railway Locomotive Engineers. These groups were formed of a cross section of the brightest and the best in these fields and became centres of knowledge, where research could be discussed, probed and developed. For those

William Jackson, Lord Allerton (left), who 'gambled' on Gresley and appointed him Locomotive Engineer and Oliver Bury, General Manager, who was party to this decision and remained a supporter when he became one of the GNR's directors in 1912.

with active, questioning minds, such as Gresley, these bodies provided an essential service which he constantly contributed to and used whenever possible. IMechE also provided a forum where senior railway engineers, no matter where their company loyalties lay, could forget their tribal bonds for a time and openly discuss new developments and assess their relative merits.

With men of the calibre of George Churchward, Henry Fowler, Dugald Drummond, William Stanier, Vincent Raven and John Robinson as fellow members, not to mention the leading lights from other industries or academia, the depth of discussion was extensive and would contribute

Goods traffic provided a primary source of revenue for any company, none more so than the 0-8-0 locos run by the GNR. Here engine number 401 gets to grips with an exceptionally long load.

greatly to Gresley's deepening knowledge and desire to experiment. Amongst those he became acquainted with through learned institutions were Edward Hopkinson, who specialised in electrification projects; Henry Hele-Shaw, an automobile engineer of note who became a leading light in aviation, designing the variable pitch propeller; and Joseph Petravel and Richard Glazebrook, both Directors of the National Physical Laboratory at Teddington. However, these men were only a small part of his ever-increasing circle of scientists from across many fields and each new contact produced even more links, some of which would grow in their usefulness as the 1920s gave way to the '30s.

Two of these were the science graduates Frederick Johansen and Thomas Herbert, both of whom were sponsored by the NPL's Director as they passed through King's College, London, and Cambridge University respectively. Johansen, from the earliest, had been fascinated by gas, air and fluid motion and formulated some of the earliest principles of aerodynamics, which he applied to aircraft design, including Supermarine's S type racing aircraft and the Spitfire. Meanwhile Herbert, an ex-Marlborough man, was noted for his work on heat, structures and metallurgy. In both cases, these were subjects that Gresley realised could have wider application in the railway world and he often sought out these two young man whenever he could to discuss these issues.

The common ground between these three men was immense and each was also imbued with the need to experiment, test and explore the potential of new ideas at each stage of development. It was a theme Gresley would return to many times in his career, especially when pursuing, with great determination, the creation of a dedicated loco test centre. For Johansen and Herbert, such facilities were a basic part of life and they would, in time, take their knowledge and skills to the LMS to help in their development programmes. Remarkably, the change in employment status didn't stop Johansen continuing to act as an advisor to Gresley as he developed his P2s and A4s.

What becomes clear from all this is the level of Gresley's scientific curiosity and his desire to experiment. The railways were central to his working life, but he looked more broadly and took a wide interest in many areas of research. In some ways, he probably found the world of steam locomotives confining, because the science they espoused, though still just active in the early twentieth century, could hardly be called cutting edge and was probably in an early stage of its death throes. But with a country run on cheap and plentiful supplies of coal significant changes were unlikely.

Gresley was undoubtedly a man who thought deeply about the future, as good scientists do, and perceived a world unbounded by present day constraints. In many ways, the railways still reflected a hidebound approach to the future, which he must have found frustrating at times. Though gainfully employed and achieving much, his talents went far beyond the area in which he worked. If he had been a young man between the two world wars he would probably have taken his great talents into one of the emerging fields of science and engineering, aviation for example. As it was, he made the best of what was on offer and sought to develop the dying science of steam locomotives as far as possible, with a nod to the future in considering such things as aerodynamics. We are a product of the age in which we live and have to work within the limits imposed by the masters of that time but even so, Gresley did seek to push back boundaries and develop new ideas, as his record of patents bears witness; a practice he continued at regular intervals until 1930, shortly after his wife's death.

Although all his patents were railway oriented, they covered a wide range of subjects, each demonstrating his keen grasp of design and the science involved. They included improvements to articulated rolling stock; superheaters; lubricators; boilers; valve gear; pony trucks; and booster engines to the development of axle-trucks or buffers combined with draw-gear as couplings. In addition, he frequently presented papers to the institutions to which he belonged, encouraged others to do so as well and invariably assessed other people's papers with honesty, great insight and understanding, drawing out themes that the author might wish to consider. His inclusive approach was in marked contrast to Francis Webb and demonstrated a desire to encourage discussion and innovation without thought of personal aggrandisement, but to achieve an advance for the collective good. It takes someone with immense self-confidence to do this and a remarkable lack of ego for such a strong, dominating personality.

Gresley was also an early member of the Institution of Locomotive Engineers, formed in 1911. In some ways, it was an offshoot of IMechE and would grow considerably in its membership through its regional branches. During 1918, a branch in Leeds came into being and Gresley was elected its Chairman. On 11 May he gave an inaugural address that summed up some of his emerging thoughts and philosophies on design. But, rather strangely, he left out a number of key issues which by 1918 were important features of his work. These were engine types and his growing interest in the Pacific configuration, the number of cylinders to be employed and valve gear, which by 1918 had already resulted in one patent:

'In the days of strenuous competition the Great Northern has always more than held its own; this is largely due to the comfort, speed and punctuality of its services, for which the Locomotive Department has principally been responsible. For these results my predecessors are responsible, and I have only to carry on their good work.

'It is now 25 years since I started at Crewe Works in an atmosphere of compounds in the locomotive engineering profession…. But there was no lack of enterprise in those days; a triple expansion engine was tried, an 8 figure firebox, and several boilers with a water space underneath and at the sides of the ashpan were built….Then I remember an attempt to do away with coupling rods, by the provision of a friction wheel, held up tightly between the coupled wheels by a steam cylinder, and which was to be released once the engine got away with its train… I could quote many other experiments of great interest, some of which have failed, and some succeeded, but all added to our experience.

'The locomotive of today is a very different machine to those to which I have just referred.

A period of transition can be difficult, but when Ivatt gave way to Gresley he left the company's locomotive and rolling stock fleets in good order as the picture here of Atlantic No 1456 and a new rake of carriages demonstrates. The engineering is up to date and the looks are modern.

The evolution of locomotives on the GNR in the years before Gresley arrived on the scene. Many of these classes were still plying their trade in the years before and after the Great War. The new CME would take locomotive design to a new level.

The improvement is chiefly due to a kind of continuous evolution. During the past ten years this has been greatly accelerated by the introduction of superheating. I am not going to say much about superheating beyond this - its full advantages have not yet been appreciated.

'The power of an engine depends upon its capacity for boiling water. The boiler is therefore without question its most important feature, but many engineers still compare the power of engines by their tractive force only and not the boiler. As a measure of the power of an engine, tractive force is useless unless the boiler is able to supply the necessary steam for long and continuous service.

'A boiler which will supply steam when an engine is notched up to 20% cut off, and which fails to do so when the engine is let out on a long incline and has to work at 50 or 60% cut off, is too small for the cylinders on that particular work, although it might be quite large enough were it only on shunting duties.

'Tractive effort, per se, is useless as a comparative measure of the power of engines. On the GNR

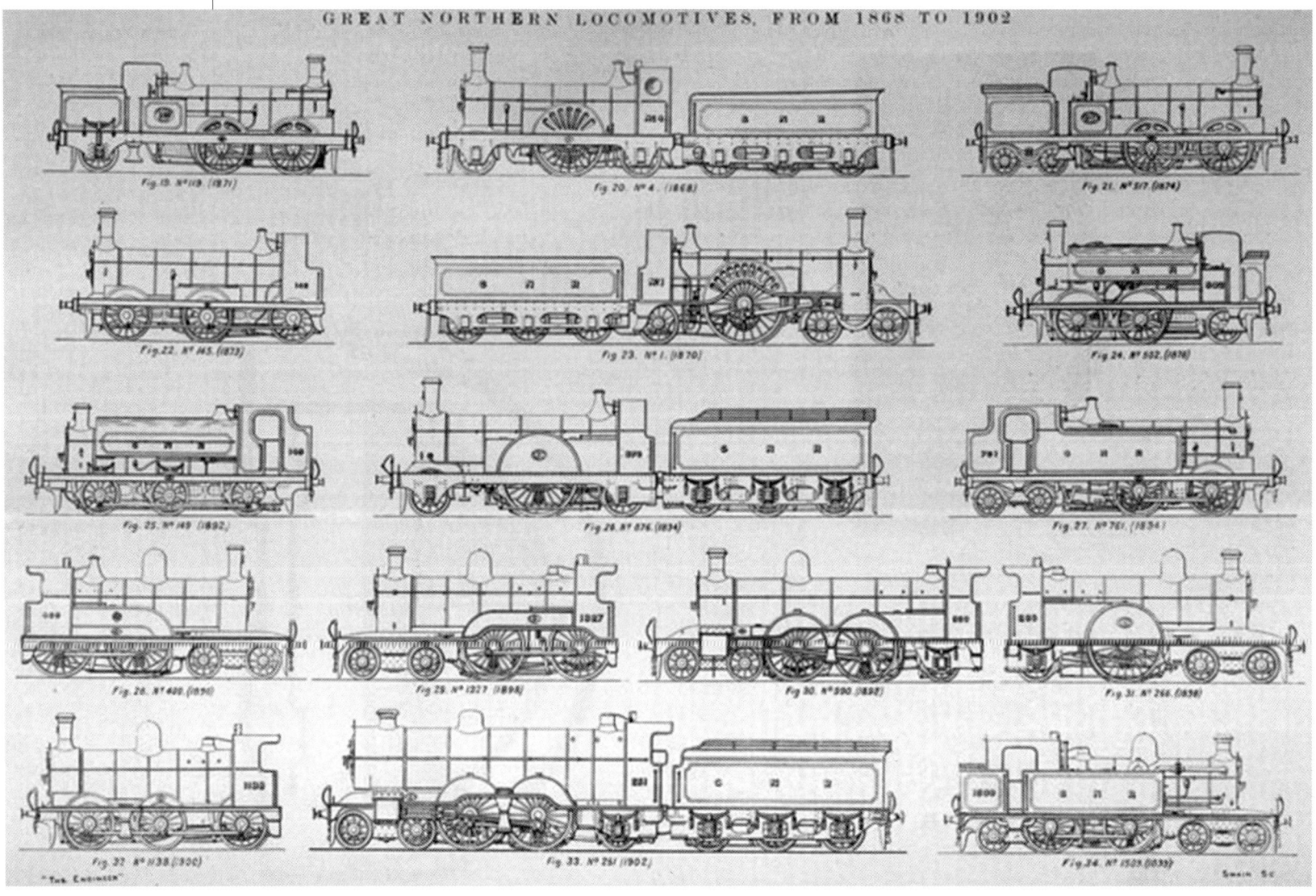

there are two very instructive examples of this fallacy.

'Mr Ivatt's first Atlantic engine had comparatively small boilers according to present day practice. The heating surface was 1,442 square feet and a grate of 26.75 square feet. The large boiler Atlantics have 2,500 square feet of heating surface and 31 square feet of grate. Except for the boilers, the engines are identical so far as boiler pressures, cylinders and wheel diameters are concerned. Therefore, the tractive powers are equal, but the large boilered Atlantics have proved to be much more powerful as express engines and are able to haul much heavier trains and keep time.

'Then later on when the 2-6-0 type was introduced the first ten had smaller boilers – 4ft 8in diameter. The later ones had boilers 5ft 6 in diameter, but the grate area was the same in each case, and the engines in other ways were identical. During the last year's work the ten engines with the smaller boilers consumed about 5lbs. more coal per mile for the whole year than the engines with larger boilers.

'Talking about fireboxes, it may be of interest to record that the wide fireboxes of the Atlantic engines introduced by Mr Ivatt are more economical from the point of view of life, and I think also from the point of view of efficiency. Recently I had to condemn one of these large fireboxes which had run 420,000 miles. Although the first engine of this type was built 16 years ago none of the boilers have been scrapped, and the first boiler is still running. This is fair proof of satisfactory design and work done in connection with the wide firebox and large boiler.

'The work done by these engines is as heavy as that done by any passenger engines in the country, and the trains hauled by them often exceed 500 tons behind the tender today. These engines have the biggest boilers and smallest tractive power of any working on the principal railways of this country.

'Then there is the much debated question of Belpaire and round topped boilers. I have tried to find some explanation for the apparent conviction of certain engineers in the superiority of the Belpaire type. There must be some explanation of this. I venture to suggest that this conviction is the result of experience. In the case of almost every railway which has adopted the Belpaire box, the firebox roof of the old round topped boilers were stayed with roof bars, which are well known to be objectionable on account of the difficulty in keeping the firebox top free from dirt. Naturally, when they introduced Belpaire boxers with direct roof stays, many of the troubles disappeared and the improvement was put down to the adoption of the Belpaire type boiler. On the other hand, the use of general stays in round topped boilers has been the general practice on other railways. To such the Belpaire boiler offered no advantage; in fact, on one line it was tried and abandoned. I have, therefore, come to the conclusion that, from a maintenance standpoint, the Belpaire boiler offers no advantage over the direct stayed round topped boiler, whilst undoubtedly its first cost is greater. This view is supported by the experience of American and Continental engineers, where the use of the direct stayed round topped boiler is generally adopted for all new engines.

'Another feature worthy of note in modern engines is the tendency towards greater accessibility of working parts. Outside cylinders, and particularly outside Walschaert valve gear, offer great advantages. It is possible to secure better cross-bracing of the frames, to say nothing of easier oiling, inspection and maintenance of motion. With such an engine it is not necessary to put it over a pit before leaving the shed and the essential parts can be better examined in a good light, a very important consideration.

'The use of mechanical lubricators for axleboxes has also tended to simplify the work of the enginemen, the oiling of all boxes being controlled by one lubricator. There has been a marked decrease in the number of hot boxes and an economy in the consumption of oil, due to the fact that when an engine is standing no oil is being used. It is an important point that the mechanical lubricator should be connected to a point in the motion which has a constant travel and not to a valve spindle, of which travel is reduced as the engine is notched up.'

Having carefully described some of the ideas central to his work Gresley then turned his attention to the future and outlined some of the issues he believed important. He began with a simple statement of intent – 'I am a strong advocate of standardisation in principle, but not necessarily of standardised locomotives'. But to this he added a brief rider, suggesting that, with the war still taking a heavy toll of the country's resources, now was not the time to push forward these ideas. Instead, he turned towards the subject of engine size, before returning to the theme of boilers:

'A few months ago I was reading a very interesting address, given to one of the American Societies, in which the writer said, with regard to locomotives, that it has been comparatively easy to make them bigger and heavier, but a greater and far more difficult problem faces us today, viz., that of making every pound of weight justify itself in terms of power. Undoubtedly engines are approaching their maximum weights and sizes in this country, but are a long way from attaining their maximum power. We can, and shall have to, get more power per unit of weight.

'The most efficient boiler is one which absorbs the maximum amount of heat from the coal burnt per unit of weight; to produce more power without increasing the weight is one of the problems to be faced. How is this to be done? One obvious way is to pre-heat the feed water; very little has been done so far in the matter of really satisfactory feed water heating. Many arrangements have been applied, but none have yielded such striking results as to justify their general adoption. In most cases, owing to the heaters getting blocked up, their efficiency is so much reduced that there is no return for the extra cost of fitting and maintenance.

'But the possibilities are far greater than is generally recognised. It is calculated that roughly three quarters of the heat which is generated in the firebox of a locomotive is wasted up the chimney. This doesn't mean that a locomotive boiler has an efficiency of 25% only – the efficiency is somewhere nearer 70%, because of the heat wasted up the chimney, more than two-thirds is in the exhaust steam and the rest in the flue gases.

The economy to be obtained by the introduction of a really satisfactory feed water system is second only to the economy which has resulted from superheating….. but to secure the ideal result the temperature of the feed water must be pre-heated to that of the water already in the boiler; troubles such as leaking tubes and broken stays would then practically disappear, and the amount of water evaporated per pound of coal would increase to a surprising extent.

'The locomotive boiler should not be required, as it is today, to heat up its feed water, and should only be called upon for evaporation and superheating; but the problem is by no means easy.'

He then discussed the means by which the problem might be solved, analysing the benefits of exhaust or live steam heaters, with or without top feed, stating a preference for the live version. But he didn't develop the debate any further and quickly moved on to the design of grates, which he believed had 'shown no marked improvement for many years', adding:

'This is a very important point in locomotive design to which no special attention has been paid, yet in giving the leading dimensions of an engine the grate area has always been one of the cardinal points. Grates cannot be made much larger, but they can be made more efficient. American engineers have been devoting considerable attention to this subject. Conditions requiring the maximum power demand that air spaces between the bars shall be as large as the character of the coal burnt will permit without actual waste of unburnt coal through the spaces between the bars. I know lately some considerable progress has been made in the design of grates and also ashpans. In the arrangement of the ashpan itself, unless properly designed, the advantage which might be expected from an improved grate may be nullified.

'Considerations of ease of maintenance have largely influenced firebox design. If more units of work have to be obtained per unit of weight out of locomotive boilers, the fireboxes will have to be designed to give more complete combustion and possibly with the provision of combustion chambers and auxiliary air supplies.'

And so his paper ran to its end, touching on such things as the use of pulverised coal, which was becoming a part of life in wartime when the quality of coal available was slipping, and rolling stock design. But by this stage his key messages had been fully aired and he ended with an exhortation to those present:

'The energies of everybody here must be concentrated on the work of the moment – the winning of the war. When this is accomplished, I say, will be the time for the locomotive engineers to bring their broadened experience to bear on the problem of transportation, and apply the engineering knowledge, experience, and, most important of all, the engineering adaptability, which this, the greatest of all wars, has taught us.'

As an address rather than a formal presentation, Gresley did not face any rigorous questions and it was left to Colonel Kitson Clark, the Vice-Chairman, to summarise the

During 1913 Gresley had developed his theories on superheating to an advanced level. A key part of this work was his twin-tube superheater which contained 34 flue tubes, with an external diameter of 4in, with each element being in two flue tubes. This arrangement placed the saturated header above the tubes and the superheated header below. This design was used most successfully in the N2 0-6-2 tank engines, having first been trialled in one of Ivatt's N1s, No.1598.

speech and thank the presenter. However, Gresley did pick up a number of remarks made whilst he spoke and added one final comment before the session ended:

'There is just one point. It is in reference to an observation made by my friend on the left. He asks, "Why not a wide firebox?" The answer is that we have not had an engine to build which was big enough. If, and when, it is necessary to build an engine of this type it will certainly be considered.'

In the weeks before his presentation, Gresley clearly gave a great deal of thought to a number of issues and those he covered he chose most carefully, bearing in mind the nature of the audience. In some ways, his script is a statement of intent, with the years beyond the war seen as offering infinite possibilities to be explored and exploited. Nevertheless, Arthur Stamer, who was in the audience, was surprised that Gresley didn't touch upon alternative forms of motive power, particularly electrification with the

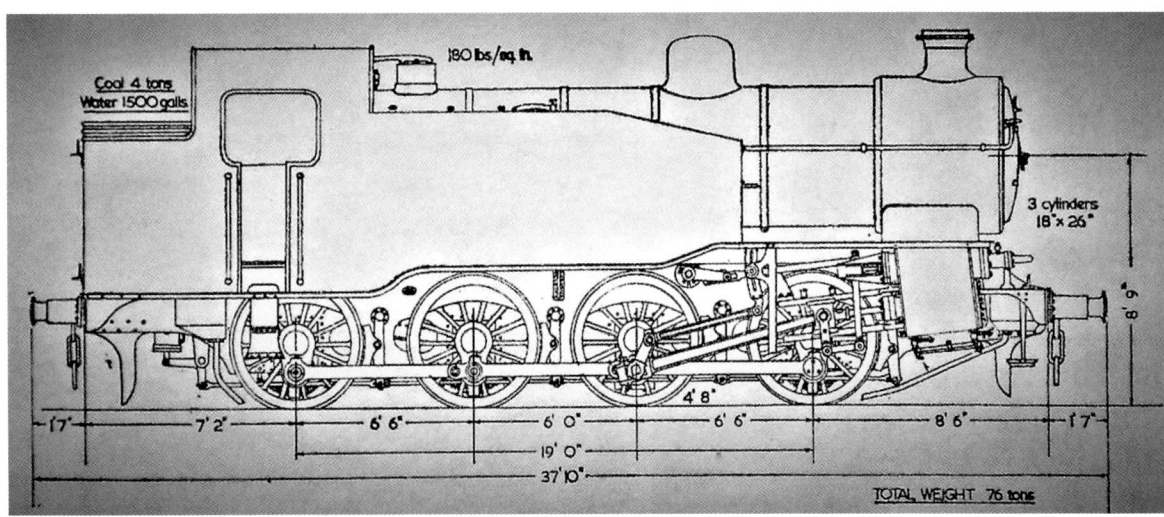

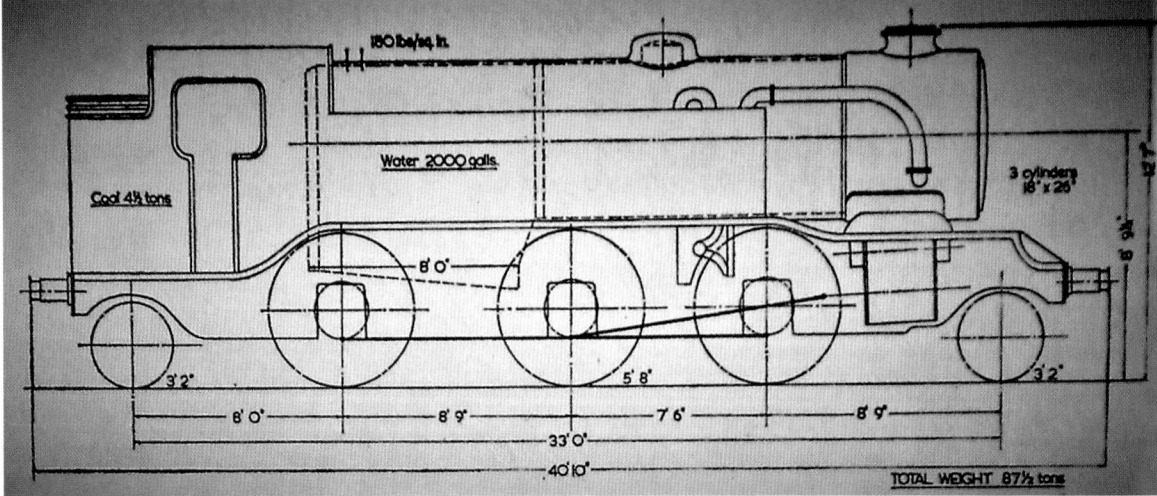

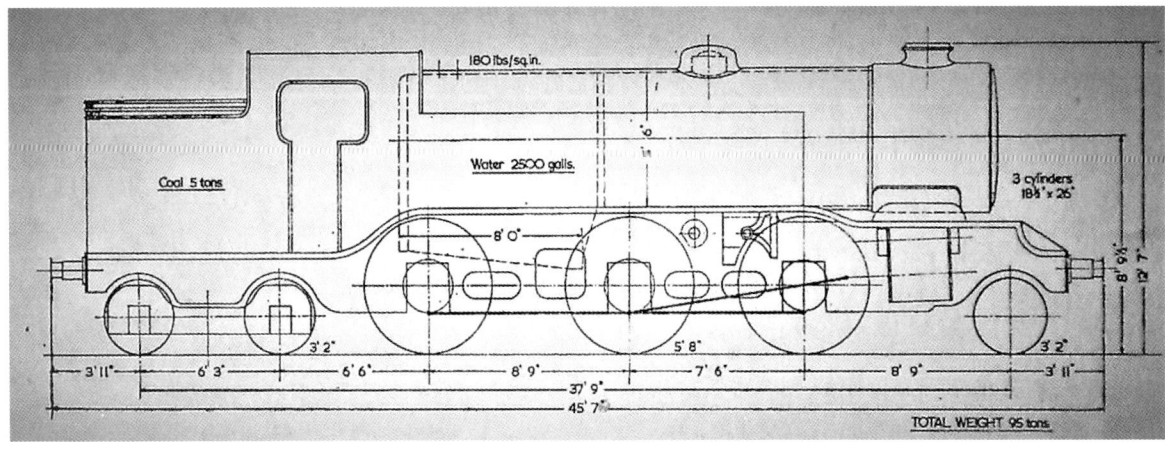

With the war dominating all that the railways did, construction of new locomotives and rolling stock was subordinated to the needs of the conflict. But planning for a return to peacetime life still went ahead and various concepts were investigated by Gresley and his staff. This resulted in a number of new designs being considered including these examples of three cylinder tank engines that were drawn between 1917 and '18.

GNR and NER making advances in this field. The speaker didn't respond to this statement, perhaps not wishing to be held a hostage to fortune or simply because he realised that the chances of it happening in the foreseeable future were slim. Yet years later, when he was elected President of this Institution, he stated emphatically, that:

> 'I should remind our members that this is an Institution of Locomotive Engineers, not an Institution of Steam Locomotive Engineers; all kinds of locomotives, steam, oil and electric, are our concern.'

There doesn't seem to have been any trace of regret when he said this, because he goes on to say that electrification has proved to be a viable option on the Southern Railway and on the Continent too. But, despite this, he believes there is still a place for internal combustion engines, such as diesel, and steam traction, if both undergo improvements. This is very much the voice of a forward-thinking man, but also a pragmatic moderniser eager to embrace all sciences, though recognising the

Gresley's New World (1912–22)

The first new engine to appear following Gresley's promotion to Locomotive Engineer. The H2 2-6-0 mixed traffic tender engine concept was still largely untried in the UK until the GNR, GCR and the Midland Railway bought some examples from the USA, where its use had been widespread for many years. Though these imports were not particularly successful, they encouraged British companies to experiment with the type. The GNR would build ten H2s (later re-classified K1) between 1912 and '13.

economic and political pressures that exist. He espoused all three technologies but realised that the change from steam to diesel or electric would be a slow one. In 1912, this was still far in the future and when he took office steam still reigned supreme. So he set about improving the stud of locomotives under his control, modifying existing stock, continuing to build Ivatt designs and building some new ones that reflected his own ideas.

The first two 'Gresley engines' to emerge appeared in 1912 and 1913 respectively, passing through the workshops alongside more N1s and J2 mixed traffic 0-6-0s amongst others. The first, a 2-6-0 mixed traffic locomotive, was produced in such a short timescale that it is likely to have been on the drawing board when Ivatt was still in charge and the new Locomotive Engineer on long term sick leave. Either way, he played a significant role in its development and the engine that emerged reflected the evolutionary process Gresley described in his paper during May 1918, as did the second type, a 2-8-0 heavy goods engine, brought out to supplement the Ivatt 0-8-0 'Long Toms'. Although these had proved successful, they were finding it increasingly difficult to meet the growing needs of freight traffic the GNR was attracting. It had soon become apparent that something stronger was needed to haul heavier trains.

It is interesting that his thoughts should turn to 2-6-0 and 2-8-0 classes for his first designs. Neither had played a significant part in Britain's locomotive history up to that time, though their use was becoming slightly more commonplace. Both types had been widely developed in the USA during the last decades of the nineteenth century and in the early 1900s had begun to find some supporters in Britain. Perhaps the most important of these had been Churchward, who led in designing the GWR's successful Class 2800 2-8-0 that first appeared in 1903. As a disciple of the Swindon man, Gresley would have taken note of all that was happening there and followed his example if it met the needs of his own railway company. But the Great Central Railway's 8K 2-8-0, designed by their talented CME, John Robinson, also provided an example that Gresley could not fail to have observed when they began appearing in 1911.

With the 2-6-0, his reasons for taking this design route are less clear, especially when considering the company's experience when purchasing twenty of the type from Baldwins of Philadelphia at the turn of the century. These were all withdrawn in 1915, after only 15 years of fairly mediocre service, so hadn't set a particularly good example to follow. However, the 2-6-0 still offered many advantages that the GWR, in particular, under William Dean, then Churchward, began to recognise and exploit with their Class 2600 in 1900 and Class 4300 ten years later. In fact, between June 1911 and the early 1930s, the company would, after an initial batch of 20, build another 322 4300s, so successful was the design. Once again Gresley would have seen this work going on at Swindon and considered their move to be a sound one. But in Gresley's hands it turned out to be a slightly different beast being fitted with Walschaerts valve gear to match its two outside cylinders.

The first locomotive, No.1630, designated H2, appeared in August 1912 and went through a period of evaluation before nine more were ordered the following year. In due course, Gresley reviewed his design and decided that a bigger boiler was needed; a move that mirrored Ivatt's work on his Atlantics a decade or so earlier. But in this case the H2 concept was modified from a 4ft 8in diameter boiler with an 18 elements superheater, producing a pressure of 170psi, and a tractive effort of 22,070lbs, to one with a 5ft 6in diameter boiler producing 170 lbs of pressure, a 24-element superheater and a tractive effort of 23,400lbs. This new engine, designated the H3, first appeared in 1913 and by 1921, seventy-five had been built. It was an evolution that would carry on through to the end of Gresley's life and be taken on by his successors, in one form or another, as they sought to extract the maximum performance from the 2-6-0 design.

The 2-8-0, or Class 01 as it became known, was another design that would undergo change. It adopted many features included in Gresley's Moguls – two cylinders, 21in by 28in, coupled to Walschaert

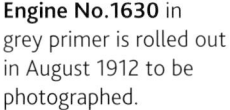

Engine No.1630 in grey primer is rolled out in August 1912 to be photographed.

One of Gresley's H3s, in this case modified to burn oil, a concept that the CME toyed with for a time. With coal cheap and plentiful any gains from conversion tended to be swallowed up by the extra cost of oil. It was a theme that would occasionally be re-visited over the years.

valve gear and a 24-element superheater. The design also mounted the largest boiler so far built by the GNR and owed much to Ivatt's work in this field. It had a combined heating surface of 2,654sqft and the engines produced a tractive effort of 31,860 lbs. This exceeded Ivatt's Q series, including those modified by Gresley during 1913 and '14, by replacing their saturated type boilers with superheated versions, by a margin of between 2,000 and 5,000 lbs.

Described by some commentators as 'simple and strong', they appear to have performed excellently but the impact they made was probably muted by being built in two groups – five before the war and fifteen afterwards. It was the sort of engine perfectly suited to wartime use, where the ability to pull exceptionally heavy loads and be easily maintained were paramount. Instead, 129 of Robinson's 8K 2-8-0s, followed by 521 8Ms, a derivative specially built for the War Office, filled this requirement, whilst 84 of Churchward's Class 2800 did sterling work over GWR's metals.

In May 1918, Gresley added a three-cylinder version, the O2, constructing one single locomotive, No. 461, to test the principle. In many ways this was his most ambitious design because it brought together many ideas he would go on to use regularly over the years in his search for greater efficiency and better performance. The war made speculative new construction very difficult but didn't stop him or his team considering the future as a paper exercise at least. As the hostilities wound down and a return to normal business seemed likely, Gresley was encouraged to develop his thoughts and begin building locomotives again. No 461 became the focal point for these

Gresley's second design was the two-cylinder Class O1, 2-8-0 heavy goods engine. Twenty were built in two batches (five in 1913/14 and fifteen in 1919/20) to provide a sturdier goods engine than Ivatt's 'Long Tom' 0-8-0s to meet an ever-growing demand for freight trains.

efforts and came to be considered as a test bed for new ideas.

Basically, he took the O1 design and fitted three smaller in line 18in by 26in cylinders with external Walschaert gear connected to the inside cylinder by a conjugated valve gear. It was a concept that Harold Holcroft, one of Churchward's gifted young engineers on the GWR, had patented in 1909, but allowed to lapse in 1913. His work had explored a concept initially investigated and patented in the 1870s by David Joy, a mechanical engineer and inventor of note, when working for Barrow Shipbuilding Co. In 1880 he presented his findings in a paper to the IMechE, but his death in 1903 opened his patent and his research up for others to explore. This gifted designer had sought to link three cylinders in a triple expansion engine for use at sea. Gresley was also aware of this research and Holcroft's work, considered the concept and took it further, resulting in his patent, number 15769, being submitted during 1915. In essence, his solution used a rocking valve to control the valve on the inside cylinder. It was described as a 2 to 1 lever that derived the motion for the central valve from the motion of the two external Walschaert valve gear. To make this possible, it was soon discovered that the cylinders would have to be set at a steeply inclined

Gresley wanted to take the O2 design a step further and produced this single three-cylinder version in 1918. He poses with his new engine, No. 461, shortly after it rolled out of the shops prior to testing. It would be three years before another 10 appeared and new construction would continue, on and off, until 1942/43.

angle, with shorter connecting rods than those used in the O1s.

Throughout the design process, Gresley considered that the advantages to be gained by using three cylinders, rather than two or even four, greatly outweighed the complexity of the valve gear he patented. He believed that three cylinders achieved the same power as two larger cylinders, but created far less wear, so reducing maintenance requirements and achieving longer life.

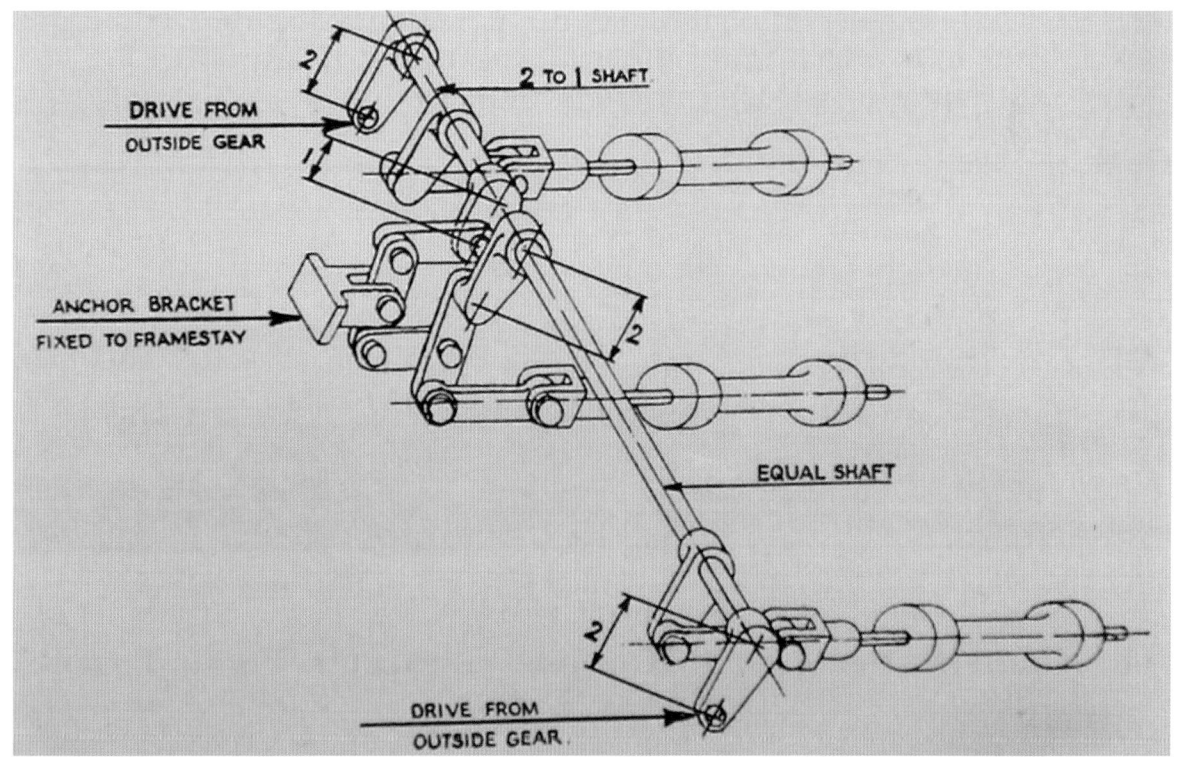

Spencer's drawing of the Gresley valve gear on engine No. 461.

The coming of war in 1914 meant that the workshops at Doncaster took on a variety of other work. Two Class N1s were purchased by the War Office to power armoured trains to help protect the east coast. The conversion work, it seems, was completed under Gresley's direction. Another key piece of GNR and Gresley's wartime work was to produce hospital trains, as portrayed here, and munitions to support the Army and Navy. In recognition of this the CME was awarded a CBE in 1920.

In the trials that followed on a number of routes, though primarily hauling heavy coal trains between London and Peterborough, the engine showed itself to be superior to the O1s and as the trials progressed, Gresley began the process of refining his ideas, seeking out Holcroft to discuss the concept, for which they shared credit. At the same time, Holcroft, by now serving with the South Eastern and Chatham Railway, was invited to join the ILocoE and in November 1918 presented a paper on the subject which Gresley was unable to attend, though they eventually met two months later.

In his book *Locomotive Adventure*, Holcroft makes only a passing reference to these events but he does leave an interesting thought hanging in the air suggesting a hint of displeasure with himself, for being too slow in completing his research, but also Gresley for adopting it in his patent:

'As regards the three-cylinder valve gear, the Record Office said that the time was getting short in which to draw up and lodge the Complete Specification at the Patent Office, so this had to be attended to at once. During my absence [in Canada and the USA] they had made an extensive search and found that David Joy had applied a form of conjugated valve gear for operating the middle valve of triple-expansion marine engines, and therefore my claim could not be for entire originality, but would have to specify particular ways of operating the middle valve, accompanied by drawings of them. I set to work but, what with the need to make haste and some loss of enthusiasm over the device not being altogether original, and there was no prospect of a three-cylinder engine being built in Swindon, all possible forms in which the invention could be applied were not fully exploited, with the result that H.N. Gresley of the GNR found a loophole a few years later on, which a little more thought might have closed.'

If he did feel that Gresley had muscled in on his work, the GNR man did smooth things over to a certain extent. Holcroft, later in his book, describes their meeting in a positive way:

'He wrote later and invited me to meet him at his King's Cross office in London at 2.30 pm on January 19th, where I presented myself for what proved to be an historic occasion. Gresley was very frank and went straight to the point; he said that the performance of his 2-8-0 and No 461 had satisfied him as to the superior results obtained by the use of three cylinders. Now that I had given him the key to the solution of the problem of applying his simple combination to any type of engine, it was his intention, henceforth, to build nothing but three cylinder engines.

'We then got down to details, and I pointed out that placing the inside steam chest in a

Harold Holcroft when serving with the GWR before the Great War. He was an exceptionally talented engineer who went on to serve the Southern Railway with great success under Richard Maunsell then Oliver Bulleid as CME. Yet he could have so easily ended up with Gresley at Doncaster and, possibly, played an even more important role there, especially with the LNER's ambitious steam locomotive programme taking root.

horizontal position at the side of its inclined cylinder and giving the steam ports a twist in so doing would present no difficulties. The passage of steam would not be affected by the shape, whilst any skilled patternmaker could deal with the shaping of the ports. As regards the crank axle, this would have to be moved round through an angle of approximately 7 degrees in relation to the two outside cranks to give six equal pulses and exhaust beats.

'The position of the combination was then discussed; my proposal was to locate it behind the cylinders so that it would not obstruct

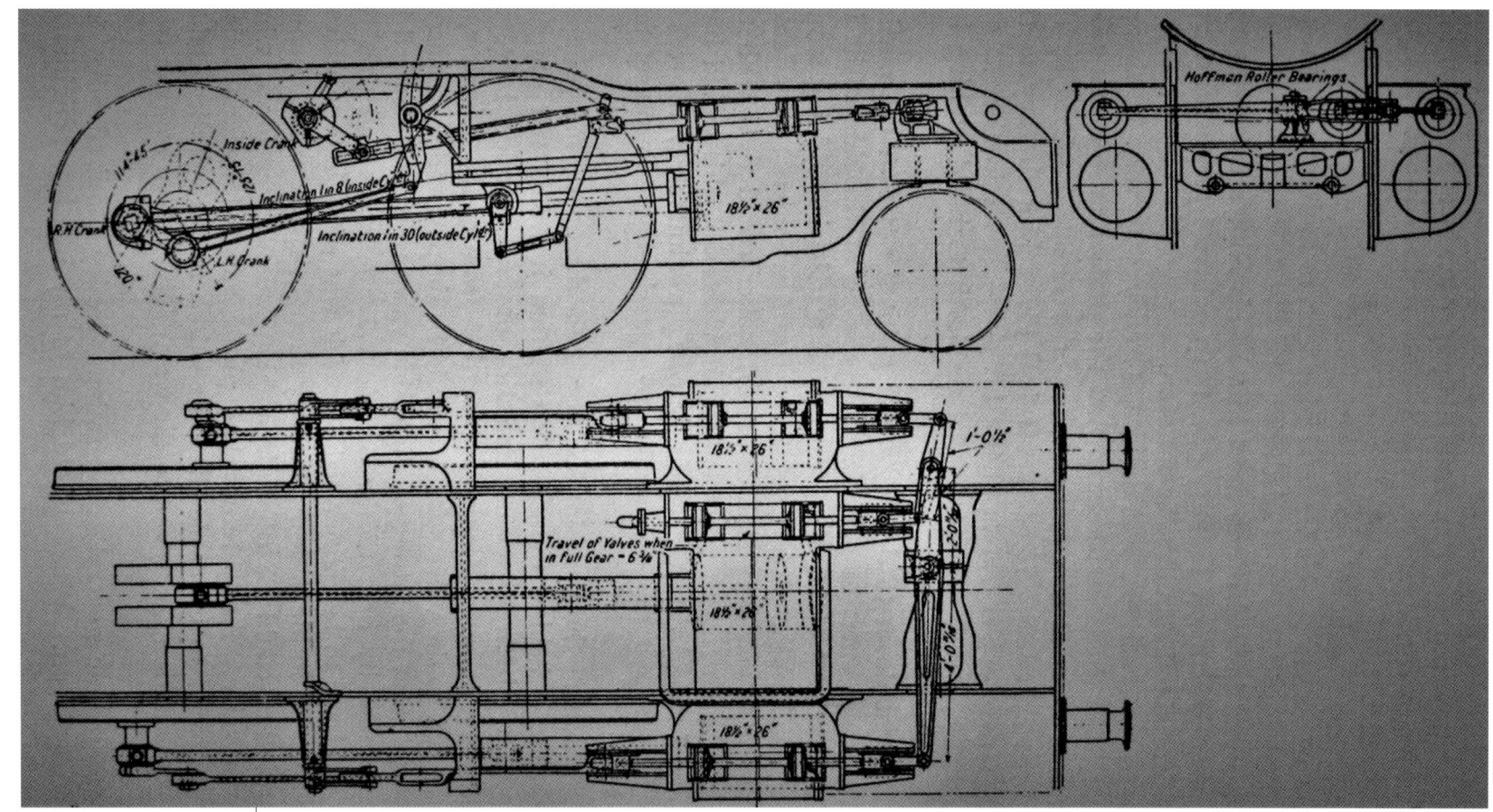

Shortly after engine No 1000 appeared this diagram was published showing its valve gear layout as developed by Gresley and his team at Doncaster. It went on to be used by the GNR, then LNER for its three cylinder engines. In his papers Harold Holcroft kept copies of his and Gresley's work with many comments transcribed across them delineating possible proprietary rights.

withdrawal of piston valves or the inside piston. Gresley, however, preferred that the levers should be placed in front of the cylinders, as the connection to the valve spindles would be simpler and more direct. I pointed out that the setting of the inside valve would be affected by the lengthening by heat of the outside valve spindles and that the gear would have to be dismantled before it was possible to withdraw piston valves or inside piston. Gresley thought that the lengthening of the spindles would be offset by making allowances for it when setting the valve. As to removal of piston valves for examination, he was prepared to uncouple the connections to the spindles and to lift the combination bodily out of the way. This was how matters were left.'

It seems to me that Gresley regarded these discussions as a means of marking the boundaries between his and Holcroft's work; to identify and make plain the differences. If so, he may have felt vulnerable to an accusation of plagiarism from the younger man or at least some criticism from within his own profession. But he was a strong leader and a man of great substance and people like that tend to prefer negotiation of a sensitive issue and offer some inducement or flattery to help achieve settlement. Holcroft went on to record that:

'Following our general conversation, Gresley inquired what job I was engaged on. When I told him my wartime activities he exclaimed, "But you ought to be on locomotive work…..we could do with you at Doncaster." I explained that I was still attached to Ashford and that if he thought anymore of the matter it would be necessary to approach Maunsell in the first place. With that we parted, both feeling highly pleased with the results of our collaboration.'

I expect Gresley may have been the happier of the two. However, there was an interesting follow up which Holcroft also reported:

'The next time I saw Maunsell after the King's Cross meeting, I informed him of my interview with Gresley, but he made no comment then. About a week later he said very tersely, "By the way, I have seen Gresley and told him that I propose to construct some three cylinder engines and shall need your assistance here." On my telling James Clayton (Maunsell's Personal Assistant) of this, he hinted that there was more to it than what was said to me and that affairs had been somewhat heated!'

The meeting in Leeds of the ILocoE during which Holcroft read his paper had one interesting attendee, Bert Spencer, who had only just been elected a graduate member at the end of his apprenticeship. In 1918 he had already joined IMechE and the dual membership was most unusual for someone so young and inexperienced. To have reached this stage so early in his career bears testimony to his talents and Gresley's backing. What he and his immediate colleagues had spotted isn't recorded, but he seems to have been a man singled out for special attention and from here the opportunities to enhance his career grew rapidly, at first from within the Drawing Office at Doncaster.

Although proving to be a success, No. 461 didn't immediately lead to more O2s being built. Ten were eventually constructed for the GNR by the North British Railway Company in 1921, then 15 more followed from Doncaster Works during 1923/24, with another 41 gradually appearing, in three more batches, by 1943. It wasn't a massive programme, but the railways had had to absorb many hundreds of ex-War Office 8Ms when the conflict ended, so the need for more GNR O2s was hardly a pressing one. No. 461's real significance lay in encouraging Gresley to push ahead with his proposals for more three-cylinder designs, which he did with great enthusiasm, starting with a new 2-6-0 Mogul that appeared in 1920 and with it the distinctive look of a 'Gresley engine' began to emerge.

Evolution will often see a number of small, almost imperceptible changes being made before a perceived master work appears and so it was with Gresley. But with this locomotive there was a step change which marked a boundary between the past and the future and it was a feeling visually reinforced when the first of the new H4 class engines, No. 1000, appeared in the early months of 1920. With an immense 6-foot diameter boiler, the largest to appear on a British locomotive up to that time, the new engine was imposing, yet the project had taken quite a long time to reach fruition. This was partly due to restrictions imposed by the war, but also the need to develop the concept of a three-cylinder engine with a conjugated valve gear. There were also concerns that an engine with such a large boiler couldn't stay within the maximum loading gauge permissible on the railway. As these problems were gradually resolved, the design came together and as O.S. Nock reported, in his classic book *Locomotives of Sir Nigel Gresley*, word soon spread through the railway world that something special was on the way: '…after the Armistice the news got about that a 'super' main line locomotive was under construction at Doncaster; everything pointed to a Prairie at least, if not a Pacific, and then No.1000 came out. This remarkable engine created quite a stir at the time…'

There was clearly a sense of expectation which may have been carefully sponsored by Gresley and the GNR. As events would soon prove, PR had been more widely embraced by a country grown used to high levels of propaganda of one sort or another during the war. With these new found techniques reputations could be built and prestige enhanced, not solely with the aim of increasing demand or profits. In Gresley's new locomotive there was much to attract attention and be exploited, even though only ten were built by 1921 and were initially employed on fast freight duties. Here they proved themselves to be effective engines, especially during the 1921 coal strike, when wage reductions were imposed on miners. Many engines of different types, the H4s amongst them, were pressed into service to ensure that a supply of coal was maintained from docks and stores. Once this was over, they began work pulling passenger trains between Doncaster and London. With their immense strength and a tractive effort of 30,031lb, loads of 600 tons were not uncommon.

1920 and the new Mogul makes its appearance at Doncaster.

The second H4 in action on the down train from London passing Potters Bar in 1921 or 1922. It appears to be making light of its load, which is recorded on the back of the print as being 9 carriages.

Records show that even with substantial loads, they could keep to scheduled times, maintaining an average speed of 50mph in the process. However, their riding qualities were described as 'lively at speed', which may well have been an understatement. Nevertheless, the crews must have relished being able to ride on the footplate of such strong engines with their reserves of power no matter what the load.

The H2, H3 and H4 designations for these 2-6-0 classes would disappear in 1923 when the LNER was formed and they became the K1, K2 and K3. Only the last of these would continue in production, with another 183 being produced between 1924 and 1937, proving themselves to be all Gresley hoped that they would be.

Gresley's third design as Locomotive Engineer focussed on the need for an improved shunting loco. These classes tended to be Cinderellas within a company's railway fleet – often ignored and taken for granted, but essential for day to day operations. The GNR tended to favour 0-6-0 saddle tanks for this work, such as the J13, but it was felt that a loco with side tanks offered greater adhesive weight in areas where steep gradients existed, most notably in the coal mining districts of the West Riding. So, in 1913, the first of a new class of 0-6-0, the J23, made its appearance. With two inside cylinders, 18 in diameter and 26in stroke, a 4ft 2in boiler, a combined heating surface of 1,119sqft and 4ft 8in coupled wheels, they produced a tractive effort of 23,630 lb, well in excess of the J13s.

Gresley's plan was to produce the class as cheaply as possible, without sacrificing performance in any way. One measure of economy involved re-using 4ft 2in diameter boilers removed from Ivatt's 0-8-2T when this class was being uprated with new, larger boilers. The barrels had to be cut down to fit the J23's shorter wheelbase, but this didn't seem to present any significant problems. A 16-element superheater was fitted to one of the first batch of ten built to test its effectiveness, but it didn't improve the performance to any great extent and the trial came to an end with the other members of the class remaining saturated steam versions.

Thirty of the class were built between 1913 and 1919, but the programme went on in fits and starts until 102 had been constructed, though the later ones received larger boilers when surplus 4ft 5in diameter units became available. These were fitted to the next batch to appear and this pattern continued until the programme came to an end in 1939. When the LNER came into being in 1923, the first 30, with the smaller boilers, were re-designated Class J51s and the remainder J50s. In these forms some lasted in service until 1965 and were always regarded as steady, capable performers.

The first J23 in service. This locomotive would later become one of the LNER's J51s.

When peace returned, and with it many of the engineers who had gone to war, such as Bulleid, Thompson, and Peppercorn, the railways could again look to the future. One key issue that quickly re-emerged was the need of employees wishing to commute to towns and cities, but particularly London, for work. The level of traffic was expected to rise as the economy returned to normal and servicemen were demobbed and returned to work; or, at least, this was the hope, because no one could predict with any certainty how quickly Britain's industries would recover. But business has to plan well ahead and assume that the economy will grow, recession will be avoided, and demand will increase. Politicians in these post-war years also predicted a rapid growth in suburban housing, caused in part by the rail networks which had opened up a vast swathe of land for development. The GNR was aware of this and planned for an increase in traffic using the N1 0-6-2 tank engine pulling a rake of high-density commuter carriages as their model. Other railways would develop electric trains for this work, especially those around the south of London, but this involved a high capital cost that would be hard to justify in a time of austerity. So Gresley and his team set to work in the immediate aftermath of war to update engines and carriages for this task.

To be truly effective, these engines had to be capable of pulling large loads through the commuter belt, managing frequent intermediate stops to pick up or put down passengers. To do this, they needed good brakes and to be able to pull away quickly so that narrow time slots in high density schedules could be met without the network becoming snarled up. To achieve this, the basic concept of the N1 was taken and from this the N2 was developed, appearing in 1920 and '21. Before this happened, though, Gresley and his designers did consider other options, such as a 2-6-2T and a 2-6-4T, but these were rejected on weight and length grounds.

The N2 bore a strong resemblance to its predecessor, but they did differ in some important respects. They both had two inside cylinders and the same size boilers producing virtually the same pounds per square inch of pressure. Their grate areas were both 19sqft and the main wheels 5ft 8in in diameter and the trailing wheels 3ft 8in. They could both carry four tons of coal and the axle loading of the N2s was 19 tons compared to the N1s' 18 tons. The N2s were all superheated, but only eleven N1s would be similarly equipped between 1918 and 1928; when Gresley sought to upgrade some of the class. The piston sizes also differed. The N1s were 18in by 26in and the N2s 19in by 26in, with the N2s being fitted with piston valves to control the flow of steam rather than slide valves. The N2s could also carry more water – 2,000 gallons as opposed to 1,600 gallons – and produce greater tractive effort – 19,945lb compared to the N1s' 18,427lb, in original condition, or 17,900lb., when superheated.

The N2s were more powerful and economic to run than the N1s and proved themselves to be superior in every way, or so it seems. By 1921, sixty were in service, fifty of them built by North British, the remainder at Doncaster. Another forty-seven would be added by the LNER between 1925 and 1929, some produced at Doncaster and others by Beyer, Peacock, Hawthorn Leslie and the Yorkshire Engineering Company. It is said that Gresley would have preferred to have built a larger tank locomotive than these for commuter work and there had been a great deal of planning work at the end of the war to create other designs but these came to nothing and the N2 appeared instead. Nevertheless, this class proved to be one of his most successful designs part supported by Francis Wintour who had led in producing the N1s.

In many ways, all these classes of locomotives, no matter how successful, are now perceived as a series of minor or major steps in Gresley's rise to prominence. Stride by stride he seemed to be heading for something of greater significance – something that would come to define his career. As the war ended, he was reaching the peak of his powers and could begin to shrug off the shackles of that terrible conflict and plan for the future. Gresley had played an active part in the conflict by organising the works at Doncaster to support the war effort, for which he was awarded the CBE in 1920, but this had been a distraction from his and the GNR's main purpose. Now they faced up to the future with a railway and a workforce badly worn down by conflict, with little prospect of major investment in an infrastructure that had been sorely tested by war. Change would not

The changing scene at King's Cross with N2s dominating North London's commuter trains.

be quick, especially with central government having brought the railways under their control for the duration. Although the Armistice had been signed, long term peace couldn't be guaranteed and so they were loath to release the companies until this was assured at Versailles in June 1919. So, in the meantime, the J23s, N2s, 2-8-0s and 2-6-0s kept appearing, but more ambitious plans remained on hold. At the core of Gresley's strategy lay designs for bigger, more powerful engines and a desire to explore the Pacific concept.

In many ways, engineers in the USA led the field in experimenting with different locomotive designs. 2-6-0 and 2-8-0 wheel arrangements amongst others can be traced back to their late nineteenth century building programmes. Designers in other countries may have taken this work further, but the foundations were often laid Stateside and the development of the Pacific 4-6-2s was no different. They were part of an evolutionary process as engineers sought to improve performance with bigger boilers and fireboxes.

In some cases, this could only be achieved by extending the frames and providing trailing wheels to help distribute the weight better. In 1887, engineers from Baldwin Locomotive Works, employed by the Lehigh Valley Railroad to construct and maintain its engines, fitted a new firebox to one of its 4-6-0 locomotives and found that this caused a severe imbalance which could only be counteracted by fitting a rear bogie. It was an experiment which proved of minimal value and wasn't pursued, but ten years later the Chicago, Milwaukie and St Paul Railway followed the same path, though achieved little more. News of these attempts spread slowly and in 1901, the New Zealand Railway Department, following an outline specification issued to the Baldwin Locomotive Works for thirteen new engines, were persuaded to allow the company to build a Pacific class to ensure the firebox required could be effectively mounted and supported and from this work the first truly successful 4-6-2 emerged.

Reports written at the time suggested that the Pacific wheel arrangement could offer greater strength and stability, particularly at speed, produce a higher tractive effort and achieve greater efficiencies and economies. In many ways, these issues amounted to being the Holy Grail for engineers and by the 1930s more than 6,500 Pacifics, of ever-growing potency, had been built for service in the USA and Canada. European companies were not slow in seeing the potential and began investigating its possibilities, though any advance was limited by the austerity inflicted by war.

Not surprisingly, it was the GWR under Churchward where the first significant step in producing a Pacific locomotive for Britain's railways was taken. In some ways it

The four-cylinder 'Great Bear', No. 111, as she appeared on the drawing board in 1906 with a typical GWR tapered boiler (above) and (right) as she was portrayed by the publicists a year later in a very popular post card sold at stations.

was an unusual step for a company that seemed firmly wedded to an ever-growing programme of 4-6-0 classes. But during 1906 and '07, the company's designers gave very serious thought to the concept and a year later a single experimental locomotive rolled out of the workshops at Swindon. Bert Spencer recalled that this engine clearly impressed Gresley:

'Sir Nigel occasionally spoke about Churchward's 'Great Bear' and it certainly lay at the heart of his own plans for just such a locomotive. Whenever the subject of the Pacifics came up the CME would occasionally recall a letter he had received from the GWR man in 1922, when the first of the GNR's engines appeared, suggesting he could have had their 4-6-2 for a very good price and not built his own! I suspected that the two men had discussed the GNR's plans and at some time Gresley had acquired many of the GWR's drawings. There was an album of photographs of the engine as well, taken during construction and then running on various duties. It had a dark green leather jacket and GWR embossed in gold centrally on the cover and resided in the CME's office. I believe it was a personal gift from Churchward and was passed to Arthur Peppercorn in due course, who, I seem to remember, kept it when he retired in 1949. It wasn't unusual for 'rival' companies to share information in this way. When speaking to Tom Coleman (the LMS's Chief Draughtsman) years later he recalled that Stanier had a set of drawings and album too from Churchward, though he didn't say if Churchward's work had been used in any way.'

Despite the GWR's early work, there was no rush to develop or build more examples by other companies in Britain and the GWR, though testing their example, didn't feel the need to develop the concept further. So the programme stalled and the coming of war deflected any serious attempt to resurrect the concept, although in the United States, their programme continued to gather pace. Gresley had clearly been engaged by the idea, foreseeing the day when more power would be needed to drive ever larger trains. During 1915, the GNR's first scheme was drawn out, and like the 'Great Bear' it showed a clear lineage back to the engines on which each company had come to rely.

It isn't clear if the sketch reproduced here was one of a number prepared with the aim of allowing Gresley to refine his ideas, though it does bear some unmistakable signs of being part of an evolutionary process. If so, the basic concept would change considerably before his first Pacific locomotive appeared in post-war Britain. The 1915 design envisaged an engine operating with a 5ft 6in

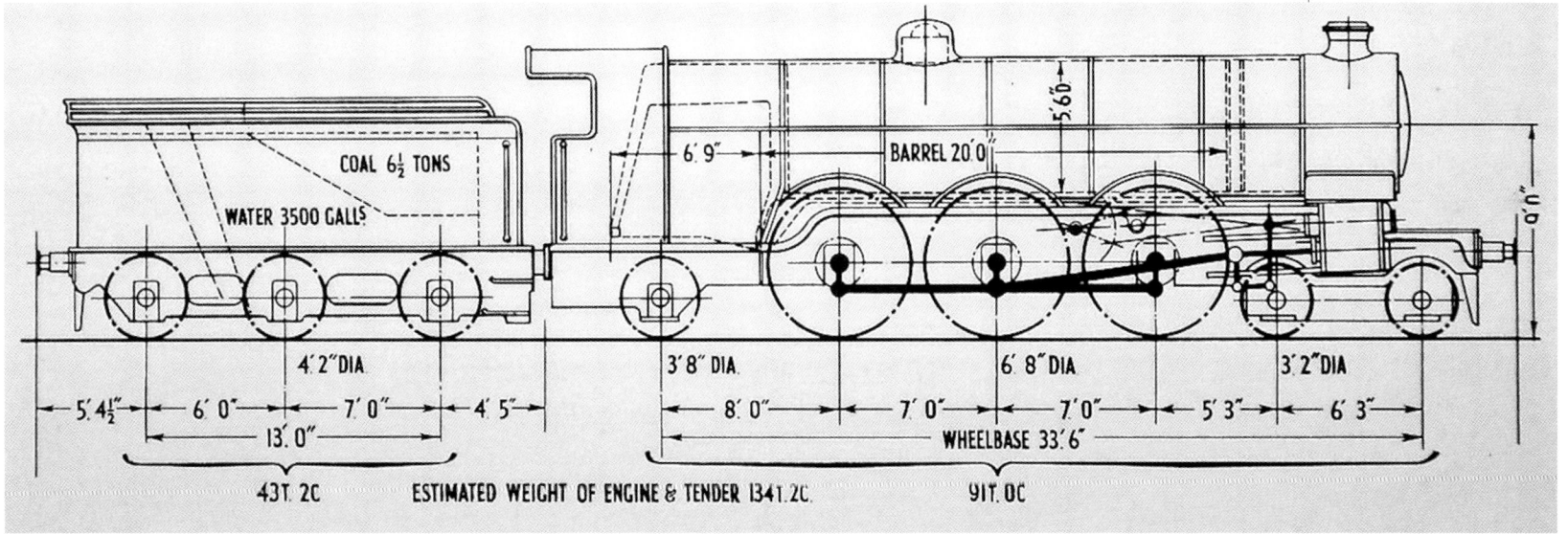

The GNR's 1915 concept for a Pacific showing a strong family resemblance to the H2, H3 and H4s.

diameter boiler and four cylinders, 15in by 26in. Considering Gresley's growing attraction to three cylinders, it is an interesting development and may suggest some uncertainty about this concept. Although too young to be involved in this first Pacific design Bert Spencer remembered Gresley saying:

'…..in all seriousness that his effort took the best of Ivatt's Atlantics and Churchward's '"Great Bear"' and married them together. The cylinder and valve gear arrangement certainly bore some Swindon hallmarks and the cylinders were also the same size, as were all the wheels. However, on the GNR locomotive the two inside cylinders were inclined to allow a clearance between crossheads and the leading axle to be maintained. Piston-valves were also to be included with rocking shafts from the outside Walschaerts valve gear actuating the inside valves under the cylinders. It was a slightly clumsy solution and would undoubtedly have been replaced before the engine had gone into service.

'The '"Great Bear"' was known to produce a tractive effort in the region of 28,000lbf and the GNR engine would have been significantly less at 21,130lbf. But the GWR engine was seven to ten tons heavier, had a greater axle loading and a wheelbase a foot longer, which contributed to its limited route availability. The GNR engine, if built, would probably have faced far fewer restrictions and been able to access many more corners of the network.

'In terms of general appearance, the "Great Bear" looked like what it was, a stretched Star Class 4-6-0 and appeared ungainly as though the trailing truck was a last minute addition. The GNR engine had a more balanced look.

'To test his theories Sir Nigel authorised the rebuilding of Atlantic engine No. 279 with this four-cylinder design and a boiler modified with a 24 element superheater. A series of tests followed, using a GWR dynamometer borrowed from Mr Churchward, but these only seem to have been moderately successful, if the test reports I read later are to be believed. Certainly the results were not sufficient to justify further work at that stage and by then Sir Nigel had moved on to his three-cylinder designs with larger boilers, aided by his patent for the conjugated valve gear which was granted in 1915.

'Another undoubted influence upon him was the Pennsylvania Railroad's K4 series of engines that began appearing in

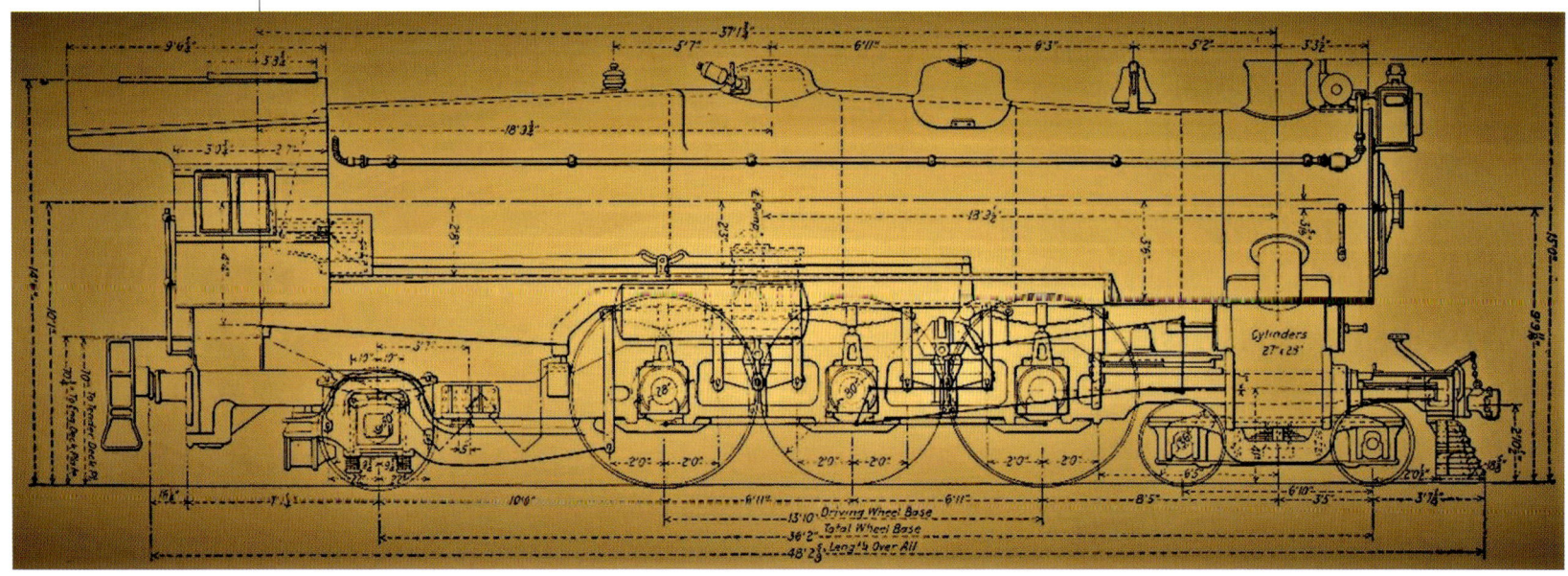

One of the K4 drawings kept by Bert Spencer.

America during 1914. Their use of tapered boilers with wide fireboxes and a three-foot-long combustion chamber was an important development noted at Doncaster as were their three-bar pattern slidebars, hollow-ground piston rods and heat treated nickel-chrome side rods. The sidebar idea was adopted by the GNR and proved so successful that it became a standard fitting on all Gresley's outside cylinder locomotives. An article appeared in *The Engineer* in 1916 which described the K4s in great detail, a copy of which was passed to me when I joined the drawing office a few years later, such had been its impact.

'It had a 7ft 5in diameter boiler which tapered to 6ft 6 ½ in which was considerably heavier than our loading gauge would allow and so we set about building a scaled down version for the first GNR Pacific. This appeared, in due course, to the maximum size allowable by the loading gauge and proved more than adequate for our needs.

'The American design had resulted from data collected at the Pennsylvania Railroad's Altoona test plant when evaluating an experimental Pacific design produced for them by the American Locomotive Company. Altoona had established the relationship between diameter and length of boiler tubes, heating surfaces and the volume of the cylinders and their recommendations led to the K4s' tapered boiler. *The Engineer* reported that with its wide firebox and combustion chamber there was always an ample supply of steam enabling the engines to maintain 60mph as long as required working at cut-offs exceeding 50%.'

The new Pacific passed through its design phase in a form that brought together all of Gresley's evolving and heavily influenced thoughts. There were three cylinders measuring 20in by 26in, linked by his conjugated valve gear and piston-valves restricted to an eight-inch diameter.

The connecting and side rods, plus the hollow-ground piston rods, all adopted the nickel-chrome solution favoured by the Pennsylvania Railroad. The boiler had a diameter of 6ft 5in tapering to 5ft 9in, giving a heating surface of 2,930sqft to which a 32 element 'Robinson' superheater added another 525sqft. The 1915 design envisaged tube lengths of 21ft, which was reduced to 19ft in this engine. However, all the wheel sizes remained the same as those proposed in the earlier design – leading bogies of 3ft 2in diameter, driving wheels of 6ft 8in and trailing bogies of 3ft 8in.

Bert Spencer was closely involved in all this work and found his star rising as a result. He would later recall these days with great affection:

'Sir Nigel would often visit the Drawing Office and happily discuss with one and all his ideas. He liked to give tasks to the young and inexperienced men, to test them and see how they would react. It may have

The engine diagram produced in 1922 to show, in simplistic form, the shape of the new Pacific. Two locomotives were authorised initially and the first, No 1470 *Great Northern*, appeared in April. The second engine, No 1471 *Sir Frederick Banbury*, rolled out of the workshops in July.

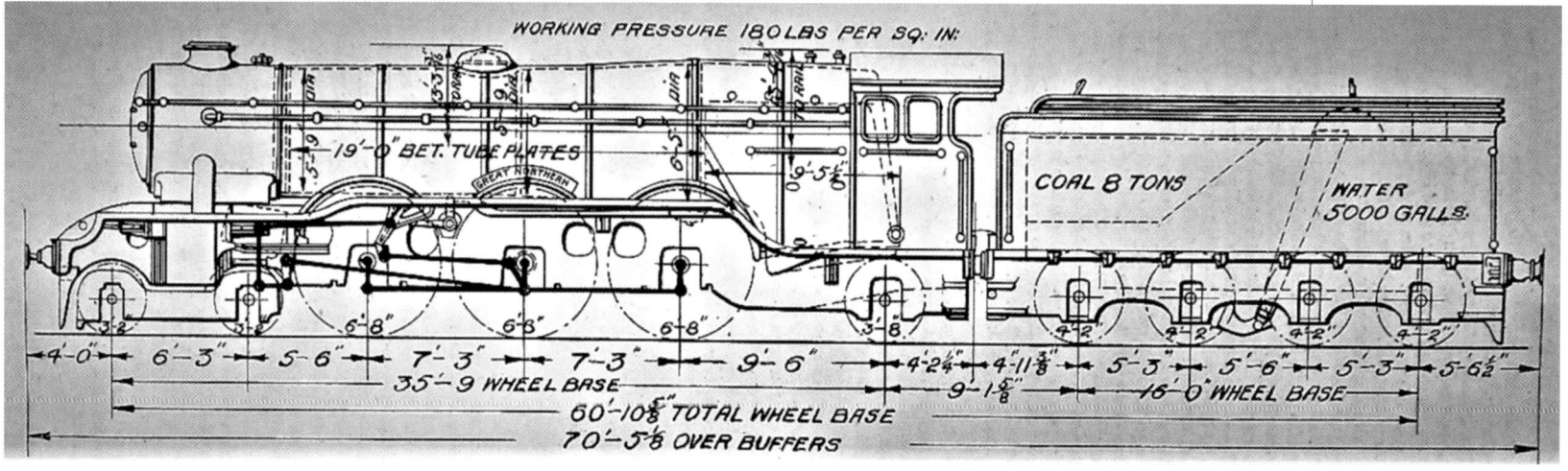

been one of the ways he learnt himself when starting out and it certainly worked. He would set aside time in his very busy schedule to listen to their answers and proposals, with the full agreement of the Chief Draughtsman, who might in other circumstances have felt by-passed. Harry Broughton, when in charge, was very keen on the newcomers getting involved in this way and even encouraged us to raise issues we thought important, provided that we were sure of our ground. When I was drawing out the Pacific's cab I adopted a side-window layout similar to those seen on some Great Eastern engines. I was pleased with the result and showed Sir Nigel during one of his visits. He liked it and ordered it to be fitted in place of a traditional GNR cab. After that the number of small tasks he set me increased.

'Sir Nigel always paid close attention to all parts of a design, whether large or small. He took a particular interest in the cab arrangements for No.1470 and a full-size wooden model was erected in the pattern shop at Doncaster before the engine was built. This was inspected by all and sundry, but particularly the 'top link' drivers and firemen who were encouraged to voice their opinions, and these we considered in refining the layout. But before building this model there was much discussion over the most suitable height at which to place the firehole of the new class in

Great Northern named but not numbered approaches the end of her construction in late March 1922.

relation to the cab footboards. To obtain a better idea of this Sir Nigel had chalked upon one side of a Drawing Office desk an oval shape representing the firehole. Then towards this he shovelled imaginary coal with his walking stick until he was certain that we had the correct height for a fireman of average build. When the wooden model and then the locomotive were built he would examine them with the same critical eye, making changes as necessary. He was a perfectionist.'

With Gresley's project coming to fruition, the world in which the new Pacific would operate was undergoing profound change. During the war, control of the railways had passed into the hands of central government and the state had retained control as the country returned to a peacetime existence. By this stage, the 100 or so companies of varying sizes that made up the network had become the focus of much attention, with a general consensus forming that the system was unwieldy and ineffective. Many senior politicians had reached the conclusion that nationalisation or a scaling down of numbers was essential if the system was to survive as a going concern. To the Minister of Transport, Eric Campbell-Geddes, fell the responsibility for leading a review and recommending changes. This resulted in the 1921 Railway Act which fell short of nationalisation but confirmed the creation of four large private companies and a number of smaller 'joint railways'. This Act was passed into law in August that year and 1 January 1923 was set as the date for this amalgamation. From that date, the London, Midland and Scottish Railway, the new Great Western Railway, the Southern Railway and the London North Eastern Railway came into existence

Generally speaking, the four big companies would attempt to gather together regional businesses and those that followed particular routes, but it wasn't always this clear cut. For example, the GWR and SR both ran from London to the West Country and the GWR forayed into Midland territory as well. These compromises were deemed essential at the time, even though they continued a replication of services that many thought unnecessary.

It became clear to Gresley very early in these deliberations that the GNR would be absorbed by a group that would probably

The three current CMEs who could conceivably have taken over the top job in the new LNER if Gresley had not proved suitable. Left to right – Vincent Raven, John Robinson and Alfred Hill. All men of huge standing and skill.

Gresley in 1922.

include the Great Eastern, North Eastern and Great Central Railways, plus the Great North of Scotland Railway, North British and the Hull and Barnsley Railway Company. Inevitably, this would mean a significant number of changes in management structures and some rationalisation. If the new companies were to survive and make good the depredations of war in the process, there would be cuts and there would be a degree of business streamlining. But first, the new structures had to be created and a jockeying for position became unavoidable. Being an ambitious, resourceful man, Gresley would have observed all this going on and assessed his chances of becoming Chief Mechanical Engineer of the LNER. There was certainly strong potential opposition from John Robinson with the Great Central, Vincent Raven at the North Eastern and Alfred Hill with the Great Eastern. In addition, there was always the chance of 'fresh blood' being brought in from outside this circle of companies.

Gresley was a good company man who had learnt how to manage in such situations and soon began a campaign of persuasion, coaxing and encouragement to improve his chances of taking the top job; by his performance with the GNR he had clearly established his credentials. It wouldn't be lost on him or his likely challengers that the GNR had pushed ahead with a modernisation plan that shone very clearly, now topped by a most imposing new Pacific class of locomotive. Its appearance during these deliberations could not have been better planned, but only time would tell if Gresley's case was strong enough and during 1922 this was far from clear.

Chapter 4
A TIME OF POLITICS AND AN AGE OF SCIENCE (1922–28)

Very little of any true worth came from the Great War. Such unbearable losses left little untouched for it to be otherwise. Those who survived the Front were forever depleted by its horrors and the world to which they returned could offer very little solace, being itself bankrupted, emotionally and financially, by the effort. But this war, with its ever-increasing cycle of violence, demanded that science produce ever more powerful weapons to enhance the speed of killing and secure victory. Yet between 1914 and '18, each side only managed to extend the stalemate as each new advance was balanced by another new development on the other side of the line. It is one of the strangely compelling aspects of conflict that the speed of scientific change it engenders can often have a profound impact on the peaceful years that follow and it also raises expectation that the changes wrought by science and the social upheaval of war will lead to better lives, especially for those who have sacrificed so much. In 1919, these were deeply held views and the sense of anticipation was palpable and pressing. Better homes, better pay and no return to the old order, where privilege was for the few and not the many, were key issues. Science became the vehicle to reinforce these hopes, encouraged by a burgeoning number of illustrated magazines and newspapers eager to publicise each new advance and raise expectations even further.

Science had a new glamour, with aviation and cars leading the way. Few could expect to fly and rather more learn to drive, but for the masses, flight and vehicle ownership remained aspirations. Alongside these developing forms of transport lay the railways, a fading allure perhaps, but an allure nonetheless and an everyday form of transport open for all to experience as social and political change slowly gained momentum.

A confident and established man photographed at the height of his powers. Gresley in the late 1920s secure in his position as CME within the LNER and entering the most important phase of his career.

Post-war, the interest in each new locomotive or high-profile trains found a ready audience eager for news. It was in this atmosphere that the new 'Big Four' companies were launched and Gresley's large and impressive Pacifics made their first appearance. They seemed to

Before the big Pacifics could get into their stride the LNER began launching high profile services with great fanfare. In 1923, the King's Cross to Harrogate Pullman service came into existence and was publicised widely. More were to follow, each launch carefully managed by the LNER's Publicity Department.

embody a new world that many hoped would replace the old. An illusion of course, but a very potent one which the new companies would seek to exploit in an effort to boost trade.

In amalgamating so many companies in so short a time, each with its own history, structures and traditions, there would inevitably be a scramble for positions in the new organisation. A new top structure was formed for the launch with William Whitelaw, Director of the Bank of Scotland and the Highland and North British railways, as Chairman and Ralph Wedgwood, the late General Manager of the North Eastern Railway, as Chief General Manager. Between them, and a new Board of Directors, their first task was to decide who would be recruited into the next layer of management and who would be discarded. It was the crucial position of CME that taxed their minds most. Yet, in reality, there was only one clear leader in this particular race. Raven, Robinson and Hill were all men of great experience and skill, but age was against them. In 1923 they were 65, 67 and 61 respectively. If any of them had been chosen, they would surely have been a stop gap measure only. The task was too dynamic and important for that and there were few other younger candidates of sufficient skill and experience, in the other railway companies to be wooed and recruited. If there were, these competitors would undoubtedly have fought to keep them. So at the comparatively young age of 46, and with an impressive record behind him, Gresley became the only realistic candidate to be the LNER's first CME. Robinson would later claim that he had been offered the post, but it has been suggested that his advancing age and reducing mental capacity may have confused him into believing that this may have been so. We shall never know, of course, but in the eyes of a chairman and directors eager for success, a man fast approaching 70 would offer little long-term competition to someone who was in their prime and had a great deal to offer.

Sometime during 1922, Gresley would have been informed of his promotion. Then within days, he would have set about the complex task of assessing all tasks coming into his area of activity, select staff and try and establish what goals Whitelaw and Wedgwood intended to set him. Just as importantly, there were budgets to be discussed and a plan of action to be agreed. All this would be set against a background of oversight from Westminster and a Ministry of Transport itself going through a huge period of change as its political head changed five times in three years. Eric Geddes went in 1921 having authored the Railway Act, to be replaced by David Lindsay who lasted only a year. He gave way to John Baird who stayed in post for fifteen months, to be swiftly followed by Harry Gosling for nine months and then Wilfred Ashley, in November 1924, who managed to stay for nearly five years. With amalgamation being a key government policy,

The railway's new enemy as advertised in brochures produced by the LNER's own Publicity Department. By the 1920s, and despite austerity, the number of vehicles on the roads exceeded half a million and was growing rapidly. The war had created a huge surplus of ex-military lorries and these shaped a boom in road haulage that would soon challenge the railway's dominance. The years between the two world wars would see power shift to the roads and the Big Four would struggle to break even, let alone make a profit. And, at the same time, they had to pay huge amounts to restore their infrastructures to a pre-war condition and attempt to modernise to meet a changing market.

With all the problems faced by the LNER and Gresley in particular, the first two GNR Pacifics provided a vision of the future and a beacon of hope. Here engine No.1470 gently sizzles awaiting a turn of duty at Doncaster in late 1922.

each Minister regularly intervened or interfered, depending on your viewpoint, in the work of the 'Big Four', adding a level of scrutiny which would tax each chairman and their senior managers to the limit at times. Fielding political questions and appeasing these masters became a key part of Gresley's life, and it was a game at which he proved to be particularly adept. He wasn't only an exceptional engineer and leader, but also a skilled 'company' man with a weather eye for all the nuances and subtleties of politics. Without this, his achievements over the next 18 years might have been significantly less.

As CME of this new company, Gresley was expected to move his place of work from Doncaster to the new LNER HQ at King's Cross. He'd worked there in the past, retaining a small office for occasional use, but this was a permanent move 'that took him away from day to day contact with men at coal face' as Bert Spencer called it. Gresley recognised that the dynamics of the organisation had changed beyond all recognition and the more sheltered world of the GNR could no longer persist with so many amalgamated companies likely to vie for position. So, Gresley couldn't be seen to favour one over the others but sit centrally taking objective control. Whatever his own thoughts or preferences he had to show impartiality and mould all these groups into a single unit, if at all possible.

The task he faced was daunting by any standards. All these diverse teams, containing tens of thousands of men and women, had to be brought together as well as the locomotives, rolling stock, workshops, machinery and much more that they managed and operated. In addition each company had evolved in different ways, creating engines and services to meet the specific needs of their lines. There was common ground, of course, and quite often the engineers had followed similar paths in creating new locomotives.

Amalgamation presented the new CME with 7,399 engines of many different types, so the programme of standardisation, that he, and Ivatt before him, had sought as time and money allowed, was suddenly a much bigger problem to resolve. With so many classes, each with their own needs and requiring specific spares, his ability to thin out types and numbers presented a problem of almost epic proportions. According to the LNER's own records, there were also 21,218 carriages for many different purposes and 281,748 trucks of various types to consider, with much of this stock dated and unsuited to the modern age that grouping was supposed to herald. When the company was launched in January 1923, the extent of these problems would have been only too apparent to Gresley, though the solutions were barely glimpsed even by someone so astute.

The company's management structure came in a number of tiers, with the CME's team working directly to the Chief General Manager, alongside accountancy, legal and general administration groups. There were also three Divisional General Managers reporting directly to Wedgwood, each taking on a specific area of business – Southern, North Eastern and Scotland. They each bore responsibility for such things as passenger and goods work, hotels, engineering, other than that related to locomotives and rolling stock, and other day to day operating issues. But they were also accountable for all the Running Sheds and their Superintendents, so had a key influence on the type

King's Cross Station between the wars. First the GNR then the LNER's London Headquarters. It was designed by Lewis Cubitt and opened in 1852.

When Gresley became the LNER's first CME he was based at King's Cross and moved his family to Camlet House near Hatfield in Hertfordshire. He sometimes commuted to work by train and would meet Bulleid en route holding his '*Times* out of the window indicating that his assistant should join him'. This is a story he later recounted to John Click, one of his assistants when CME with the Southern Railway.

of locomotives and rolling stock to be provided. This was a potential flash point in any organisation and it was one which made locomotive development difficult for many years. But Gresley, Wedgwood and his Assistant General Manager, Robert Bell, seem to have navigated this particular path with diplomacy and tact, allowing the CME to decide the best way forward.

It seems that Gresley chose his own team wisely from staff available in the amalgamated companies. Arthur Stamer combined the two roles of Assistant CME with Mechanical Engineer Darlington. At the same time Walter Chalmers, Robert Thom then Tom Heywood covered Scotland and Charles Glaze then Edward Thompson filled the Mechanical Engineer post at Stratford. Finally, Gresley's old stamping ground of Doncaster continued to be managed by Francis Wintour, but he was superseded by Robert Thom in 1927, who came to this crucial post just as Gresley's plans for the future came to fruition. Beneath these major figures lay 30,000 or so other workers, of many specialities, to be marshalled and led to ensure the new organisation was a success. In a past age, when workers' rights were poorly defined and were so muted as to be unheard, subservience was natural and enforced by the threat of dismissal without references. Soldiers returning from the war claimed rights their forebears thought impossible to achieve. Inevitably, this led to disputes as employers tried to reassert old values over a generation shaped by conflict who rightly demanded some return for their sacrifices. So the 1920s became an industrial battleground over which Gresley and his like had to pick their way if the railways were to run efficiently and attempt to return a profit. In the coming years, this conflict would present him with extremely stern tests which would push his leadership skills to their limit, none more so than in the General Strike of 1926. By comparison, the task of modernising locomotive and rolling stock fleets would appear at times to be a simple logistical exercise. Yet it was this side of the business against which his accomplishments were measured. A far greater achievement, I believe, was his sensitive and practical management of a huge number of people at a time of great social and economic upheaval and the part he played in these reforms shouldn't be forgotten. Many of his contemporaries took a very hard line indeed, but he chose a moderniser's route instead. Not for him a hardnosed approach but one of understanding, an openness for negotiation and seeking improvement wherever possible.

Social, economic and political considerations will always be the lot of those in charge of a large organisation, but the end result must always be a profitable output. For the railways, this meant attracting trade and finding engineering solutions to boost capacity. For this, Gresley could rely on many good people, but any leader needs an immediate entourage to act as filters or troubleshooters, and in this he would turn to Oliver Bulleid.

In his perceptive book *Master Builders of Steam*, Henry Bulleid described how this working

A united team enjoying a day out at one of the many sports related activities encouraged by the company to foster better labour relations. The LNER, and Gresley in particular, were keen supporters of these pursuits and the company's senior managers were regular attendees, as seen here. Front row (left to right) – Gresley, Whitelaw, Wintour and Wedgwood. Back row – Thom, Peppercorn, Brown, Eggleshaw and Firth.

As soon as the LNER had begun to settle down to its new existence the PR Department began the process of issuing booklets describing new engines and trains. The most popular of these proved to be one containing this large pull out drawing of Gresley's Pacifics. A later version was colourised.

relationship developed and its effect on the new organisation:

'In April 1923 Gresley and Bulleid moved into the new LNER CME's offices near the junction with the overbridge and main departure platform No. 10 at King's Cross. They set up a small Drawing Office for scheme, detail and checking work; after checking, Gresley signed the loco drawings and Bulleid the carriage and wagon drawings. New design was almost entirely done at Doncaster: the other Drawing Offices merely continuing with the usual stream of minor and detail work, standardisation, etc.

Doncaster had thrown a double six as far as the new engineering bosses were concerned; and since both Gresley and Bulleid were inclined to be technically arrogant, a trait which tends to flourish in their 40 to 50 age group, Doncaster methods were in and the other constituents could like them or lump them. The directors poured a little oil on the fires of unfairness by choosing GNR green as the LNER passenger loco colour instead of, say, Great Eastern blue.'

To this mix the 25-year-old Bert Spencer was added in 1924 and

the following year he was joined by his new wife Elsie, moving into a terraced house in Barnet. Here he was within a short drive of the Gresley family at Camlet House, near Hadley Wood, now in the Borough of Enfield. Meanwhile, Bulleid and his wife had also moved to this area of London, creating a small LNER enclave allowing some meetings to take place away from the glare of directors and staff in the King's Cross HQ. Spencer later recalled that:

'Occasionally there was a pressing need to discuss new plans and projects or the

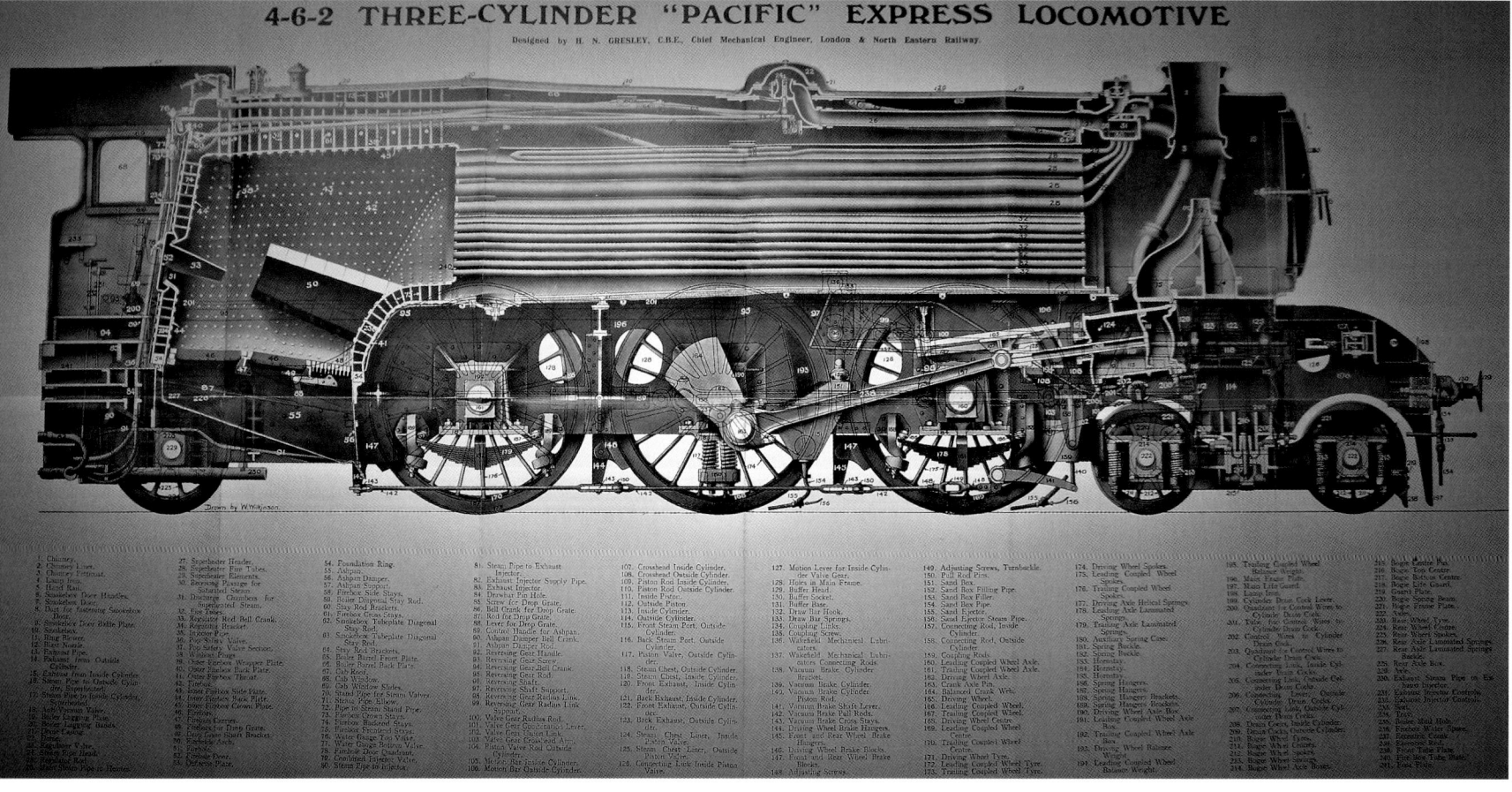

In parallel, and perhaps in competition with Gresley, Vincent Raven developed his own Pacific Class for the NER. The first two appeared in December 1922 eight months after the GNR's first A1 and five months after the second. Whilst Gresley's engines became the centre of public attention the Raven Pacifics slipped into comparative obscurity, although three more were built after the LNER was formed. Here the final member of the class, 2404, City of Ripon, is captured at rest between turns at York.

performance of different offices or workshops. This could best be carried out at Camlet House in Sir Nigel's study where we could work undisturbed. It came to be a regular practice especially when the W1 and then P2 were in planning. Neither project had wide support and were seen by some as costly distractions.'

Bulleid, who had known and worked for Gresley off and on since 1912, provided an interesting insight into the CME's personality and way of working when he wrote:

'Gresley was the best Chief I had been under and our relations were the happiest. He was incapable of ill-temper, but what I appreciated most was his wide interest in all engineering. He was always ready to adopt any suggestion, but only after consideration. It could be felt that if he agreed to try anything it would almost certainly be a success. He had a wonderful memory, was extremely observant, and amongst other things could read a drawing in a way given to few. Disloyalty was the one thing he did not tolerate. After all the head of a department deserves loyal, unremitting service and obedience. He has also to be given every possible help to lighten the burden he assumes.

'He gave me orders when he should. He asked my opinion if he wanted it. He expected to receive suggestions and to be given particulars of any development in any field which might not come to him direct.'

They seem to have enjoyed a frank and honest relationship, the essence of which Henry Bulleid captured in his book:

> 'Humanly, they sometimes discussed their wisdom, and sometimes the stupidity of others. They did not always agree: once Gresley took up his fireside position quite indignantly, wanting to know how it was that none of his assistants ever seemed to come up with any suggestions. "By the way," said Bulleid casually, "You remember that draughtsman you agreed to see last week" – "Of course I do, the damned fool." "Well, there you are," said Bulleid, "Do you think he'll come back with another suggestion?" Gresley was slightly penitent; each found it easier to see brusqueness in the other than in himself.'

If he was brusque and gruff at times it was a front that hid a remarkably equitable personality. He was undoubtedly a strong, focussed man, but at the same time understood human nature and possessed a warm and generous personality. However, Roland Bond, a leading light within the LMS, later wrote, 'I was given to understand from some of my LNER friends that Gresley was not easy to talk to – but I found the reverse to be the case,' adding that, 'when visiting the CME at King's Cross or Doncaster it seemed that many of his staff were quite cautious when approaching him, suggesting that he might have ruled with a firm hand'.

Gradually, the leaders in each of his new departments began to understand their chief's way of working, aided by the very experienced Stamer, Bulleid, Spencer and Frank Day, who moved to King's Cross on promotion from the Drawing Office at Doncaster to advise Gresley on carriage and wagon issues. There was undoubtedly a bedding in period, but this soon passed, allowing the CME to begin the main task at hand – to review the engines and rolling stock at his disposal and form plans for the future. In fact, one part of this picture had already been brought into focus before the LNER had come into being. One of the last acts of the GNR's Board before it disbanded was to approve the construction of ten more Pacifics, which were well in hand during January 1923. This largely untried design had to be tested before entering service in even greater numbers and as part of this process, they could also be compared to the Pacifics designed and built for the NER by Vincent Raven, which now passed into Gresley's control.

The NER man, having missed out on the new CME post, retired on the eve of its creation, though was held 'on the LNER's books' for a year as a technical advisor, extending his long-standing relationship with Ralph Wedgwood for a brief period. But his departure was inevitable, especially with the cancellation of electrification projects, which had become the raison d'être of this far-seeing man. And with this he became a director of Metropolitan-Vickers, where other forms of motive power were being developed. But he left Gresley an interesting legacy. There were his two Pacifics, which were rushed into traffic in December 1922, eight and five months after the GNR's 1470 and 1471, but, perhaps of greater significance was a report he wrote for the LNER's Board in 1923 which tried to predict future locomotive needs, based on what was currently available and their condition. The report concluded that most of the stock had an average life expectancy of 40 years. If so, this would necessitate the construction of only 185 or so new engines each year to keep the fleet refreshed and replenished. Sadly, it was a summary too simplistic in its judgement, being based on pre-war traffic figures and expected growth and not a realistic view of current and future trends. There was also the issue of engineering advances, with the drive for better performances and economy to consider and how all this might affect numbers in the future. It also failed to take full account of the long-term effect of the recent conflict and the true level of wear and tear it had inflicted on the stock, as well as the infrastructure.

In truth, the fleet contained many effective locomotives, though in some cases an increase in traffic was severely testing their strength and schedules were likely to suffer in due course. There were also other engines that were unlikely to meet future needs. With the conclusions reached, one wonders whether Gresley had been involved in the review at any stage. If not, he would not have appreciated the limits the paper sought to impose on him and would undoubtedly have been concerned

The two new Pacifics inherited by the LNER. The NER locomotive, on the left, was essentially a stretched version of Raven's three-cylinder C7 Atlantic class engine. Gresley's Pacific, whilst owing much to his earlier work, was a design of greater originality. In 1923 engine No.2400, *City of Newcastle* and the third A1, No. 1472, *Flying Scotsman*, entered a comparative trial running between Doncaster and King's Cross. The results were fairly conclusive in judging the A1 to be superior in terms of coal (52.6lb/mile to 58.7lb/mile) and water (38.3gal/mile to 40.4gal/mile) consumed. The A1 also produced a higher drawbar horsepower of 928 to 875. These tests weren't repeated and, if they had been, the results may have varied one way or the other. However, there were other issues to consider, one being the reaction of the drivers and firemen. On the whole they rated the A1 a better engine to drive, though modifications to the last three Raven Pacifics did narrow the gap. Looking back one can only wonder why three extra NER type Pacifics were constructed in 1924, especially when so many more of the superior A1s were already being built?

that his hands were being tied. A cost-conscious chairman and board would inevitably quote the figure of 185 in any future debate over locomotive disposal and construction programmes and seek to impose a limit on Gresley's considered assessments of need. It may have seemed that Raven had left him a poisoned chalice. In reality, Raven was probably only stating the obvious – make do with what you have because the economics of your position are unlikely to support anything else. Gresley was too much of a realist to believe otherwise and so fell back on a number of basic principles to guide him – principles he eluded to in his Presidential address to the I MechE in 1931. In describing improvements that could be made to steam engines, until electrification could realistically take over, he set four targets. 'Enable locomotives to remain

Engine No. 2400 whilst undergoing trials in April 1923. Here she is seen south of Alnmouth, with dynamometer car, apparently making light work of a heavy load and steady climb upwards.

available for traffic for longer periods. Reduce maintenance costs. Greatly improve thermal efficiency and reduce fuel consumption and running costs.'

They were practical steps, easily understood by professional and lay people alike and in the attainment of these goals lay his justification for change. But thanks to Raven's assessment and 1920s austerity, it would be a difficult path to follow. Make do with what you have can be a sensible strategy, but rarely, if ever, matches capacity to changing needs. Eventually, any limitations on experimentation and change can be self-defeating and appear absurd with hindsight. So the astute Gresley watched and waited for any opportunity to arise that might be exploited to push through change. And he wasn't slow in using positive PR whenever necessary to speed up the process. The *Railway Gazette* became one of his many regular outlets for news, with a five-page spread appearing in the April 1922 edition describing the A1. In December, the same magazine covered Raven's Pacific in a single page, which contained nothing except a brief technical description and not a single compliment. Your plans, intentions and achievements are of little use in a highly political environment if they aren't publicised and feted. Gresley was proving to be a master of this art, taking time to discuss these projects with journalists and giving them open access to this work in all its phases. Of course, this could be a double edged sword, with failure gathering as much publicity as success, but the risk seemed worthwhile and the press generally worked in his favour.

A common scene in the LNER's first year of operation – a Gresley H3 No 4668 awaits departure at King's Cross. Very soon the railway would find Pacifics dominating the heavier, more prestigious trains.

The April report was peppered with many positive messages:

'Mr Gresley has succeeded in producing a remarkably fine locomotive, embodying in its design all the features necessary for the realisation of the highest efficiency in the handling of very heavy express trains at high average speeds, and maintaining punctuality therewith when circumstances are adverse; at the same time providing a locomotive which in outward appearance is characterised by symmetry and a well-balanced disposition of the various outstanding parts.

'Many difficult problems arise in the design and construction in a locomotive such as this, and in going over the features of the engine with Mr Gresley and Mr Wintour we were greatly impressed by the manner in which difficulties of no ordinary character had been overcome. At the moment it must suffice to say that the engine reflects the greatest possible credit upon those responsible for its design and construction, and demonstrates again the efficient character of the company's plant at Doncaster.'

King's Cross in 1925 with the Doncaster built engine No 2557, *Blair Atholl*, about to be manoeuvred onto a train. This locomotive only entered traffic on 28 February that year and so was barely run in when this picture was taken.

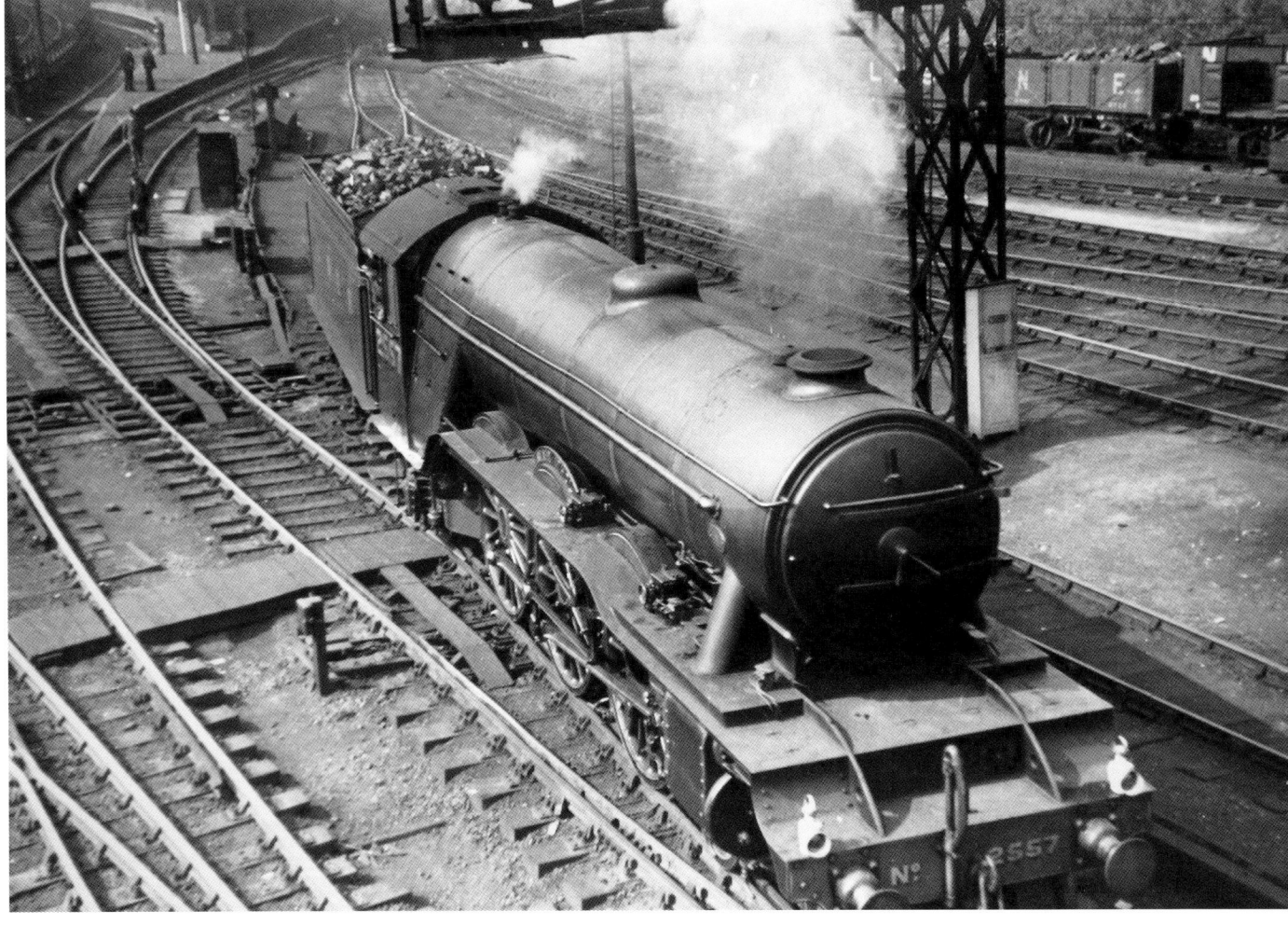

The editor then went on to describe many of the technical details of the first engine before being directed, by the CME, to an appraisal of the 'new E.C.J.S. twin sleeping car built on Mr Gresley's patented articulated system and containing 20 sleeping berths', which was just making its appearance. So in five pages of compliments, accolades and technical analysis the *Gazette* made a strong case for Gresley and his ideas. Undoubtedly this would have pleased the directors, but at the same time it underpinned the seriousness of the CME's intent in building a locomotive and carriage fleet for the future.

Bert Spencer observed all this from the wings and later wrote of the problems they faced beyond the shining words of journalists:

'The early years were difficult. With so many different types of locomotives to operate it was impossible to establish how well they met the company's needs. There were more than enough in number but not necessarily of the right type. So from the beginning Sir Nigel continued building those introduced before amalgamation until the future became clearer. Forty more A1s were built between 1923 and 1925 – twenty of these at Doncaster and another twenty under contract by North British – as well as another three more of Raven's Pacific at Darlington in 1924. In addition, there were more N2s, O2s, J50s and H4s (now re-designated K3s). If my memory serves me well new construction of these engines totalled 80 in 1924 and 63 in 1924. This period was

A Time of Politics and An Age of Science (1922–28)

Although at the time based in Scotland, Robert Thom carefully recorded all new locomotive production in a large leather and felt bound book from which this page was taken. He kept this book going until 1936. In it he logged each newly constructed or reconstructed engine as they appeared from each Works. Occasionally he would gather a group of engines together if they were of identical design and being turned out within a few weeks.

A1 locomotives

Numbers 2563 to 2582 were built by North British under contract to the LNER. 2563, *William Whitelaw,* is seen here suspended over 2568, *Sceptre,* towards the end of their construction in July 1924 at the company's Hyde Park Works in Glasgow.

2547, built at Doncaster, was released to traffic on 30 August 1924. This photograph was, apparently, taken shortly afterwards.

noted for being one of hard work on new designs but also of the need to convince the powers that all was not well and could be improved.'

The number certainly fell far below that predicted by Raven, but probably reflects uncertainty over the future and a degree of caution in hard economic times. But the A1s did, at least, have the benefit of garnering huge amounts of publicity and re-vitalising the long-distance routes from London northwards where the Atlantics were beginning to struggle as trains grew heavier and in more demand. From this starting point, Gresley began working to develop new concepts and engines, at the same time seeking to boost the performance of inherited engines to ensure they could best meet future needs. Not everyone agreed with his three-cylinder engine policy and for decades, criticism abounded within his own team and outside. Some of this was forensic in nature, to be sifted and analysed long after the event, but in other cases it was, at the time, the root of significant differences of opinion within his profession. He seems to have turned a deaf ear to these debates and stuck to his ideas with a singular determination. And who could argue when his locomotives were perceived to be so successful.

In 1924 and 1925, two British Empire Exhibitions were held at Wembley to celebrate the country's gradual recovery from the Great War. The major railway companies were invited to exhibit items that reflected the technical advances they were making. The LNER wouldn't pass up the opportunity of displaying Gresley's third Pacific, No. 1472 Flying Scotsman, on both occasions. To achieve this she was taken out of commission for two months to prepare her for the occasion. She was exhibited in the Palace of Engineering where she was joined by the GWR's *Caerphilly*

In 1924 and 1925 two British Empire Exhibitions were held at Wembley to celebrate the country's gradual recovery from the Great War. The major railway companies were invited to exhibit items that reflected the technical advances they were making. The LNER displayed No. 1472 on both occasions. Here the engine is seen in the Palace of Engineering where she was joined by the GWR's *Caerphilly Castle* in 1924 then *Pendennis Castle* in 1925. These displays provided an interesting comparison of styles and engineering solutions.

Castle in 1924 then *Pendennis Castle* in 1925. These displays provided an interesting comparison of styles and engineering solutions.

In 1925, he took his ideas a step further forward and led in designing a freight engine of unparalleled size and strength for this country. The 02 class had been a great success, but Gresley envisaged a new generation of locomotives that could pull much larger loads. At the same time, he wished to experiment with the 2-8-2 Mikado configuration that had first appeared in America in 1884. The concept reached its zenith there with production of the impressive Pennsylvania Railroad's L1 series between 1914 and '19, when 574 were built. Experiments had shown that this wheel arrangement allowed a larger boiler to be mounted onto the frames, but it also meant that the firebox didn't have to ride above the rear driving wheels. This enabled a wider, deeper firebox to be fitted, which created a greater rate of combustion and steam generation.

This gave the design greater potential and Gresley followed the 2-8-2's development with great interest. During 1924 he began experimenting with the concept and obtained authority to build two freight engines as a means of investigating the design's potential. There was some justification for such a large engine with the ever

A Time of Politics and An Age of Science (1922–28) • 117

An L1 is part of the collection of the Railway Museum of Pennsylvania in Strasburg, PA. When photographed, engine No.520 was in stripped down condition awaiting restoration, but in this state it does at least provide an interesting view of some elements of its engineering. These two cylinder locomotives could produce a tractive effort of 61,465 lbf and were capable of pulling the heaviest coal and mineral trains unaided on mountain routes on the railroad. They were also used to test booster engines on the trailing truck to improve adhesion and traction at starting or when moving at low speed in demanding conditions. It was an idea which Gresley also explored when designing his P1 2-8-2 engine.

Gresley's first P1 on one of its usual coal train turns. It strongly resembled the A1 with its graceful lines only spoilt by the Westinghouse brake system located midway along the boiler.

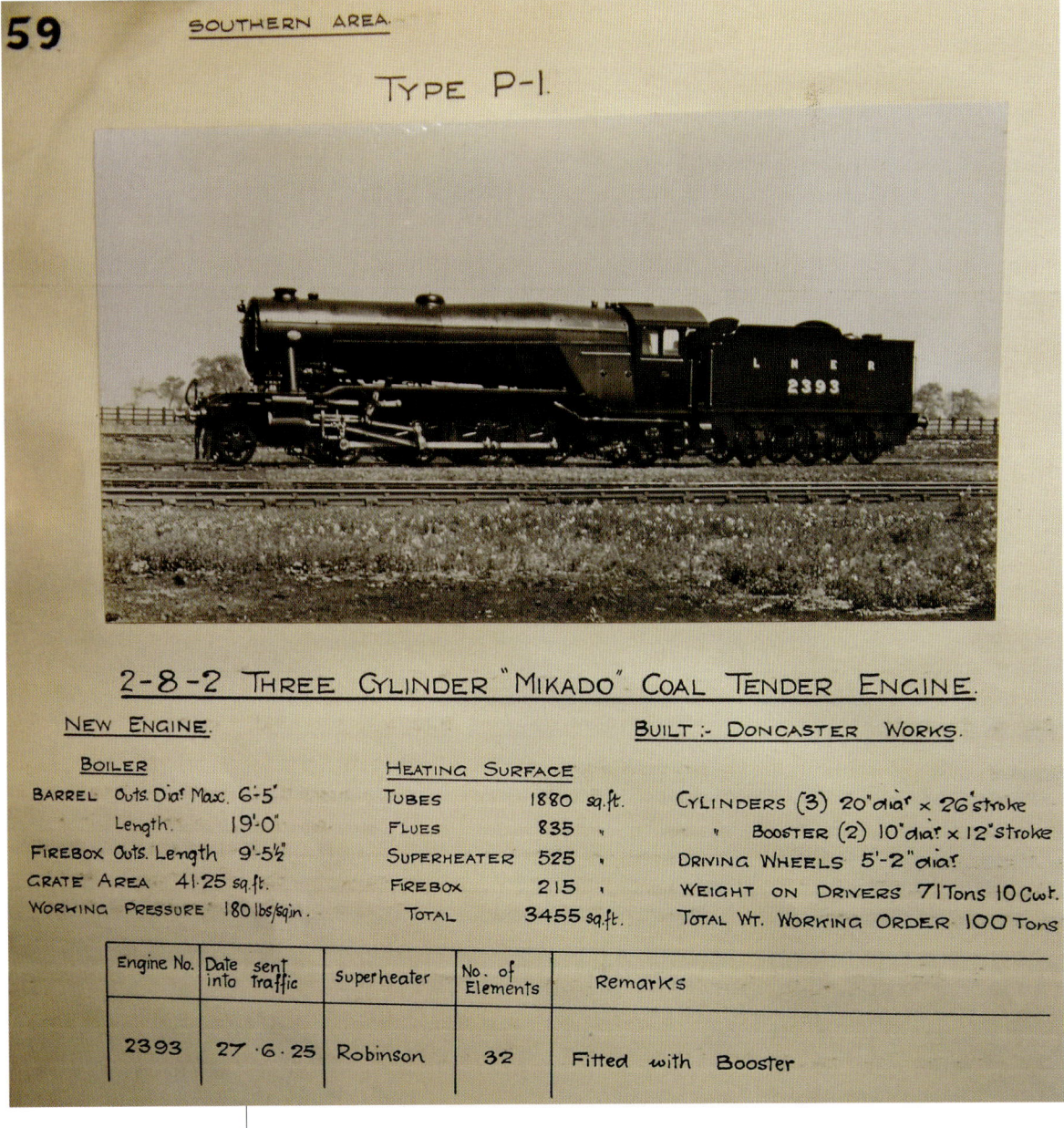

Robert Thom's personal record of locomotive production, this time the first of the two P1s is carefully logged.

growing demand for coal to be hauled between Peterborough and Ferme Park sidings in North London. Loads of up to 1,600 tons were common and existing freight locomotives struggled with such a weight, spread over 100 or so wagons.

So Gresley took the 2-8-2 configuration and added a boiler basically the same as the model attached to the A1 Pacifics. To this he added a two-cylinder booster engine to the trailing wheels, as per the American L1, and Westinghouse brakes. Doncaster turned out the two engines in June and November 1925 and they quickly went into service and proved that 1,600 ton loads were well within their capabilities. But just as they began to prove themselves the requirement changed, and the loads were reduced on the Peterborough to London route. This was partly due to market forces, but also perceived problems associated with 100 wagon trains, which were proving too long for safe running through passing loops on the line. These two factors convinced George Thurston, the Southern Area General Manager, and his Goods Manager, that shorter trains were the best solution, and these could easily be dealt with by the smaller freight engines or the H4/K3s. After this, the P1s tended to slip from view, though continued to work for another 20 years. However, the concept wasn't forgotten by Gresley, who continued to see potential in the Mikado layout and would, in due course, produce his P2 express passenger locomotive. In this he was following an example set by designers in France. In the years following the Great War, they had embraced 2-8-2 designs more fully than in Britain and begun producing their 141 series of engines, as the Mikados were designated, in great numbers. Gresley, Bulleid and Spencer, who all read widely and absorbed lessons learnt in other countries, seemed to have been particularly fascinated by this design work in France.

In particular, a very close professional and personal relationship would grow up between them and Andre Chapelon, who in the mid-1920s was just beginning to make a name for

himself on the other side of the Channel. This very able engineer, who was born in Saint-Paul-en-Cornillon in October 1892, was educated at the renowned École Centrale Paris. His time there was interrupted by the Great War, in which he served with distinction in the front line as an artillery officer with the 106th Regiment, then as a strategist and instructor. Returning to civilian life in 1919, he completed his course at the École Central and graduated in 1921, finding work with the PLM Railway in their Rolling Stock and Motive Power section.

In many ways, this period of his life was an apprenticeship in which he learnt the more practical elements of design; this he did in the capable hands of Etienne Tribolet, a senior mechanical inspector at Lyon. It was during this period that he began delving into the area of thermo-dynamics in some depth, developing theories that would underpin much of his later work. By the mid-1920s, when he first came to Gresley's attention, he was formulating ideas, based on the work of Kyosti Kylala, a Finnish engineer, on locomotive exhaust systems. This would result in the Kylchap model being developed, which would seriously impact on

The second P1 here recorded as 'pulling a 100 plus trucks and 1,600 tons of coal and making light of her full load'.

Andre Chapelon later in his career and by then a person of huge stature and influence in the engineering world

Gresley's work and that of many other steam locomotive designers in the future. It was shortly after this that two men met for the first time, in a meeting called by engineers at Davey, Paxman and Co of Colchester. The two designers were investigating a new valve gear jointly produced by Hugo Lentz and the company for use in static engines, which with modifications was being adapted for use in steam locomotives. Chapelon was visiting the company's Essex works at the same time as Gresley. Whether the meeting was pre-arranged or simply a chance encounter is unclear, but it was the beginning of a relationship that would have a profound effect on locomotive development on the LNER.

1925 proved to be an increasingly busy year for Gresley with a number of ideas forming in his mind for investigation and development. A man with such a fertile imagination and drive wouldn't be constrained unnecessarily by restrictions on budget or any other limitations lesser men might seek to impose. With a team of clever designers around him it was always possible to consider new ideas at the same time as make current programmes work. Speculation has always been linked to accumulation, though this involves an acceptance of risk, but now was the time to push boundaries in the search for improved performances and greater economy. It is in times like this that great men and women come into their own, being able to free themselves of shackles others accept too easily.

The next stage of the Mikado development was clearly in his mind

Experimentation and analysis of different ideas lay at the heart of any designer's work. Gresley was constantly seeking different and better ways of achieving a desired output. So different schemes came and went in this endless search for the perfect solution, though many came to nought or were simply a step in a long process of discovery. Spencer discussed many of these in his 1947 paper, but two others were added by A.F. Cook, who although not a member, attended Spencer's presentation in London. The first of these, above, was a 2-8-2 tank engine based on the standard O2 2-8-0 and P1. It would have weighed in the region of 100 tons. Cook didn't provide any details of the use to which such a specialist engine would be put, but heavy coal trains were the most likely. The second (opposite above) was a 4-6-0 engine against which Cook recorded '..prepared at Doncaster in about 1925 when Gresley was still hoping to build a large taper-boiler for the GE Section'. It bears a very strong resemblance to the LMS Black 5 which appeared nine years later.

A Time of Politics and An Age of Science (1922–28) • 121

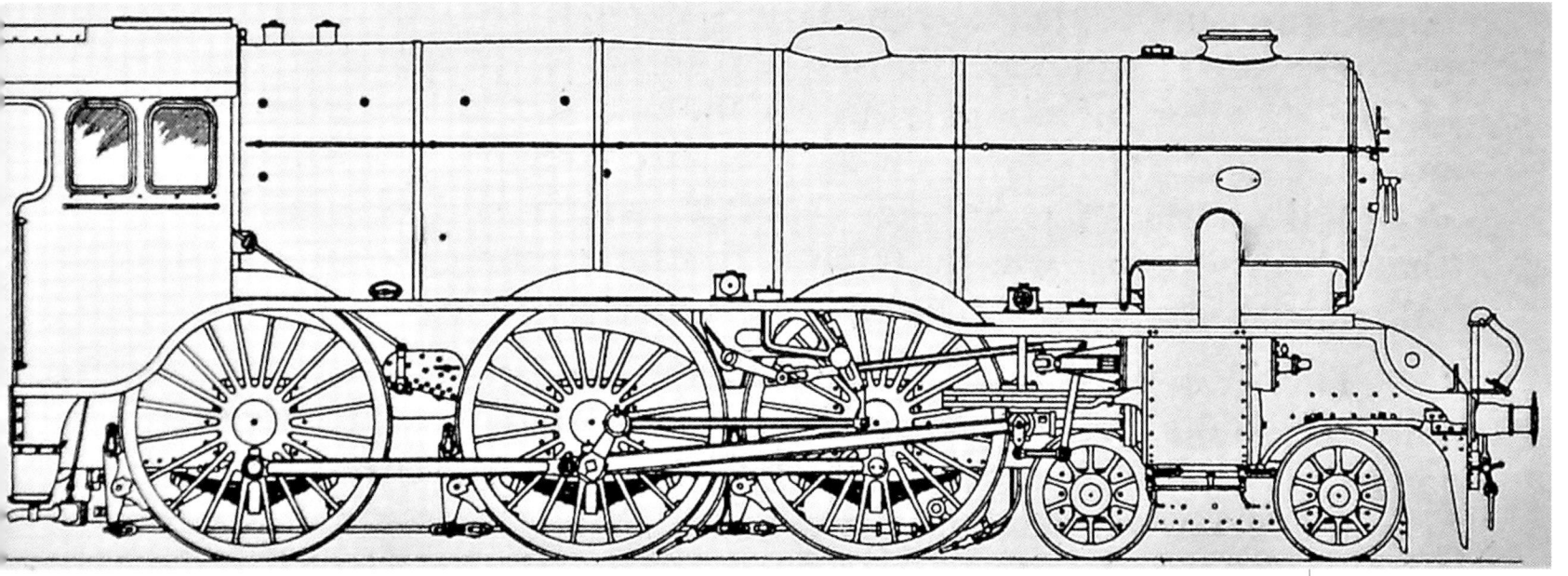

Thought to be No.1401 the second locomotive produced by ALCO when experimenting with high pressure boiler technology. This research clearly impressed Gresley, who began working towards a British version in 1924 and perhaps even earlier.

The unique Beyer, Peacock Class U1 locomotive under construction at Gorton Works during 1925 and (below) as it appeared in June of that year. The 7ft diameter boiler was fed by two Gresham and Craven injectors, and the engine had a firebox and 45 element superheater that provided a combined heating surface of 3,518 sq ft. In its banking role it proved successful and it lasted on the Worsborough branch line until the line was electrified when, after a General Repair, it worked on the Lickey incline south of Birmingham for a time, being converted to burn oil rather than coal during 1952 in the process. It didn't prove to be a popular engine in either guise when crewed by BR LM staff. After a period in store the engine was finally withdrawn from service in December 1955 and scrapped at Doncaster three months later.

during 1925 as was the next stage of the Pacific design. In addition, he was searching for an alternative type of boiler to take locomotive performance to another level. In this case, he envisaged using technology more usually seen in the maritime world, which had been adapted for use on a prototype locomotive designed by John Muhlfield and built by ALCO in America during 1924 for the Delaware and Hudson Railway. Here, a 350psi high pressure water tube boiler had been mounted on a 2-8-0 chassis and linked to a two-cylinder compound expansion system. In its development, Yarrow and Co, the Clyde Shipbuilders, who were specialists in this field of engineering, had acted as consultants to Muhlfield. The product of their joint effort, engine No.1400, *Horatio Allen*, rolled out of ALCO's Schenectady Works in New York at the end of that year. It was quickly followed by other versions that refined the technology and performance.

Gresley became aware of this work and saw in it a possible means of reducing running costs, especially the amount of coal consumed. Even before No. 1400 had been completed he had begun corresponding with and then meeting Yarrow's engineers to discuss a UK based project. Despite the speed of development in America, progress in Britain was more measured, probably reflecting the amount of work Yarrow's and the LNER were already undertaking. It would take another two years before a boiler would appear and late 1929 before an experimental engine had been constructed to test these theories. Bert Spencer remembered that:

'Arthur Stamer had developed a close association with Yarrows over the years and much of the planning work for the W1 was undertaken at Darlington. He and Sir Nigel were both fascinated by these ideas and, I believe, Stamer visited the United States at some point in time to see the American engines at work. There was certainly a great number of papers circulating from him with many of his comments attached. He then played an important role in getting the new boiler manufactured and then engine No. 10000 at Darlington and tested. There was concern in some quarters that the engine was something of a red herring, but both I and Bulleid believed it was a worthwhile experiment

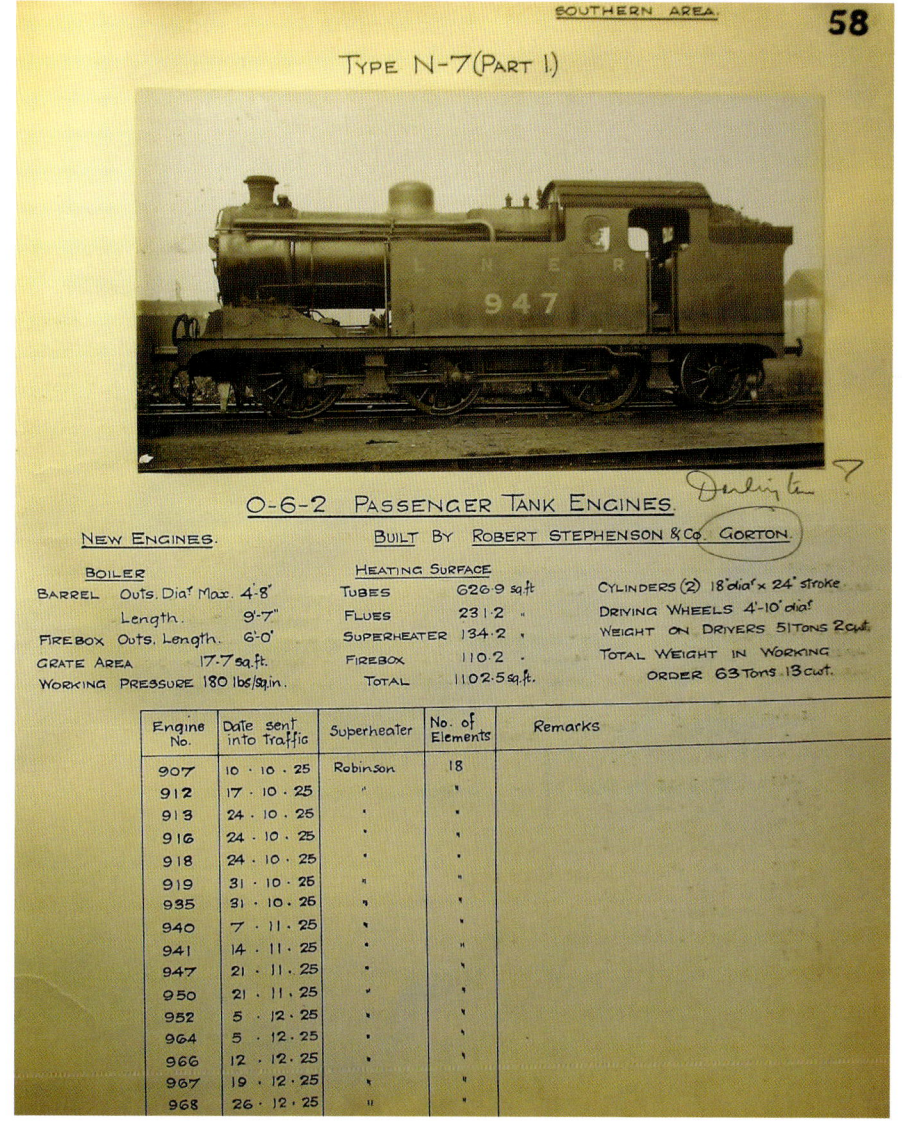

One class inherited from the Great Eastern was the 1915 introduced N7 0-6-2T for North London suburban services designed by Alfred Hill and his team and first called the L77. It proved so successful that production carried on until 1928 under Gresley until 134 of different types had been built. The last of these versatile engines were withdrawn in 1962.

that might have borne fruit. Gresley's trust in the new system can be gauged by the patent he and Harold Yarrow submitted in December 1928, to which they gave the title 'Improvements in Locomotive Boilers'. I don't think it earned them any money.'

In 1925, much of this work was still far in the future. In the meantime, Gresley and his team pressed on with other tasks. One of these was an interesting departure for the company, but once again it demonstrated how widely Gresley looked in exploring potential ideas. In this case, it involved a requirement for a banking engine to eliminate the need for double-heading. Having established need and sought approval to proceed, a specification was submitted to Beyer, Peacock and Co of Manchester. This company specialised in designing and building articulated 'Garratt' type locomotives which were of immense strength and more than capable of undertaking this specialist work. Spencer in his 1947 paper to the ILocoE described this project:

'The only LNER "Garratt" type locomotive, No.2395, went into service in 1925 for banking duties on the Worsboro' branch, between Wentworth Junction and West Silkstone, a distance of approximately three miles on a gradient of 1 in 40. The engine is of the 2-8-8-2 type and has six cylinders 18½ in by 26 in. and 4ft 8 in. diameter coupled wheels, the cylinders and most of the running gear being interchangeable with the three-cylinder 2-8-0 type O2 class mineral engines.

'In the original "Garratt" proposal, based on providing the equivalent of two GC Section O4 class 2-8-0 engines of the well-known Railway Operating Division type, each unit was to have two outside cylinders 21 in. by 26 in., giving a tractive effort of 62,650 lb., but the existing six-cylinder design which provides a tractive effort of 72,940 lb. was adopted in order to provide a greater margin of power for dealing with the heaviest trains.'

1925 also saw the LNER drawn into a competition with the GWR in which the A1 would be compared to their Castle Class. Why the LNER's board felt it necessary to sanction these trials is unclear, because the two companies did not compete on the same primary routes. It may simply have been a case of hurt professional pride, the GWR having claimed on a placard at the Wembley Exhibitions that their Castles were the most powerful locomotives in the British

GWR engine No 4079, *Pendennis Castle*, and the LNER's 4475, *Flying Fox*, posing before the first comparative trial on the East Coast main line. Unfortunately, 4475 'ran hot' on the first day and was substituted by No. 2545, *Diamond Jubilee*. The A1 appears to dwarf the GWR loco, yet the Castle performed better in each trial.

Isles – a boast that the press quickly picked up and publicised widely. With the ever-increasing search for good PR, this may have thrown down a gauntlet which the men at King's Cross felt unable to ignore. Bert Spencer later observed and recorded a more considered view of these events:

'At the time it was thought by many to be an unnecessary distraction. The tests were not scientifically based recording only timings and fuel consumption, so offered little to analyse or compare. There was a suggestion that the full range of analysis available through the use of dynamometer cars should be brought to bear, but this seems to have been ignored by all except Sir Nigel. As a result, I do not think he involved himself in the trials willingly, seeing little value in them from a scientific point of view, and so was bowing to pressure from Whitelaw and Wedgwood. However, the issue of the Pacific's coal consumption had become a topic of some discussion, with views being expressed that it could be improved. The GWR trials were seen by some as helping bring this debate to a head.

'My personal view was that this problem was more likely due, in part, to the drivers who were more used to the Atlantics and adopted their practice of long cut-off, with the regulator partially open, when driving the Pacifics. There was also an issue, which I raised with the CME, about the valve gear employed on the A1s. When being interviewed by Sir Nigel before becoming his Technical Assistant at King's Cross, we talked at length about the Pacifics. He was interested in work I had been doing, under Francis Wintour's guidance in the Drawing Office, on possible

An unnamed Gresley Pacific, with her number obscured, gathers a large crowd before departure from Paddington on a test run in May 1925.

modifications to the valve gear. When in post the CME brought the subject up again and looked at the drawings I had prepared a few months earlier. It seemed to me that he had been considering changes to the extent of valve movement for some time, being aware that the original design was flawed, but was loath to change the design until the engines were due for general repair. The trials in 1925 did help speed the rate of change though.'

During his 1947 presentation he expanded on this issue and underlined the impact it had on locomotive design within the company:

'April and May of 1925 saw events which had a far-reaching effect on the development of LNER locomotives. An exchange of engines took place and trials were carried out on both LNER and GWR lines between Gresley's Pacific with three cylinders 20in by 26in, a boiler pressure of 180lb/sq in, and a tractive effort of 29,835 lb, and Collett's 4-6-0 type 'Castle' class with four cylinders 16in. by 26in., a boiler pressure of 225 lb/sq in, and a tractive effort of 31,625 lb. The GWR engine, weighing less than 80 tons, proved to be lighter on coal than its 92 ton LNER rival and, as a consequence, Gresley decided to revert to the use of long lap valve gear as it was clear that this feature of the Castle class design was mainly responsible for its superior performance.

'In preparing the design for the original Pacific valve gear (which was based on experience gained from the H4/K3 class) Gresley decided to fit valves with 1¼ in, lap and to restrict the full gear cut-off to 65%., with a maximum travel of 4^9/16in., in order to minimise the possibility of over travel on the valve of the middle cylinder. In actual practice the short lap valve gear made it necessary to run the Pacifics at comparatively late cut-offs and towards the end of 1924 consideration was given to the fitting of long lap gear to permit the earlier cut-off working. The scheme was not proceeded with as it was not felt that the extensive alterations to the outside valve gear then proposed could be justified in view of the successful performance of these engines on heavy main line duties. Early in 1925, however, the centre valve was given an additional 1/16 in. lap to counteract the effect of over-travel on the centre cylinder output at high speed.

'Following the exchange tests Gresley began to experiment with long lap valves on the Pacifics. The valve gear of engine No.4477, "Gay Crusader", was modified and trials were carried out with valves having 1.5/8in. lap. The results were most satisfactory in spite of the fact that only the minimum amount of alteration had been made to the existing valve gear.

'The success of this experiment led to the fitting of the completely redesigned outside valve gear originally proposed in 1924. The outside valves were given a lap of 1.5/8 in. with line and line exhaust and 1/8 in. lead, but the centre valve had an additional 1/16in. lap in accordance with practice instituted in 1925. Full gear cut-off continued to be restricted to 65%, but the maximum travel was increased from 4.9/16in. to 5.3/4 in. The first engine to be fitted with the valve gear in 1927 was No. 2555, "Centenary", and in comparative trials with Pacifics having the original short lap gear the average coal consumption with trains of approximately 500 tons between Doncaster and King's Cross reduced from 50 to 38 lb. per train mile.

'All existing Pacifics were subsequently altered in a similar manner to No. 2555 and the modified gear was fitted on all future engines of this type. The improved engine performance thus made possible was an important factor in the successful running of the non-stop "Flying Scotsman" between London and Edinburgh, inaugurated on 1 May 1928 and the high speed trains which went into service some years later.'

In a letter dated in May 1962, he summed up the improvements this change wrought by stating, quite simply, that it made 'an outstanding locomotive even better'. It would be hard to argue with him about this, but at the same time it is difficult not to commend him for his part in the work. He was a naturally reticent man to whom claiming credit was anathema, but to him must go many plaudits. He saw the problem and recommended a practical solution in such a way as to support his greatly respected leader. It is of little wonder that they enjoyed such a long and fruitful professional relationship; they were most probably friends as well. A totally trusted assistant is like gold dust and Spencer carried this with him into old age, long after Gresley had died and, in theory, released him from any bond of trust.

1926 was again a busy year, but this time production seemed to centre on two classes of 0-6-0 6F tender engines – the J38 and J39. Whilst express locomotives attracted publicity and plaudits, it was the unglamorous goods or tank engines, busying themselves dragging freight or commuter trains around the country, that provided essential, profit making services for company and country. During the mid '20s, the need for additional engines in these classes proved irresistible as a long delayed economic recovery was expected, despite the General Strike of 1926.

The J38 was built in response to increasing freight trade in the Scottish Area, though the initial requirement for 103 locomotives was scaled down to 35 engines when it was realised that a larger wheeled version, the J39, could prove more useful. The J38s were all built at Darlington in 1926, but the J39 would prove so successful that its construction programme would last from 1926 until 1941. During this period there would be year by year new production, except 1939 and '40, until 289 of these versatile engines were in service on mixed traffic as well as freight duties. Darlington Works would be responsible for producing the bulk of the J39s, but in later years some work was subcontracted to Beyer, Peacock.

During a good scientist's career, they will invariably investigate many ideas in a bid to develop solutions to specific problems. Sometimes the ideas will be their own, but more often than not they will have to delve into research undertaken by others in a bid to find solutions. History is dotted with many examples of apparently unconnected developments coming together to produce something each participant

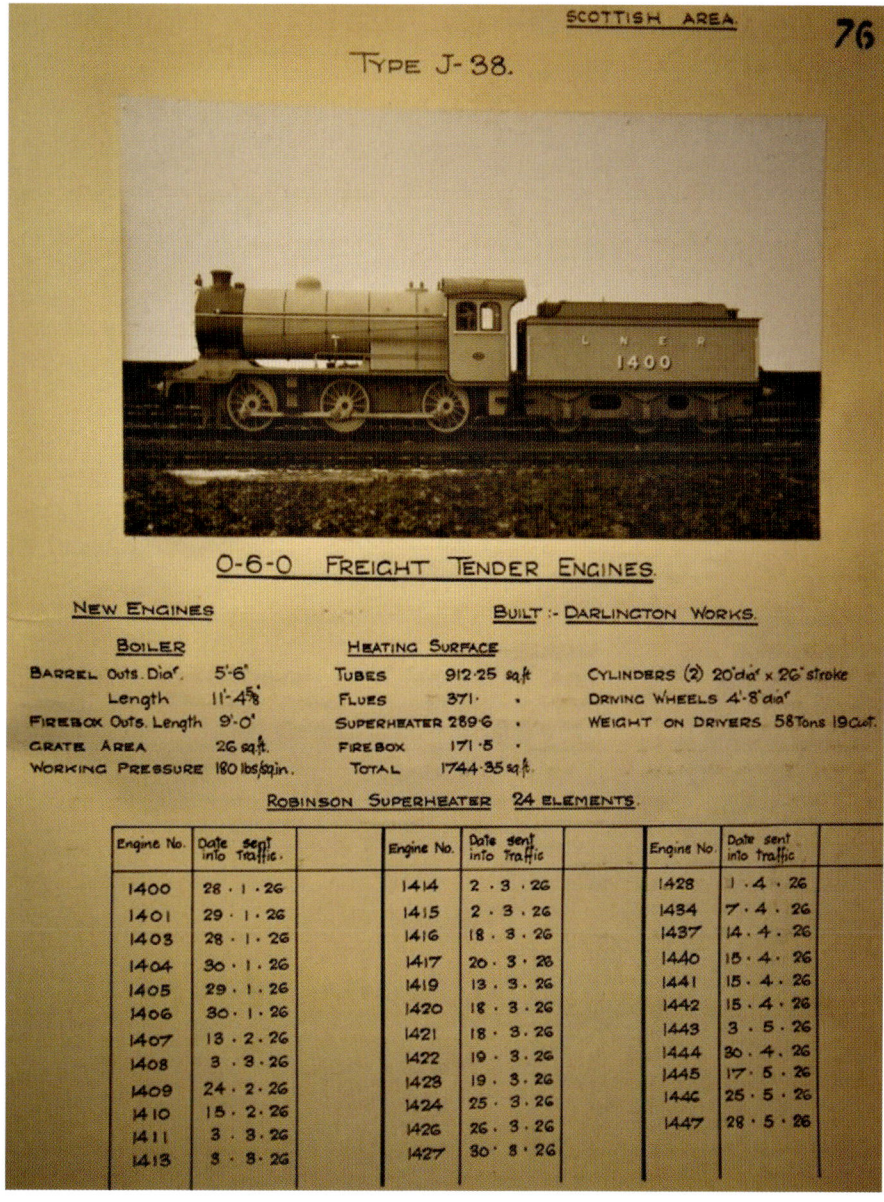

Robert Thom's summary of the J38.

J38 No. 1440, the first of the class, passing through one of her regular haunts, Gorgie to the west of Edinburgh, in July 1926 when only 6 months old.

J39 No. 1298 as she appeared when new. This locomotive was one of the second batch constructed at Darlington in 1927. The increased wheel size from the J38's 4ft 8 in. to 5ft 2in., not only improved these engines' performance but gave them a powerful more balanced look. They proved so successful that some lasted in service until 1962.

probably couldn't visualize at the time of their discovery. These inventions can be spread over many centuries before a final piece of a jigsaw is found to allow a new picture to form and a host of ideas fall into place in a new and significant way.

The development of railway locomotives is no different – the creation of fire coming a long way before the conversion of steam to powered motion and so on. There are many incremental advances, small and large, on the path to invention with ideas being tried then discarded or accepted on the way to the creation of something significant. In his career, Gresley came to personify this approach, his ever-fertile mind searching for something seemingly out of reach, but slowly becoming attainable. During the 1920s in particular, this became a religion to him, stimulated by his profound sense of scientific curiosity. But inevitably there were financial, political and operational pressures at work within the LNER which acted as a brake on his design ambitions. Yet within these constraints, he still followed many routes and considered and tried a variety of ideas in a bid to improve or refine the breed.

In his A1 and P1 designs, these elements are most clearly seen and each locomotive he produced also played some part in this process. As the 1930s approached the speed of these developments began to reach a peak, aided, in part, by the support and advice of Chapelon, Bulleid, Spencer and Robert Thom, who in 1927 transferred to Doncaster. Francis Wintour had proved to be a valuable and committed supporter of the CME, but his age was beginning to tell and retirement beckoned. In his place Thom would bring new energy and greater dynamism.

It was during this period that Gresley pursued another idea in

The design of the J39's footplate probably owed more to Worsdell than Gresley. Spartan and compact but functional, affording the crew excellent visibility.

Engine No. 1791 as fitted with the Weir feed pump – on her port side just forward of the cab. She ran in this condition until 1924 when withdrawn and the pump removed. Records mapping the performance of the engine at this period do not seem to have survived, but one may assume the pump produced sufficient improvement to warrant further tests with alternative systems.

his bid to enhance his engines' performance. Feed-water heaters were a firmly established principle in steam boilers but had not been exploited to any great extent by locomotive designers. The idea is a simple one. Keeping the water level in a steam boiler constant is essential for its safe and efficient running. This is achieved by having a continuous flow of water from a tank or tender. The cycle this creates is deemed to be an irreversible one under the 2nd law of thermodynamics because there is an inability to achieve 100 per cent efficiency in energy transfer. In essence, water, when introduced into the boiler, will be considerably cooler and cause thermal shock to the boiler's metal. Heating the injected water will also absorb more energy generated by the boiler and reduce its efficiency still further. So, pre-heating the water to the highest possible temperature before it enters the boiler can in theory improve its thermodynamic efficiency and reduce long term shock damage. A pre-heating unit in a locomotive also has the benefit of capturing steam exhaust from the cylinders, which was lost to the air, and re-cycling it to heat the water as it passes from the tank into the boiler. There will still be heat loss in the system, but the level of loss is reduced. It is this principle that Gresley and his team wished to explore having seen a Weir-built feed-water heater and pump fitted to Great Eastern Claud Hamilton Class Atlantic, No. 1791, in the years immediately after the war: a process set in motion by Alfred hill when that company's CME.

It was an idea that had been in his mind for many years and had formed part of his 1918 address to the ILocoE, but it wasn't until he became the LNER'S CME that he began to test the theory in a more practical way. Whilst the Davies and Metcalfe exhaust steam injectors were already in use and acted as a form of pre-heater, Gresley felt that there was still room for improvement. So, in 1926, he arranged for Worthington feed pumps to be fitted to an ex-GER Holden Class B12 4-6-0, No. 8509, and an ex-North British Railway Reid Class C11 Atlantic, No. 9903, to test his theories. The trials that followed suggested that some benefits might accrue and so

Engine No. 8509 as she appeared shortly after being modified with the ACFI water heater system. It was an ungainly attachment that did little for the looks of the locomotive, but the potential savings of coal and water seemed worth striving for.

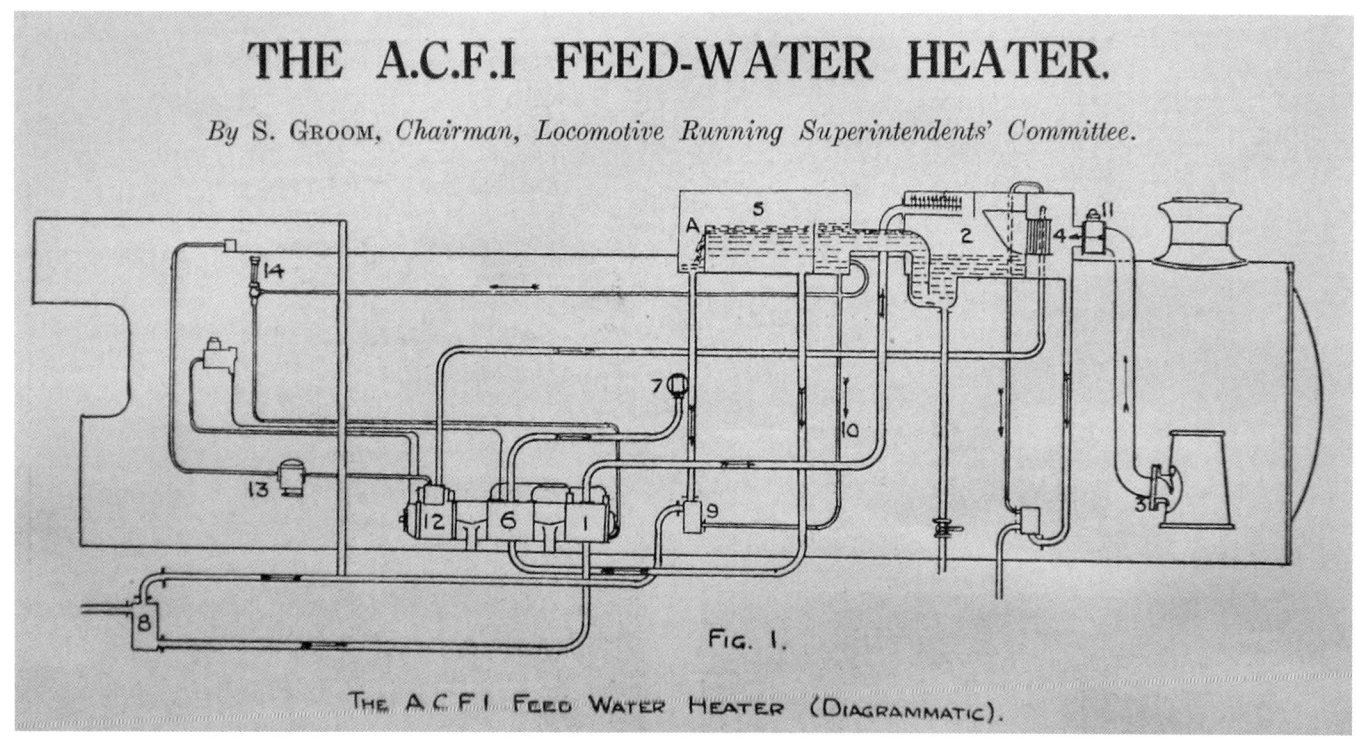

THE A.C.F.I FEED-WATER HEATER.

By S. Groom, *Chairman, Locomotive Running Superintendents' Committee.*

FIG. 1.

THE A.C.F.I FEED WATER HEATER (DIAGRAMMATIC).

The ACFI equipment in close up and as portrayed in the LNER's journal.

Shotover as she appeared in 1929. The modified ACFI is far less intrusive and by the time it equipped the first P2 2-8-2 express engine it had been further refined and moulded into the body shape a little better.

extended into 1927, but this time using versions of the ACFI (Société Auxiliaire des Chemins de fer et l'Industrie) designed heater system instead. Gresley had noted its growing use on the continent and saw that the manufacturers claimed economies of 10 to 12 per cent in coal burnt and 15 per cent less water used. With such obvious benefits, he was eager to push ahead with trials, purchased some of the French-built units and fitted them to four more Holden 4-6-0s – 8504, 8517, 8519 and 8523. In addition, two ex-NER Atlantics, No. 728 and No. 2206, were also equipped with the pre-heaters as a means of comparison between classes.

Then over a period of some months, in 1927-8, all these engines were put through their paces on the Eastern Section of the company's Southern Area. The results seem to have been encouraging, though no record appears to have survived in public hands to confirm this, so success or otherwise has to be measured by other means. One way of doing this is to see if the experiment continued or the unit became a standard fitting on more locomotives. E.A.S. Brown, in his book *Nigel Gresley – Locomotive Engineer'*, concludes that 52 more B12s were modified, plus two Pacifics – A1 No. 2576, *White Knight* and A1, No.2580, *Shotover*, both in mid-1929, fifteen months after 2580 was rebuilt as an A3 at Darlington. The B12s cannot be confirmed but the Pacifics were definitely customised and ran for a time with this equipment in a modified form, which allowed it to be fitted inside the smokebox. During 1934, ACFI was also fitted to the first of Gresley's P2 express engines.

All this suggests that the CME continued to see potential in the system and clung to the concept to draw out as much as he possibly could from it. Here again, Gresley

A Time of Politics and An Age of Science (1922–28) • 133

The valve gear arrangement for the D49 class saw the gear placed behind the cylinders due to space limitations.

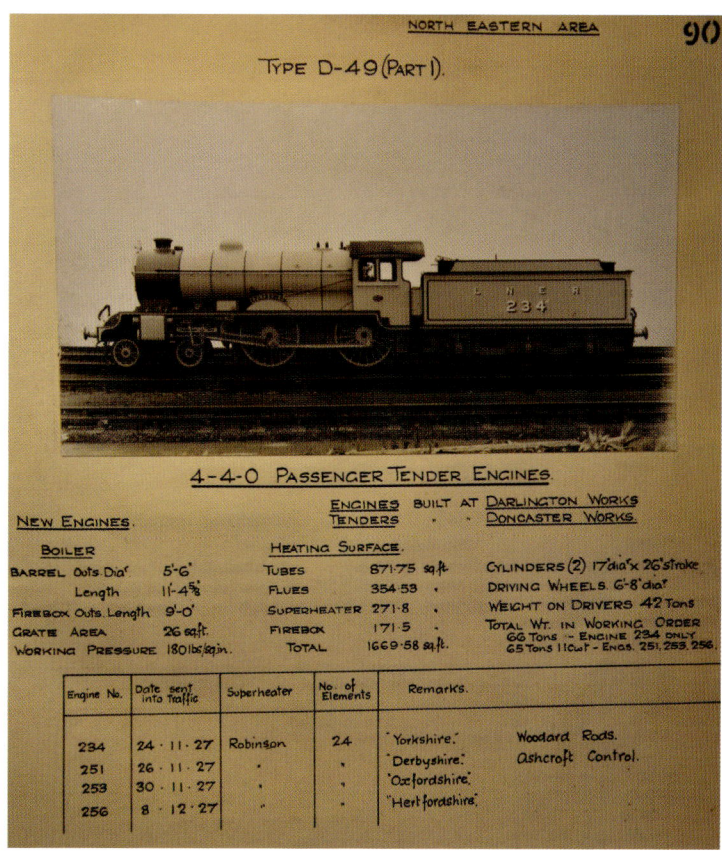

Robert Thom's record of the first batch of D49s that appeared in late 1927. Their construction went on at Darlington until 1935 by which time 76 had been built.

displayed his tenacity in pursuing an idea when those around him had given up or moved down another path. In any business, simple economics will eventually dictate whether an experiment continues or not. In this case, it seems that the idea was dropped when potential savings failed to materialise, or it was realised that any achievable savings were cancelled out by the purchase price and then increased maintenance costs of the system itself. If so, the conversion offered no real advantage that accountants could accept. Feed-water pre-heaters continued to play a part in steam locomotion on the continent, but never found wider favour in Britain, despite Gresley's best endeavours. It was another case of what might have been.

Another idea of worth which Gresley and his team pursued with great vigour at this time concerned the type of valve gear to be used. Bert Spencer described this work in 1947:

'For the lighter passenger services in the North Eastern and Scottish Areas, Gresley introduced the three-cylinder, 4-4-0 type "Shire" class express engines. The first of the new series, No.234, "Yorkshire", classified D49, left Darlington works in September 1927. These engines have 6ft 8in. diameter coupled wheels and the three 17in. by 26in. cylinders are arranged in line above the bogie, thus making it possible to accommodate the Gresley gear behind the cylinders. This arrangement avoids the necessity of disconnecting the gear for valve examination and also eliminates the effect of outside valve spindle expansion on the centre valve. The boilers of the D49 class carry a working pressure of 180 lb. per sq inch and are interchangeable with those of the J39 class.

'The valve events were difficult to maintain and the engines were fitted with piston valves when the cylinders required renewal.

'Although the D49 class engines were fitted with poppet valves operated by oscillating cams driven from the Walschaert valve gear, Gresley felt that the full advantage of such valves would not be realised unless a simple rotary gear was developed. In 1929 two D49 engines, No. 336, "Buckinghamshire" and No. 352, "Leicestershire", were therefore fitted with an experimental arrangement of rotary cam valve gear designed by Messrs. Lentz Patents in collaboration with the LNER.

'Engines fitted with each type of valve gear were selected for comparative tests carried out between Newcastle and York in November-December 1929, each engine [Nos. 352, 236, 239 and 352] being tested for five days on the same trains. From the results it will be seen that engine No. 352, with rotary cam operated poppet valves, was a little lighter on coal per drawbar horsepower hour than either the piston valve [236] or the oscillating cam poppet valve engine [329].'

Spencer then went on to describe all the test results in fine detail and any reason for the variations, before reporting that forty more engines with rotary cam gear were built between 1932 and 1935. He passes no comment on the wisdom of doing this, which suggests he wasn't in total agreement with this course of action or others where the CME seemed too innovative.

This impression is confirmed to a certain extent by his next comment:

'During development of the three-cylinder 4-4-0 type, D49 class engines, Gresley considered the possibility of constructing a six-cylinder 4-4-0 type geared locomotive, of similar tractive effort, having 6ft 8in. diameter coupled wheels, a boiler pressure of 200 lb./sq in and a tractive effort of 21,520 lb.

'A six-cylinder 'uniflow' engine arranged in 'Vee' form with three cylinders on each side of the smokebox drives twin crankshafts with cranks at 120 degrees. Rotary cam valve gear operating 3in. diameter double seated poppet valves by stepped cams gives four ranges of cut off in fore gear. The main casting incorporates the crank case,

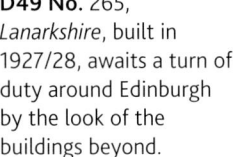

D49 No. 265, *Lanarkshire*, built in 1927/28, awaits a turn of duty around Edinburgh by the look of the buildings beyond.

saddle and jackstaff supports…. The 'uniflow' engines were to have a crank-shaft speed of 700 rpm at 70mph and the drive from the twin crankshaft was to be transmitted by bevel gearing to a jackshaft. The provision of a suitable bevel drive presented difficulties and the scheme was not proceeded with.'

One can almost hear a sigh of relief. At times working alongside a dynamic personality must have had its drawbacks. The highly creative will always have 'flights of fancy' which will take them in many directions, some of which may eventually prove to be successful, whilst others become unwanted distractions from the main business at hand. Yet this was part and parcel of Gresley's personality and way of working. The papers that have survived from this period show how he involved himself day by day in the process of design and construction, taking an almost minute interest in the fine detail of a project. In many cases he contacted his Mechanical Engineers at Doncaster and Darlington and the Chief Draughtsman on a daily basis suggesting changes or seeking updates on work. And to this was added regular visits in which progress was undoubtedly discussed. Luckily, he behaved diplomatically and fully understood the pressures his staff were under, so didn't ruffle feathers when asserting close control of all this work. At times, it must have been a difficult balance to achieve as Bert Spencer suggested when he wrote:

'The pace of work was relentless at times. Up to

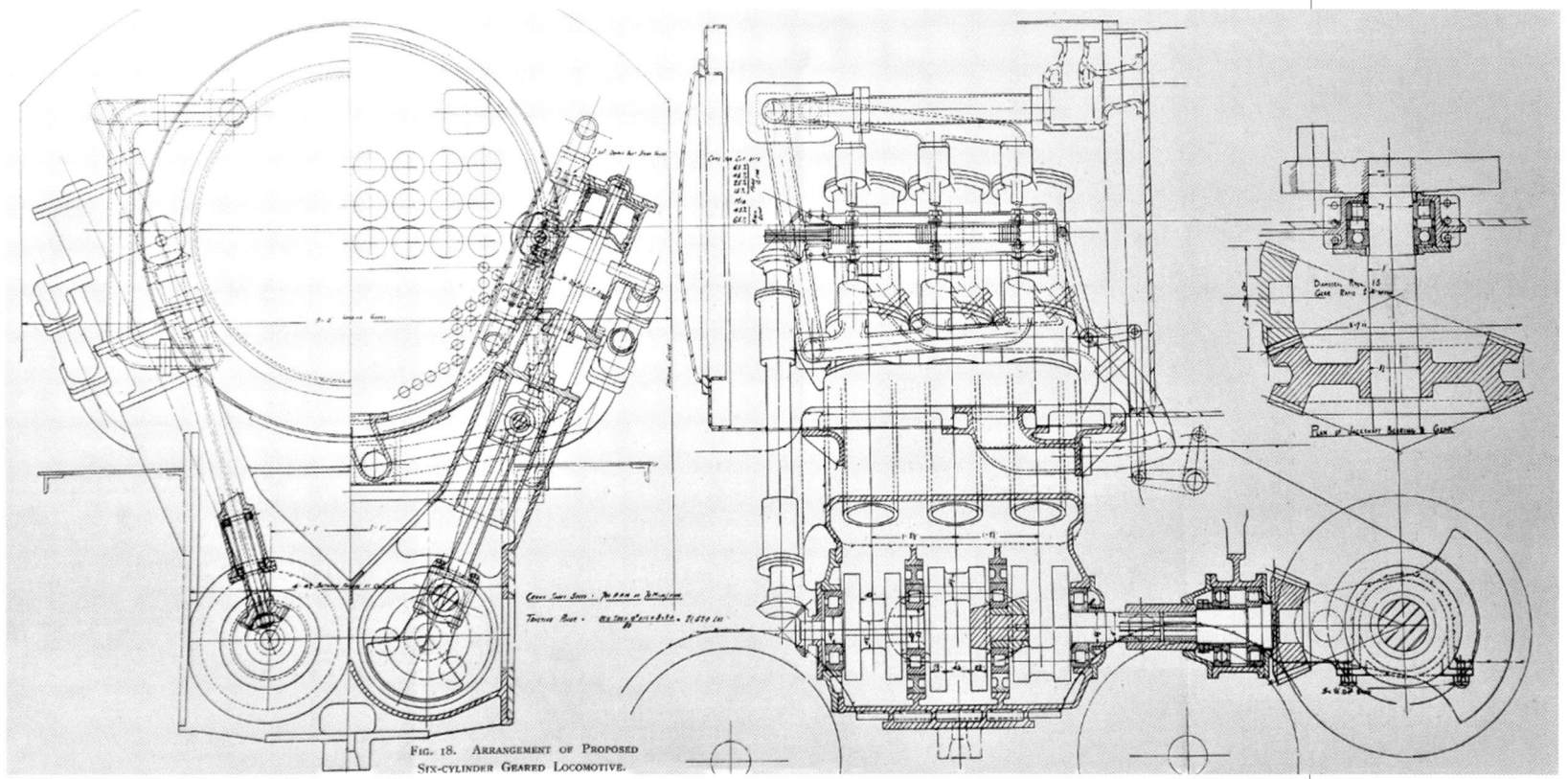

The initial design for Gresley's experimental six-cylinder 'uniflow' engine. Bert Spencer, it seems, took his CME's rough sketches, and scribbled ideas, and produced the drawings that ended up forming part of his 1947 presentation to the ILocoE. Although taking this preparatory action he reported the proposal didn't get beyond the drawing board phase. A distraction killed off, perhaps, or a far seeing idea that might have proved a success if not unnecessarily terminated. As with any unusual idea the weight of other work, plus a degree of scepticism can prove impossible to overcome. It is hard to say how strong Spencer's influence was in these matters, but he does seem to have been a voice of reason and assumed the role of long stop on much that Gresley contemplated.

1929, on an almost daily basis, Sir Nigel would produce new ideas or improvements to other designs in sketches or short written statements as his agile mind appraised all that was going on around him. Many of these were filtered out at King's Cross or underwent modification before reaching Thom, Stamer or the Chief Draughtsman. But he would also contact them directly on many issues they may already have had well in hand. There was little friction though, such was the high regard in which he was held.'

And one could add to this his strength of character and management style.

The D49s seem to have been successful engines, particularly in the inter-war years, a fact confirmed by their continued production until 1935. But the oscillating cam Lentz poppet valves proved to be less successful in service than hoped. They were modified over the next decade but without achieving the hoped-for improvement. So from 1938 they were replaced with standard piston valves when the cylinders fell due for renewal. Although some of these engines lasted in service until 1961, the ever-increasing size of loads, particularly during the war, meant they were gradually relegated to lesser duties. It was a process that gathered pace as the LNER began producing its heavier duty B1 4-6-0 mixed traffic engines during 1942.

As the decade drew to a close, four locomotive projects continued to grow in significance, along with all the other tasks facing Gresley in managing such a substantial area of work. There was the next phase of his Pacific programme and this was followed by a more powerful class of passenger engine for the Eastern Section of the LNER. Then there was the next stage of the Mikado programme and the Yarrow experimental high pressure boiler project. This design was reaching fruition in 1928 and only awaited an order from the LNER to allow construction to begin. Before this could happen, Gresley and his team had to design a locomotive on which the boiler could be mounted. But neither the Mikado or the W1, as the LNER/Yarrow engine would be classed, were high priority projects in the eyes of the board of directors or the Locomotive and Traffic Committees chaired by William Whitelaw. Instead, they gave greater priority to the more immediate need for additional Pacifics and a new

Batch two D49 No. 329, *Invernessshire*, built in 1928 and fitted with oscillating cam poppet valves, is photographed at Grantham sometime during 1932 on a visit from her home shed of Eastfield in North Yorkshire.

4-6-0 passenger engine to meet an ever increasing demand for more powerful locomotives on the old Great Eastern lines running from Liverpool Street Station.

Even with an ever growing fleet of Pacifics to play with, traffic demands were increasing sufficiently to justify building more. While many people in Britain were still profoundly affected by austerity in the 1920s, there was still a middle and upper class still seemingly able to enjoy a high standard of living and this meant that long distance passenger services on the railways for work and pleasure were still drawing a large number of customers. In addition, the military which still held many hundreds of thousands of men in establishments strung out along the main lines, continued to have a pressing and increasing requirement for the railways. One of their primary needs was to ensure the effective movement of these forces and their equipment, whether on duty or on leave, and the railways were still seen as the best way of ensuring this would happen. So for various reasons, the LNER believed that an expansion of this modern class of engine was fully justified.

By this stage, the A1s had proven their value but the design was undergoing change and refinement in an effort to improve their performance. Long lap valves had been tried, tested and introduced as standard equipment. But their boilers, which produced a pressure of 180psi, and superheaters containing 32 elements, were thought insufficient for the long distance work planned.

By comparison, the development of a boiler producing 220psi of pressure, with an enlarged superheater containing 43 elements, seemed to offer enhanced performance and endurance. So, in 1927 Gresley sought permission to modify five A1s with the new boiler to test these theories further. In July, the first of these, A1, No. 4480, *Enterprise*, emerged from the workshops, nearly four tons heavier, to begin a series of comparative runs that would measure the benefits of each boiler/superheater combination. Shortly afterwards, 4480 was joined in these trials by the second modified engine No. 2544, *Lemberg*, at which point Spencer takes up the story:

'The only differences between the new and original boilers were an increase in the thickness of the barrel plates, a closer pitching of the firebox stays and an increase in the number of superheater elements from 32 to 43. The cylinders of No. 4480 were not altered, but those of No. 2544 were reduced to 18¼ in. diameter (to give the high-pressure boiler a tractive effort approximately equal to that of the standard 180lb. Pacifics), the tractive efforts being 36,465 lb. and 30,362lb. respectively as compared with 29,835 lb. on the standard A1 Class.

'Engine No. 4480 proved highly successful in service, the increased power due to the use of the higher pressure with 20in. diameter cylinders enabling the engine to be worked at relatively early cut-offs on the heaviest trains.

'Comparative trials were carried out between A1 class No. 4473, 'Solario', with 180 lb. pressure and No. 2544 with 220 lb. pressure (during February 1928, over a two-week period on the hardest duty of the time – the 10.51 am from Doncaster to King's Cross and return at 16.00 hrs). Both engines had long lap valve gear. Engine No. 4473 made six return journeys on consecutive days (312 miles per day) and engine No. 2544 made five return journeys the following week.

'Whilst the coal consumption per mile and per ton-mile showed a substantial economy in favour of 2544, there was little to choose between the two engines when comparing coal and water consumption on a horsepower basis. Engine No. 4473 did more work during the trials owing to greater wind resistance which adversely affected its coal and water consumption per mile and per ton-mile, these comparisons giving no credit for the extra effort due to weather conditions.'

Many years later Spencer touched on another issue Gresley and his team considered at the time when judging whether to proceed with the boiler producing 220psi pressure:

'There were concerns over the comparative maintenance costs between boilers operating with different pressures – higher pressures costing more or having shorter lives. Thom had presented a short paper

Comparative Tests between Pacific Engines with 180 & 220 lbs/▫" Boiler Pressure   FEBRUARY 1928

A series of comparative tests have been made between two Pacific engines of equivalent tractive effort, one having smaller cylinders than the other but fitted with a boiler carrying a higher pressure and having a larger superheating surface, the object of the trials being to see what economy in coal & water consumption could be obtained by the use of the higher pressure boiler.

Engines 4473 & 2544 were selected for the trials, the leading particulars of the former which has 180 lbs/▫" boiler pressure, are shewn on Sheet 1. The mileage run by this engine up to Jan 31st. since its last general repair was 5020 but prior to the tests the valves and pistons were examined, the valves were tried over to check the settings and any necessary adjustments made, and the percentage cut off graduations shewn on the reversing gear in the cab were checked. The safety valves were adjusted, the boiler and steam chest pressure gauge checked, and it was seen that the injectors and other auxiliaries were working satisfactorily. The brick arch and firebars were looked to, any leaky joints were made tight and the engine generally put in good running order.

The high pressure engine No 2544, its leading particulars are shewn on Sheet 2. Its mileage since last repair was 5088 up to Jan. 31st, and it was examined and treated in an exactly similar manner to Eng. 4473. On each engine the boilers were washed and the tubes brushed on alternate days.

The trials were carried out on express passenger trains running between King's Cross & Doncaster, one double trip being made daily. They extended over a fortnight, Eng. 4473 being tested the first week. Two sets of men were employed & in order to have similar operating conditions with each engine the men were changed in the middle of each week.

A supply of Rossington coal was put to one side for the two engines, it was weighed on & off daily, a supply for lighting up and making up the fire being kept separate in bags, the amount of fire in the box at the commencement and end of each trip being kept as nearly alike as possible.

The tenders of both engines were metered out so that the capacity in gallons for each inch in depth of water was known, & this depth was measured by means of a dipping pipe in the tender connected to a water gauge in the dynamometer

---

SHEET 3

Comparative Tests between Pacific Engines
Eng. 4473, Type A1, 180 lbs/▫" boiler pressure. Results of tests on 11-4am Doncaster to King's Cross, Feb. 13-18th 1928.
Distance 156 miles   Booked Running Speed 55.4 M.P.H.
Number of booked intermediate stops 1.

General Running Conditions

Record No.	Train Tons	Axles	Actual Speed m.p.h	Signal & P. Way checks	Extra Stops	Weather	Wind M.P.H.
1177	427	56	54.9	1		Showery	Nil
1179	430	56	54.8	1	-	Fine	Nil
1181	425	56	53.3	2	1	Showery	10.0 W.S.W
1183	440	59	54.8	2	-	Showery	8.5 SW
1185	432	56	56.1	2	-	Fine	13.0 W
1187	456	59	55.7	1	-	Fine	5.5 W.S.W

Average Locomotive Performance

Record No.	Press. lbs/▫ Boiler	Press. lbs/▫ Steam C.	Cut off %	Steam Temp °F	Drawbar Pull Tons	Drawbar Horse Power
1177	172	163	22	571	1.90	622
1179	172	160	22	562	1.95	638
1181	174	162	22	573	2.28	727
1183	175	161	24	566	2.32	762
1185	174	162	25	579	2.23	748
1187	174	158	25	575	2.18	726

Average Water Consumption on Trip

Record No	Pounds Evaporated Per hour	Per Drawbar HP hour	Per sq. ft. of HS/hr Evap.	Per sq. ft. of HS/hr Total	Per Mile	Per 1000 ton train ml.	Feed water temp. °F
1177	17390	27.9	5.93	5.03	316	742	47
1179	15750	24.7	5.38	4.56	287	668	46
1181	17390	23.8	5.93	5.03	325	765	49
1183	18520	24.3	6.32	5.36	337	767	50
1185	17750	23.8	6.06	5.14	316	731	46
1187	17710	24.4	6.04	5.12	318	697	47

The results of the trials in February 1928 found a very simple voice in the back of a small notebook kept by one of the officers involved, two pages of which are portrayed here. Their simplicity and lack of scientific depth helped convince Gresley of the need to introduce a fully equipped test centre.

on the subject to the A.R.L.E [Association of Railway Locomotive Engineers] when Gresley was President between 1926 and '27. He compared 180 and 200 lb. psi boilers and this led to a great deal of discussion by members each describing their own experiences. With the likes of Gresley, Thom, Stanier, Fowler, Beames and Bulleid in attendance there couldn't have been a more expert group of people, but even so no final conclusion could be reached.

However, the consensus, led by Stanier, seemed to be that there would be no appreciable difference in maintenance costs and the benefits of running with a boiler with higher pressure would outweigh any small difference, if it existed at all. With that assurance Gresley felt able to argue the benefits of conversion.'

Armed with this limited information, Gresley sought authority to modify the rest of the class and apply these changes to a new batch of Pacifics which had been authorised in late 1927 by the Locomotive Committee. Lack of data also reinforced his view of another subject that was increasingly taxing him – the absence of adequate test facilities available to the LNER. As a scientist of note, he was only too aware of the need to test any new idea rigorously 'on the road' and in the laboratory, so that its merits, both short and long term, could be assessed and compared. In Britain there had been very little focus on this issue; a lack of foresight and effort which clearly rankled with the CME, as he made clear in a Presidential address made to the ILocoE in 1934:

'About six years ago the French engineers [Chapelon amongst them], who were fully alive to the benefits which could be derived by the provision of a testing station, were able to persuade the French Government that it was necessary to have such a station. Just over 12 months ago the French station at Vitry, near Paris, was opened.

'This experimental station is the most perfectly equipped in the world for carrying out analytical and scientific research….There are also four new dynamometer cars fitted with the most modern recording appliances, attached to the station. These are available for use in connection with trials in service on any French railways, and can be used for checking the results of innovations which have been introduced as a result of research in the locomotive experimental station…The establishment of the great new experimental station at Vitry is evidence of the confidence and conviction of the French engineers that progress can only be secured by full and complete research.

'What have we here in England? A small locomotive testing plant of 500 hp capacity, installed at the Swindon works of the GWR 30 years ago… The Swindon plant is, however, much too small for modern locomotives. [And] there are four dynamometer cars in existence on British railways, all of which I regard as almost obsolete when compared with modern cars.'

To him and many others it seemed unbelievable that as science advanced and solutions became more complex, a two dimensional testing system, more suited to Victorian times, was their sole means of refining design. He was only too aware of the many nuances and variables contained in the process of development and the pressing need to understand all elements of a design and their inter-relationships so that all possible outcomes could be considered. And here he looked to other emerging worlds such as aviation and aerodynamics, which, during the 1920s, were reaching far into the future and pushing back boundaries. They were aided in this by scientists working at RAE Farnborough, the National Physical Laboratory and major aircraft manufacturers such as Hawker and Supermarine. In these places, advanced testing methods had become central to all they did and Gresley wished to bring this approach to the railways, where considerably more money was being invested by the companies involved in new equipment programmes.

Through membership of IMechE, he had gained access to scientists at the NPL in particular and appears to have read their published papers with great interest. He, according to Spencer, became an occasional visitor at their rapidly expanding facility at Teddington and made the acquaintance of many of the leading lights there. These included Sir Thomas Stanton, the Superintendent of the Engineering Department, the aviation specialist William Duncan and, as mentioned earlier, Frederick Johansen.

Born in 1897, Johansen joined the NPL in 1922 shortly after graduating from King's College London with a degree in Civil and Mechanical Engineering; to which he added an MSc then a PHD later. He so impressed Stanton and Duncan with his knowledge and skills that they swiftly directed him towards researching the effects of element flow around moving bodies. This work, and his growing understanding of aerodynamics and

Cigarette cards were a familiar sight during the inter-war years and in a scientific series they included this picture of Frederick Johansen working in the NPL's wind tunnel.

Robert Thom records the arrival of the first few A3s. Such a famous class of engine seems to deserve greater fanfare than this, but any lack of internal publicity was soon replaced by extensive press coverage.

internal and external streamlining, proved of interest to Gresley and he began to seek the younger man's advice on many issues relating to locomotive and carriage design. As the decade drew to a close, this working relationship was beginning to bear fruit and would reach a peak in the 1930s, supported by the advanced test facilities at Teddington. If the railways didn't wish to invest in adequate test and evaluation facilities, he was determined to make use of anything else that was available to improve the breed. But by the end of the decade, only the Yarrow/Gresley W1 project would benefit to any extent by this connection.

Meanwhile, the Pacific project moved into its next phase, encouraged by recent test results. This led to the development of the 'Super Pacific', as some called it, though in reality it became the A3, with the remaining A1s eventually being upgraded to the same standard. At the time, it was regarded as Gresley's masterpiece and over the years this description has become fixed in the public consciousness; by any standards, it was and is worthy of this title as proved by the first engine, No. 2743, *Felstead*, when she appeared in the summer of 1928 to be shedded at Doncaster. She was followed by the other nine of this first batch, all of which were earning their keep by April the following year.

The arrival of these A3s coincided with the introduction of a non-stop service from London to Edinburgh and with it a long-held ambition of the LNER was finally realised. But the new service owed more to the development of eight wheeled corridor tenders capable of

A Time of Politics and An Age of Science (1922–28) • 141

holding nine tons of coal than the new Pacific, allowing, as they did, the crew to be changed whilst the train was in motion. The A1s, which by this time had proved themselves more than capable of such arduous work, having been modified with long lap valves, were allocated to this duty. Memorably, engine No. 4472, *Flying Scotsman*, one of five locomotives prepared for the task, took the inaugural train northwards on 1 May 1928 with Gresley on board. The engine, the train and the LNER were showered with publicity in the days and weeks that followed. Bert Spencer 'who was present on this trip' recalled the day in a very brief way:

'There were a sizeable number of journalists on board as well as Sir Nigel, some of his family and many representatives from the railway. The journey passed without incident though at one stage it was suspected that a tender axle box might be overheating. But, if so, it didn't slow progress or delay the train in any way. Gresley and I took a number of parties up to the cab through the tender much to the CME's great pleasure, especially when taking the controls for short periods. By this stage he was becoming increasingly concerned about his wife's health and the first non-stop run to Edinburgh provided some distraction.'

While the *Flying Scotsman* and the other Pacifics were the centre of so much attention, other equally important locomotive

1 May 1928 and 4472 begins to pull away from King's Cross. For nearly two months before the inaugural run she had been in the works under 'general repair' making sure she was on the 'top line' as Bert Spencer called it. The design of her new tender was kept a closely guarded secret in case the LNER's main opposition got wind of the development and tried to steal a march on them.

Luggage labels and much more was soon produced to advertise this premier service.

developments were taking place. They may not have had the glamour or prestige of the non-stop, high speed runs, but they were equally important to the LNER and the fare paying public. And sneaking almost unnoticed through the design and construction process were the first of the B17, 4-6-0, class engines.

With loading gauge restrictions in place on many of the old Great Eastern lines, only locomotives up to a certain size could be accommodated and these didn't have the capacity to pull the heavier passenger trains then becoming more common. Classes from other areas were tried, such as the K2 2-6-0s, but these proved little better. Very quickly, the service on many routes declined and the company faced considerable criticism. In the face of this censure, the LNER responded by commissioning a new class and the Doncaster drawing office was given the specification, with many of Spencer's drawings and notes attached. This centred on building a three cylinder 4-6-0 engine which would include the cylinder and motion arrangement from the D49. It had to have a maximum axle load of 17 tons, yet be capable of producing a tractive effort of approximately 25,000 lb. For some reason, the solutions produced by the Chief Draughtsman didn't find favour with the Locomotive Running Department. In the discussions that followed, it was agreed that the design work would be contracted out to the North British Locomotive Company, who would also have the incentive of a contract to build some or all of the engines if their design was accepted. They began work in December 1927 and in February the following year submitted their proposals to Gresley.

NBR also struggled to meet the loading parameters set by the LNER and so presented two designs for consideration, both of which exceeded the 17 ton limit. With time pressing, the engine which exceeded this loading restriction the least was chosen.

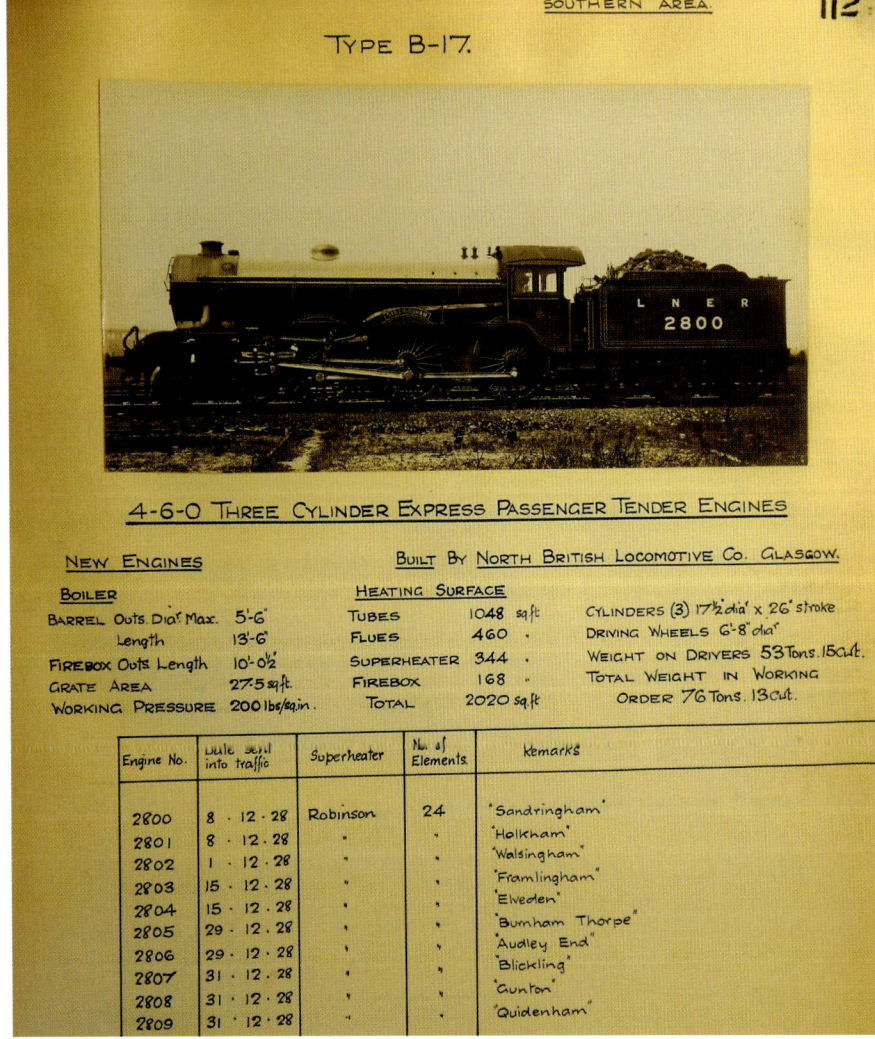

Robert Thom's B17 summary for 1928.

Their solution is said to have drawn heavily on the experience they'd gained four years earlier when constructing twenty A1 Pacifics. Certainly, the driving wheels were the same size and the valve gear arrangement was adopted, added to which the cab and cylinders bore similarities, but whereas the original A1 boilers produced 180 lb. of pressure, the B17 achieved 200lb. And with a design finally approved, the LNER placed an initial order for ten locomotives, which North British delivered in November and December 1928. Bert Spencer briefly mentioned the B17s in his papers, picking out only one interesting element in their design:

> 'The B17 class have conjugated valve gears behind the cylinders, as on the D49 class, and are the only Gresley three-cylinder engines to have divided drive, the outside cylinders driving on the second coupled axle and the inside cylinder on the first. This arrangement was necessary in order that the weight distribution of the engine should conform to the limits imposed by the engineers. Operational requirements also made it necessary to restrict their overall length and the original GE type six-wheeled tender was therefore provided. Later engines had the larger standard 4,000 galls tender.'

These engines performed well but were noted for their rough riding qualities. There were also problems with cracked frames which modified lighter springing on the driving wheels combined with stiffer spring on the bogies failed to resolve. The problem continued and eventually horn blocks were added to the middle driving axle, with improvements being made to axlebox lubrication at the same time. It seems that this reduced the problem, though records suggest that it wasn't eradicated entirely and it did little to reduce their poor riding characteristics.

As the end of the decade approached, Gresley could look back on his first seven years as CME with some pride. There was clearly much more to do, and the decade ahead would be equally challenging. He had moulded an organisation from a number of different companies into one that worked and developed a locomotive and rolling stock programmes of substance and potential. Yet behind all this, he still wished to push back the boundaries of what was possible, pursue innovation and take his science to new levels. All his ambitions would come together in the W1 project, but as it evolved and reached fruition he had to cope with a tragic and crippling loss of almost unbearable proportions.

B17, No 2808, 'Gunton', which entered service in December 1928 appears to be making light work of a twelve coach load (date and place are not recorded on the negative).

Chapter 5
A NECESSARY DISTRACTION (1929–31)

Ethel Gresley died on 5 August 1929 after a long battle against the slow spread of cancer of the womb, bladder and mesentery. For many months she had been afflicted with an undiagnosed pain, keeping her increasing discomfort secret from her family and perhaps even her husband. Victorian stoicism was a hard mould to break and silence and forbearance took immense courage but eventually her pain and increasing fragility could no longer be disguised and her decline became only too apparent. In the 1920s, there were few treatments available to help those suffering from cancer. A radiation regime, though having its origins in the 1890s, was still in its infancy with few understanding how it worked or the collateral damage that could be caused to healthy tissue. Surgery remained the only realistic way of tackling such an invasive set of illnesses and this only become possible with the gradual refinement of anaesthetics in the Great War. The dangers inherent in this course of action were considerable and even in the hands of a skilled surgeon there was a high risk that the patient might die or the cancer might not be removed in its entirety.

Gresley sought the opinion of his friend Sir Maurice Cassidy, a surgeon and cardiologist of note, who was based at St Thomas' Hospital in London. He visited the patient and, it seems, recommended surgery to remove the cancer. Gresley had his dressing room stripped and converted into a make shift operating theatre, preferring this to the risks of moving her to a local hospital or the debilitating effects of transporting Ethel to St Thomas' for treatment. Cassidy carried out the surgery himself, with the family GP and a privately employed nurse in attendance. It seemed for a time that she would survive this ordeal, but her condition deteriorated and her life came to an end with 'no pain', according to her death certificate.

Ethel was buried in Netherseal, within a few feet of her late parents-in-law and other members of her husband's family, under an oak tree planted by the Reverend Gresley in 1869. A plaque nearby informs the casual visitor that this tree is the great grand-daughter of the Boscabel Oak, in which the future King Charles II hid following his defeat at the battle of Worcester in 1651. True or not, it does add a sense of history and permanence to this quiet spot at the heart of the village.

Spencer recalled the impact of Ethel's death on her husband:

'For some weeks Sir Nigel was rarely seen and Arthur Stamer took over many of the CME's duties. The reason for his

Gresley in the early 1930s. He seems to have lost the exuberance and confidence that characterised so many of his earlier portraits.

The eminent surgeon and physician Sir Maurice Cassidy who fought to save Ethel Gresley's life. He was an old friend and golfing partner of the CME and in 1930 became Physician to the Royal Family, such was the respect in which he was held. Later on he would become personal physician to George V and George VI until his death, following a car accident in 1949. Gresley, it appears, remained his patient until his own death in 1941.

absence was known by some, but was kept to a very small circle. When his wife died the impact on him was profound, as one might expect. In all the years I had known them they appeared to be a devoted couple and her loss must have seriously exhausted his reserves of energy and blunted his sense of purpose. When he returned from a trip to the USA with his eldest daughter the changes in him were plain for us all to see. He recovered to a certain extent, but never again displayed the same energy or vitality. For many months there were rumours that he might retire and there was much speculation about who his successor might be.

'It seemed to me that the W1 locomotive, which was nearing completion in the latter part of 1929, provided him with a brief distraction and brought him back into the fold. Its development had interested him for many years and seeing it so close to completion in the Works fascinated him, as it did us all.'

In the immediate aftermath of Ethel's death, Gresley, who had planned to visit North America for many years, took Maurice Cassidy's advice and booked passage for himself and his daughter Violet, on the Canadian Pacific liner *Empress of Scotland*, to Quebec for a prolonged break from work and the worries of home. They sailed from Southampton on 31 August and didn't return to Britain until nearly the end of November. Their schedule seems to be lost to time, but the holiday soon became a working break with Gresley taking whatever opportunity came his way to observe locomotives in operation. One in particular caught his attention, the Canadian Pacific Railway's oil burning *Selkirk* 2-10-4, which had begun entering service earlier that year and clearly impressed him.

The first twenty of this class were designed and built by the Montreal Locomotive Works specifically to haul loads on a long and gruelling route through the Selkirk Mountains of British Columbia. In their distinctive maroon, grey and black livery, they dwarfed anything built in Britain or Europe and so impressed Gresley that he felt moved to record his impressions. Later on, he submitted this material to the *Railway Gazette* for publication. This was quite a departure for someone who had limited himself to writing learned papers for institutions or simply inviting journalists to view his work. Yet his writing style was both fluent and articulate and, if granted a healthy retirement, one wonders whether he might have written more widely on a subject that clearly enthralled him. As it was, his article captures many aspects of his personality, from being a keen observer and analyst to someone who still took a boy's joyful interest in locomotives and engineering no matter how grim his personal circumstances might be:

'During my recent visit to Canada I saw some of the new 2-10-4 engines under construction in the Angus shops at Montreal, and the officials of the CPR were kind enough to make the necessary arrangements to enable me to travel on the footplate of one of these engines over the Rocky Mountains. The first two of these engines of the class, 5900 and 5901, are fitted with boosters. The remaining 18 engines (of the first batch built) are not so fitted, but the trailing truck is so designed that the boosters can readily be applied.

'While staying at Banff during the first week of September

Although a tall man Gresley appears diminutive beside the massive bulk of a Selkirk engine in September 1929. His daughter Violet leans out of the cab clearly enjoying the experience of riding on the engine's footplate. Before leaving for Canada, the CME was clearly aware of this new class of engine being built and deliberately sought them out, travelling right across Canada to do so. There is little evidence that the design influenced his own work, although he did make much of the oil firing technology, but the visit does demonstrate his fascination with engineering and the constant need to assess potential and learn new lessons.

I travelled on the footplate accompanied by my daughter, from Field to Golden – a distance of 35 miles – which is all down grade, with some very sharp curves. The engine ran easily and appeared to negotiate the curves very smoothly without lurching. The speed, of course, was not fast – during the whole trip it did not exceed 30mph. West of Golden the line was practically level, so I travelled on the train as far as Beavermouth, which is at the foot of the long incline leading over the Selkirk Range of mountains, where we rejoined the engine.

'The gradient is about 20 miles at 1 in 45; the load behind the engine was 950 tons. After a few miles a slight drizzle started, causing the rails to be greasy, and the engine began to slip to such an extent that it seemed as though the train would come to a stand. When the speed had got down to about 4mph the driver put in the booster and speed was regained up to about 12mph, when the booster was taken out. This performance had to be repeated five times before reaching the eastern end of the Connaught tunnel. This is five miles long and dead straight, and being perfectly clear, it was possible to see the exit when we entered it. There are two tracks through the tunnel and it is interesting to note that here the English rule of the road is followed, in that the train is on the left hand line, the reason being that as the driver's seat is on the right side of the engine, he has more air and a better view on the side away from the wall of the tunnel.

'We took about 13½ minutes to get through the tunnel, and on arrival at Glacier on the other side, I joined an eastbound train. It was extremely interesting travelling on the footplate of this great engine during the night and being able to see about half a mile ahead on the straight with the assistance of the powerful headlight. The cut-off was kept at 50%; the engine is oil fired, and there was no difficulty in maintaining steam. The boiler pressure varied between 250 and 275 lb. per sq in.

'I was told the tender carried 4,000 gallons of oil, and that on the 126 miles between Field and Revelstoke the consumption works out generally at 1,400 gallons for the trip, the equivalent to about 11 gallons per mile, with trains of an average weight of 1,000 tons.'

Refreshed, if not renewed by his visit to North America, Gresley returned to work part time in early November, though as Spencer recalled 'these were only fleeting visits to his office at King's Cross to catch up with work' but grief moves with you and he found living

at Camlet House difficult to bear and so moved into a service flat in Cadogan Square in Knightsbridge; a place he appears to have used over the years when working late or attending evening meetings. Here he was within a short taxi ride of King's Cross and the IMechE's headquarters in Old Birdcage Walk on the edge of St James' Park. In the months that followed, he would often be found there in the library or talking to fellow engineers. A refuge it may have been, but it continued to stimulate his scientific curiosity and over the next few years he attended many meetings and contributed to a number of papers for this institution and the ILocoE. At the same time, it seems that his desire to invent and submit patents had evaporated. This was probably a result of grief, but a busy work schedule would not have helped either.

As 1930 dawned, he allowed his professional life and the LNER's ever-present demands to re-assert themselves. For the recently bereaved, this isn't necessarily a bad thing, but the need for a distraction can lead to restlessness and over commitment of time and energy. Nevertheless, he appears to have coped with this transition and threw himself into many tasks and he was welcomed by many eager to see him 'back in the saddle'. Robert Thom summed up this feeling by simply recording the words 'the Chief is back' in a short memo written in January 1930.

If his visit to Canada had re-opened his eyes to developments overseas, it was a theme established during the 1920s. His growing relationship with Chapelon, as the Frenchman grew in stature, was one sign of this. He also watched with great interest advances being made in Germany, but here he was less certain of the direction in which they were going. The Great War was still too recent to be ignored and the conflict too vicious for trust to be resumed quickly. For some, appeasement was in the wind and the 1930s would see an uncomfortable bond growing in certain quarters, despite the obvious threat generated by the rise of Nazism. Gresley it seems had an open mind on technical issues, though not the political ramifications arising from dealing too openly with an old enemy beginning to embrace militarism again. In 1927, he astutely touched on this subject at a meeting of the IMechE at its North-Eastern Centre in Leeds. He spoke of German progress in designing new locomotives, which he'd witnessed in a recent visit, but the words he used had a much wider meaning:

'Unfortunately the Germans are ahead of us in certain things,

No 5920 was the first of the second batch of Selkirk 2-10-4s which appeared later in the 1930s and were given the classification T1b. These two outside cylinder engines weighed 365 tons (10 tons lighter than the first batch), could produce an immense tractive effort of 78,000 lbf and maintain a boiler pressure of between 275 and 285 lbf/sq in. Two engines from this second batch have been preserved.

and they are ahead of us in that great revolutionary alteration of the design of locomotives through the introduction of the superheater. I do not want them to be ahead of us in new things that are coming along.'

This attitude would help drive his research and development programme into the 1930s. The results of which may be seen as a direct response to emerging German ambitions. If so, he was well ahead of many of his contemporaries for whom very close ties were being formed in 1930 and would last until war became inevitable. Gresley, for one, seems to have admired German technical achievements but suspected their motives and abhorred their methods so, throughout the 1930s, he showed great caution in entering too eagerly into an active dialogue with men who would soon be wholly committed to Hitler's regime.

When by necessity he was obliged to greet a German delegate or discuss their technical work, as he did when Dr R.P. Wagner, the German engineer, was invited to address the ILocoE in 1935, on developments in his homeland, he was very forthright and barely disguised his feelings. However, he was by then President of the Institution so had to exercise a degree of diplomacy, but in doing so balanced this by praising the 'wonderful speeds that are attained on the French railways.... know the engineers well. Many of them are old friends of mine'. He then added:

'Of course, Dr Wagner, you know when you come to England we criticise you freely and very openly, and you must take it in good part. Another criticism I have to make – you will think I am rather captious – is that you are talking of a 220 ton train, and I do not exactly remember what the weight of the locomotive is, but it is not far short of the train. It is a big engine with an 80 ton tender and the engine weighs 120 tons, making a total of 200 tons of engine for 220 ton trains.'

Having questioned the validity of this concept he then went on to criticise other aspects of Wagner's work leaving him, one assumes, in no doubt about where Gresley stood, with his admiration of his French counterparts clearly expressed, all wrapped up in polite disdain for German efforts.

When Gresley returned to work full time in early 1930, these events were still only glimpsed on the horizon, to be noted, but not ignored. In the meantime, he was again absorbed by the development and improvement of the LNER's locomotives and rolling stock. In the first year of the decade this involved the W1 project, a new 2-6-2 tank engine for passenger services, plus production of the next batches of A3s, B17s, K3s, J39s and J50s and the acquisition of a number of 0-4-0 Y3 and Y10 shunting locomotives from the Sentinel Wagon Works based in Shrewsbury. In addition, a number of locomotives underwent modification, most notably the ex-GER B12s, D15s and D16s, plus a batch of J52s. To this was added one of Raven's five A2 Pacifics, which in late 1929 had been turned out of Darlington Works in a rebuilt form in an effort to improve its performance. Much of this new production work was routine in nature and long planned, but it still held elements that greatly interested Gresley, with the 'high pressure passenger tender engine' at its core.

Few contemporary accounts now remain that describe this development programme. However, in January 1931 he was invited to address a meeting of the IMechE on the subject of 'High Pressure Locomotives'. In doing so he provided a broad outline of his work. By all accounts the preparation for this presentation absorbed him for many months, as he studied his new creation and then wrote in the third person, and third person and then circulated a confidential copy to members before the meeting.

He begins by describing the various attempts made worldwide to develop such an engine. He started with the Delaware and Hudson locomotive of 1924 and ended with the Schwartzkopff-Loffler three-cylinder locomotive which appeared in 1930. In each case, he points out the potential benefits of these schemes. After this long preamble he turned to his own work, re-written here in the first person to avoid confusion:

'The first British high pressure locomotive to be built is the four-cylinder compound engine of the LNER, which was completed at the end of 1929. Unlike my Continental colleagues, in designing this engine I thought it advisable to be content with what may be regarded as only a moderate increase in boiler pressure to 450 lb. per sq. in. In coming to this decision I was largely influenced by consideration of maintenance costs and the desirability of advancing by stages. Past experience of revolutionary designs has been that the spectacular advancements have not always been justified by results, and, consequently, I deemed it wiser to seek progress on a less ambitious scale. I also recognized that as the pressure increases the economies to be expected in fuel consumption are in a diminishing ratio.

'I decided to adopt a boiler of the water-tube type, in view of the successful application of such boilers to high pressures in marine practice and in large power stations. In September 1924 I accordingly approached Mr Harold Yarrow, of Glasgow, whose firm are so well known as designers and builders of water tube boilers, and suggested to him a design of boiler of the water-tube type which might be applied to locomotives. This involves a radical departure from the usual design of such boilers for marine and land purposes, and upwards of three years of work on the part of Mr Yarrow and I resulted in the completion towards the end of 1927 of the final design, which was patented in our

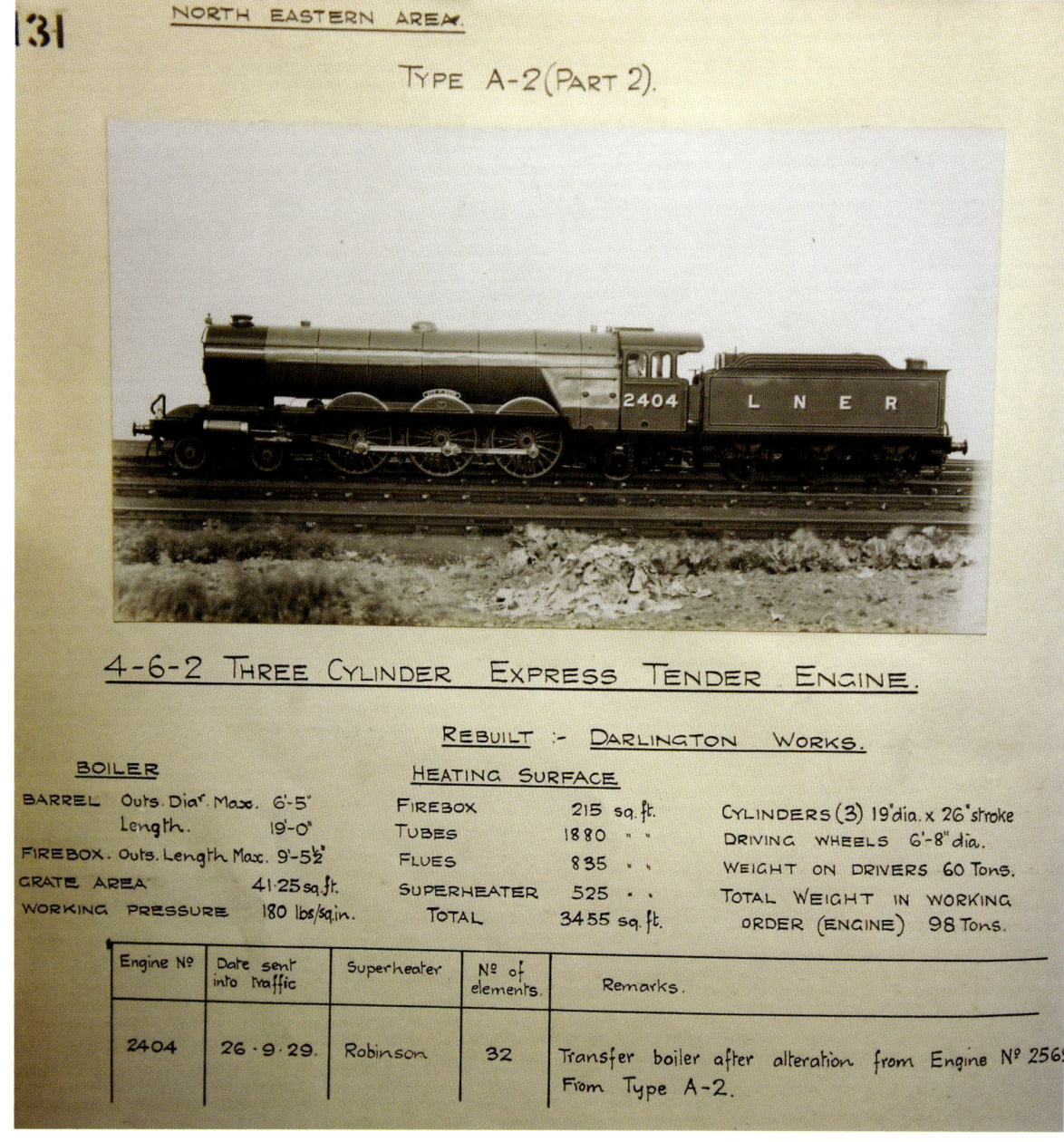

The A2s, as Raven's Pacifics were called on amalgamation in 1923, were certainly the poor cousins in the LNER's Pacific fleet and probably didn't deserve this reputation. They were all based at Gateshead, then York for the whole of their working lives. From these two sheds they worked in the North-East up to Scotland, then took on secondary express trains on the East Coast main line. In 1929 when 2404, *City of Ripon* was due for a general repair at Darlington the decision was taken to rebuild her using a spare A1 boiler from engine No.2569, *Gladiateur*. Spencer believed that Arthur Stamer may have been instrumental in this, hoping, one assumes, that these improvements would extend the life of engines he had played an active part in creating. Sadly, this didn't work and in the few years following his retirement in 1933 all were withdrawn from service (three in 1934 and two in 1936) to make way for Gresley's A4 Pacifics. In his album Robert Thom captured the elegant lines of 2404 following reconstruction.

joint names. Early in 1928 an order was placed with Messrs. Yarrow to proceed with the construction of the boiler, which was completed and tested in October 1929. The engine was built at Darlington Works and ran its trial trip on 12th December 1929.

'The considerations which govern the design of marine or land boilers are so entirely different from those required in a locomotive boiler….In the ordinary water tube boiler resting on foundations, the boiler can expand freely in any direction, and the tubes, not being subject to vibrations and racking stresses, are not liable to leak. In a locomotive, the boiler must be so secured to the frame that in addition to standing the shocks and vibrations consequent upon the engine running at high speed upon a railway, it must be capable of withstanding the shocks which occur when a locomotive is shunting, or comes into contact with buffer stops, or possibly becomes derailed.

'It is necessary also to have due regard to the fact that the boiler provides an important structural element in the construction of a locomotive and contributes to its rigidity. It will be seen in this boiler that a large steam-drum forms the backbone of the boiler, from which the tubes and the small drums depend. At the forward end this drum is carried in a cast-steel cradle into which it is firmly secured by large strap bolts, and any fore-and-aft movement is entirely prevented by stops which are machined on the lower side of the drum. The cradle in turn is secured to the engine frame by 1 inch steel plates extending downwards inside the main engine frames, to which they are securely riveted. The steel drum must be free to expand longitudinally, and accordingly the back end is secured to the top of a triangular-shaped transverse plate which in turn is secured at its lower extremity to the engine frame. The drum therefore, whilst being free to expand longitudinally, is constrained from side or vertical motion.'

At this point some might have expected that Gresley would have discussed the rationale for adopting a 4-6-4 wheel layout to carry this water tube boiler, but he doesn't and quickly moves on to describe the practical issues involved in its use. Yet the reasons behind this choice were interesting, though not, perhaps, for the particular audience of pre-dominantly non-railway engineers he had in mind. Initially, and for simplicity's sake, he hoped that an A1 chassis would be sufficient for this purpose. To this, as he described in his paper, there would be two key additions:

'Reciprocating pistons have been adopted in all the latest high-pressure locomotives, as this form of conversion of energy appears to be the most advantageous for meeting all conditions which a locomotive is required to fulfil. Owing to the high range of temperature and the consequent losses by condensation in a simple

The final production W1 boiler nearing the time when it would be fitted to the engine's frames. The photo, which appears to have been taken at Yarrows, shows its unconventional shape from the cab end. Eight down pipes have been shaped to allow space for the firehole to be fitted.

engine, the use of a compound or 'Uniflow' system is essential.'

As to the number of cylinders to be used, he appeared to have an open mind simply stating that, 'in the high-pressure locomotives produced during the last five years, both two, three and four-cylinders compounds have been adopted.' Initially it seems that Gresley favoured three cylinders, so continuing a pattern set very early in his career. On this issue and more and more he sought the advice of Professor William Dalby, who was an IMechE Council Member and later its Vice-President. Correspondence and meetings between the two seem to have been fairly frequent, especially during W1's construction.

Gresley and Professor Dalby seem to have formed a close friendship and by the mid-1920s began each letter with 'My dear Gresley (or Dalby)'. They had much in common, having both chosen to become railway apprentices when teenagers. Dalby entered the GER's Stratford Works in 1876 under William Adams and eight years later he had risen to become Chief Assistant in the Permanent Way Department at Crewe. On the way, he was awarded a Whitworth Scholarship, which allowed him to study for an external London University degree. As his studies deepened, he became attracted to academia and, in 1891, became assistant to the eminent physicist Professor Alfred Ewing, who was then in the process of setting up the Engineering Department at Cambridge University. This led, two years later, to the award of an honorary MA for the work he had undertaken during this challenging phase. More appointments and honours followed and by the 1920s he had become Professor of Engineering at London University, worked on various government commissions, seen war service as a consulting engineer to the War Office and Admiralty, and been elected as a Fellow of the Royal Society. Yet throughout this time his fascination with steam locomotives remained a constant of his life, with his 1902 book *The Balancing of Engines* becoming a key reference source in the industry. While researching he became a close associate of both Francis Webb and John Aspinall, so providing another link with Gresley.

It is little wonder that he and Gresley developed a strong bond and the younger man often sought the guidance of such an established figure. This was especially so when concerns about the form such an engine should take and the question of achieving sufficient balance came up. In July 1926, Dalby wrote to the CME in response to a request for advice, suggesting that a 'three cylinder, high pressure, two stage compound locomotive' would seem sufficient for his needs. So the initial design envisaged one high and two low pressure cylinders producing 350 psi and 180 psi respectively, generating a power output expected to be similar to an A1. Dalby's advice is of particular interest because in his 1902 book he contended that:

'The balancing of locomotives is carried out in a traditional way, and the compromise that makes a hammer blow on the rails a necessary accompaniment to approximate uniformity of tractive force is accepted by Railway Engineers as the best possible solution to the problem. The advent of the four-cylinder locomotive, however, brings with it practical possibilities of balancing the inertia forces….. The reciprocating masses in a four crank locomotive may be arranged to balance amongst themselves without the use of balance weights at all. Under these circumstances, always supposing the revolving masses to be balanced, there will be no variation of rail-load, no unbalanced force, and no horizontal swaying couple. The engine will, in fact, be perfectly balanced.'

In the intervening years, and the advent of Gresley's three-cylinder

Professor William Ernest Dalby, a noted engineer and academic who forged a close personal and professional relationship with Gresley. This, most notably, proved of value when problems connected to the development of W1 came to the fore.

October 1928 and the new high pressure locomotive takes shape in this outline proposal. In looks it was thought to be a stretched A1 suitably adapted to take the new boiler. But in reality the changes were rather more complex than that. Bert Spencer kept a copy of this drawing, which with age and constant opening was held together by tape which has stained the paper. It is included here, though damaged, for its authenticity and historic interest.

engines, Dalby must have been swayed by the CME's arguments that his solution was a better one. If so, it is interesting to consider the discussions that must have taken place over the years, especially during Gresley's visits to Dalby's substantial home at 50 Park View Road in Ealing.

During 1926, as the boiler design began to be refined and take shape, consultation with Yarrows began to reveal that it would be longer than expected. As a result, it was calculated that this would leave insufficient space for the cab and crew if the A1 frames were used. An adequate working area could only be achieved by moving the boiler forward which created potential balancing problems. At this point, Gresley seems to have accepted that a different approach was needed and again consulted Dalby, Arthur Stamer, Robert Robson, the Darlington Chief Draughtsman and, surprisingly, Sandham Symes, the LMS Works Manager at Derby and one-time Chief Draughtsman there.

The link with Symes seems to have been sparked by similar experiments the LMS, under Henry Fowler, were pursuing with high pressure boilers, in partnership with the Superheater Company. In due course, this resulted in an experimental three-cylinder compound 4-6-0 locomotive, No. 6399, *Fury*, being constructed on behalf of the LMS by the North British Locomotive Company in Glasgow. Despite the great rivalry between the two companies, there does appear to have been a sharing of ideas and experience, which Symes, presumably with Fowler's agreement, continued to practice.

Armed with the views of these specialists, the design was re-worked with the trailing two wheeled bogie being doubled in size to four and the frames extended. This allowed sufficient space for the cab and the extended boiler to be fitted and thus maintain sufficient

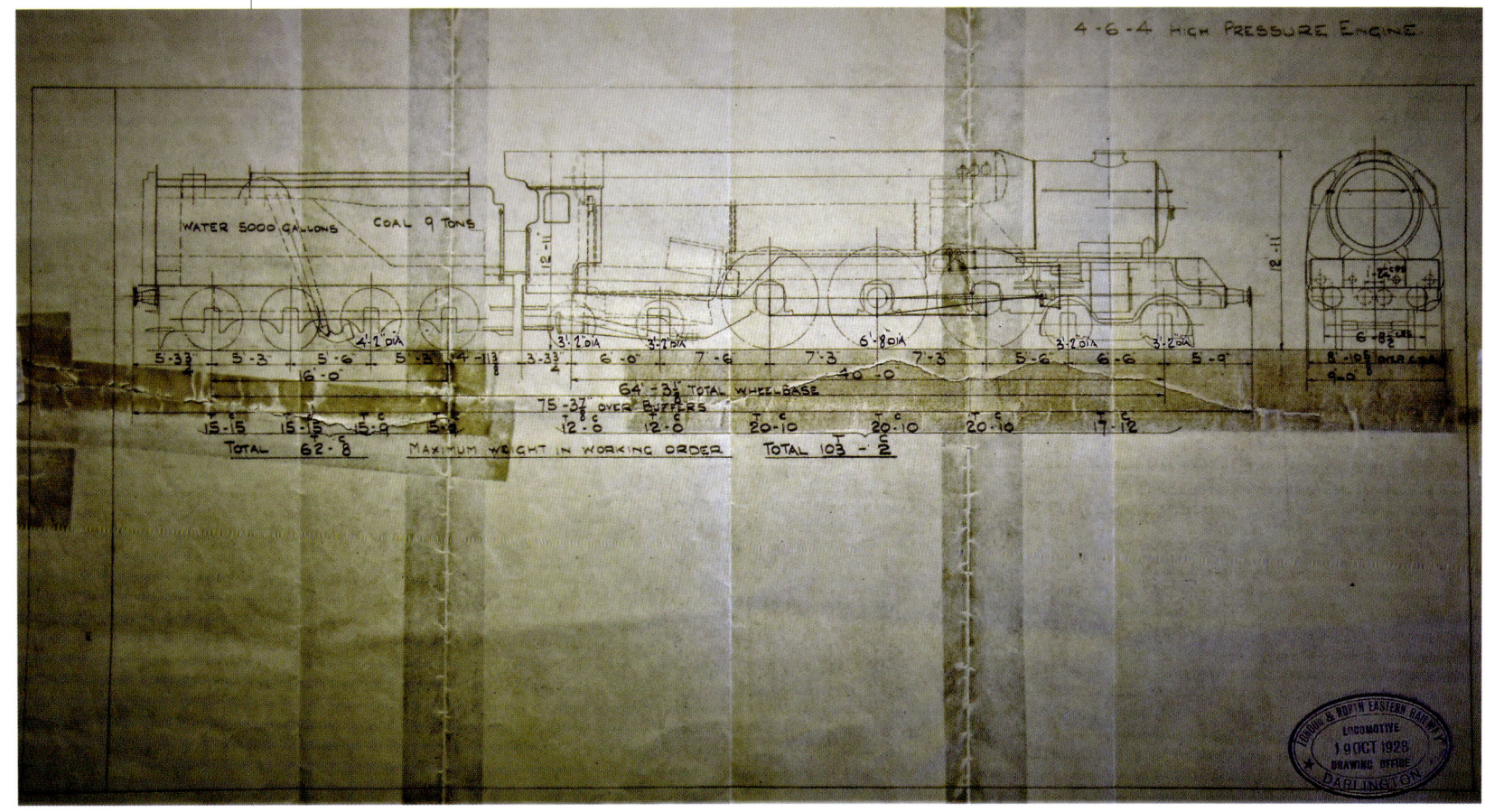

balance, but the proposals went further and included the provision of a fourth cylinder, which, according to an internal LNER memo in early November, would create a more even starting effort. The contention seems to have been that in W1's case, the load forced on three might prove excessive and be poorly balanced. True or not, on 9 November 1926, the change was made and the 4-6-4 configuration was accepted, although how willingly or not Gresley did so is not recorded. In this early stage of the project it might simply have been the case that he wished to consider all options and see how far each might be developed. He could then take a reasoned decision with all the available evidence to hand. One thing is certain though; the need to make a final decision in 1926 was hardly a pressing matter. Such was the lack of urgency given to this project that it would take until October 1928 for the Drawing Office at Darlington to produce the first serious attempt at a layout.

With the engine's outline still in a state of flux, Gresley then described, in his 1931 paper, how the focus of attention fell on the need to maintain the boiler's efficiency in operation:

'In adopting a water-tube boiler I was not unmindful of the troubles which might reasonably result from scale formation in the tubes....In order to prevent this as far as possible I decided to introduce the feed-water at the highest possible temperature.... The water is supplied from the tender by means of two ordinary injectors, and is

As the W1 project gradually progressed this schematic was apparently produced and circulated amongst senior LNER staff as a simple reference guide.

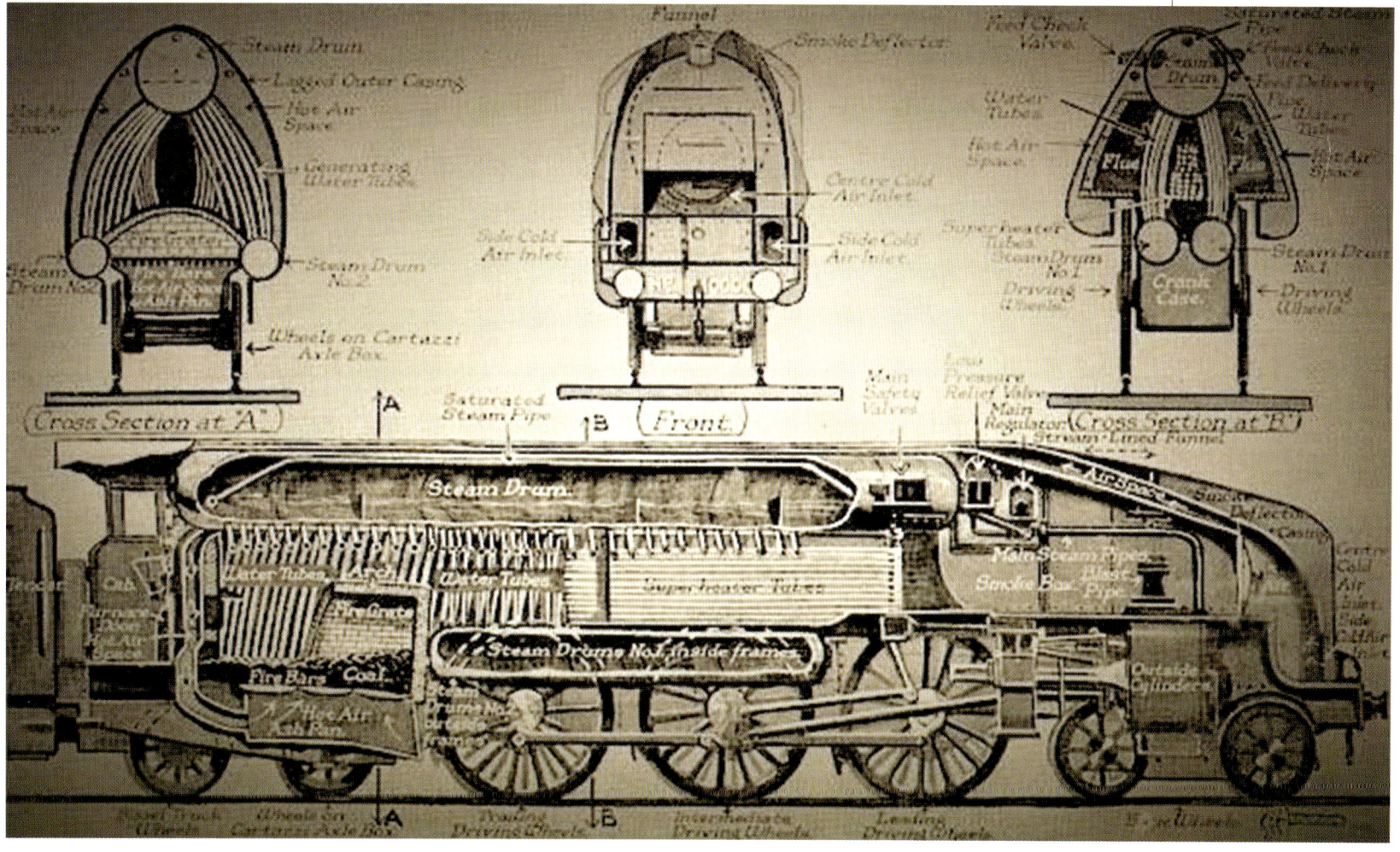

delivered into the forward space of the top drum, after passing through a form of injector heater. The latter has two sets of cones in which the injector action is repeated by steam from the steam space in the boiler. Heat is absorbed to such an extent by feed-after that its temperature when delivered into the water chamber is 400 degrees F. and is therefore about 50 degrees F. less than that of the saturated steam in the boiler. Much of the scale and mud is consequently thrown down in the forward portion of the top drum.'

With these and several other issues being resolved, Yarrows and Drawing Office staff gradually pushed ahead with the design, with periodic management meetings conducted by Gresley at King's Cross to gauge progress and discuss and agree any changes to the design. These sessions, chaired by the CME, supported by Stamer, Bulleid, Robson, A.L. Mellor from Yarrows and Spencer, who took and circulated notes, proved to be crucial to the project. Without this small working party there was a good chance that progress would have stalled and the project be swamped by the remainder of the LNER's very busy design and construction programme. As it was, progress was still painfully slow and it wasn't until late 1928 that a boiler could be ordered and final assembly and operational running be contemplated. As this day approached, the engine's final form had to be refined, with the odd shape of the boiler providing a challenge. In his 1931 paper he described how this problem was resolved, though didn't mention the part played by staff and facilities at the National Physical Laboratory:

'In order to provide sufficient length for the water-tubes, it was necessary to have the top steam-drum as high as the limits imposed by the load gauge permit, consequently there was no room for a chimney of the conventional type. Engines having large high-pitched boilers can only have very short chimneys and trouble has been experienced in such engines owing to smoke and steam beating down on the front windows of the cab and interfering with the driver's view of signals. I enlisted the assistance of Professor W.E. Dalby and constructed a wooden model of an engine of this type. This model was placed in an air flume, and powdered chalk was blown up the chimney at the same time as a current of air was drawn through the flume at 50mph. Observations through a glass window slowed the course pursued by the powdered chalk, and as a result of various modifications, the design finally adopted was arrived at.'

When he wrote these words, much of the work the NPL did was highly classified or simply commercial-in-confidence, so necessitated the highest level of security. The identity of the scientists who did

The final design.

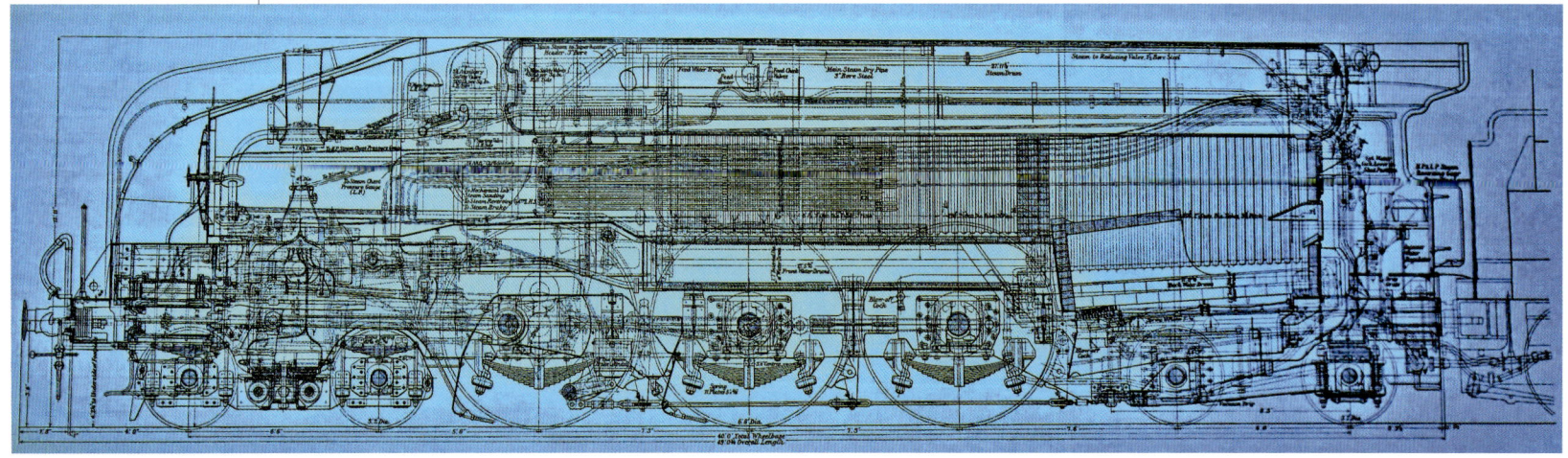

Frederick Johansen (left) preparing a late stage scale model of W1 for a series of tests in the wind tunnel at Teddington. Records that survive suggests that this process went on for some time with a variety of models being used. Gradually a sufficiently effective shape was produced.

this work was similarly shrouded in secrecy so in his paper, Gresley had to be guarded in what he wrote. In reality, Sir Thomas Stanton, the NPL's Superintendent of Engineering, who in a long career had specialised in fluid flow, the effects of friction and, latterly aviation, actively encouraged the CME in this field of research and in so doing allowed Gresley wide access to the facilities at Teddington and the specialists there.

Stanton and Gresley had much in common as scientists, but the NPL man had been luckier in-so-far as he worked in an area where the value of research and testing, using the latest tools available, was accepted as the norm. Without them Stanton argued 'it would have been impossible to anticipate engineering problems'. By comparison, railway engineering was far behind, much to Gresley's growing frustration. Best of all, the NPL had a Duplex wind tunnel, which, during the 1920s and '30s, played a key role in developing the science of aerodynamics and, amongst other things, the development of the Spitfire and Hurricane. This provided Gresley with an invaluable facility for use in his experiments. At the same time, it brought him into contact with Frederick Johansen and his rapidly developing ideas and research, with its possible application to locomotive and rolling stock design. W1 would be the first occasion in which both men would work together; though for Johansen this task would be sandwiched between work for Supermarine in the design and construction of their S series Schneider Cup racing seaplanes.

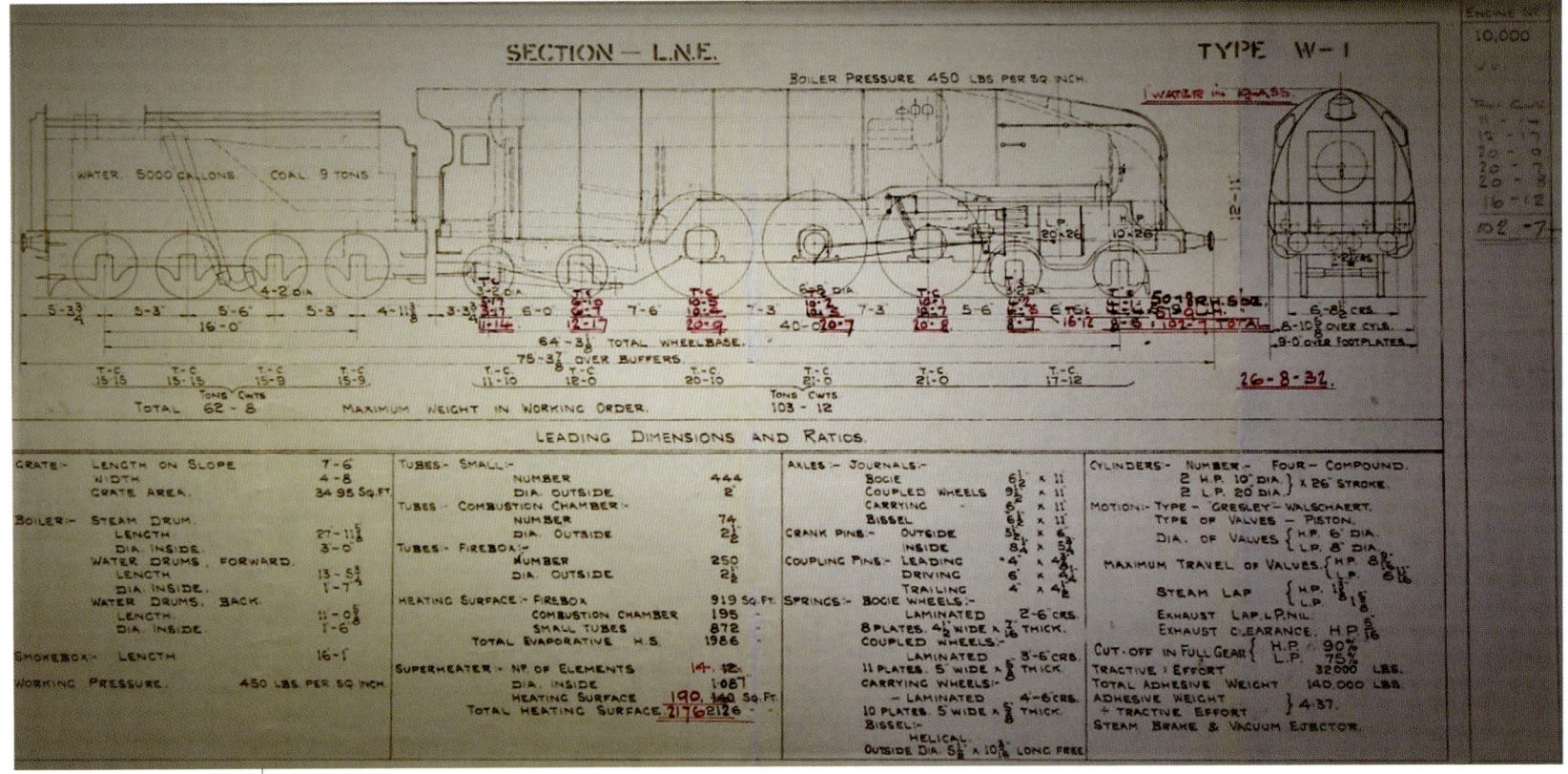

Locomotive diagrams were prepared for each engine showing variations and design criteria and became a ready source of information for staff. This is Bert Spencer's overwritten copy of W1.

In his paper, Gresley, due to time constraints and the need for security, glossed over the way the locomotive's final design gradually evolved and the effort it took to do so. In fact, it was a process that went on for quite some time, with a great deal of modelling and then re-modelling taking place as the shape was refined. Johansen, with his growing understanding of these issues, became central to this work; his ideas and suggestions playing an increasingly important and largely unrecognised part in shaping this locomotive and others that would follow. In time, the term streamlining would enter the locomotive engineers' vocabulary, as it did in other design spheres from cars to ships and much more.

It was in many ways a misnomer because such a complex science couldn't be explained by such a simplistic description but in the late 1920s and through the '30s, it was hijacked by publicists seeking a good headline. And so 'streamlining' became a passing fashion that hid a very serious subject that scientists and engineers were only then beginning to understand and exploit. Gresley, Stanton and Johansen were only too aware of this and attempted to promote a more studious approach to the subject especially in its application to the railways.

They were successful up to a point, but for every follower there was a critic of such ideas, including Oliver Bulleid. In the early 1930s, after W1 had made its first public appearance and Gresley was pursuing the concept with some vigour, he was reported in the press as saying:

'The thing [streamlining] is no more than a fashion, but as such it cannot be ignored by any self-respecting designer who wishes to be in the swim…. Streamlining is a necessity for aeroplanes, as vacuums of air turbulences would mean loss of stability and speed. But with railway trains it is a different matter.'

Nevertheless, W1 became the first of Gresley's locomotives to go through this process and be modified in accordance with these principles and it wouldn't be the last. On one level, Johansen's wind tunnel experiments may simply have been useful in lifting away the engine's exhaust, so that the driver's forward view was not obscured. But it seems realistic to believe that it was more than this and represented Gresley's determination to pursue new ideas to the point at which their benefits become clear or the concept could be rejected. As a true scientist, his mantra would inevitably be to seek, explore and push back boundaries and this was very much the case with W1.

When the engine was completed she certainly looked like something from the future, emerging from the works painted in grey primer. But the last 12 months of construction had been a slow process, with the engine's frames, cylinders and only four driving wheels fitted, at Darlington before being shipped to Yarrows in the spring of 1929. Here the boiler work was completed and encased in wonderfully curved panels secured by straps, which remained unpainted. In this near complete state she was photographed, with dummy middle driving wheels, and returned to Darlington for final assembly, 'sheeted up' to keep her form and function a secret. But finally, all work was complete and she was ready for her first trip on 12 December. Over the next few weeks, her mileage gradually built up, as did confidence in her performance. On 22 February 1930 she arrived in Edinburgh, receiving a great deal of press attention in the process.

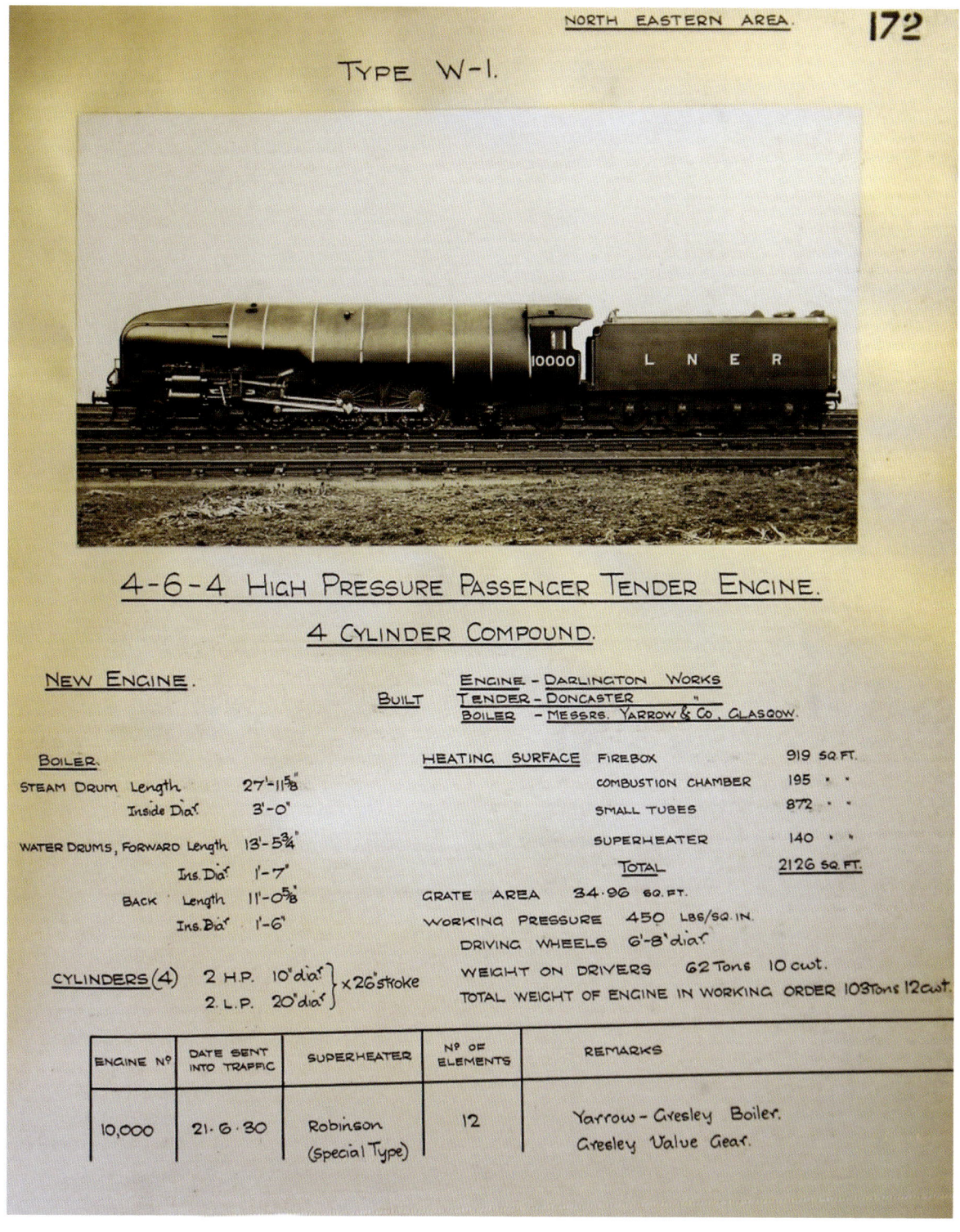

W1, No. 10000, as recorded in his papers by Robert Thom.

W1 just before her first trial run from Darlington. The three men inspecting the engine are reported as being Gresley, peering 'in to the works', Arthur Stamer pointing at something of interest or concern, whilst turning to talk to A.L. Mellor from Yarrow's. A dynamometer car was attached, but any data collected that day hasn't yet come to light.

Next day she ran a test run to Perth pulling a 406 ton load, but she developed problems with the high pressure injectors, which wasted a considerable amount of water. As a result she arrived 22½ minutes late. On the return trip the engine performed better but still arrived late. Apart from problems with the injectors, the only other cause for concern was the engine's propensity for wheel slip. But drizzle and slight rain had been consistent throughout the day and may explain this problem, as did the crew's relative inexperience on W1's footplate.

Inevitably there were teething problems and a full testing programme was planned, but in 1931 Gresley was able to record a very optimistic message about the future in his paper to the IMechE. He concluded by writing:

'The locomotive has worked trains of over 500 tons weight for long distances at express speeds with constant success and reliability, and although it has not been possible so far to carry out any extensive trials, there is every indication that it will prove more economical in fuel consumption than express engines of the latest normal types. Any economy effected in maintenance cost will only become fully apparent after the engine has run for a few years.

'It has been ascertained that the cost of a water-tube boiler similar to that fitted on this engine will not be appreciably greater than that of the ordinary wide firebox type as fitted on Pacific engines. The most expensive components of the water-tube boiler are the solid-forged steam and water-drums. These are not subjected to the action of fire, and consequently may be expected to have a long life. On the wider firebox type of ordinary boiler, the copper firebox is the most costly section, and it is well known that its life is short and its renewal an expensive item. Again, in the ordinary type of locomotive boiler tubes and firebox stays are sources of trouble involving costly maintenance and occasional failures. In the design of boilers under consideration there are no stays; the tubes are more effectively secured, and are not subjected to variations in temperature and stress at the points where they enter the drums.

'In conclusion, I submit that, with the moderately high pressure and simple design, which I have adopted, economy both in fuel and maintenance costs will be secured and at the same time the reliability so characteristic of British locomotives will be fully maintained.'

When he wrote these words two more years of testing lay ahead, with measured trials taking place in December 1932 and August 1933,

Gresley and his daughters Marjorie (left) and Violet when W1 appeared at King's Cross on 8 January 1930.

By this stage she had received her top-coat which Bert Spencer described as 'a mixture of dark grey and green'.

And so to London where her every movement in early 1930 was captured for the movies and the press.

following periods of maintenance when various modifications were undertaken. In between times, she ran normal duties on a variety of lines, including, on occasions, the 'Flying Scotsman'. Gradually, conclusions were reached about Gresley's great experiment, best summarized by Bert Spencer in 1947:

> 'The evaporative heating surface of the boiler was small for the usual smokebox vacuums and satisfactory steaming only occurred when the engine was developing high outputs at long cut-offs with a smokebox vacuum in the region of 6 in., at which figure the smokebox temperature was too high. Some improvement was effected by fitting twin blast pipes.

> 'The engine was weak during acceleration when working compound after a stop as the superheat took some time to build up and, as a consequence, the LP cylinders could do little work owing to condensation and the HP cylinders were unable to provide sufficient power alone.

> 'Difficulty was experienced in maintaining the airtightness of the boiler walls owing to the variation in the temperature of the plates, and this frequently led to steaming troubles owing to air being drawn through the defective joints instead of through the grate. Considerable modifications were also made to the arrangement of the baffles to ensure that the flue gases came into contact with the whole of the water tubes, as experiments with a full size model of the forward portion of the boiler revealed that short circuiting of the gases had taken place.

> 'Notwithstanding the various alterations carried out, the use of high pressure and compounding on engine No. 10000 did not prove economical and in general working the engine was burning considerably more coal than the standard Pacifics. In 1937 it was therefore decided to rebuild the engine as a three-cylinder simple and substitute a boiler of a similar type to that used on the P2 class.'

Despite Gresley's drive and determination, W1 became a project impossible to sustain, there being

London & North Eastern Railway—Record of Locomotives. No. 10,000

Class **W.1** Type **4.6.4** Length over Buffers **75 ft 3 7/8 ins.** Cylinders No. **2 HP 10" / 2 LP dia. 20"** Stroke **26" / 26"** Class of Boiler **Sup. Water Tube.** Diagram No. **103.**		
Description **Passenger Tender** Dia. of Driving Wheel **6 ft. 8 ins.** Brake **Dual (Steam & Vacuum)** Heating Surface **2176** sq. ft.		
Maker **L.N.E.R., Darlington** Weights (Empty) T.C. (Loaded) **166.0** T.C. Valves **Piston** Grate Area **34.95** sq. ft.		
Date Built **June 1930** Tractive Effort **32,000 lbs.** Tons Lubricator **Mechanical** Working Pressure **450** lbs. per sq. inch		
Nameplate Rebuilt Heating Apparatus **Steam** Superheater		
Injectors { R. **D&M No.8 (Live Steam)** / L. **-do-** } Ejectors **Davies & Metcalfe.**		

Ref. to Repairs.	NATURE OF REPAIRS.	Boiler Reg. No.	Date Repairs Commenced.	Date Repairs Completed.	Mileage.
NE.1/3	NEW ENGINE	18193	–	20.6.30	
	Light repairs & alterations. New superheater etc.	"	16.8.30	17.1.31	
	White Metal cleaned from cylinders, etc.	"	26.1.31	3.2.31	
	Light repairs.	"	24.3.31	10.4.31	
	Alterations, etc.	"	9.6.31	30.6.31	
	Light reprs. & alterations. H.P.Cyl. welded etc.	"	3.8.31	25.11.31	
	Adjustment to Bissel Truck etc.	"	15.2.32	22.2.32	
	Boiler repairs etc. New type reducing valve.	"	29.3.32	28.4.32	
	Repairs & alterations.	"	9.5.32	27.8.32	
	Nil repair. Cylinders examined etc.	"	14.3.33	17.5.33	
	GENERAL	"	29.5.33	13.6.34	70,000
	Nil repair. H.P.Valves.	"	26.6.34	10.7.34	
	Light repair. Fitted with 'Salamanderite Joints'	"	16.7.34	27.8.34	
	Nil repair. Examination of low pressure superheater elements.	"	4.1.35	9.1.35	17,000
	Light repair. Crack in R.steam chest. Cyls. welded, tested etc.	"	24.1.35	10.5.35	18,000
	Nil repair. Minor adjustments etc.	"	22.5.35	29.5.35	19,000
	Nil repair. Alteration to front end to secure better smoke clearance, etc.	"	14.6.35	10.7.35	20,000
	– continued –				

no provable benefits to be derived from this ambitious, but apparently flawed design. Eventually, even the most optimistic person has to conclude that there is little point in continuing if there is nothing to gain. As it was, Gresley managed to keep the experiment going long after others had walked away. How the LNER's Board of Directors viewed this project is not recorded, but their thoughts are, perhaps, not hard to divine. With the pressing demand of a railway seeking to survive and make a profit at a difficult time, such speculation when a more than effective solution, in the form of the A1/A3s, is already in place is an unwanted outlay. However, Gresley must have been disappointed when a halt was called; it had, after all, become a significant part of his scientific life. He was an inventor and anyone with these skills wishes to take the lead in the process of change, if possible, by making a leap of the imagination that considers fundamental principles and questions perceived wisdom. The common man will say 'stay as we are, all is well', the scientist will ask why and perceive a future that can improved by their talents and wisdom, while in the middle sits business, which tends to follow a star if it quickly brings a pot of gold to the coffers. Gresley knew all this and attempted to take a

A copy of W1's records for 1930 to 1935, as kept by Bert Spencer. Although the content is brief it gives a clear view of the work carried out on the locomotive as Gresley sought to prove the design worthy of his efforts.

W1 photographed on shed at Neville Hill Depot, Leeds, in July 1935. By this stage her front end had been modified with, amongst other things, a revised smoke lifting solution.

path between these conflicting views, using all his skills to reach into the future and find new and better solutions to perennial problems.

With W1 in service and creeping towards eventual reconstruction there were more pressing matters demanding Gresley's attention. Amongst them there were three other development projects to engage him.

'Bread and butter work' is a staple part of any life. For the engineer, this means the procurement of essential and sustaining work to fuel and expand an organisation. It might not be too advanced in concept and may simply build on what has gone before, but it supports healthy growth, feeds the business and encourages production. For this reason known quantities are often more desirable than any speculative, cutting edge work. A new 2-6-2 tank engine built at Doncaster between 1930 and 1940, certainly fitted this bill.

While the N2s and inherited tank engines, such as the Great Central designed 4-6-2 A5s, did sterling service on suburban commuter lines, their limits were exposed on the Edinburgh district and Glasgow to Helensburgh routes in Scotland. In response, Gresley and his team proposed a new tank engine with a tractive effort of 22,464 psi, some 2,500 lb. more than the N2. During his years as CME, he had toyed with a number of large tank engine designs, including this one. Spencer

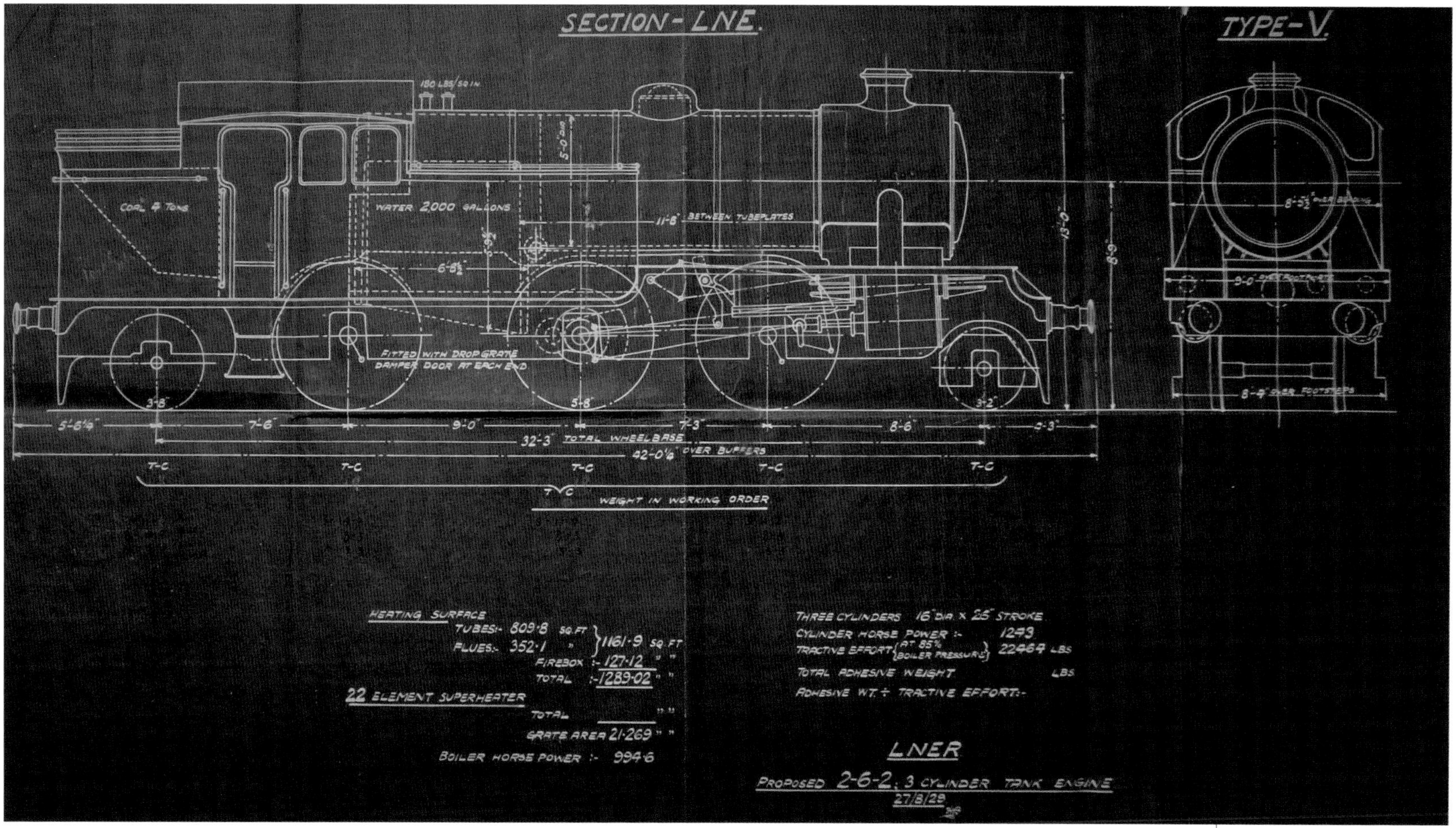

The design and the reality. The V1's graceful, well balanced lines were often commented on by engineers and lineside enthusiasts alike. But its good looks disguised a truly effective performer.

touched on this issue and described some of the attempts made by Gresley to create a more effective tank engine:

> 'In 1925 a scheme was prepared for a three cylinder 2-6-4 type tank engine for the GN Section London suburban services incorporating the K3 class cylinders, wheels and running gear, together with the 5ft 6in. diameter boiler used on the GN Section K2 class, 2-6-0 type two cylinder engines. The tractive effort at 85% boiler pressure was to be 28,431 lb. It was not found possible to alter the layout at Moorgate Street Station to permit the use of engines of this length in conjunction with suburban train sets and the proposal was not developed.
>
> 'In 1927 the use of tank engines on the GE Section Southend lines was considered for services usually worked by the B12 class, 4-6-0 type, with inside cylinder engines having 6ft 6in. diameter coupled wheels and a tractive effort of 21,969 lb. A two cylinder 2-6-4 type tank engine of similar tractive effort was proposed having 6ft 2in. diameter coupled wheels and 20in by 26in cylinders with the 5ft 6in. diameter boiler used on the J39 and D49 classes, but the project was abandoned in favour of additional B12 class tender engines.'

To this could be added several other designs, including the three cylinder 2-8-2 tank engine to pull heavy mineral trains. But the V1, as the new class became known, finally gave Gresley the opportunity to take all these proposals and construct a locomotive of this type. The 92 built proved to be excellent performers, with the last members of the class lasting in service until 1964. Unlike W1, it was a simple, uncomplicated design based on well-established principles and practices. It had three 16in by 26in cylinders with conjugated valve gear, 5ft 8in coupled wheels, a 5ft diameter boiler producing 180 psi of pressure, the Robinson superheater, a leading double swing truck used on the K3 and a radial trailing truck based on the N2 design. However, the boiler was a slight departure from Gresley's usual practice. Initially it was planned that the H2/K1 4ft 8in diameter, 180 psi type would be used. But after further thought, and possibly in the knowledge that some spare units were available, attention turned to the type of boiler fitted to the North British Railways Class K (LNER D34) design, built between 1913 and 1920, which carried 5ft diameter, 180 psi boilers. This design, in modified form, would be carried by the V1s. Change would come in time, in the form of a boiler producing 200 psi, which were fitted to the final batch of locomotives produced in 1939/40 and re-designated V3s in due course. Many of the V1s would also be modified in this way.

V1, No. 2909, built at Doncaster between 1930 and '31, pulling a mixed bag of carriages on a date and at a place not recorded. It is presumed to be on the edge of Glasgow whilst undertaking one of the engine's usual passenger duties.

It was also during this period that Gresley revisited the concept of articulation, this time applying these principles to locomotive design; an idea he tried first during 1923 by converting Ivatt C1 Atlantic No. 4419. Spencer described this second experiment in an article he wrote for the *LNER Magazine* in 1932:

'The CME has carried out a most interesting conversion with two of the C7 type 4-4-2 express passenger engines of the NER, built respectively in the years 1911 and 1913. These engines have three single-expansion cylinders driving the first pair of coupled wheels, and they have now been rebuilt and fitted with a bogie placed behind the coupled wheels under the cab, this being the first example of articulation between engine and tender in which the rear end of the front end of the tender are carried on a common base. The arrangement has greatly improved the riding of the engine and eliminated the relative lateral movement between the engine and the tender. The booster bogie has a side play of 4½ in. each side, controlled by a pair of coil springs, having a compression of 2 tons.

'During recent tests with engine No. 727 on a 300 ton train a speed of 19mph was obtained in 8 minutes on a gradient of 1 in 70 with the booster out of operation. With the booster in operation a speed of 25mph was reached in 5¾ minutes. On a level road the engine with the booster out of operation was able to start a load of 496 tons, the drawbar pull being 9 tons. With the assistance of the booster, a load of 746 tons was started with a drawbar pull of 12½ tons.'

Little more seems to have been written or recorded about this experiment, beyond the two locomotives being re-classified as C9s and entering service. But it seems that adding a booster was seen as a way of supplementing the number of locomotives available to pull heavier passenger trains. However,

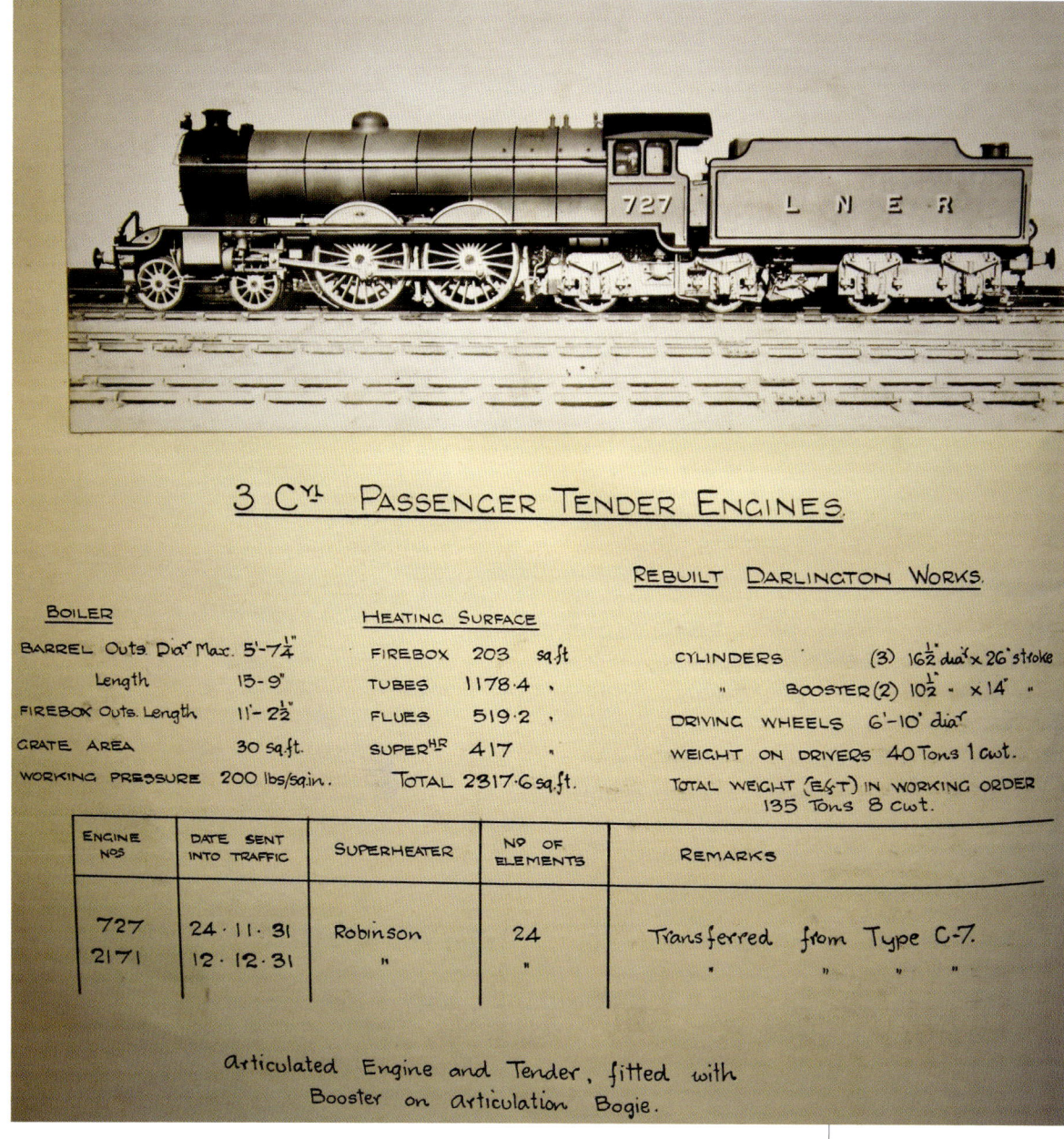

Thom records the C7 experiment.

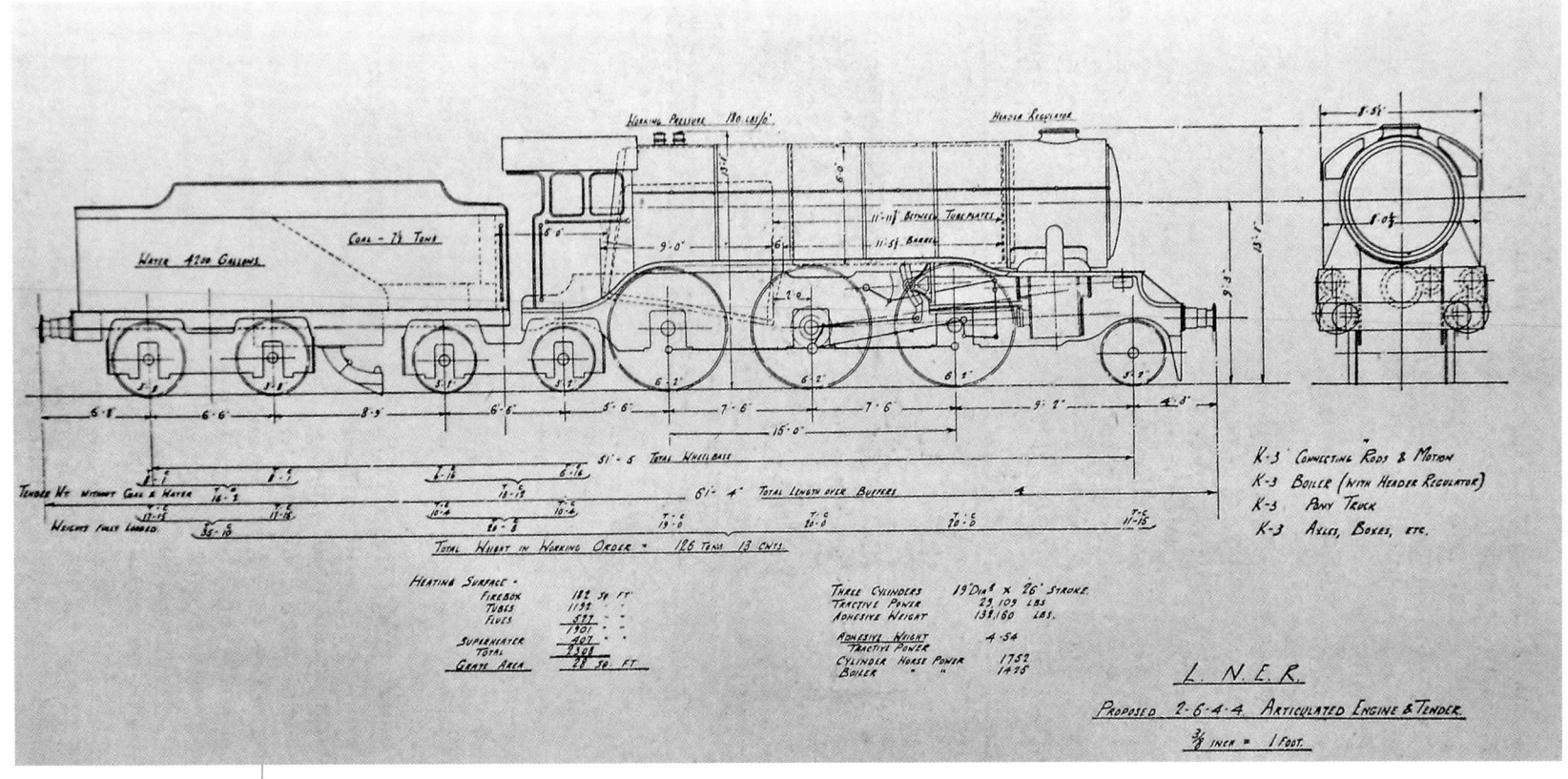

Gresley's proposed 2-6-4-4 articulated locomotive of 1935. It adopted the boiler, valve gear, connecting rods, pony truck, axles and axleboxes from his K3 design.

with the advent of more Pacifics this need fell away and both engines continued to operate in this guise until late 1936, when they were returned to their C7 state. It was a minor experiment which summed up Gresley's approach to engineering, but also his desire to keep researching an idea he felt had untapped potential. Articulating would remain a subject close to his heart and continue to find an outlet in carriage design and, as Spencer recalled, one final attempt at creating another locomotive. This time it was a three–cylinder 2-6-4-4, but on this occasion it never reached production, being 'abandoned in favour of the more powerful V2 class engine'.

The two years following the death of his wife must have been extremely difficult for Gresley and the hope he placed in the W1 project, and the effort he expended on the engine, clearly acted as a distraction. But life goes on and the demands on his time were unlikely to diminish in the foreseeable future; these demands were so clearly reflected in the parlous state of the LNER's finances. The post-war recession had begun to lift very slightly in the late twenties only for these early signs of recovery to be dealt a crushing blow by the Wall Street Crash of 1929, which led to the slump that engulfed still fragile European economies. Businesses, none more so than the railways, suffered

from a sudden drop in consumer demand and saw their finances come under huge pressure. The LNER, in particular, witnessed their passenger traffic drop by nearly 9 per cent and freight by about 8.4 per cent in this period. The effect of this was to reduce their net annual income from £13m in 1929 to £7.2m in 1932, making them barely able to manage day to day business needs let alone growth. With this the need for cuts and economies became the order of the day, with long term plans retarded until the future became a little clearer. With this in mind, many senior figures considered their futures and had to decide if now was the time to depart and seek pastures new, leaving the

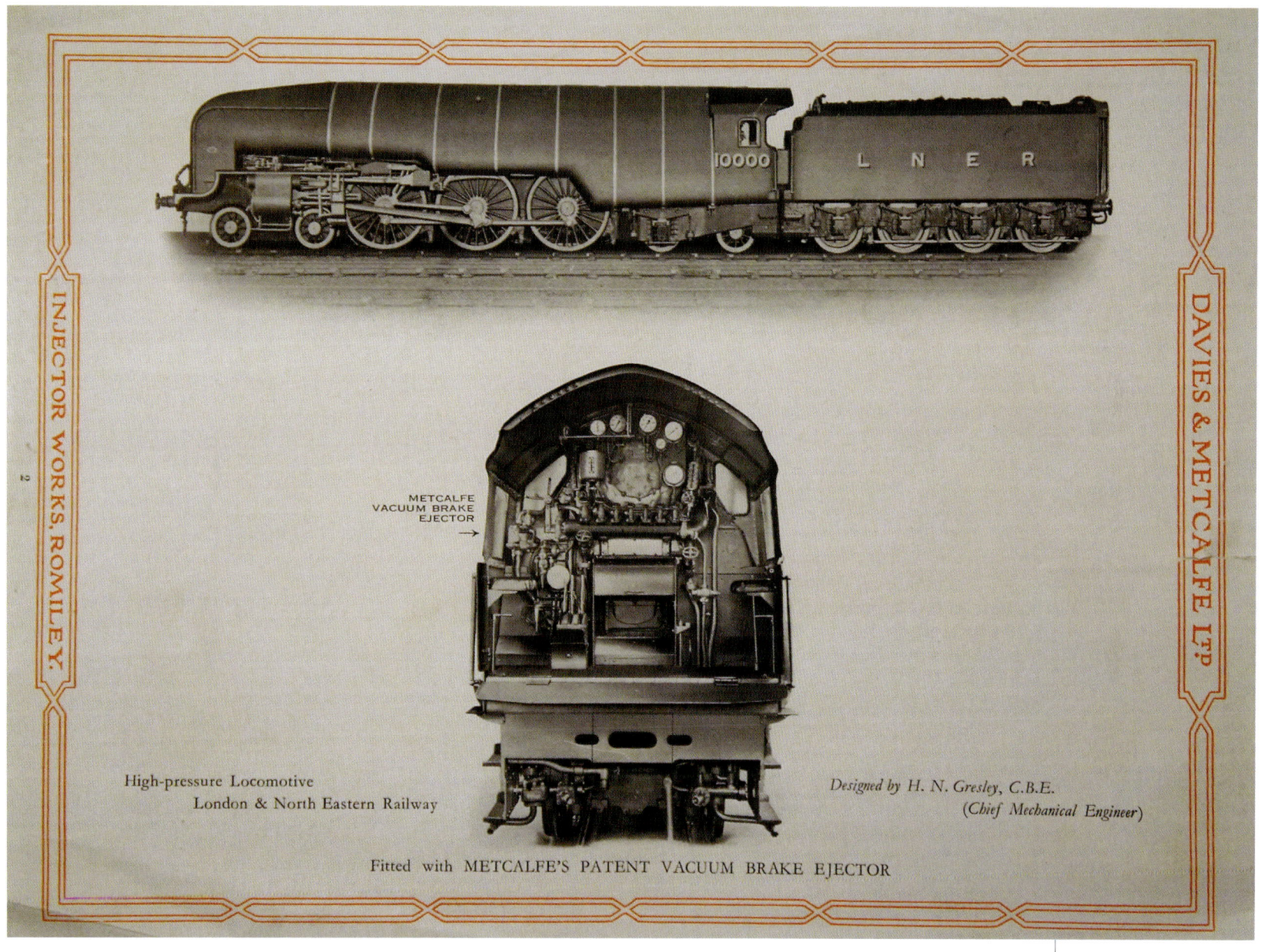

Even though W1 didn't fully meet expectations and was eventually rebuilt in a more conventional form, its modern looks and novelty found an outlet in many adverts of the period. It did much to help the LNER's PR team sell the company as a modern and vibrant concern. It also, as displayed here, proved very popular amongst the company's supply chain when seeking to promote their products.

field open to younger people with greater energy and will to fight.

If, as Spencer believed, the CME did contemplate retirement in these two years, still suffering from grief, then it would have had immense consequences for him and railway history. His interest in W1, I believe, played a significant part in re-engaging him after the tragedy of his wife's loss and enabled him to carry on to greater glory and receive the laurels his achievements richly deserved.

Chapter 6
A MASTER AT WORK (1932–34)

Fate and good luck can be immeasurably beneficial in life, but if the stars do not line up to favour you then great talent may not find its outlet or destiny. Yet there are so many other influences that contribute to success. Training, experiences, contacts, politics, economics and opportunity are just some of them but even with all these working in your favour, there is that unpredictable element that will always come into play and mark some out for greatness and others for obscurity.

Gresley in his professional prime. He was described by Spencer as having 'a clear and incisive view of life and science'. If so, his expression in this picture captures these traits to perfection.

Many of Gresley's achievements clearly arose as a result of his engineering skills, his drive, ambition, perseverance, business sense, political acumen and exceptional executive powers but he also had the blessing of fate. He was lucky to be in the right place at the right time; to be armed with the best tools available, with a team of people, above and below, who supported him extraordinarily well, even when business was stagnating and life was difficult. In the years 1932 to 1935 these elements came together to help produce a masterpiece of design. Yet this period started off fairly quietly in terms of locomotive development, with W1 still the main highlight, while more existing types were produced by the works. Between 1931 and 1933, new V1s, D49s, O2s, K3s, B17s and J39s appeared in modest numbers, with the workshops continuing a modification programme of existing types – D14s, D15s, J52s, C7s, A8s and B12s amongst them. With the company's revenue dropping, such a careful programme was essential. It wasn't until 1934 that the LNER felt able to initiate a slightly more ambitious building programme with a final batch of nine more A3s being built, suggesting that some confidence was returning.

It was certainly a period when expenditure on innovation and experimentation proved difficult to achieve, although some did go ahead. However, the design programme was still heavily influenced by the need for large express locomotives, whilst Gresley's fascination with aerodynamics showed no sign of diminishing, despite a lack of support for these ideas by some, including Bulleid. Spencer recalled that:

'It became a point of difference between the two men. Bulleid was highly critical of the research being undertaken by Dr Johansen, which I don't think endeared him to Sir Nigel, though he did not appear too concerned at the time. But the CME saw many benefits to be derived from these ideas and wind tunnel experiments. These included partial or complete

streamlining to reduce wind resistance in motion at high speed and the dissipation of drifting smoke and its effect on forward visibility. From the late 1920s until the end of his life it remained an important issue and even when Johansen was employed by the LMS at Derby he continued to consult him. Sir Nigel, I believe, had a much clearer view of the future than his principal assistant.'

The relationship between Gresley and Johansen remained a close one, with the CME sponsoring the younger man's research and helping his development as a scientist. When elected President of the IMechE in 1936, he confirmed this by inviting Johansen to submit a paper entitled 'The Air Resistance of Passenger Trains', highlighting the results of his work. He also made the point when opening the debate that followed the presentation in London during 1936, that this area of research had some of its origins in experiments undertaken by John Aspinall thirty-five years earlier. He added that, 'The work described here is a considerable amplification of the results which Sir John had obtained…. This paper is most valuable.'

In doing this Gresley underpinned the fact that such studies had a sound historical base

Despite the arrival of many A3s between 1927 and 1935 the A1s still provided an essential backbone to the LNER's express services until rebuilt. Here engine, No 2546, *Donovan*, is caught whilst waiting for departure from York.

One aspect of the air resistance debate that seemed to achieve a degree of acceptance concerned the role of smoke deflectors and body shape in lifting exhaust away from the locomotive to improve a driver's visibility. Johansen conducted wind tunnel tests for the LNER, LMS and the Southern Railway in the late 1920s and early 1930s using models of the SR's Schools Class, the LMS's Royal Scot and the LNER's A3s. Some of this work found expression in live trials on several A3s which were modified in a number of ways, as portrayed here in a photo kept by Bert Spencer, who appears to have added a brief note. Although none of the A3s remained in these states for long the work Spencer recalled 'contributed greatly to Gresley's thoughts on streamlining'.

Smoke lifting trials March 1933

in the development of the railways and were a continuing part of their evolution. With sceptical souls such as Bulleid in the audience, who questioned the basis of this work and wind tunnel experiments in particular, this made it very clear that he believed in these long-established principles and 'trusted that his [Johansen's] research would be carried much further'. But Bulleid wasn't swayed and again made disparaging comments about this work in front of the CME at this very public forum. Who was right and who was wrong is probably immaterial, what is important though is the distance that appears to be growing between the two men.

Nevertheless, Gresley was determined to pursue this area of research and explore its potential as far as he could. He wasn't alone in doing this because designers in many countries around the world were following a similar line. Yet to some, like Bulleid, it was merely the latest fad encouraged by the growth of aviation and Art Deco styling, which was having a huge impact on many aspects of life in the 1930s. To others, though, it held great potential and pointed a way to develop locomotives and trains, powered by steam, oil or electricity, in the future. This was nowhere more apparent than in Germany, where Hitler had taken power and declared the state's intention to pursue an age of great scientific advance to be trumpeted as one of the virtues of the Nazi state.

Modern weapons were his chief aim, but this 'endeavour' filtered down to other areas, most notably the railways. So began a race to create cutting edge locomotives to challenge other countries' achievements. And so over the next few years, a race of sorts began in Europe with Gresley's Pacifics being measured against the latest products of the Deutsche

Hamburg Station with the SVT 877 on the left and a new steam railcar on the right, waiting to depart for Lubeck. The Flying Hamburger was built by Waggon-und Maschinenbau, of Gorlitz in Saxony, and contained two 12 cylinder diesel engines, one in each car, and was fully wind tunnel tested before being constructed. The unit could reach 100 mph and maintain an average speed of 77.4mph on the comparatively easy route to Berlin. It was a prototype in a programme that evolved into the slightly more powerful SVT 137, of which 33 were built.

Reichsbahn-Gesellschaft, in particular the Class 05 4-6-4 express locomotive that first appeared in 1935. There was also a high speed two car diesel-electric unit, built in 1932, to run between Berlin and Hamburg. In very short order it was nicknamed the 'Flying Hamburger' (SVT 877) such was its speed. Gresley, on a brief visit to Germany, took the opportunity of traveling between the two cities on this train to gauge for himself its abilities. He was clearly interested in the concept, and having seen the SVT 877 at work Gresley was able to compare it to a rival produced by the Bugatti Factory in Alsace, which appeared in 1933. Its designer, the Italian born Etorre Bugatti, was a specialist in car design, but as the world dipped into recession and demand fell away he turned to the railways where there was still investment and profits to be made. He focussed on railcars in the belief that alternatives to steam were being sought. As a result, he came up with a modular solution that could be arranged in a number of combinations to suit customer needs – single, double or triple – powered by two or four

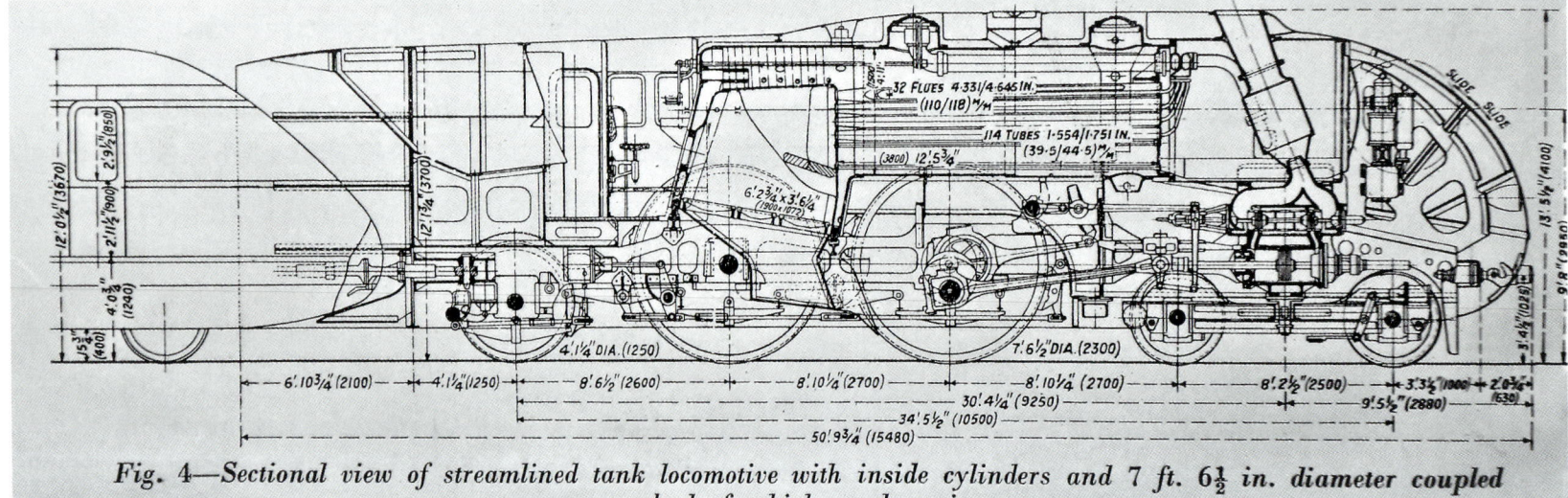

Fig. 4—Sectional view of streamlined tank locomotive with inside cylinders and 7 ft. 6½ in. diameter coupled wheels for high-speed service

Two examples of German attempts to produce streamlined steam locomotives in the early 1930s. The engine above was designed by Henschel & Sohn AG to run at speeds up to 100 mph with two carriages. Left – an early attempt at building a streamlined Pacific showing how access could be gained to the wheels and motion to aid servicing (on this occasion a modified Class 01 4-6-2).

petrol driven 12.7 litre engines as required. Depending on the formation chosen, they could carry between 36 and 144 passengers in seats. Their performance was impressive and one, designated the 'Presidential' was recorded reaching 122mph in 1934. Success followed and by 1938 Bugatti had built and were maintaining more than 100 railcars – work that eclipsed road vehicles in scale and financial return.

During 1933, Gresley and Bulleid were invited by Bugatti to view the prototype railcar at work on the Paris-Deauville line, presumably in the hope of gaining orders. If so, he would be disappointed, because the CME was more interested in the aerodynamics of these vehicles and the wind tunnel testing programme Bugatti had put in place. Its curved, wedge shape nose certainly bore all the hallmarks of the principles he and Johansen were doing so much to develop. But apart from that, the visit was a pleasant interlude in an otherwise busy schedule.

Much has been made about the influence Bugatti and the design of these railcars may have had on Gresley's work, particularly the A4. By this stage, judging by Johansen's research papers held in the National Archives and information contained in his submission to the IMechE, its shape was one of many already laid out and wind tunnel tested at Teddington. This isn't to say that Bugatti's work didn't find favour with Gresley. His cars were the product of a master and in the 1930s so obviously embraced streamlining and their part 'Bugatti' blue livery was similar to the colour that eventually graced many A4s. But more than that, the connection, though a quixotic one, has many weak links. If anything, the key effect of this railcar and the SVT 877 was to throw down a gauntlet to Gresley. It seems that he returned home eager to prove that his engines could outperform these new vehicles as well as the more conventional steam locomotives being built in both countries. He was aware of the extreme propaganda being peddled in Nazi Germany, particularly, and saw an opportunity to regain the initiative.

Railcar developments were not the exclusive province of Germany and France at this time. There were many examples of this technology being developed elsewhere in the world to interest Gresley and his team. The first of these was in Italy where the Societa Anonima Italiana Ernesto Breda of Milan were developing a new type of twin engine diesel units capable of speeds more than 100mph. But of greater significance were two Art Deco inspired trains that appeared in the United States during 1934, both of which drew heavily on

A popular postcard produced in the mid-1930s to publicise Bugatti's new railcars. Its shape was thought to have influenced Gresley's work, but the link is tenuous at best, because by this stage extensive research and modelling by the LNER and the NSP had produced an outline that would be adopted by the company.

technology being developed for the aviation business. Such was the nature of their design that many would refer to them as aircraft without wings. These two articulated designs, called M-10000 and the Zephyr, were produced by Union Pacific and the Budd Company respectively. These multiple carriage sets were capable of 100mph and could carry passengers in great comfort. In fact, the Zephyr on one test ran for 1,015 miles at an average speed of 77mph, at one point reaching 112.5mph, clearly demonstrating its power and endurance in the process. Such was its impact that in the months following launch it became known as the 'Silver Streak'. Whilst the LNER doesn't seem to have shown much interest in these American designs, the LMS did. A party of their officers visited the States and rode on both designs. This led to an experimental diesel unit being successfully constructed in 1938. But for the war, this might have led to greater development and wider use.

Whatever their professional differences, it doesn't seem as though Bulleid tried to discourage Gresley too firmly on the issue of streamlining, but assumed the role of a good deputy, pointing out any flaws in his reasoning and identifying any potential problems that might arise. In any case, the CME, though a man who sought collaboration not confrontation, was very much in charge and, as pointed out by Spencer, 'he was very genial, but didn't suffer fools gladly and, at times, disliked criticism.' In the circumstances, it would have been politic for Bulleid to choose circumspection over criticism. So the working relationship continued and focussed on the next big project, which was led in part by Gresley's continuing interest in the 2-8-2 Mikado concept, plus a growing realisation that an express engine of this type might meet the need for a more powerful engine to tackle heavier loads over the hilly terrain of the LNER's line between Edinburgh and Aberdeen. On this difficult route, where the largest loads were in the region of 480 tons, Pacifics were deemed more than adequate for the task, but now loads up to 550 tons were proposed. This would impose the extra expense of double-heading, or so the Running Department's head believed and he submitted a request for a larger locomotive capable of working this line by itself.

As 1933 dawned, it was nearly eight years since the two P1 heavy mineral engines had made their first appearance and over the years many questions had been raised about their performance. Amongst other things there were criticisms of their coal consumption, the boosters proved troublesome, the flue tubes in the boilers suffered from frequent cinder blockage, the 100 truck trains the engines were designed to pull were deemed too hazardous and discontinued, and the crews appear to have disliked working the two engines. In considering if the design could be adapted for express train use, Gresley authorised a trial, with engine No. 2394, on the King's Cross to Peterborough line. It worked the semi-fast 7.45 am service and reached a speed of 65mph in the process and performed fairly effectively, though riding on the footplate is recorded as being uncomfortable.

As an experiment, it would have told Gresley little that he didn't know already, the engines' performance being fully understood by then. But as a demonstration of potential it had great value, perhaps helping persuade a reluctant Board of Directors, and the Locomotive and Traffic Committee, that here was an idea worth considering in trying to solve an operational problem in Scotland. Of greater significance may have been the continuing development of more 2-8-2 locomotives in the USA and France, and the lessons learnt from this work, which received wide coverage in the railway press. But

Breda's high speed diesel powered railcar which was in wide use in Italy by 1935.

Gresley seems to have been the only British designer to have pursued these ideas to the point of building an engine, presumably because 4-6-2, 4-6-0 or 2-8-0 classes were seen as providing sufficient power and speed for most express and heavy goods needs. If so, one must admire his determination in exploring this concept so doggedly, though others might have considered it a case of obstinacy. In fact, he had thought more widely than an express engine by proposing a 2-8-2 heavy tank engine in 1930 to replace Ivatt's aging R1 Class 0-8-2Ts. (a re-working of a design first put together in 1925 as described earlier in this book). Nothing came of these plans, but the work undertaken added to his growing knowledge of the type.

Added to this slowly developing interest, Gresley gave instructions for a simple drawing of a 2-8-2 express locomotive to be prepared in late 1931. Not surprisingly it strongly resembled his Pacifics, but did not take into account any of the ideas his and Johansen's research had begun to throw up. Then in early 1932, Spencer, it seems, took this first effort and quickly revised the layout to produce something strongly resembling the eventual shape of the new engine. But it took until late 1933 for Gresley, with Bulleid and Spencer's support, to refine his thoughts on the requirement and begin to engage Robert Thom and Harry Broughton, at Doncaster, in the design process. The specification issued to them included a requirement for 6ft 2in driving wheels, an adhesive weight of 80 tons 12 cwt, a 6ft 5in diameter boiler producing 220 psi of pressure, a 43 element superheater of the Robinson type, 50ft of grate area, three 21in

Union Pacific's M-10000 (above) as advertised in the mid-1930s. M-10000 had a short life being withdrawn and scrapped in 1942. Budd's Zephyr was much more successful and ran on into the 1960s spawning the development of more units along the way

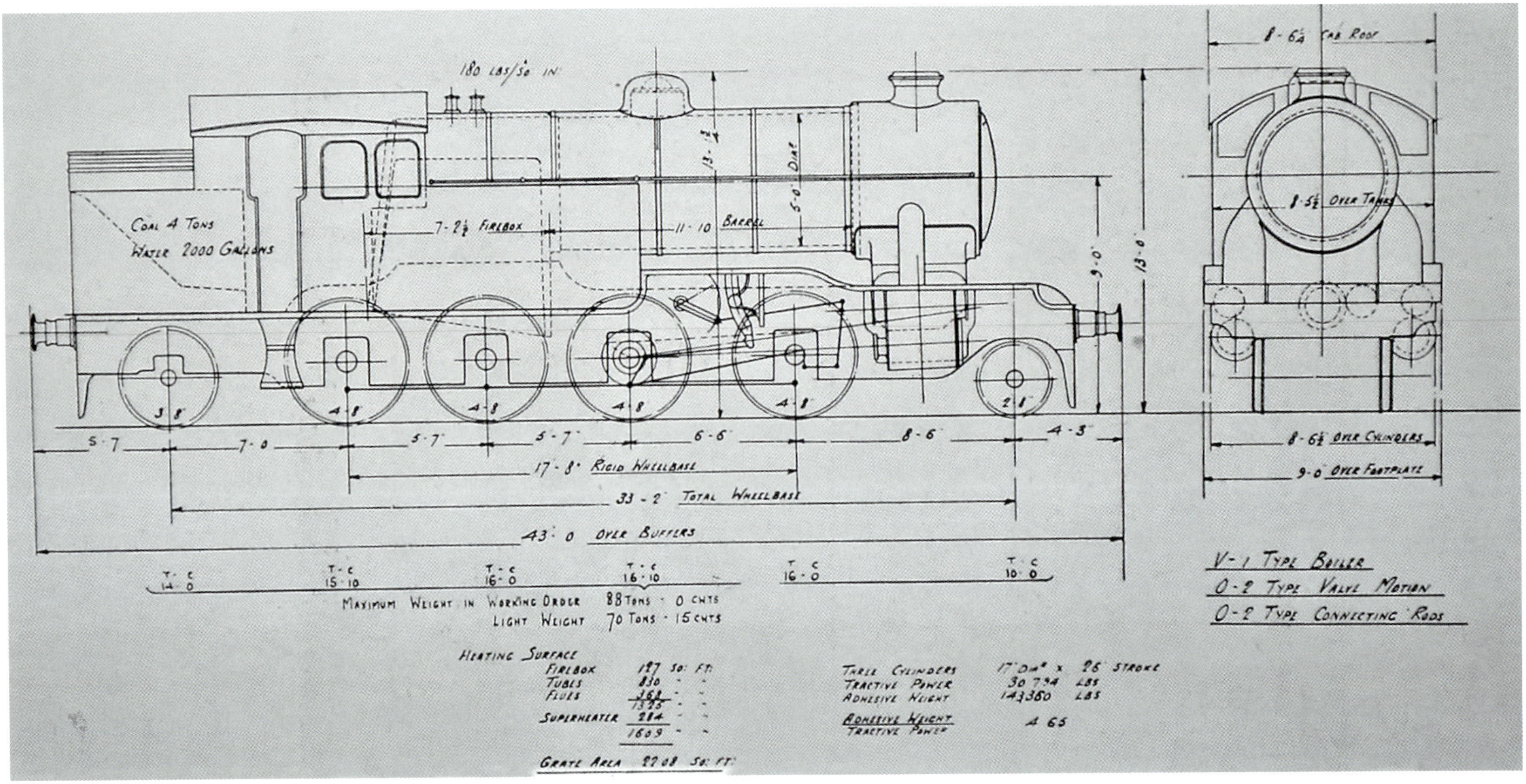

Gesley's experimental 2-8-2 tank engine design produced in 1930 but not proceeded with.

by 26in cylinders, a double Kylchap exhaust system in the smokebox and the ACFI feedwater system. One interesting addition to this was described by Spencer:

'Steam distribution on the first engine (No.2001) was by Lentz rotary cam poppet valve gear, the diameter of steam and exhaust valves being 8in. and 9 in. respectively. Gresley's decision to fit such large diameter valves was influenced by his talks with Chapelon, whose four-cylinder compound Pacifics on the Paris-Orleans Railway were putting up remarkable performances. These engines had poppet valves operated by oscillating cams, the diameters of the steam and exhaust valves on the low pressure cylinders being 8.66 in. and 9.45 in. respectively.'

Many years later he added a brief note to this:

'To test the benefits to be derived from the Lentz rotary cam gear Gresley had, over a

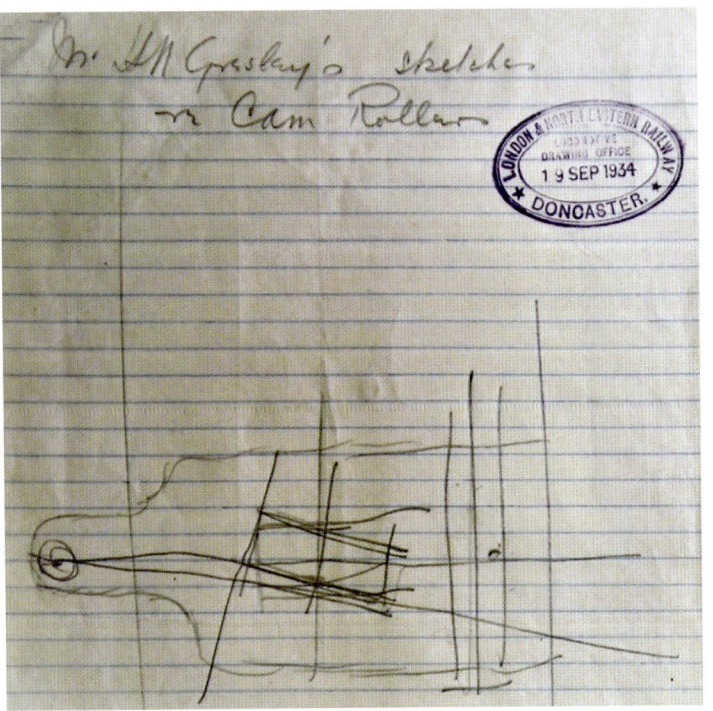

One of a number of Gresley's rough sketches that Spencer kept. He would present these to his Assistant on a daily basis when a major project was underway. His job was to convert them into a more detailed form for the Drawing Office to expand. The originals were then returned to Spencer to be archived at King's Cross.

number of years, authorised its use on various classes of locomotive – D49s and B12s amongst them. But as work on the P2 gathered pace the gear was installed on two C7 Class Atlantics which were often used for testing items of auxiliary equipment. The results were good and it was decided to go ahead with No. 2001 on this basis.'

In February 1933, the Drawing Office were set the task of providing a schedule of material needed for construction of two P2s and placed orders. They then began preparing detailed drawings even though Gresley had yet to complete his deliberations on a number of issues. Worried about the slow progress and delays, Thom set out a draft production schedule in September 1933 so that workshops and manufacturers could plan their work. But even at this stage, the final design was far from completion or agreement. On the 6th, he received a letter from Bulleid which he hoped would be the CME's final views on the requirement. Bulleid also enclosed a 'sketch' prepared by Spencer showing the locomotive's proposed final outline, which seems to be the first time either Thom or Broughton had seen it. He wrote:

'I enclose pencil sketches showing the proposed side elevation of this engine. As the top of the clothing behind the chimney will require to open for inspection of the feed water heater, it will be necessary for a horizontal line on the bend to show where the lagging plates are hinged, and in view of this Mr Gresley has been considering whether it would be advantageous to do away with the ordinary

Though the date is barely legible (February 1932?) and the drawing is badly marked by creases and dirt, this seems to be one of the earliest surviving sketches of the P2 prepared by Bert Spencer.

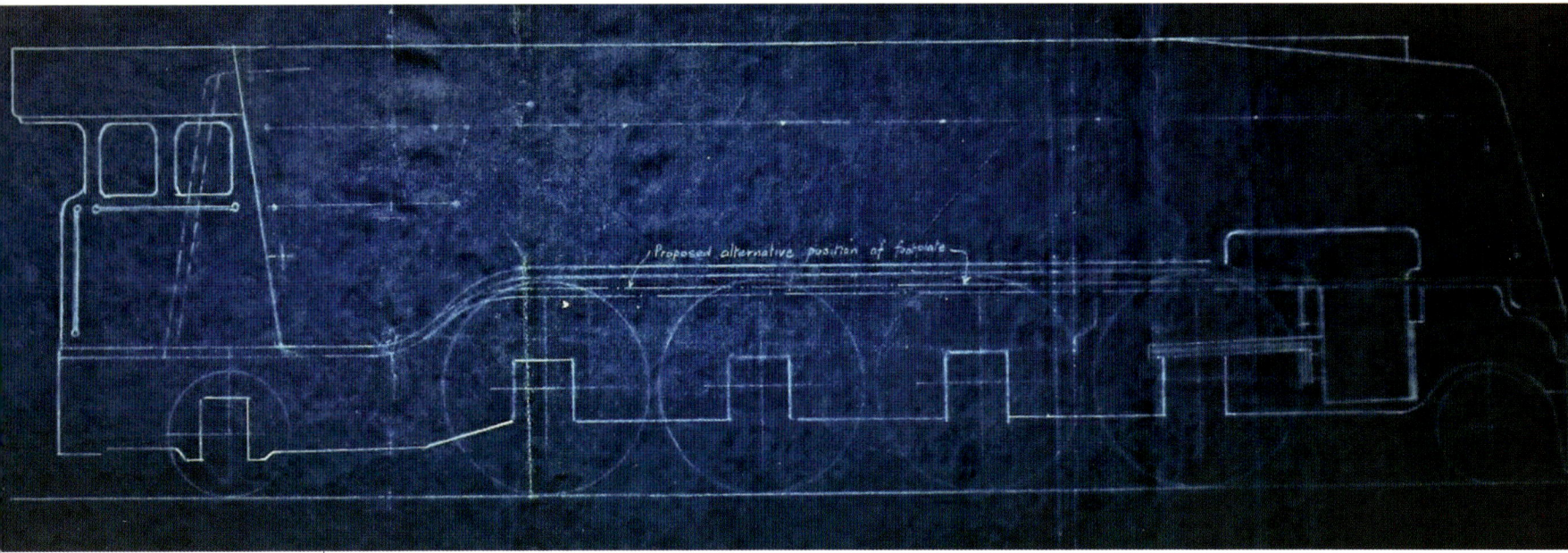

One of Spencer's 1933 drawings showing the proposed layout of Gresley's Mikado No. 2001.

type of clothing and fit clothing secured by horizontal bands, thereby improving the streamline appearance of the engine.'

As a small aside to this, Spencer sent Broughton a short note on 17 September accompanying a ream of rough sketches, on any old piece of paper that came to hand, prepared by Gresley when clarifying his thoughts on the cam gear. Spencer normally took these almost indecipherable drawings and used his draughting skills to translate into them something much more legible. But on this occasion time was pressing and he sent the originals with 'Mr H.N. Gresley's sketches re Cam Rollers' written at the top. These surviving examples tell us much about the way Gresley worked, the level of detail he involved himself in and the value of having someone as talented as Spencer beside him to ensure

his thoughts were conveyed and refined effectively.

With the first locomotive due to be ready by May 1934, Gresley finally approved all the drawings on 17 October, though up to its launch he was still tweaking the design, often focussing on some of the most innocuous items. It was almost as if he thought this locomotive might be the principal achievement of his career and so fussed over every small item and often visited Doncaster to see the work in progress. But in the capable hands of Robert Thom, the programme was carefully and effectively managed. Miraculously, to some, he achieved this alongside all the other tasks in progress there and despite the high number of requests he received from Gresley for information about the P2 and other tasks being undertaken at Doncaster. The few files that remain in public or private hands show the extent of correspondence he received almost daily for action

from King's Cross, often beginning with the words 'the CME would like to know what progress is being made on…' or '..see attached the CME's sketch/comment/proposal on..' But the phlegmatic Scot, who was known to stand little nonsense from anyone, was more than capable of managing Gresley and Bulleid, together or individually and in his hands, the P2 project was brought to fruition, No 2001 appearing on 22 May 1934 and No 2002 on 6 October, the second engine being fitted with piston valves instead of the Lentz gear.

The locomotive's launch, then inaugural run from King's Cross took place on 1 June, following an appearance at Doncaster's Open Day on 26 May. And with this the locomotive quickly passed into the hands of the Running Department with Gresley, Bulleid and Spencer watching closely how she performed. Each of them, it seems, also took the opportunity of riding

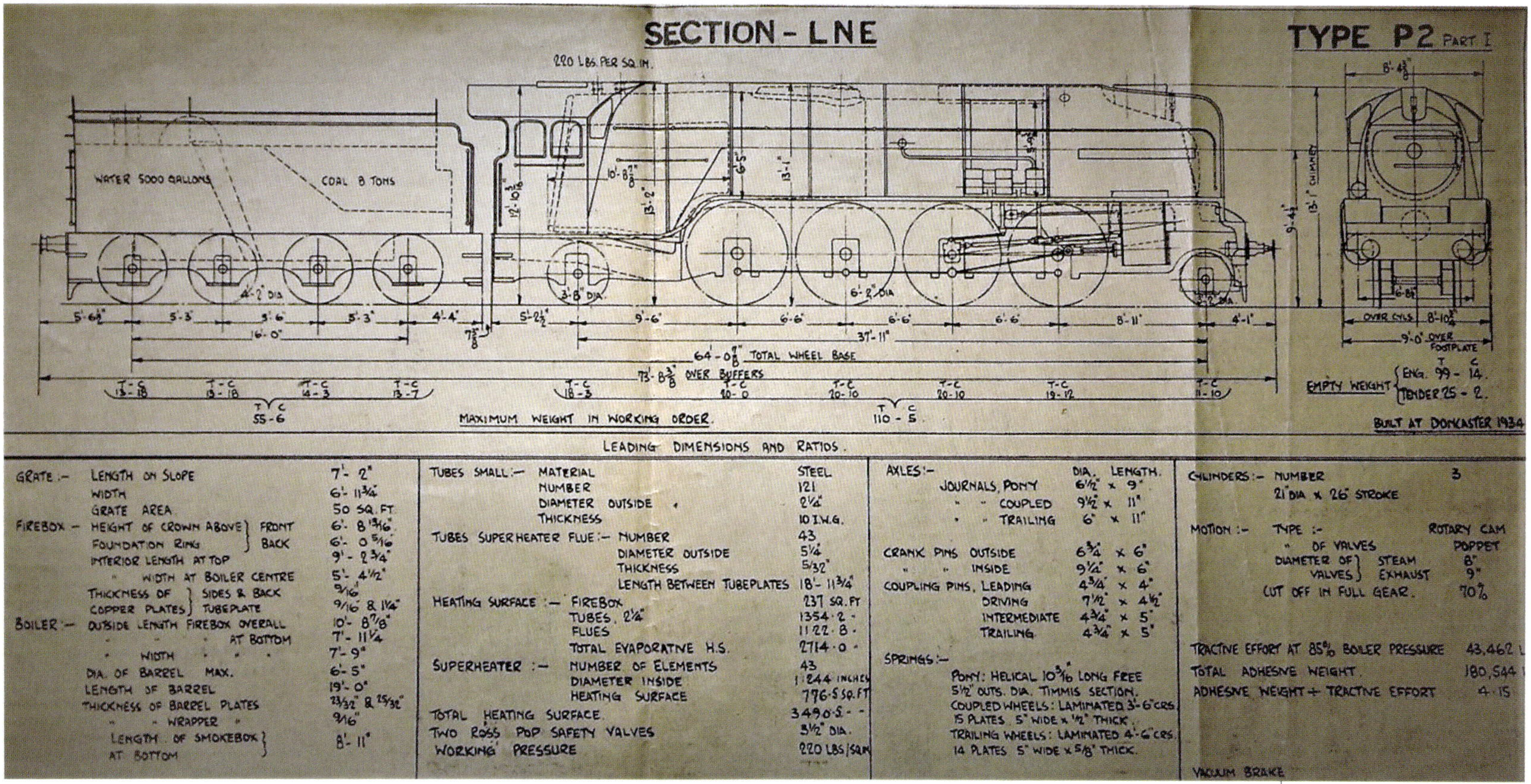

A Master at Work (1932–34)

The final diagram of engine No.2001 issued in early 1934.

on the footplate to make their own assessments. Gresley also sought out the crew to gauge their views and reactions to this engine, now named *Cock O' the North*. On 13 June, he put some of their thoughts down in a letter to Robert Thom:

'The engine is found to be very hot in the cab, and the enginemen find it necessary to run with the front windows on the first catch. Will you please look into the question of fitting additional ventilators on each side of the cab in the upper portions of the front plate not occupied by the window.

'The men are also complaining of the heat from the firehole

The first P2 nearing the end of construction at Doncaster. Much remains to be done but the engine's distinctive shape is now well established.

1 June at King's Cross and a group of VIPs stop to admire the new locomotive before its departure. Bert Spencer can be seen in the group of three in the foreground (smiling and wearing a light coloured felt hat) and it is said that Gresley is in the group gathered around the cab.

Stratford Works May 1935. 2001 makes an appearance at the Works Open Day with a small crowd gathered around, many of whom seem to be showing greater interest in the photographer than the engine.

door, and I should be glad if you would consider fixing a short screen on the fireman's side in addition to the large screen on the driver's side to give extra protection.

'Some modification is also required to the large screen, as when opened it interferes with the movements of the fireman.

'The enginemen also call attention to the cock fixed on the tender for filling the water bucket. It is too low and difficult to get a bucket under easily. This arrangement should also be modified on the other tenders of this type.'

It seems to me that most of the great railway engineers had an easy way with people of all ranks in their organisation. They could put their seniority to one side and talk man to man in a way that encouraged others to be forthcoming with their views and opinions. In this way, the leader could often discover snags they hadn't foreseen or simply view a problem from a different angle. Gresley, as he grew older and more aware, developed this ability and relished contact with footplate crew in particular and respected their assessments. As in this case, he didn't simply note the issues raised and move on, but promptly took action to improve the engine's design and the crew's working conditions.

On 19 June, the P2, having completed a few running in turns to iron out any faults, was deemed ready for her first formal trial. She was scheduled to pull a 649 ton load, including a dynamometer car, from King's Cross to

On her early visits to King's Cross 2001 became the centre of much attention being photographed and filmed by the PR Department, the press and enthusiasts alike. With such an imposing look this isn't surprising.

Grantham, then on to the Barkston triangle, returning later in the day. With these runs successfully accomplished, with little recorded in the brief report that might be considered critical or flattering, Gresley took stock of all that had happened so far and authorised more trial runs. On 22 June, he wrote to Thom:

'As soon as the indicating gear is fitted I want you to take a complete series of cards at slow speed throughout the full range of cut-offs.

'As regards the running trials, I have made provisional arrangements with Mr Barrington-Ward that the trials will be carried out on the 11.4 am from Doncaster and the 4.0 pm from King's Cross beginning on Monday July 2nd. 'The trials on the 2nd and 3rd July should be carried out with the ordinary load of these trains, but on the 4th and 5th weights of the trains should be made up at Doncaster and King's Cross to just over 600 tons, including the dynamometer car.

'The engine is to be indicated and the water consumption taken on each trial. Arrangements should be made to record the superheat at the header, steam chest and exhaust. Smokebox and ashpan vacuum should also be taken.

'During the recent runs the ACFI thermometer did not appear to be recording correctly. This should be put in order as I wish the feed temperature to be taken on the trials.'

While the engine's power and load pulling capacity could not be criticised, and it had proved itself capable of high speed, there is a note of concern creeping into Gresley's correspondence that all might not be as well as expected. This was translated into the need for more extensive tests and a growing belief that 'on the road' trials were insufficient for his needs. This was a theme that he had been pursing for many years in the hope that the Ministry of Transport might sponsor construction of a test centre along the lines of the facilities at Altoona in the USA or Vitry in France but his words had fallen on deaf ears,

P2 undergoing test in July 1934 – the wooden shack to protect engineers is shown clearly. Spencer described it as a 'Heath-Robinson contraption that was dangerous and inefficient'.

with the recession being given as a reason for inaction.

Now he cast envious eyes towards the Paris centre which had opened only a year earlier, its facilities being highly praised by Chapelon in his letters to the CME. It may have been him who initially suggested that the P2 visit Vitry and be assessed in the more extensive facilities there. If so, it was a thought encouraged by a collision on 18 July 1934 when the test shelter, built around the engine's smokebox to protect engineers recording data, was damaged. The shelter was strengthened, but it brought home to Gresley just how ramshackle and unsafe this testing system was.

Things moved quickly and on 24 July, the CME had discussed 'the proposal to test the P2 type engine on the Locomotive Testing Plant at Vitry with Monsieur Place'. This memo then went on to describe all the items required for the trials, from customs declarations, modifications to the engine and any restrictions in place. All this suggested that Gresley had had this in mind for some time and carefully managed the exercise to greatest effect, gaining approval to proceed in the process. So detailed planning began and a programme was agreed with Monsieur Pierre Place at Vitry, the Engineer in Charge, with a start date of December 1934; timed to allow the second, slightly modified P2 to enter service.

In the meantime, Gresley kept in regular contact with Chapelon by letter, phone and occasional meetings, to discuss the P2 but also other projects, including W1 and the Pacifics. Clearly the CME found this most valuable, but a meeting of like minds will have this effect. There was no other agenda between them other than to debate their science away from the politics of their own organisations, something both men must have found refreshing. During a telephone call on 22 October, Gresley seems to have expressed his concerns to the Frenchman about P2, because on the same day Chapelon wrote:

'I have examined the case of your locomotive No.2001. I am surprised that this engine can produce sufficient steam with blast pipe tops 6 in. in diameter and with the shortest bars 11/16 in. long and 1.1/16 in. wide. The total sectional area for the steam through the two tops is therefore 327 square cm., whereas from my experience with French locomotives, this section would have to be at most 250/270 square cm. to get perfect evaporation up to the highest rates of firing of 800 kg. per sq metre of grate area per hour.

'This difference may be due to the quality of the coal; my experience makes me think it might not be so great, however. I think, therefore, that if 2001 does, in fact, steam often properly up to the highest rates of firing with the present sectional area of 327 square cm. this area ought to be retained without alteration and the thickness of the fire be reduced as a consequence at the lowest rate of firing. Our practice is to run with very thin fires when the working engine allows,

Early in 1934 the LNER began distributing material to publicise the new engine's launch. This painting was particularly popular and captures the magnificent looks of the engine especially when coupled to the company's green livery.

The fireman takes a breather as the engine appears to coast. Although fleet of foot with its eight coupled 6ft 2in driving wheels it would be unlikely to compete in the speed stakes with Gresley's Pacifics. But their intention was a high average speed on the winding, hilly track north of Edinburgh, not to race down Stoke Bank as *Mallard* so famously did.

2001 more appropriately dressed for her 'home' line.

and to run with thick fires only when the engine is being forced.'

After a great deal more advice, he ended with a short, supplementary note, 'the design of the double exhaust for engine No. 10000 is finished and the drawings will be sent at the end of the week.' This is very revealing, because it hints at the depth of Chapelon's involvement in Gresley's work, not simply the CME's observed conclusions. It is hard to say, from the limited material available, whether the flow of advice was a two-way process, but one suspects it may have been. Someone with Gresley's great engineering skills and love of experimentation would have much to say and suggest to a fellow designer.

Before the P2 was transferred to Vitry, the engine spent a week or so in Scotland to be tested on the line for which she had been designed. Norman McKillop, a driver at Haymarket and a great fan of Gresley's Pacifics, was instructed to collect the engine from Doncaster and participate in the trial runs. Later in life, he often wrote about his experiences and amongst these recollections he recorded his memories of 2001, beginning with his first impressions, written in draft form and later much modified for publication:

'She looked impressive….I stood back and took her all in. There and then I ticked off what I didn't like. The four coupled drivers were too close together for some of those curves I knew so well. I could almost hear the squeals as that semi-rigid mass did a spot of cavorting round acute bends. I did not like the small 6ft. 2in. wheels and the short connecting rods.

'It was arranged that I should work the engine on the 4.5 am from Edinburgh to Aberdeen the following morning. I was to take the train to Dundee then work the engine to Dundee depot for examination before returning.

'One look at "Cock O' the North" told me she was powerful, but wouldn't have the agility of a Gresley Pacific. Inside me I knew that this new engine would be a near miss and I was disappointed.

With barely a whisper of smoke, 2001 pulls away from King's Cross.

Engine No. 2002 makes her appearance whilst her sister began tests at Vitry. Here she is seen before her front-end was modified with the addition of extra smoke deflection plates.

The truth was that Gresley's engines had become to me something in the nature of an answer to every high speed driver's prayers. The first was sufficient to verify all my fears. We left Edinburgh with fourteen coaches and a technical officer in the cab. I never allowed the engine to touch anything higher than 65 on the short straight stretches and nursed her around the curves, but two-thirds of the way to Dundee I was smelling heat. My technical companion advised me to "come off", but I thought otherwise. So we timed the train to Dundee to find three of the coupling rod bushes cutting to such an extent that there was a broad line of 'gold' from the nave of the wheel to the rim, where the brass and oil had run from the bush.

'This first run was the start of a series of tests I made with 2001. After each run I reported on her and I reported plenty. All the bushes had to be eased on big-ends and coupling rods, but what could not be eased was her terrific appetite for coal.

'The engine became something of a star attraction to all, except the lads who had to fire her…. She could haul any two trains if you cared to tie them together – haul them up any gradient in Britain - but no matter how a driver tried to economise, she swallowed a hundredweight of coal to the mile, where a Gresley Pacific was doing her job on anything from 28 to 35 pounds on the same road with a slightly smaller train.'

It seems the line north of Edinburgh was increasingly seen as the wrong place for the P2 to operate, but it was hoped that the trials in France would highlight any deficiencies there may have been and any modifications that might improve this situation. So, the engine was shipped across the Channel during the night of 5 December, taking a number of trucks containing Ashington coal and a brake van with her. The ferry berthed at Calais at 8.20 the following morning with the loco being unloaded by 12.30. Steam was then raised and the engine

2001 is positioned on the rolling road at Vitry and the guard rail has been removed whilst doing so. One of the figures peering from the cab is said to be Bulleid, but it is difficult to confirm this.

moved under her own power to the local depot escorted by Bulleid and a small team from Doncaster. From here she was moved to Vitry and testing on the rolling road began shortly afterwards. In the weeks that followed, Gresley and Spencer occasionally visited France to observe the tests in progress and, on one visit, brought a range of spares with them as well. Spencer kept notes of all he saw and Bulleid made copious notes too, recording progress and problems encountered. These he sent to the CME almost on a daily basis, when he himself wasn't in France but back at King's Cross. All this was supplemented by frequent phone calls in both directions, suggesting that Gresley kept a very tight rein on the whole programme.

When testing came to an end on 8 February, the engine had undergone 24 trials on the rolling road, supplemented by trips on the main line between Paris and Orleans. However, the whole programme was jeopardised by a series of problems related to the driving wheels' axleboxes, which repeatedly overheated necessitating removal, replacement or repair. On numerous occasions, the engine's wheels had to be dropped and this involved 2001 being taken to the Paris-Orleans works. Just as Gresley and Bulleid believed the problem had been resolved, it re-occurred. So, very few of the early tests could be completed and it began to seem that no useful purpose would be served by continuing. Bulleid's diary described each days events, gloomily reporting each breakdown, each repair and the

This photo is believed to have been taken during one of 2001's many visits to the Paris-Orleans Works to allow the main driving wheels to be dropped to give access to the axle boxes so they could be replaced or repaired.

time away from the test centre. Finally, on 10 and 12 January, the locomotive completed two full days of testing, but after that the axlebox problem crept back and two more wheel drops were necessary to allow more repairs to be made. On this occasion though, at Gresley and Bulleid's instigation, the method of re-metalling the boxes was changed, following a visit from a Mr Murphy from J. Stone and Co who reviewed their work and recommended changes, and this appears to have been successful.

After so many false starts and such extensive repairs it was decided, reputedly based on Chapelon's suggestion, that the engine should be subjected to a period of main line running to allow the axle boxes, wheels and motion to 'bed in'. So on 26 January, she ran on the Paris-Orleans line, pulling three other engines set in back gear to produce measured resistance. Regular inspections during the day found the boxes to be 'cool' and the problem seemingly resolved. This process continued until 7 February, with the section of track between St Pierre des Corps and Orleans becoming her regular haunt.

With these runs rapidly eating away the time available, but proving useful in so far as the engine's reliability was concerned, Gresley approved a shortened programme for rolling road tests at Vitry. So on the 8th 2001 returned

P2's power graphically displayed. Spencer recorded that 'the whole building seemed to vibrate and shake most violently when the locomotive was running near to its maximum output. The noise had to be heard to be believed'.

to the plant. Here a successful day's work was accomplished in which, after two hours running, 'the regulator was fully opened and it was found that at 90kph 1,600 horse power was developed.' More tests were planned for the 9th, 10th, 11th and 12th, but three of these were curtailed or cancelled. This was due to the engine's inability to maintain steam pressure, a loss of cylinder efficiency due to excessive clearances, failure of the ACFI, severe slipping of the wheels on the rollers and on the 11th the left hand leading axlebox overheating again. So back to the Paris-Orlean Works she went for the wheels to be dropped and the box to be re-metalled for the last time.

Once this work was completed, preparations for her return to Britain were put in place, but first she would go on display at the Gare du Nord in Paris and then Nord Station. With this PR work over the engine was embarked at Calais on the 21st and arrived in Harwich the following morning her sojourn to Vitry not deemed a great success. Bulleid prepared a number of memos for Gresley and Thom highlighting some of the issues the tests had identified. In the coming weeks, a rather brief action plan was produced which led to a number of modifications being made to the first two engines and four others of the class that would be built in 1936. In addition, Gresley wrote several memos to Thom and Tom Street, now Chief Draughtsman, Harry Broughton having retired during 1935,

A photo given by Stanier to his Chief Draughtsman, Tom Coleman, in 1935. Coleman wrote on the back 'the ghostly figure is the CME getting too close for comfort'.

highlighting changes he wished to make. These included producing lateral play in the leading and trailing wheels, improvements to the firehole door, a longer combustion chamber, firebars designed on a French model, improvement to the lubrication system to the axleboxes and so on. Modifications to the poppet valve gear also became an issue in June. But it seems that the resounding success the CME had hoped for with his new engine was proving elusive. Meanwhile, engine No 2002, *Earl Marischal'*, had entered service and was herself undergoing various tests between London and Doncaster. Bert Spencer, who appears loath to have expressed an opinion on these engines, wrote:

'As originally turned into traffic, No. 2001 had continuous cams, but after approximately 10,000 miles service trouble was experienced owing to the point of contact of the follower rollers breaking down the casehardened surface of the inlet cams. Stepped cams were fitted, but the valve events were consequently restricted to six ranges of cut-off in fore gear. On an engine of such high tractive effort the large difference in power between cut-off positions proved inconvenient and was not conducive to economical working. The second P2 was fitted with 9 in. diameter piston valves and had outside

2001 draws many interested spectators at the end of her time in France, on this occasion at Amiens Station.

Walschaert gear with Gresley gear for the inside cylinder in order that a direct comparison could be made with the poppet gear on No. 2001.

'At early cut-offs No. 2002 would not clear the smoke and it was necessary to modify the front end arrangement. As a result of further wind tunnel experiments (overseen by Frederick Johansen, who was by then employed by the LMS) a second set of deflector plates, positioned about 18 in. from the inner plates, were fitted and shaped internally to deflect air upwards to the rear of the chimney. This unsightly arrangement proved successful.

'With smaller clearance volumes and an infinitely variable cut-off No. 2002 proved lighter on coal than No. 2001. Numbers 2003 to 2006 were therefore fitted with piston valves as was 2001 in April 1938.'

It seems that Spencer was following the old adage 'if you can't think of anything nice to say, say nothing', when describing the Mikados. However, much later he did add a brief comment that 'these engines would have performed better if they had been allowed to operate in the south where their great power could have been harnessed

2002 now modified with extra plates, which seemed to have had the desired effect and lifted the smoke sufficiently to improve the driver's visibility.

without fear of doing damage to the track or the driving wheels. But overall, they proved costly to run and were difficult to maintain in good running order. I recall it being said that for every day spent out of service by the A3s and V2s the P2s had two or three.

So the two engines went into service, receiving a mixed reception in the process, especially from those like McKillop who happily expressed a preference for Gresley's Pacifics. Bulleid, though, remained a committed advocate of the class and years later would discuss these engines with his staff on the Southern Railway when CME. John Click, who served as a premium apprentice under Bulleid, then became one of his assistants and remained a corespondent to the end of Bulleid's life, recalled many conversations they'd had about the P2:

> 'I was left with the impression that Bulleid more than Gresley had been instrumental in getting a 2-8-2 built. He would say that "it was the one engine in which I got a lot of my way" and was always talking about it. He added, on one occasion, "it embodied a lot that was new, but lacked the one thing that would have made it truly successful – a way of casing its long coupled wheelbase into curves by building the front with a Helmholtz or Zara type truck. This was a common solution on the Continent and would have helped the engines considerably when running north

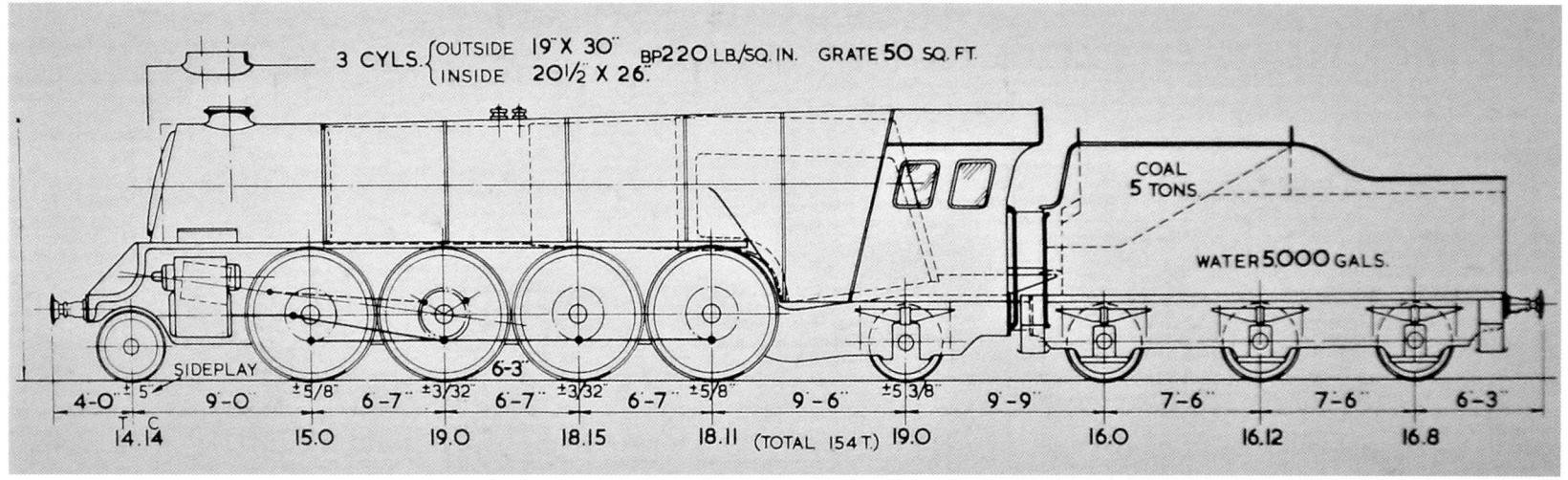

Two of Bulleid's attempts to design a Mikado for the Southern railway showing his reluctance to give up on the 2-8-2 configuration.

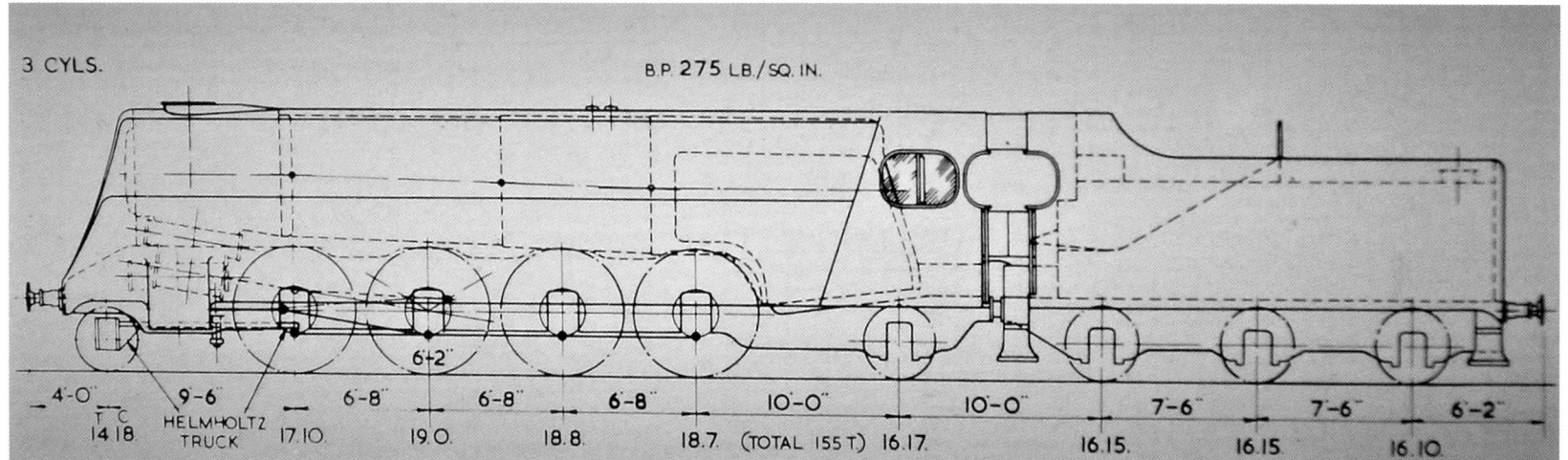

of Edinburgh. I wanted this and suggested it on many occasions to Gresley, but he felt there were enough new features built into the loco already and one more would only confuse the issue even more'".

'Such was his like of the design that he attempted to get one built on the SR before proceeding with his Pacifics. This was a three-cylinder design which included many features used in the first two P2s', but with the addition of a Kraus-Helmholtz truck which had first been introduced in the late 19th Century. This proposal was rejected by the civil engineers on the grounds of potential damage to the track by spreading, especially where a third electric rail was present. Many years later and even up to his death he frequently mentioned these engines in our correspondence and thought the French had better appreciated their virtues and developed many fine locomotives of this type.'

His pride in this work came over clearly when Bulleid commented on Bert Spencer's paper to the ILocoE in 1947 and presented an argument to counter any criticism:

'Cock O' the North had a lesson for everyone. She was

not extravagant at all, but was in fact extremely efficient on the testing plant, and compared favourably with the French engines in her coal consumption per rail.h.p., and better still, per d.b.h.p. When tested on the open road between Orleans and Tours she developed a very high horse-power, of 2,800, and again showed herself to be an efficient engine from the point of coal consumed per d.b.h.p. In service, however, she was an extravagant engine. The fundamental reason for this was that she was not put to the use for which she was designed. Instead of working trains well within her capacity over long runs, she was employed on a service such as Edinburgh to Dundee, went to Aberdeen and hung about there, and did a very poor mileage per day, with the result that she showed a heavy coal consumption, most of the coal being burnt through misuse rather than working trains.'

One thing is certain though, both Bulleid and Spencer believed these engines were used on the wrong route, yet the running department could hardly be criticised for that. They had specified an engine for the Highlands and not another to run on routes emanating from London to the North, which were already well catered for by Pacifics. To this can be added a comment made by Robert Riddles, who was to all intents and purposes British Railway's first CME in 1948. He wrote that the P2s were 'too elaborate and over engineered for the purpose required', but he was no fan of Bulleid, as later events would prove.

Despite any perceived shortcomings, four more P2s were built in 1936, which suggests that the class may not have been perceived in too negative a light. Whilst these new engines would benefit from the lessons learnt by 2001 and 2002, they picked up a theme less acceptable to Bullied and fall for what he considered to be the misconceived fashion of streamlining. While he had been focussing on the first P2s, Gresley, Thom and Street, and their respective teams, had been exploring and exploiting this concept within the limits of the technology available to them – and a locomotive to surpass the early Pacifics and P2 was well on the way - the A4.

Perhaps one of the most important outcomes of the P2 programme wasn't the locomotive itself, although it did sum up much that Gresley had considered

Bulleid's attachment to the P2s, in their original form, was only too clear. His son, Henry, recorded that this photograph was one of his father's favourites summing up, as it did, the sheer power of engine No. 2001.

and pursued during his career, but the Test Centre itself and his continuing battle to get an identical facility built in Britain. So great was his ambition to succeed that he arranged for William Stanier and Dr H.J. Gough FRS to visit Vitry in January and see for themselves engine No 2001 being tested and then tour the facility.

In 1930, Gough had succeeded Stanton as Superintendent of the Engineering Department at the NSP and became one of Gresley's staunchest friends and supporters in the intervening years. The doctor was a specialist in metal fatigue and a keen proponent of purposeful and extensive testing regimes and supported the CME's case with great determination. Gough was described as an astute, highly creative engineer and a 'man of strong convictions which he expressed courageously' and, at the same time was described as 'kind and generous to his friends'. It was a description that could have applied to Gresley himself. During 1935 they, along with the influential Stanier, backed up by the scientist Sir Harold Hartley, the LMS's Director of Scientific Research, pushed the Minister of Transport to review a programme shelved some years earlier when

Bert Spencer remained uncommitted on the virtues or failings of the P2, but he was a reticent soul especially when it came to discussing his much-admired CME. However, his feelings may be gauged by the fact that he kept this photo in a frame in a prominent position in his house.

2001 and her sister engine, No 2005, *Thane of Fife*, gently sizzle on a hot day between turns, shortly before *Cock O' the North* was rebuilt and streamlined like the other members of the class.

the economy had crashed. To help revive this matter, Gresley marshalled these 'big guns' to help argue the case.

To reinforce these efforts, Monsieur Place was invited by the CME to visit the IMechE's HQ in London and present a paper entitled 'Locomotive Testing Plants', to a large audience of 'many eminent engineers and others'. With such an influential man able to demonstrate the value of an advanced test facility, backed up by the considerable weight of many prominent scientists and engineers, there must have been expectations that purse strings might be eased. But their arguments, and the supporting evidence behind them, failed to impress and it was left to the 'Big Four' companies to initiate construction. During the months that followed, the SR board decided that electrification took priority, while the GWR contended that the test facilities at Swindon were sufficient for their needs. So the LNER and LMS had to go it alone and find funds for the work, which they did. Progress was slow, then the war intervened and it wasn't until 1948 that the first locomotive, appropriately the A4 *Sir Nigel Gresley*, became the first engine to run on the new rolling road. Sadly, it was too late for the centre's prime mover and also too late for steam locomotion, which had entered its Indian Summer and would soon face extinction.

Chapter 7
SPEED, COMPETITION, ART DECO, AERODYNAMICS AND THE SCIENCE OF PUBLICITY (1935)

1935 proved to be a pivotal year for Gresley. Work and science had always been the cornerstones of his life and these became more important after the death of his wife. It is a truism that grief may ease but will never depart and other things can appear to help fill a vacuum created by loss. And this appears to be the case for him, with change being limited to a new life in Cadogan Square rather than Camlet House and then leasing a new home, Salisbury Hall, near St Albans in Hertfordshire. Here, he could find a certain amount of peace and quiet, but it was also a place where he could entertain his family and many friends. His daughter Violet became his companion for a time and a very familiar figure acting as her father's hostess until her marriage to Geoffrey Godfrey in 1937. It is said that Gresley seemed to enjoy all the

'Speed' by the gifted American sculptor Harriet Frishworth. This work came to personify much that happened in art and science in the 1930s and spread into the world of locomotive design.

Gresley in the mid-1930s exuding the confidence of an elder statesman at the peak of his powers and authority. Bert Spencer later wrote that 'this picture caught Gresley's character perfectly – intelligent, incisive and in command'. To these words, others would add 'kind, generous, sympathetic and understanding'. Eric Bannister, who became Spencer's assistant at King's Cross, probably encapsulated best the effect the CME had on a personal level when he wrote, 'By his patience and willingness to listen to a raw recruit he won my loyalty and respect. He made me want to give him all the help I could – and that unsparingly.'

trappings of the country gentleman that went with this life but, in due course, he found this large rambling house too much for his needs and joined his newly married daughter at her home in Watton-at-Stone, near Hertford.

With some stability in his personal life, and the support of his daughter, he could focus more fully on many professional issues as he approached the last years of his life. During September 1934, he was elected President of the ILocoE for twelve months and then President of IMechE in 1936. These prestigious positions carried great weight and were much more than honorary titles. They also entitled the recipient to choose a subject of their own choice and address this in a very public way, And on 27th September he took to the dais in London and spoke in depth about the railway industry and picked through subjects close to his heart. One of these was, of course, the need for a Test Centre and he heaped pressure on the powers that be with a well-argued, impassioned speech, urging them to action, but there was much more than this and he set out his creed and the issues he thought important:

'Before concluding my address, it is appropriate to refer to the tendency today towards the

Salisbury Hall as it appears today surrounded by a moat in which lived wild ducks Gresley was famously photographed by the water here with a mallard in 1937. During the war the Hall was taken over by de Havilland Aircraft, whose main works were based at Hatfield, and became one of its design offices.

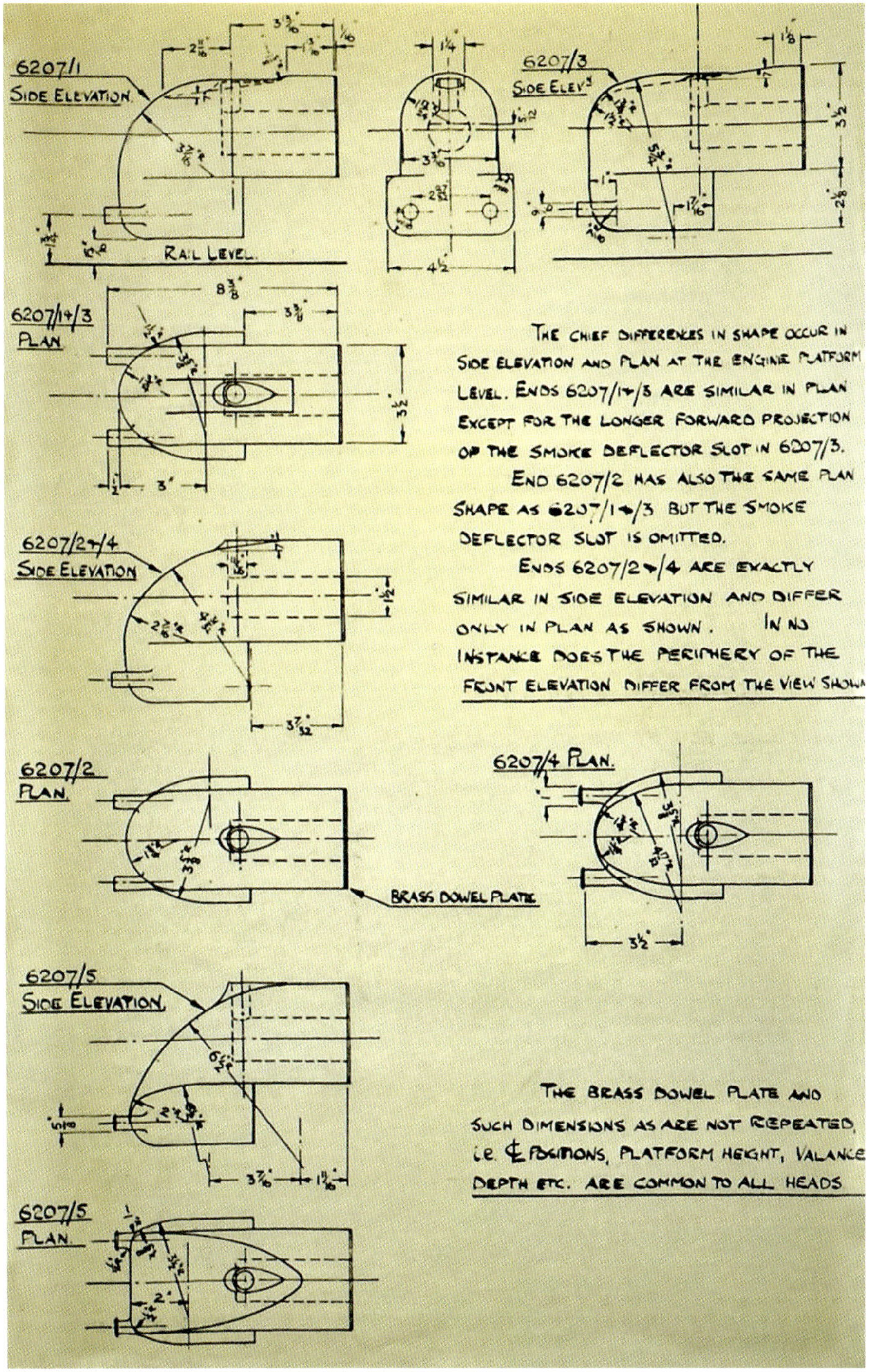

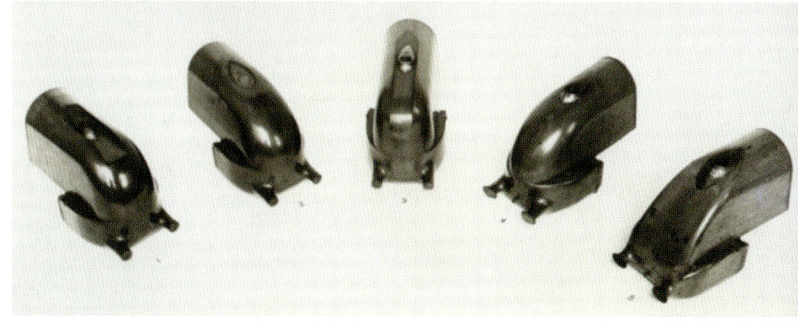

Drawings and photographs produced by Johansen in the early 1930s, when working concurrently for the LMS and LNER, to back up his research into locomotive shapes and reducing the effects of air resistance. Drawing and model number 5 clearly show the shape adopted by Gresley for the A4s and the later P2s, whilst the top right-hand drawing bares a strong resemblance to engine No. 2001 as built in 1934. Each drawing is numbered with a batch two Princess Royal Class engine number to be built in 1935. During 1934/35 the LMS were contemplating its streamlining, something that didn't take place. Tom Coleman, at Derby, was a major contributor to this work.

speeding up of all trains, and to make some reference to the extra high-speed passenger trains which have recently been introduced abroad. In this matter Germany has taken the lead. In France a similar service has been started on the Nord, between Paris and Lille, and Bugatti cars are running on the Etat and PLM. In Holland and Belgium, a number of diesel-electric high speed units are working, but the speeds attained are not so great as in Germany.

'The question is naturally asked; why has nothing been done here beyond speeding up the existing steam-operated trains? The answer, of course, is the difficulty in finding space on our congested railways for a path for trains of such exceptional speeds. The permanent way of the British railways is well known to be the most perfect in the world, as is also the method of signalling, and there is no question that trains of the highest speed contemplated can be run with safety and comfort on our railways.

'It is not suggested that speeds much in excess of 100mph can economically be maintained. The air resistance, notwithstanding scientific streamlining, absorbs so much power. Experiments with models of existing types of coaches carried out by the NPL show that air resistance of trains of average length, say twelve coaches, at 100mph, is approximately double that of trains at 70mph. In the case of the "Flying Hamburger" it is calculated that 85% of the power generated by the diesel engines is absorbed in air resistance when running at 100mph. Streamlining is essential at extra high speeds because the air resistance of trains increases approximately as the cube of speed, but it is of comparatively negligible value at lower speeds, up to, say, 50mph. I think the day is not far distant when heavy trains consisting of one class will be run at speeds not less than the best speeds of today, and that short extra high speed trains will be run between London and the big industrial centres. The steam locomotive, however, of greatly improved efficiency, as a result of the establishment of a locomotive experimental station, will still continue as the chief power unit operating on our railways.'

As this was a Presidential address, a discussion period did not follow so no alternative view could be expressed, but the reaction may be gauged by William Stanier's words when seconding the vote of thanks.

'The work Mr Gresley is doing is an inspiration to all of us who are trying to follow in his footsteps.'

These men may have been commercial rivals, but they were also fellow engineers eager to push back the boundaries of their science. At this stage, the LNER and LMS were entering the most competitive phase of their rivalry, which makes such a close collaboration even more surprising but it continued on many levels. Tom Coleman, Stanier's Chief Draughtsman, often met Robert Thom to discuss different projects and the LMS man even rode, as a guest, on LNER Pacifics. Frederick Johansen, having been recruited by Harold Hartley for his expanding Scientific Department in 1932, still continued to do work for Gresley until 1936 or '37, using his connections within the NPL to gain access to the wind tunnel there and there are several signs that many of his reports on aerodynamic issues were circulated quite widely within both companies, with similar locomotive shapes being suggested, following wind tunnel trials. With this in mind, it is possible that a Stanier Coronation could have ended up with an A4 front end or vice versa.

Nowadays, such sharing of information would be unthinkable, commercial pressures being so intense, but it seems to have been quite common with the NPL and Johansen in particular during the 1920s and '30s. It extended into the aviation world as well, with his involvement in the design of Supermarine's Schneider Trophy aircraft which evolved into the Spitfire, at the same time as he was assisting Hawkers' in their development of its Hawker Hurricane. Both companies came to him for advice, supported by wind tunnel testing at Teddington, even when he was working for the LMS full time. One wonders how any degree of confidentiality could be maintained, but perhaps the companies he dealt with saw no problem with this. Yet between 1934 and 1937 the business rivalry between the LMS and LNER was intense. During these years both companies were trying as hard as they could to exploit the lucrative passenger trade from London to the North. The LNER had taken a clear lead during the 1920s with its new Pacifics and non-stop express services but very slowly the LMS had begun to catch up and during 1933 introduced its first two 4-6-2 Princess Royal Class engines to a flood of publicity. Although only two compared to Gresley's 79 A1s and A3s built by 1935, the LMS had also developed a substantial number of powerful 4-6-0 express locomotives to boost their service. But it was the two Princesses that threw down the gauntlet and within two years ten more had been added and a non-stop service from Euston to Glasgow, to rival the LNER service to Edinburgh, became a real possibility and with it the setting of speed records.

It was a race to the north that had a sound economic base, but it revived memories of an earlier competition on the lines to Scotland in the 1880s between the Great Northern and the London and North Western Railway. But in this case speed records, streamlining and glamour became this new competition's common denominators. In so doing it mixed scientific research with a

The mid-1930s saw more new B17s, D49s, V1s, J39s and the last batch of A3s appear. Here B17 No. 2856, *Leeds United* gets turned at Neasden shortly after being built.

PR campaign which cared little for studied analysis and more for a good headline. Both Gresley and Stanier responded to the challenge, rose to the occasion and produced two new classes of locomotive that encapsulated all that they had hoped to achieve in their careers – the A4 and Princess Coronation respectively. But races can be fought on many different levels and the LMS, though slow to embrace Pacifics and non-stop running, were ahead of their rivals in other ways, such as the depth of research they undertook.

While Gresley continued to press the case for the new test centre, his development programmes did at least have the support of his very talented staff, dynamometer cars testing and an ad hoc arrangement with the NPL and Johansen. In addition, there was the informal advice he could seek from fellow members of the institutions to which he belonged and from those such as Chapelon. Beyond this, he was restricted in whom he could employ. Meanwhile, the LMS had taken the concept much further with the creation of its Department of Scientific Research under Harold Hartley, who was recruited by the company's forward thinking chairman in 1930. This eminent chemist was able to put together a team of highly qualified scientists under Tom Herbert and in the mid-1930s he centralized this group at Derby, where they would be of greatest use. They then set them to work on a whole host of tasks in well-equipped laboratories. This included a continuation of research into the effects of air resistance, refinements in locomotive design, improvements in thermal efficiency and much more to do with the effective running of the railway.

Gresley could only look on and admire the work they were doing and perhaps envy the facilities at their disposal. But during the late 1920s he met a most unusual father and son who would strengthen his scientific arm and close the gap with the LMS. First of all, he encountered then employed Professor Thomas Turner, who was a pioneering expert in the world of metallurgy, as a consultant through the good offices of the NPL. Then, while undertaking this work, Turner senior introduced his eldest son, also Thomas, though referring to himself professionally as T. Henry Turner, to the CME. He, like his father, was a highly qualified specialist in metallurgy. Being impressed by what he found, Gresley decided to recruit him as well, though this time on a permanent basis as Chief Chemist and Metallurgist in his department. Here, during 1931, he was placed in charge of four small district laboratories, inherited on grouping, at Stratford, Doncaster, Darlington and Cowlairs; to this would be added a specialist metallurgical facility in 1932. Over the next ten years, father and son would bring a more measured approach to research, particularly in the area of metal fatigue.

When considering ideas for new engines, where the stress of high speed and long distance running reduced engineering tolerances to a fine limit, their advice would be essential and, according to Bert Spencer, it was key to the success of Gresley's locomotive programme in later years, particularly in the barely understood science of metal fatigue. So when contemplating the next generation of locomotives, Gresley had a mishmash arrangement of specialists drawn from a number of fields to assist in their design. But to this, of course, he could add the established skills and experience of Thom, Street, Bulleid, Spencer and many others. With this backing, he progressed

Thomas Turner senior was born in Ladywood during 1861 and studied at the Royal School of Mines where he was awarded the De la Beche medal. He then moved to Mason Science College (a forerunner of Birmingham University) where he continued his research into the physical and chemical behaviour of metals. During a long and distinguished career he rose to become the first Professor of Metallurgy at Birmingham, lecturing and writing widely on the subject. His work for the LNER came very late in his career, when Gresley needed a scientist's view of the problems related to locomotive design. Thomas Henry Turner (left), born in 1895, followed his father to Birmingham University where he gained an MSc then worked as a research metallurgist with Metropolitan Vickers and International Nickel Company in New York before returning to his alma mater to continue the study of metal fatigue, engine failures, corrosion and associated subjects. Employing both these men proved to be a wise move and one of immense value in the development of the CME's next generation of Pacifics in particular.

towards a project which would bring together many elements he had been experimenting with throughout his career – cylinders, valves, boiler, aerodynamics and much more – all the result of the ever increasing, and publicly fought, competition between the LNER and the LMS.

There was also the matter of national pride to consider. By 1935, Germany was in the grip of Nazism and had become a totalitarian state driving home its doctrine of suppression and expansion through propaganda, militarism and advances in science. This was nowhere more apparent than on the railways, as witnessed by Gresley himself when viewing their high-speed rail cars at work and reading of their plans for high speed, streamlined locomotives. Competition with the LMS was a key driving force, but on a personal level he had no wish to be outdone by anything the Germans could produce. As war drew near, this feeling seems to have grown in intensity.

  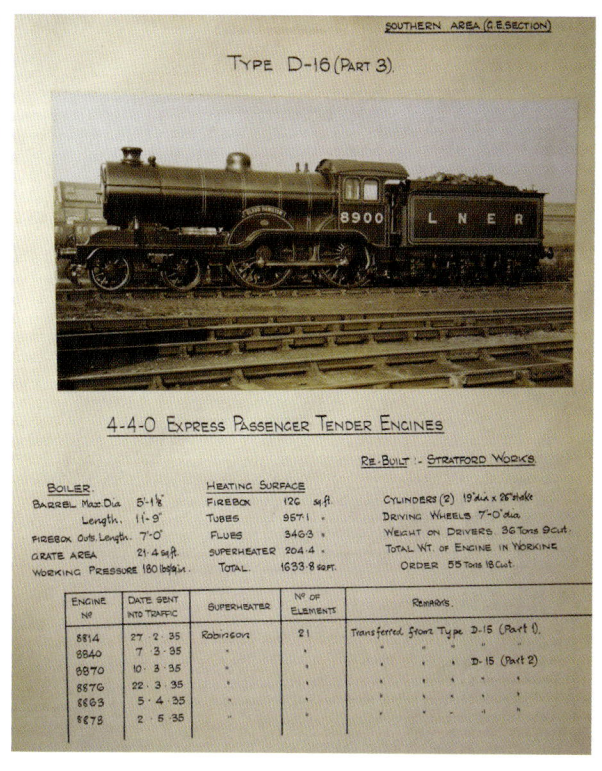

Robert Thom continued to log each year's building programme – the last A3 Pacific amongst them. But he also noted that in 1935 the LNER continued to rebuild many of the older locomotives, such as the A8s, B12s, D15s and many more. Whilst new locomotives became the main focus of attention the need to improve the whole fleet was never lost on Gresley and his team.

So, fired up with the spirit of competition and driven by a desire to achieve engineering perfection, a new Pacific was born but this time it would evoke a new age and begin to personify a style based on the Art Deco movement and its desire to throw off the shackles imposed by a rigid conservatism. For some, this would be the triumph of form over function and this was nowhere more apparent than in the railway world, where for many there could only be one well established form. For them, change could only mean more of the same but this modernist concept had many supporters and could name Bugatti, Chapelon, Coleman, Gresley and Wagner amongst its number. However, it went far beyond train design into civil engineering, architecture, car and ship design and the rapidly emerging world of aviation, all of which were very serious areas of science not noted for their pursuit of extravagant fripperies.

This coming together of art and science first found its outlet in the years immediately before the Great War and it had only just begun to make an impact when hostilities commenced. It was a slow spreading movement with its roots in visual arts that expanded into other areas of design. With its use of bold geometric shapes, matched with bright colours, fine craftsmanship and opulent materials, the effect was most striking and unusual for the time. And when the world turned from war, the Deco style acquired fresh strength and its influence became a defining feature of the 1920s. By then, it had spread into new areas where scientific research, sparked by a growing understanding of liquid flow and aerodynamics, had opened up many new possibilities. Form had indeed found a function and during the 1930s this took one more step forward, moving into a more subdued phase called 'Streamline Moderne', where curving forms became even more pronounced and central to the design process. From here, industrial designers – a generic title applied in the USA to a new breed

The opposition takes shape in Nazi Germany, as captured in these two pictures. The first of three powerful streamlined 05 Class engines built at the Borsig Locomotive Works between 1934 and 1937, under the direction of Dr Paul Wagner and Dr Litz. They appeared to great acclaim and soon began to set records. Their impact far outweighed the tiny number built.

of engineers and artisans – began the process of marrying Deco style and science when constructing new locomotives.

During the late 1920s and early '30s, the work of men such as Raymond Loewy, Norman Bel Geddes, Henry Dreyfus, Otto Kuhler and more began to flourish and their influence on locomotive design spread rapidly to other parts of the world. One member of this group, Dorwin Teague, probably summed up this link between art and science, but also hinted at its long-established principles. In 1927, he wrote about the analogies between the mathematical proportions of the Parthenon and the functionalism of modern aircraft, automobiles and locomotives. And to this he added a few words about the importance of work undertaken in the 1860s by Samuel Calthrop and 1890s by Frederick Adams into reducing the effects of air resistance on trains. Now all this work, coupled to the scientific endeavours of men such as Gresley and Johansen, would find a voice in Britain.

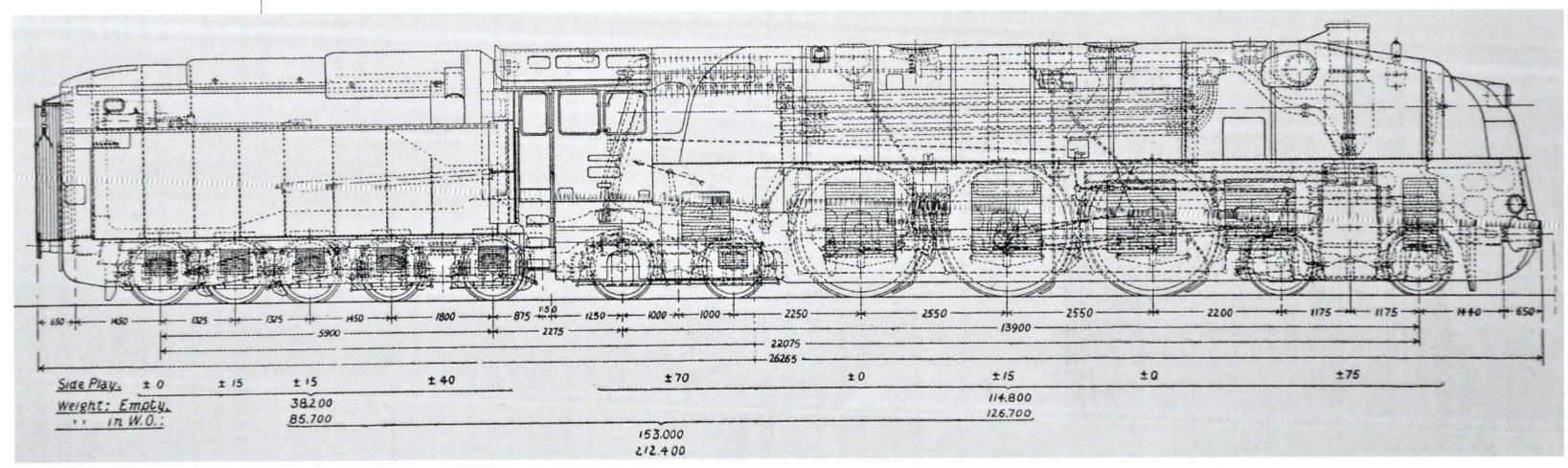

A clear statement of intent set out by the New York Central with the introduction of their 4-6-4 streamlined engine in November 1934, designed by Henry Dreyfus. Being the first was a proud boast, but other companies in Europe were already well advanced in their research. There appears to be little evidence to suggest that the Commodore was a wind-tested concept or merely the work of a talented draughtsman with a 'good eye' for shape. It remained in this form until the 1940s when de-streamlined.

The next stage in their work, and the move to a streamlined locomotive and train, relied heavily on convincing the LNER board that this was a direction in which the company should move and here, the CME relied upon the German example to push forward his ideas. When elected President of the IMechE in 1936, he described this process in his initial address:

'I visited Germany in the latter part of 1934 and travelled on the 'Flying Hamburger' from Berlin to Hamburg and back; I was much impressed with the smooth running of this train at a speed of 100mph, which was maintained for long distances, that I thought it advisable to explore the possibilities of higher-speed travel by having such a train for experimental purposes on the LNER.

'I accordingly approached the makers of this train and furnished them with full particulars as to gradients, curves and speed restrictions on the line between King's Cross and Newcastle. With the thoroughness characteristic of the German engineers they made a very exhaustive investigation and prepared a complete schedule showing the shortest possible running times under favourable conditions and then added 10% which they regarded as adequate to meet varying weather conditions and to have sufficient time in reserve to make up for such decelerations or delays as might normally be expected.

Frederick Adams' 1893 patent describing his 'wind resistant' train.

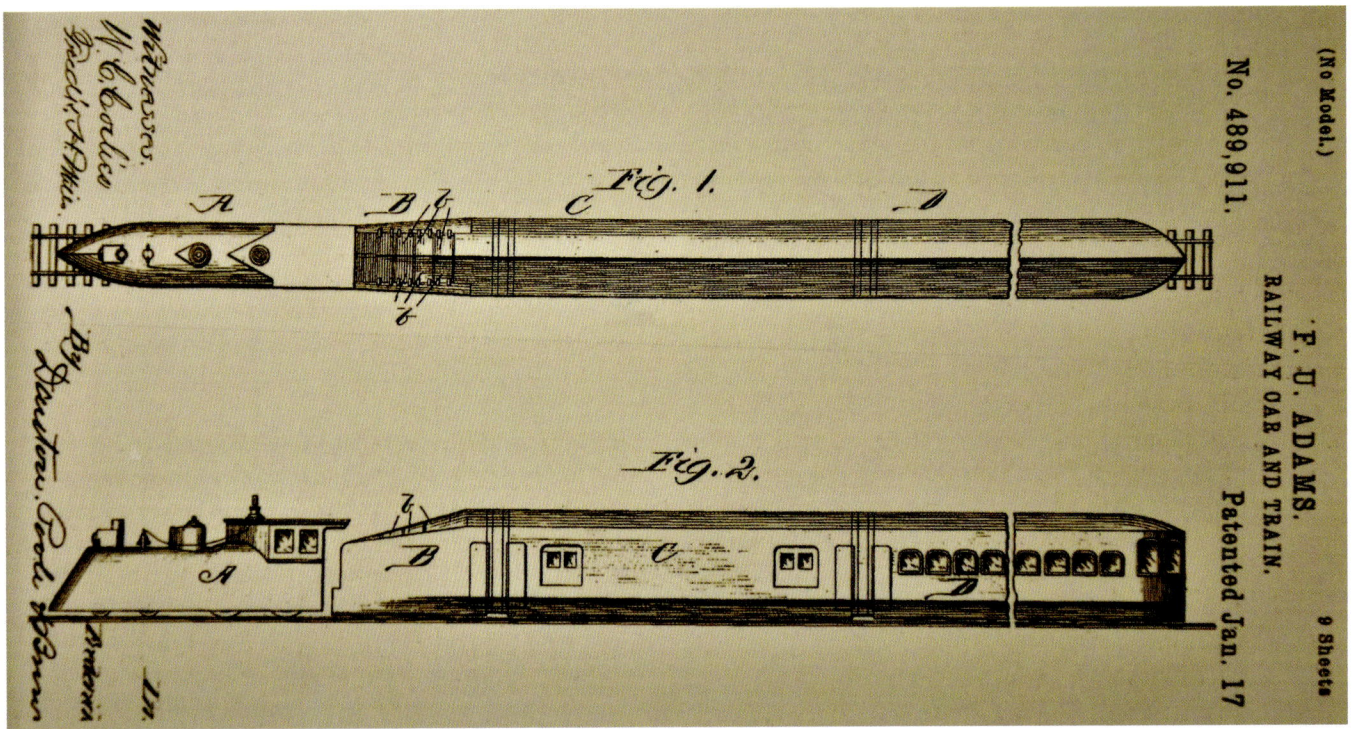

A photo of SVT 877 collected by Spencer and used to demonstrate how a version for the LNER might have looked.

While Gresley contemplated the future of locomotive design the day to day business of the LNER went on, with many designs he had inherited still doing sterling service or being developed. Here a B12, derived from the GER Class S69, and built in 1928 by Beyer, Peacock, appears to be undertaking shunting duties at King's Cross in the mid-1930s

'The train, weighing 115 tons, was to consist of three articulated coaches and to be generally similar to the German train. The times for the complete journey were given as 4 hrs and 17 minutes in the up direction and 4 hrs 15½ minutes in the down. The train provided seating for 144 passengers. The accommodation was much more cramped than that provided in this country for ordinary 3rd class passengers, and did not appear likely to be attractive for a journey occupying four hours. My Chief General Manager suggested that with an ordinary "Pacific" engine faster overall speeds could be maintained with a train of much greater weight, capacity and comfort. A trial with a train of seven bogie coaches demonstrated that the run could be accomplished with reliability in less than four hours under normal conditions.

'I felt that to secure a sufficient margin of power it would be essential to streamline the engine and train as effectively as possible, and at the same time make sundry alterations to the design of the cylinders and boiler which would conduce to freer running and to secure an ample reserve of power for fast uphill running. The design for the engine and carriages were prepared and the complete train built in the Company's works at Doncaster in the remarkably short time of 5 months.'

Some would later say that Gresley was being a little disingenuous in this statement and missed out certain details, such as

Throughout the 1920s and '30s, publicity was an art practised extensively by the Big Four railway companies, but particularly the LNER, who seized any opportunity they could to exploit this medium. In so doing they often arranged for a gleaming Pacific to be posed for press photographers, on this occasion engine No. 2546, *Donovan*, built in 1924 at Doncaster.

improvements recommended by the German builders to enhance performance. It was suggested that he deliberately found fault with their design so that any proposal to purchase their railcars would fail. His own agenda, it was concluded, being to push ahead with his streamlined steam designs at any cost and in doing so setting back the process of modernising motive power in Britain by twenty years. This was a view reinforced much later by the sharply critical Gerard Fiennes, who became an LNER apprentice in 1928 before rising to become Operating Superintendent, then joining the British Railways Board. He was probably well placed to pass this judgement, because one of his achievements in the 1950s was to drive the purchase and introduction of Deltic Diesels on the East Coast main line and retire the Pacifics.

He also pointed out in a letter towards the end of his life that Gresley '… may have been instrumental in cancelling electrification projects when the LNER was formed that Raven had championed and would, undoubtedly, have pursued if chosen to be CME'. The accusation is a clear one. Gresley wasn't a moderniser and was in thrall to steam power.

There may have been some truth in this, but any judgement must be made on reasoned and evidential grounds and this means understanding the conditions that prevailed at the time and the conflicting demands facing Gresley when making decisions about the future course of motive power development. Hindsight is a wonderful thing and can make lesser men, who did not face these complex problems, appear as great philosophers, able to exercise the judgement of Solomon. 'If only I had been managing then all would have been different' is their collective refrain.

The trouble is that critics often presume many things and misread 'facts' in reaching conclusions. Gresley was, in fact, a moderniser, as his constant search for well-reasoned and scientific answers would bear witness, but he was also a pragmatist who understood the real-life issues of economics and the restrictions this placed on all areas of his business. There were limits on what he could do, and he knew them only too well. Flights of fancy about alternative forms of motive power, whilst academically stimulating, will always come face to face with hard facts and risk assessment. And the most obvious fact was that Britain was a country almost exclusively powered by coal, or its derivatives, for most of Gresley's life. The coal industry was also the biggest industrial employer in these decades, with 1.2 million or so people in service, so any reduction in use by a move to oil would have had catastrophic consequences for the country's economy.

The LNER's decision in 1923 to cut back Raven's electrification programme when making such good progress does seem shortsighted. But with an economy almost bankrupt and a railway system severely run down by the war, there was an inevitability about their action and, of course, there were also the effects of having a workforce depleted in numbers and skill, through casualties, to be considered. Something had to give and capital expenditure on speculative projects, such as electrification, became the victim. With the post–war gloom turning to a decade or more of economic recession, the position remained unchanged for a long time. Steam was a well-practised science, coal was readily available and cheap, so it is little wonder that the railways favoured this form of power and continued its development. Gresley could hardly be blamed for this and was simply responding to the limits placed on him.

When it came to the business of acquiring 'off the shelf' diesel-electric railcars from Germany, some of these arguments still applied. As the Deutsche Reichsbahn had already discovered, each railcar could cost almost double the price of a new Pacific engine and rolling stock and this did not take into account the cost of upgrading the infrastructure to service these new units. They may have been looking to the future, but this came at a huge cost and, clearly, they were unable to carry freight traffic, which was the lifeblood of the LNER.

Fiennes also made the point that while Gresley had pursued his steam dream, the Southern Railway had pressed ahead with electrification despite the costs involved but this is an argument that fails to compare like with like. The Southern was primarily a commuter railway, operating in an area served by many power stations, with a need for high density, frequent stop and start trains, for which electric multiple units were ideal. Their profits lay in providing a rapid transit system capable of feeding London's need for millions of workers each day. The LNER, by comparison, fed the industrial heartlands of Britain, where gas power still prevailed in many homes, and long-distance travel and heavy goods traffic were key features, so required a different policy and solutions. Although the SR pressed ahead with its ambitious electrification programme, even they were forced to rein it in when austerity struck. Their only alternative was to restore its steam locomotive programme to fill the gap, such was the funding crisis it faced. Work eventually picked up post-1945 but it would be another 22 years before steam was finally eradicated from its network such were the costs involved.

The truth of the matter is best summed up in the words used by Gresley when addressing the ILocoE in 1931, '….this is an Institution of Locomotive Engineers, not an Institution of Steam Locomotive Engineers…'. This isn't the language of a hidebound man fixated on a single view of the future, but someone who understood the realities of life and made best use of what was available to him, all the time hoping and seeking something better. To prove this point, in 1935, when the economy showed signs of recovery, Gresley, with Wedgwood and Whitelaw's support, commissioned a study into the electrification of the LNER's North London suburban lines. To this was added the route from Manchester to Sheffield which was approved for conversion in 1936. In both cases, new locomotives and multiple units would be needed and the

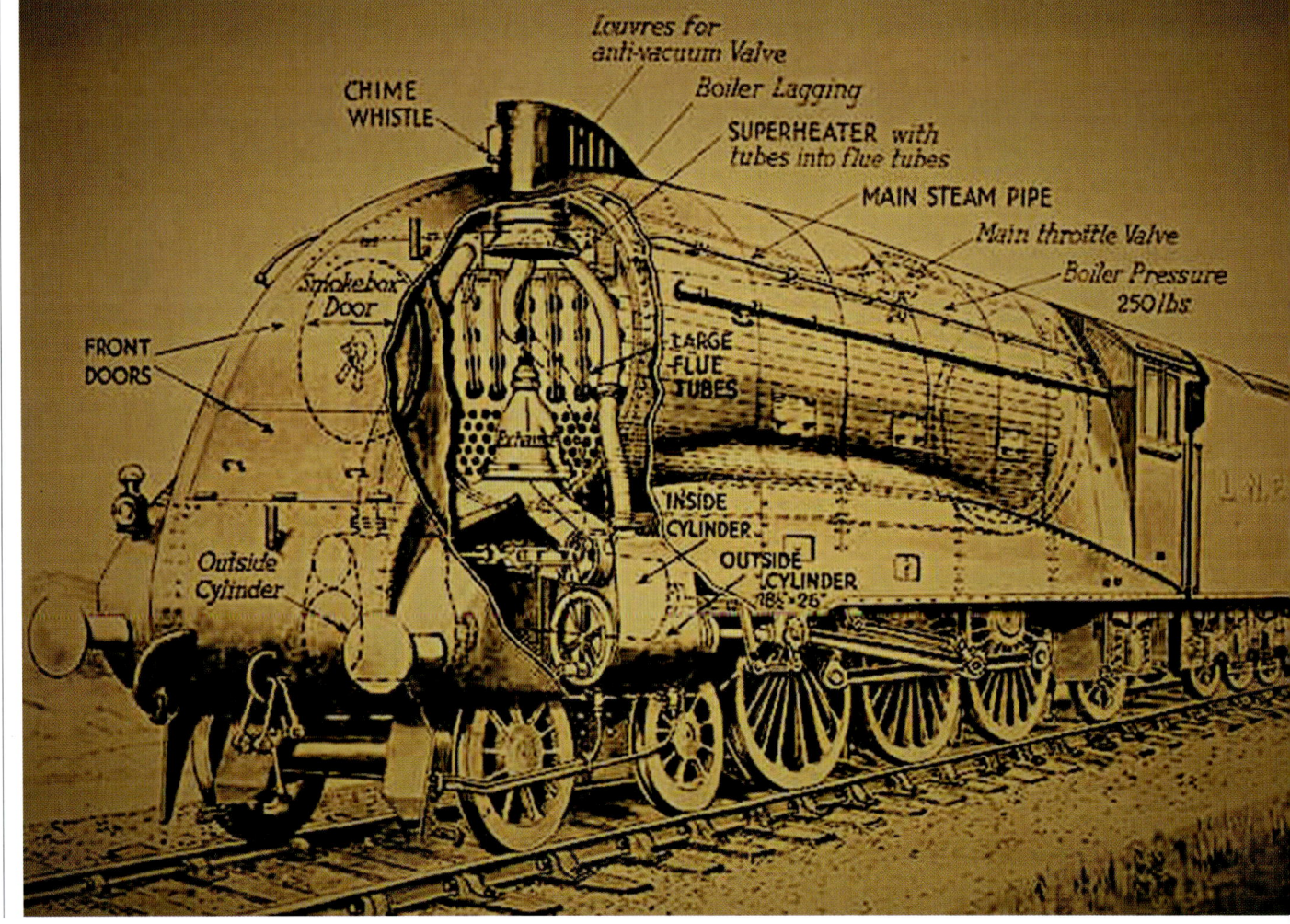

An early sketch of the new streamlined locomotive. On the back Bert Spencer has simply written 'a card produced in March 1935 to show the rough outline of the A4 for publicity purposes'.

Flying Scotsman with driver William Sparshatt standing beneath the engine's nameplate with two young cleaners hovering above. This photo was probably taken shortly before or after the test run in November, for publicity purposes.

first of these, a prototype 1500V Bo-Bo engine, appeared in 1941.

With their eyes set firmly on the future, and having rejected diesel-electric railcar ideas, the scene was set for the LNER to pursue a steam solution. But the theories expounded by Gresley and Whitelaw needed to be proved before a new locomotive could be commissioned although it is interesting to note that Spencer and the Drawing Office staff at Doncaster had begun preparing outline sketches of a new streamlined Pacific early in 1934. Also, by mid-year, they had begun ordering material for their construction, so confident were they of receiving approval to proceed.

In the meantime, a test was authorised in November 1934 that would seek to replicate the service suggested by the SVT 877's designers at Waggon-und Maschinenbau AG, but pulled by steam instead. On 30th November, 4472, *Flying Scotsman*, crewed by William Sparshatt and fireman Bob Webster, drew a special train on the outward journey from London to Leeds, of four carriages and a dynamometer car; with a scheduled time of 2¾ hours set for both outward and return journeys. On each occasion, traffic managers worked to ensure a clear path on the route to avoid any normal operational delays that might occur, so giving the exercise a slightly artificial feel. But a locomotive of such power, with such a small load was unlikely to fail and so it proved. The train arrived at Leeds 13 minutes ahead of schedule, having reached 100mph in the process; though unofficial timings taken on board suggest that 98mph was the limit. The return later that day was just as spectacular and overall an average speed of 72.2mph was maintained over both runs. The only problems recorded seemed to have occurred on the return

Gresley congratulates Sparshatt, whilst the exhausted Bob Webster looks like a rabbit caught in the headlights. Life for footplate crew was hard and these two men were tested to very uncomfortable limits on 30th November. However, in the 1930s, labour was cheap and plentiful with health and safety rarely practised in a way we would recognise today.

leg when Webster showed signs of fatigue, having shovelled some 4,000lb of coal per hour, and there were concerns over the lubrication system and possible overheating. Gresley was famously photographed congratulating the crew at King's Cross on their great triumph and the PR Department made capital out of this event, with articles appearing in newspapers and journals in the days and weeks that followed.

Despite being carefully stage managed, it was deemed a great success and supported the development of this type of service and new trains to haul them. As a result, on 4th January 1935, Wedgwood presented two memoranda to the board summarising the results of the test, suggesting an extension to the trials, but also seeking approval to finalise plans for a new locomotive and

4472 was always a good performer, or so reports suggest. One of her record cards registers few trips to the works between 1933 and 1944. Just before the test on 30 November she appears to have spent three days being prepared for this important non-stop run.

rolling stock. With time pressing, it seems to have been agreed, with these requirements forming part of that year's building programme. It was a remarkably ambitious plan and one that soon became linked to celebrations surrounding George V's forthcoming Silver Jubilee. Whether this was by chance or design is unclear but it was a remarkably good hook on which to hang the proposal and an even better scheme to publicise the new train and the services they would provide.

As planning proceeded so a second high-speed trial was held on 5th March, this time between London and Newcastle, with A3 No. 2750, Papyrus, in charge. One of the many accounts written at the time recorded the event in breathless prose:

'The LNER beat the world's record for speed by a steam train by running from London to Newcastle in under four hours. The train consisting of a dynamometer car, restaurant car, three first-class corridor coaches, and a brake van, had a weight of 213 tons, with a seating capacity of 204 passengers, and was hauled by a "Super Pacific" type engine, built at Doncaster in 1929.

'The train left King's Cross at 9.8 am and reached Newcastle at 1.4½ pm., nearly four minutes ahead of schedule. As far as Doncaster timings were inside schedule, but owing to the derailment of some wagons at Arksey, it was necessary to slow down and finally to stop, because of single line working ahead. By Darlington the lost time had been regained and the average speed for the whole journey was 67½mph. The highest speed recorded was 88mph just north of Hitchin. The driver of the outward run was H. Gutteridge and his fireman A. Wightman.

'At Gateshead sheds "Papyrus" was found to be in excellent condition and was used for the return journey with W. Sparshatt as driver and R. Webster as fireman.'

They were, of course, reprising their role from the November tests. Sparshatt was a driver known to

The key to locomotive testing in the 1930s – a fully equipped LNER dynamometer car. It didn't have the facilities or refinements of the Vitry test centre, but it did serve a useful purpose when the company wished to record a particularly fast run, or simply measure performance.

Papyrus shortly before the March run. A little earlier she'd spent five days in the works at Doncaster presumably to make sure she was fit for this big occasion. Right – setting off from King's Cross on a typical overcast day, the air laden with the beginning of a smog so familiar in London at that time. Conditions throughout the day were reported as dry, but cloudy.

push an engine to its limits and so appears to have been carefully chosen for this high-profile job, though on this occasion one way only, to spare poor Bob Webster and his shovel.

'At 3.47 pm the return journey was begun. As far as Grantham schedule times only were kept as long slack was necessary north of Doncaster at the scene of the derailed coal train, but after this driver Sparshatt took the opportunity of showing what his engine could do. For over 12 miles from Corby and down the long drop from Stoke Box to Tallington, the average speed was over 100mph and just south of Little Bytham 105.5mph was registered for 30 seconds, and for 10 seconds it reached 108mph. This it may be confidently asserted marks a world's record for speed.

'The whole journey from Newcastle to King's Cross was completed in 3 hrs 51mins at an average speed of 69.6mph. The train had thus covered 536.4 miles in 7 hrs 47½ mins.

'At the AGM meeting of the LNER, held on the 8th, in London, Mr William Whitelaw, the chairman, said the trial run was so encouraging that they would give immediate consideration to the question of putting on a record speed train, to be called the 'Silver Jubilee', between King's Cross and Newcastle in the autumn.'

The trial was again deemed a success and produced times far better than those predicted for the SVT 877 over this route and with this any interest in acquiring the German built railcar seems to have ended. But was purchase ever a realistic possibility? Probably not, on a number of counts. Even in 1935 and '36, Britain and Germany were entering into an arms race as Nazi ambitions became clearer. So, neither side would have been likely to sell new technology to each other at this time and government permission would undoubtedly have been required to do so if it had been proposed. This was nowhere more apparent than with Maybach's, who were producing cutting edge diesel engines to power tanks and half-tracks for the German army. To have sold engines of a similar type to the British at that time would have been akin to Rolls-Royce selling Merlins to the Luftwaffe. Gresley received a taste of this when visiting Germany to see SVT 877 in operation. During the tour, he was blocked from visiting the maintenance facilities and viewing the inner workings of the design and its engines.

In addition to this, investing a substantial sum of money in procuring railcars from overseas meant less new production in this country. With times still harsh for many people and industry struggling to keep its head above water, this might have meant substantial redundancies, without increased profits to offset the costs. So, to buy machinery in large quantities from overseas made little sense economically or socially at that time.

Finally, there is the question of political and cultural attitudes to address. By his own admission, Gresley saw Germany as presenting a serious technological and military threat to Britain. On one hand, this meant that the Germans were developing a more modern rail system and investing heavily in further improvements which would feed its war machine. On the other hand, it meant that the LNER would actively be supporting this regime with a large influx of foreign capital to cover production and spares supply. Gresley, like many others, probably sensed the coming of war and so would have shied away from such a substantial commercial venture with a potential enemy. Far better to go with a British built option and support the home economy, proving, in the process, and in a most graphic way, what his country could do.

While outline planning for the new locomotive and carriages had been going on for many months, the bulk of the work was only completed in the weeks following the record run in March. Even allowing for this early preparation, there must have been a scramble to get everything completed on time once the go ahead was finally given. A tremendous weight of work then fell on Robert Thom and the Works at Doncaster, as well as Tom Street and drawing office staff responsible for locomotive and carriage design. Eric Bannister caught a flavour of this time when, following his transfer to the Drawing Office in 1935, he wrote:

'This was an exciting time at Doncaster. The detailed design work was started on the A4 Pacifics by Mr E. Windle, mainly on the cylinders. The design of the 250 psi boiler was begun by boiler

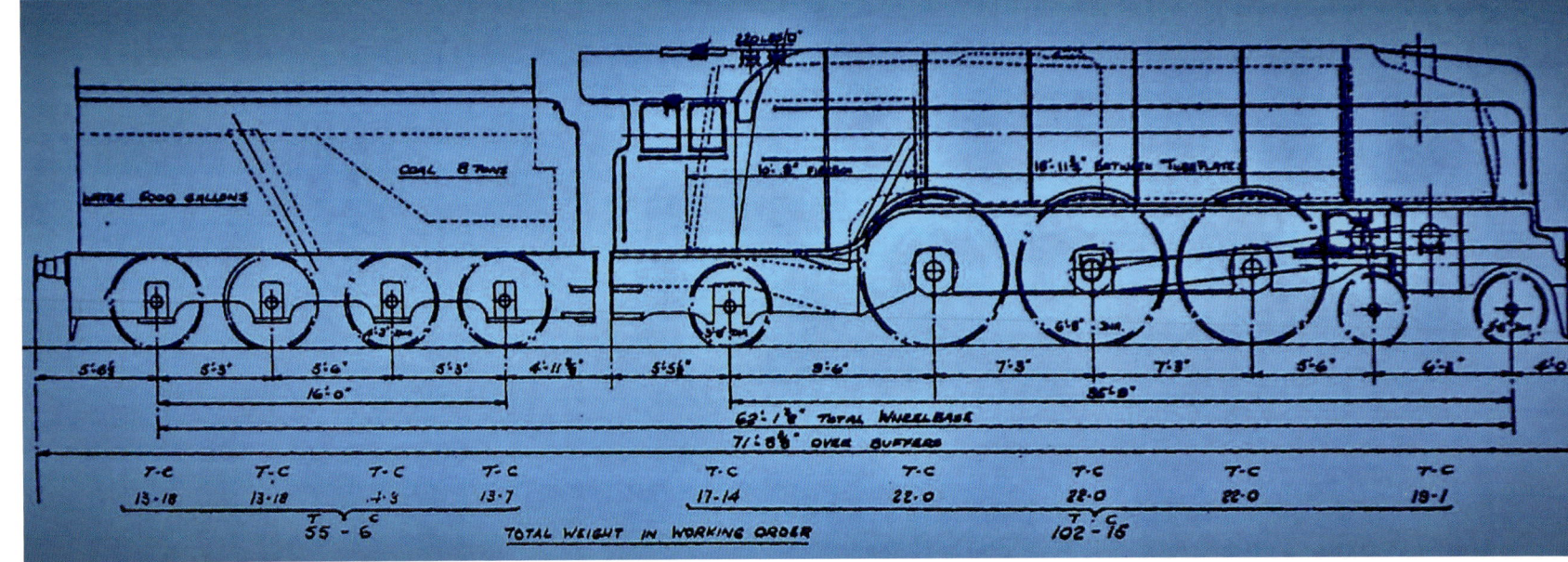

Early in the project when shape was being considered this diagram was prepared and circulated for comment. Quite simply it was an A4 with P2 outline. But by this time the P2s were themselves undergoing re-design and the Johansen tested solution came to the fore.

draughtsman, Mr Hibberling and Mr Street was working with some ideas of measuring the overthrow of the Gresley 2:1 valve gear on the centre cylinder in response to a letter from King's Cross. Mr Gresley used to do the overall designs and send most of the detailed design work to his team at Doncaster.'

With Bulleid absent in France with P2 until February, and then following this up with a period of assessment, Gresley and Spencer together pressed ahead with the A4 and its carriages. Spencer did many drawings himself, following long discussions with the CME, and was supported in this by staff in the small drawing office set up at King's Cross.

With the project being assigned the EO number 341A in 1934 to allow purchase of material to commence, work quickly got underway. With his hand on the project's pulse, Spencer was at the centre of all that happened and so his recollections are critical to understanding the 'whys and wherefores' of the process. His notes for the 1947 presentation to the ILocoE display his usual modesty and self-effacement, and describe the programme succinctly and without drama:

'The train trials hauled by a standard A3 Pacific demonstrated that the run could be accomplished in less than four hours under normal conditions. It was felt, however, that an economy in working and a greater margin of power would be secured if a form of streamlining could be embodied in the design of the engine and the train.'

Coal usage on 30 November and 5 March was calculated to have been 54lb. per mile and 45lb. respectively. Although showing a marked reduction between the A1 and A3 locos employed on these two occasions Gresley believed there was still considerable room for improvement:

'As far as the engine was concerned it was of vital importance that any modifications made to reduce air resistance should not prevent steam and smoke being lifted clear of the cab front windows when working at high speed and early cut-offs. For this reason, it was decided to adopt the horizontal wedge form of front end.

'Various forms of chimney were tried during wind tunnel experiments carried out at the City and Guild Engineering College [an institution affiliated with Imperial College and based at Finsbury within walking distance of King's Cross] in connection with

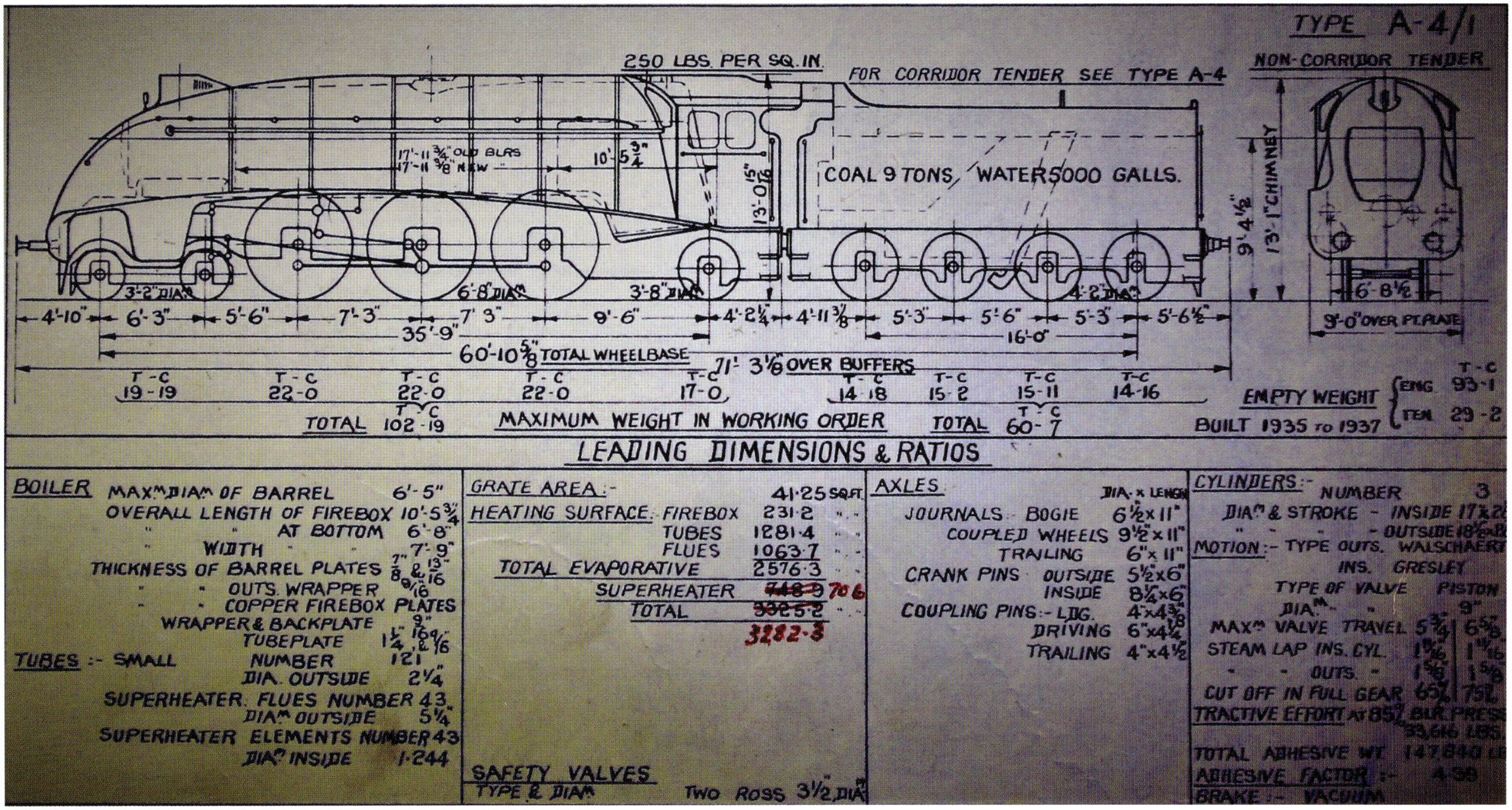

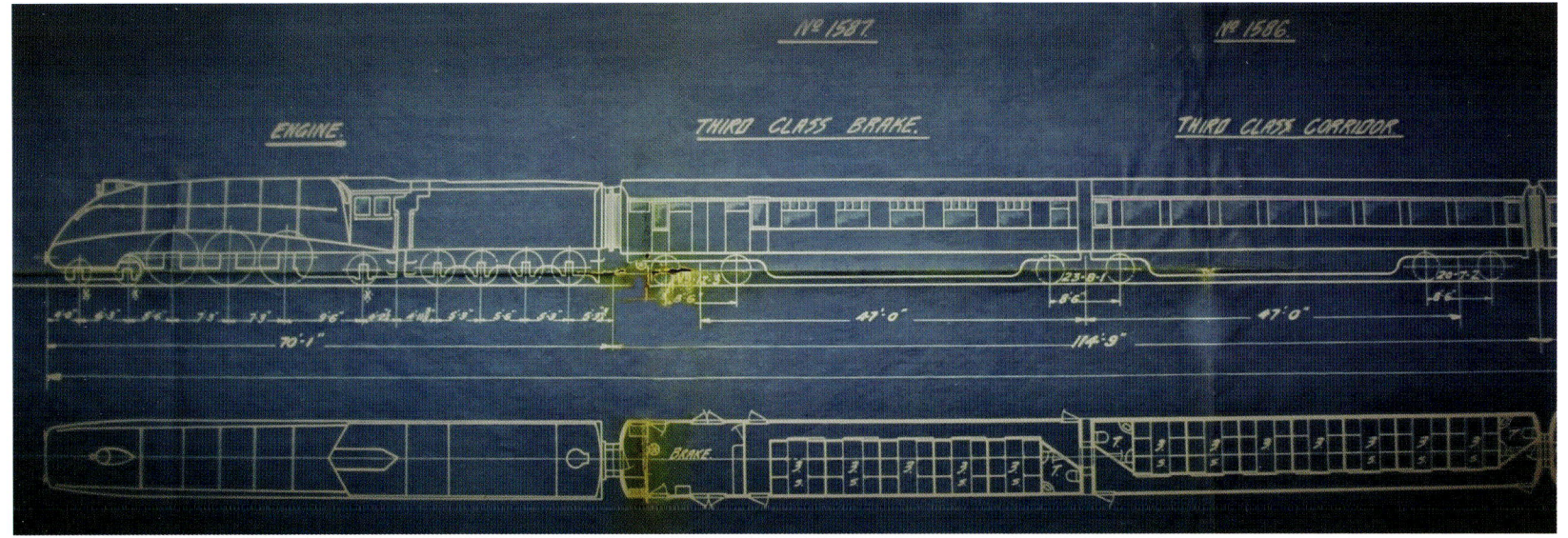

Two more drawings preserved by Bert Spencer showing the outline specification for the A4 and (below) a battered blueprint showing the engine and its first two articulated carriages. Some of the measures to reduce air resistance are demonstrated. The train is very clearly an expression of all Gresley had worked towards in his long career.

The first A4, No. 2509, takes shape at Doncaster in July 1935, the framing for her distinctive nose and cut down boiler are only too clear.

smoke lifting, before the design of the outer casing now fitted, which also houses the anti-vacuum valve, was evolved [sometime in 1934].

'It was originally intended to carry the casing back to the level of the boiler to form a straight line from the chimney top to the cab roof, but, whilst such an arrangement was satisfactory in a head wind, a wind other than head-on caused an increase in air pressure on the windward side of the boiler and a reduced air pressure on the lee side which tended to draw down the smoke and obscure the look-out. The difficulty was overcome by cutting down the casing at the rear of the chimney and this permitted a flow of air below the level of the chimney top.

'Experiments were carried out at the NPL with scale models of the streamlined Pacific engine and an ordinary Pacific engine to determine the comparative head-on wind resistance and to calculate the horsepower required at various speeds to overcome the air resistance.'

These were tests Frederick Johansen attended, according to his papers. Presumably he had slipped back

Speed, Competition, Art Deco, Aerodynamics and the Science of Publicity (1935) • 219

Even though Robert Thom was still several years from retirement when the first A4s appeared he decided to end the journal he had begun so many years earlier with this entry. Was it the high spot of his career that was unlikely to be equalled?

This posed photograph shows 2509 nearing completion in August 1935, with another Pacific on the road beside her. This presents an interesting picture demonstrating how the casing was shaped and put together. Some would complain about the time taken to assemble the casing and the way it interfered with servicing these engines. But as Alfred Ewer, who would become Running Superintendent at Doncaster after the war, said 'this may have been the case but it didn't add greatly to the time taken to turn these engines round or keep them running. In any case the men who worked with the A4s were too proud of having them in their care to grumble. They were the best and they all knew it and enjoyed the privilege'.

into his old role as an advisor to Gresley again, though employed by Hartley full-time. Once again this suggests a high degree of co-operation between competitors. However, he was using the facilities at Teddington to test streamlined shapes for the LMS at this time and was also assisting in wind tunnel tests for Supermarine and Hawkers, so the duties may have been combined. During 1936, the LMS would build their own scaled down wind tunnel at Derby and so the need for him to work at the NPL site on locomotive related tasks diminished somewhat. He still continued supporting Supermarine and Hawkers in their efforts to design the Spitfire and Hurricane respectively, but that was another matter. Spencer continued:

'Several modifications were made in the basic three-cylinder Pacific design to ensure freer running and an ample reserve of power for fast uphill working. The boiler pressure was increased from 220 lb. to 250 lb.per sq in., and a distance between the tube-plates was reduced from 19ft. to 17 ft/8in., the combustion chamber length being increased accordingly.

'The three 18½ in. by 26 in. cylinders were provided with valves increased from 8 in. to 9in. diameter and particular attention was paid to the size and shape of steam and exhaust passages. In the actual castings the passages were carefully examined and all roughness removed. Standard Pacific valve gear, with full gear cut-off restricted to 65%, was fitted.

'In order to reduce stopping distances the brake power on the engine was increased from 66% to 93% of the adhesive weight, as compared with the A3 class, and on the tender from 53% to 62% of the weight in working order. The centres of the laminated springs on the coupled wheels were increased from 3ft. 6in. to 4ft. and the flexibility was increased from .135in. to .27in. per ton to ensure good riding qualities and to limit the unloading effect in the event of the engine rolling at high speed. Forty per cent of the reciprocating weight was balanced.

'As originally built the A4 class had bogie control springs giving initial loading of 2 tons and a maximum loading of 4.55 tons at 4in. throw over. It is apparent that more wear was taking place on the flanges of the leading coupled wheels than on the driving or trailing wheels and the initial loading on the bogie control was subsequently increased by 4 tons with a maximum loading of 7 tons. At the same time, the control on the trailing carrying wheels was reduced by altering the inclination of the Cartazzi slides from 1 in 7 to 1 in 10.66.'

The construction of 2509 and carriages in time to meet the September deadline was a daunting task by any standards, especially when set against all the other work that had to be undertaken in the workshops at Doncaster. It fell to Robert Thom to mastermind the programme and drive it to a successful conclusion. Each week he was faced with myriad demands and, judging by the files that remain, he received many notes and phone calls from Gresley seeking updates, making changes or simply offering encouragement and support. Even for someone of Thom's undoubted talent and determination, it was a tall order, but imperceptibly the project gradually came together and the first two A4s progressed along the production line at Doncaster. 2510 was only marginally behind in construction and seems to have benefitted from the lessons learnt in constructing her sister, particularly in the way the casing plates were put together to achieve the streamlined shape. This issue was complicated by discussions that went on throughout the summer about the extent of aerodynamic shaping. There was a growing feeling that the practice followed in Germany and the USA, where casing continued down almost to track level around the whole locomotive and tender, then curved in under the frames, should be adopted in Britain to fully exploit the streamlining concept. But with September rapidly approaching, practicalities didn't permit this development. It is hard to say whether this was an idea Gresley initiated or not, though by encouraging Bulleid to produce side valances suggests this might have been the way his thoughts were going.

With this issue side-lined, or rejected completely, 2509 emerged in September to be admired and photographed. Journalists were invited to look over her and quickly wrote their articles, each praising the engine's unique look and speculating on its likely performance. They also described the carriages being developed in parallel with the locomotive. Quite often rolling stock was overlooked in favour of motive power, even though it provided the main commercial element of many projects. But these vehicles embraced many ideas Gresley and Norman Newsome, who succeeded Frank Day as his Carriage and Wagon Assistant in the mid-1930s, had been developing over many years, including articulation, streamlining, capacity, comfort and styling, so were worthy of closer analysis.

Speed, Competition, Art Deco, Aerodynamics and the Science of Publicity (1935) • 221

The distinctive and unforgettable shape of the first A4 emerges at Doncaster for publicity photos in early September 1935, painted in colours to celebrate the king's Silver Jubilee. Robert Thom posted these pictures in his album, with pride of place going to the lower photo which shows him and the works managers enjoying the engine's 'launch'.

The principle of articulation which Gresley had begun to develop many years earlier, and which he patented in one form or another in 1908, 1910 and 1922, came together in the Silver Jubilee design. Using axle trucks as couplings had proved successful on some commuter trains and allowed the GNR to convert old six wheeled carriages into longer more effective units. But their

2509 as she appeared in September 1935 when making her first appearance in London. Bullied later claimed that he suggested side valancing over the wheels when Gresley was reputed to have said to him 'something should be done about the streamlining of the cylinders and running board'. Whether it improved the aerodynamic efficiency of the engine is hard to assess, wind tunnel tests seeming to have been based on models without these aerofoil side valances being fitted. Some believed they were unnecessary, made servicing difficult and restricted airflow around moving parts, so losing any cooling effect.

Silver Jubilee's articulation and streamlining in close up. The skirts extend down to near track level and the gap between the carriages is covered by 'special aluminium finished rubber sheeting'.

A high standard third class compartment.

The *Jubilee's* publicity brochure.

The splendour of Silver Jubilee's first class restaurant car.

fixed nature, by comparison with carriages with simple couplings, did not always prove popular in running departments, due to lack of flexibility in stabling and use. But on the high speed, exclusive services Gresley planned they came into their own.

An article appearing in the *Railway Gazette* on 20 September 1935 waxed long and lyrical about the comfort of these carriages, luxuriating in the Art Deco colours, shapes and fittings used, before moving on to the many technical innovations Gresley had introduced. These included streamlining, of course, but also covered such things as ventilation, use of lightweight materials, insulation and much more. There is little doubt that these carriages provided a high degree of comfort for passengers in each class compartment and showed Gresley and Newsome's eye for detail.

With all this work successfully completed, *Silver Link* finally entered traffic and after the briefest of running in periods made her way to London, with her new rake of coaches, to undertake a 'press run'. Over the years these had become a major media event with companies seeking to do something special and tap into a rich and immediate vein of publicity. But it could be a double edged sword, as the LMS discovered in August 1933 on a press junket with its new Princess Royal Pacific, No 6200. Near Stafford, it suffered from an overheating driving box, which then caught fire. With the fire extinguished and with no spare engine close by to help, the engine was forced to limp the rest of the way to Crewe with its capricious passengers witnessing the debacle first hand. But they were gentler times then, with journalists seeming happy to give someone the benefit of the doubt, or they may simply have been 'sozzled' or feared being excluded from future events if too critical.

Silver Link departs from King's Cross on 27 September on what proved to be an exceptional inaugural run by any standards.

Speed, Competition, Art Deco, Aerodynamics and the Science of Publicity (1935) • 225

Power and beauty all rolled into one – a photo kept and framed by Bert Spencer.

Mid-journey on the 27th. There has been speculation that it is Gresley who is waving to those on the trackside. He was a showman by nature and would have enjoyed the occasion, so it might have been him, but confirmation is impossible so long after the event.

Silver Link arrives under the curved roof of Newcastle Station on 27 September. Gresley holds court on the footplate – one of his favourite locations - his presence reported as being enjoyed by the crew with whom he seems to have had an easy relationship.

Nevertheless, *Silver Link* performed admirably on 27 September and garnered wonderful publicity for herself, the train and the company in the process. The mood of the day was captured in the words of one journalist who wrote in his headline grabbing article:

'Yesterday afternoon on its trial run, the LNER's streamline train, "Silver Jubilee", reached a speed of 112mph. This is the fastest speed ever attained by a steam locomotive in this country. But almost more astonishing than this sudden burst of speed was the average kept up mile after mile – 104.9mph for 27 miles between Hitchin and Huntingdon, 96.9mph from Hatfield to Laxley and 921.1mph for 70 miles from Wood Green to Fletton.

'It was rumoured that the "Silver Link" – that strange looking engine that resemble, according to the mood, either a war tank coloured silver and black or a monster from the primeval age – could have drawn its 270 ton load at a good 120mph. At the highest speed the sensation was exhilarating. The train seemed to skim over the rails rather than to run on wheels.

'Sir Ralph Wedgwood, Chief General Manager of the company, expressed his confidence that the train will run at a profit. "There is complete safety," he emphasised. "This is not an experiment. It is the fastest long-distance train in this country, and if you interpret the words 'long distance' to mean over 200 miles it is the fastest long-distance train in the world – oil, diesel or steam".

'"It is the finest engine we ever had," said Driver Taylor on his return to King's Cross. "At 112mph she does not vibrate so much as other engines going at 80mph. We could easily have gone faster if we had wanted to – we were not all out by any means".

'The Silver Jubilee missed a world record by 8mph. A new streamlined steam engine, drawing a train of 200 tons, reached a speed of 119.8mph – on an official run on the Berlin-Hamburg line in June.'

Whether by design or chance, the first two DRG Class 05s had spent the months since construction in 1935, and just before 2509 appeared, undergoing high speed tests, amongst other things. In many ways, they were experimental locomotives and were maintained for trials only, with no obvious intention of providing a genuine high-speed service such as that planned by the LNER. So they were rather like racing cars, tuned up for short, sharp sprints, with longevity or endurance remaining untested, but like racing cars, they could make a 'big splash' and gather great headlines for the cause. The truth is that the A4s could do it day in day out in good or bad conditions such was the effectiveness of their design.

On 30 September, *Silver Link* began the serious business of running a challenging schedule and making money; a role she would undertake by herself until October when 2510, named *Quicksilver*

2510, *Quicksilver* at Doncaster in late September 1935 as her sister draws much attention running to Newcastle.

HORSE-POWER SAVED BY STREAMLINING.

	Horse-power required to overcome head-on air resistance.									
Speed, m.p.h.	60	70	80	90	100	110	120	130	140	150
Standard " Pacific " type.	97.21	154.26	230.51	328.49	450.92	599.39	778.65	988.95	1235.87	1520.80
Streamlined type.	56.39	89.41	133.61	190.40	261.36	347.41	451.32	573.21	716.32	881.48
Horse-power saved by streamlining.	40.82	64.85	96.90	138.09	189.56	252.98	327.33	415.74	519.55	639.32

To prove the benefits of streamlining Bert Spencer produced this chart during his 1947 presentation. It was a debate that rumbled on until the end of steam with entrenched opinions, either way, making debate difficult. To some it is a matter of aesthetics, not science. However, Thomas Henry Turner, in commenting on the paper, added one very interesting view. He was recorded as saying, 'The idea of Sir Nigel's Pacific locomotive's streamline was to blow up the dirty, opaque smoke by means of clean, transparent air. The chimney projects so that the smoke can be swept away, leaving a layer of clean air below it against the Bugatti like front end. The LNER streamline thus tends to give transparent air free from steam and smoke along the boiler and aids the driver's view ahead. It also decreases the objectionable thump when express engines meet and pass one another at speed'.

completed her work up and joined her sister in service. Soon two became four with the arrival of 2511, *Silver King* in November and 2512, *Silver Fox* in December. More would continue to arrive until the class was complete in 1938. By Christmas, Gresley could look back on a year of great endeavour and the creation of a masterpiece that few, he felt, could question, such was its electrifying performance and impact.

Bert Spencer, as a good deputy, fully supported Gresley at all times, but was not blind to any shortcomings in his work. His judgement was sound and well balanced when evaluating success. So, as one would expect, his 1947 presentation is a model of fairness and impartiality when assessing the CME's work, even when it is the A4. However, he clearly took great pride in these engines and found it difficult not to suppress his feelings on the subject, although he hinted and understated rather than praised directly:

'Thirty-five of these engines were built and in addition to working the high speed trains, took turns on the heaviest main line duties. Four were fitted with double chimneys and one of these, No. 4468, 'Mallard', attained a speed of 125mph during brake trials on 3 July 1938, with 236 ½ tons behind the tender. By 1938 the popularity of the high speed trains was firmly established and it was clear that a demand for longer and heavier trains would eventually arise.'

When any criticism of these engines or Gresley's designs in

During 1936, due to the success of the *Silver Jubilee* train set on the run to Newcastle, it was proposed that there be a similar service from King's Cross to Aberdeen. Trials with a dynamometer car were held using 2511, *Silver King*, and she is caught on a test run between Newcastle and Edinburgh at speed passing through Morpeth on a rainy day. She gathers interested glances whilst a pet dog tries to pull its owner away.

Harringay in early 1936 as 2510 thunders through. Tom Coleman, the LMS's Chief Draughtsman, kept this photo, one of many A4 pictures he acquired. Robert Thom, his friend, also ensured that Coleman rode on the footplate several times and had a set of design drawings. This is quite remarkable considering the level of competition between both companies. It is rumoured that Coleman was considered as a replacement for Thom at Doncaster and he appears in an LNER photo to mark the occasion of his retirement.

general cropped up during the discussions that followed, both he and Bulleid leapt to their leader's defence and there were many occasions when this happened – the A4, Gresley's conjugated valve gear and his preference for three cylinders. But one in particular struck a discordant note with both men during the 1947 presentation – the issue of over-running of the centre cylinder which was fitted with the Gresley gear. Spencer replied:

'No indicator diagrams were taken on the A4 class engines as the streamlined casing made it impracticable to find accommodation for an operator and direct reading instruments were not available. Diagrams had been taken on the A3 class engines and Mr Peppercorn had kindly given permission for a selection from engine No. 2751 to be published. It will be noted that the area of the centre cylinder diagram is not affected to any material extent until speeds of 60mph and over are reached at early cut-offs. Above this speed there is some difference in the power developed between the outside and inside cylinders, but the fact remains that engines fitted with this form of conjugated valve gear ran successfully and economically.'

Engineers, like any other professional group, will chip away at past achievements and analyse results ad nauseum, especially if these accomplishments were boosted by the sort of headlines Gresley's work attracted. Professional jealousy perhaps, but some genuinely believed that in his work form had triumphed over function and over the years, rightly or wrongly, their voices grew louder.

Chapter 8
FETE AND FATED (1936–41)

'After Silver Link had run so successfully and the A4s began entering production in large numbers there was a sense of anti-climax at King's Cross. There were many plaudits, of course, and much to assess, but for a while it seemed that a peak had been reached and only a downward path remained. Though full of energy and interest it took some time for Sir Nigel to find his old form and when he did it was electrification that seemed to engage him most.'

So wrote Bert Spencer shortly before his death in 1968. It seems inevitable that an individual reaching retirement age should begin to slow down, contemplate their successes and failures, then consider what might lie ahead. In Gresley's case, the A4 programme was a high point reached in a period of great enterprise and exploration which had been sparked by the death of his wife in 1929. Even allowing for the greatness of the man, these achievements were unlikely to be equalled and such an effort unlikely to be sustained with old age beckoning. But the drive and ambition which lay at the centre of all he did could not simply be switched off and, in due course, new challenges presented themselves to him. They may not have had the glamour or scientific interest of his Pacific, W1 and P2 projects, but they involved a future beyond steam and were stimulating nonetheless. As Spencer observed, electrification was back on the agenda, if it had ever gone away. The chronic restraints on money caused by the Great War, followed by the slump of the early 1930s, were finally beginning to lift and investment in long term infrastructure and equipment projects was possible. By 1936, income had increased to £9.1m from a low of £7.7m in 1933 and this rose to £10.1m the following year.

With margins slowly increasing, the LNER board felt able to move ahead with two phases of their long-planned electrification programme, to sit alongside the continuing development of steam locomotives. It was an activity also

The CME enjoying the luxury he has shaped, timing his creation in the process.

With A4s taking all the plaudits and electrification again on the agenda, Gresley's A1/A3 Pacifics continued to do their good work, rarely grabbing the headlines as they had once done.

encouraged by central government, where concerns were growing that this technology was not being developed as quickly or as cohesively as it might be. As a result, William Weir was appointed to review electrical supplies and the way the power industry managed these resources, then consider its wider usage in other industries such as the railways. A committee was formed, on which Ralph Wedgwood sat, and after much deliberation, in which Gresley participated, recommendations were produced which led to the 1926 Electricity Supply Act. Over the next decade, as the number of power stations increased, industry, most notably the railways, were encouraged to make use of the ever-expanding national grid, but with recession and stagnation biting, this proved difficult.

The first of these involved the LNER's heavily graded Woodhead Line from Sheffield to Manchester and Wath across the Pennines, which had become a major route for carrying coal, with passenger numbers increasing also. The second focussed on commuter routes from Liverpool Street and Fenchurch Street stations to Shenfield in Essex and Stratford.

In each case, scoping studies were commissioned by Gresley, with the results published in 1935/36 and both reports demonstrated, very clearly, the benefits to be derived from these proposals. There seems little doubt that the CME embraced both projects with great enthusiasm, although neither had the kudos of his main line steam ventures. So here we see Gresley as a moderniser, seeing beyond the age of steam, because there seems little doubt that the march of electrification would be unstoppable. More importantly, it would also play to Britain's industrial strengths and rely for power on a generation system based on coal and not imported oil. By the 1930s, Britain had a

A wide variety of types on shed in the 1930s before the A4s began to appear in any number. The results of Gresley's big engine policy are only too apparent.

string of more than seventy coal burning power stations, which, through the 1926 Electricity Act, produced a standardised voltage of 132kV. This had revolutionised power generation in this country and allowed industry, including the railways, to develop in many new directions and locations.

The cost of developing the Shenfield lines was estimated at £3.4m, with this outlay spread over a four or five year period. However, it was predicted that this investment would increase traffic from 1.4 million loaded train miles per annum to at least 2 million or more and reduce operating costs by a third. The Pennine link produced similar figures making both projects capable of a return on the company's investment in a 10 to 12 year period, even without the offsetting effect of any work needed to keep steam running on these routes. With the Southern Railway's electrification programme acting as a guiding light, the LNER's own experience of running a similar system around Tyneside and the savings to be achieved, the company approved both projects in 1936. While all this was happening, the London Passenger Transport Board, which had been formed in 1933, were producing their own plan for the electrification of other suburban lines and the extension of tube routes. Gresley was part of this work and acted as advisor to the LPTB, so ensuring both projects were co-ordinated and proceeded along common lines.

The CME had already begun considering rolling stock needs before electrification plans were approved, investigating possible solutions with Metropolitan-Vickers and other contractors. While tube lines in London were powered by a fourth 'live' rail, lack of clearance in tunnels not being conducive to overhead wires, no such limitation applied to the

LNER. So their commuter lines, plus the Pennine route, and any other project in the future, would be built using a 1500V direct current passed through catenary wires to pantographs mounted on the roofs of locomotives and powered cars. After many years of development by a number of companies around the world, this was a concept that was well understood and Gresley already had a team of electrical engineers in place to help him formulate his ideas. However, it was a solution rejected by the Southern Railway who adopted a third 660V DC 'live' rail solution in the inter-war period.

To lead his development team, Gresley had very astutely head hunted Henry Richards in 1924 from the Southern Railway. Before then, he had worked for AEG, then the London, Brighton and South Coast Railway as the Electrical Traction Engineer, where he'd made a name for himself developing some of the earliest electric trains. Under him as deputy was the Australian Harry Swift, recruited specifically from English Electric in 1936 to support the LNER projects. Then there were Alfred Hopking, who for many years had worked for de Havilland designing aircraft before joining Metro-Vicks, and Alexander Emerson, who had been a premium apprentice under Gresley before becoming a senior draughtsman in his Electrical Engineering Department. In addition, Tom Street and Bert Spencer had shown a particular interest in these projects and would become closely involved in this work as well. Following Gresley's death in 1941, Street would in fact become Chief Draughtsman to Richards when he was created Chief Electrical Engineer. Of these six men it would be Emerson who would do most work in preparing specifications for the locomotives and multiple units for these lines. By 1936, in anticipation of approval to proceed from the board, his work was well advanced.

In formulating his ideas, Gresley looked to Metropolitan-Vickers, English Electric and Metropolitan-Cammell for advice. Vickers had, in the 1920s, built 3ft 6 in gauge Bo-Bo and Co-Co electric locomotives for South African railways and Gresley visited that country with his son Roger to see them in

(Left) Henry Richards hovers behind Oliver Bulleid whilst on a visit to the Romney, Hythe and Dymchurch Railway. Richards was a key figure in the development of electric traction in Great Britain, but his contribution has been largely overlooked. With an eye to the future Gresley recruited him in 1924 and he rose to become Chief Electrical Engineer, before joining BR and retiring in the early 1950s.

(Right) Harry Swift was born in South Australia and attended university in Adelaide where he gained a degree in engineering. He travelled to Europe in 1913 and found employment with Siemens Schukert in Berlin and was interned as an enemy alien from 1914 to 1919. From then until 1936 he was employed by English Electric and took the lead in the electrification of railways in South Africa and also worked in Denmark and Poland

Alexander Hockley Emerson, who played a key role in the LNER's electrification plans and would later become Resident Electrical Engineer in charge of the Sheffield, Manchester and Wath project. According to Bert Spencer it was Emerson who did most of the early work on designing the motive power needed to operate services on the new electrified lines.

The Metropolitan-Vickers Company designed and built electric locomotives for South Africa, here at the Daimana running shed (now Danskraal in Natal), which Gresley and his son visited during a tour of South Africa in 1938.

operation, writing of his experiences in the LNER's Journal. However, this Bo Bo design does not seem to have played a significant part in the evolution of the locomotives built for the LNER. And during 1936, it was decided that three different types would be needed to meet all the Pennine route's needs – mixed traffic, express passenger and banking locomotives, with 69, 9 and 10, respectively, being ordered. At the same time, a study to consider the commuter trains best suited for service in London produced a plan for three car multiple units. 100 of these were ordered in 1938 – ninety-two for London and eight for the Manchester to Glossop part of the Woodhead Line.

Gresley wished to press ahead and build examples of each type so that full evaluation could begin in advance of the lines being ready for new traffic. Past experience shaped his thoughts and such a crucial project couldn't be allowed to fail simply because testing hadn't fully validated the designs and it was here that Metro-Vickers' work in designing their engines for service in South Africa proved crucial. What followed may have been designed and built at Donaster, but it had its origins in the Lancashire based company's drawing office. Metro-Vickers and its supply chain were also responsible for manufacturing many parts, such as the electrical equipment.

The first batch of these engines was commissioned in 1937, but it wasn't until August 1940 that the prototype locomotive, No. 6701, was completed, the coming of war and problems with the design causing delays and problems. By this time work on the line had also been deferred, partially due to the hostilities, but also the need to complete expensive civil engineering work on a new double-track tunnel at Woodhead. And with this the project was shelved for an indeterminate period, though 6701

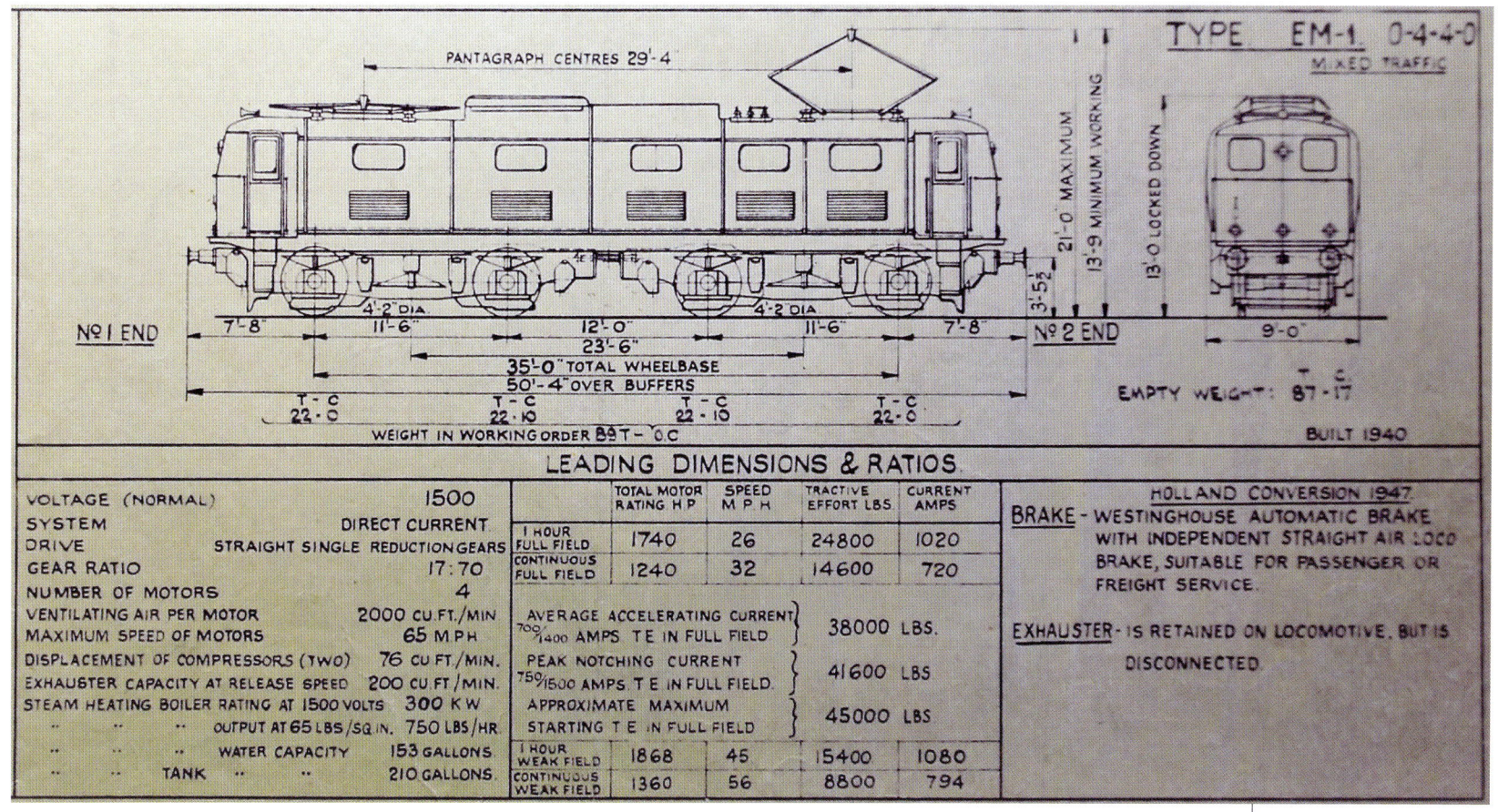

Gresley's first and last electric locomotive in detail. This prototype influenced design for many decades.

continued to be tested until October 1941 when she was placed in store 'for the duration'. Work would re-commence after the war but the long planned line only opened in 1955, long after Gresley had died.

Real progress on the Shenfield line was delayed for reasons that are unclear, but the result was that Gresley only felt able to sign the contract allowing construction to begin in 1939. With war only a few months away, further delays were inevitable and little had been completed before Germany invaded Poland. It would be ten more years before the project would be completed, but work on developing the new multiple units had advanced quite a long way before this temporary block was imposed. With many examples of this type of train already operating successfully on the Southern Railway and London's Underground system, there was considerable experience in this field and so some thought there was little merit or challenge in designing trains of this sort.

A powered box on wheels seems to have been their considered opinion, if the views expressed at the time are anything to go by. By comparison with a steam locomotive this may have been true, but to others they were the future and had to be embraced. Gresley seems to have fitted into the latter category and so the LNER design, which was capable of reaching a maximum speed of 75mph, contained many interesting features for an above ground train, including air operated sliding doors and electro-pneumatic brakes.

Design work for these units seems to have begun in 1938 at about the time Robert Thom retired. He was replaced by Edward Thompson, who had been Mechanical Engineer at Darlington since late 1933 and brought with him considerable experience of carriage design to the new post. The extent of his influence on the project isn't recorded, but one source suggests that the bogies

The LNER's prototype Bo-Bo locomotive for the Woodhead Line. Its drawgear and buffers were mounted on coupling linked bogies in such a way that there was no transmission of traction or braking force through the locomotive's body. Its design also included a regenerative braking system that allowed energy to be transferred between climbing and descending trains on steep approaches to tunnels. To provide a fine degree of control during starting and acceleration the two bogies could be controlled in series or in parallel. During testing there was found to be a problem with weight transfer when accelerating. As a result there was a reduced load on the leading bogie that seriously affected adhesion and caused wheel slip. Some believed that it was a problem that wouldn't have affected a longer, heavier Co-Co design with their two 6 wheel bogies. Early in the project this issue was discussed but cost considerations seem to have dictated the LNER's decision to go down the Bo-Bo route.

were based on his development work and much more besides. If so, in Thompson the project would probably have had a strong and experienced supporter who would lend his weight to the Doncaster based design team.

It is believed that six units were nearing completion when war was declared and were placed in store, somewhere in the Midlands, painted in a blue and cream livery. Here they remained until 1946, when the whole project was resurrected. Although these two electrification schemes were only a small part of Gresley's work, their contribution to Britain's railway history was out of all proportion to their number. In their functionality and practicality,

Fete and Fated (1936–41) • 237

These two photographs taken in 6701's cab sum up why steam locomotion had had its day. Immense power on tap and no avaricious firebox to fill, with all its attendant discomfort, and an uncluttered view ahead where everything could be seen. Some footplate crew would mourn the death of steam, but the feeling was unlikely to last when the benefits of this new technology sank in.

These two pictures were taken in 1949 when the new Shenfield service was finally commissioned. Mass movement of passengers over short stop/start routes was their primary aim, so they had to be functional in the extreme to allow large numbers to be carried. They contained a most basic standard of fixtures and fittings, with little comfort to be had, but this was and remains the nature of commuter traffic into cities during short bursts of activity each morning and evening. Even though the final design was the LNER's, the project combined the work of a number of primary suppliers. The driving units were built by the Birmingham Railway Carriage and Wagon Company at their Smethwick Works, where many of London's tube trains were constructed. Metropolitan-Cammell built the other carriages, whilst English Electric provided control equipment and Crompton Parkinson produced the 210hp traction motors.

On the way to Buckingham Palace to be knighted, his daughter, Violet, and sister, Beatrice, beside him.

they embraced the future, seeing beyond the end of steam and, for that matter, dieselisation as well. But this is how a good mind, imbued with a high degree of pragmatism and common sense, works. Always move forward in measured steps and never dwell on past triumphs or remain wedded to the stifling effects of tradition. Gresley was a master of these arts and become a man of great stature and achievement in the process.

When looking at his career, it seems that he always cultivated a wider role than simply being the LNER's CME and joined many institutions and groups that allowed him to expand his influence and interests. He was an establishment figure and a leader by nature and seems to have gravitated to roles that gave him the opportunity to use his undoubted skills to best effect. But it was during the 1930s that the level of recognition and the extent of his influence reached a peak. On one level, this meant the Presidency of IMechE and the award of a knighthood in 1936, but on another level there were a wide number of other bodies seeking to enlist his services. For a man just turning 60, whose day to day life was extremely busy and stressful, this must have been a very heavy burden indeed.

In addition to his work for the IMechE, ILocoE and IEE, he also played an active part in the labours of the International Railway Congress Association and Association of Railway Locomotive Engineers, the presidency of which also fell to him in 1936. This was no mere membership but involved presenting detailed reports on various subjects; the state of Egyptian railway workshops and improvements in steam locomotive design being just two. He may have had assistance in this work from his staff at King's Cross but the primary effort was still his. Then there were tasks he undertook away from the railway world. Following the loss of two steamships, the *Usworth* and *Blairgowrie*, during gales in the Atlantic on 14 December and 27 February 1935 respectively, initial investigations suggested that the cause might be due to the steering gear then widely in use. To aid them in their deliberations, the Board of Trade commissioned Gresley to consider this possibility by looking at this system in detail. In this he drew heavily on the NPL's expertise and trials undertaken in the testing tanks at Teddington. The committee he chaired concluded, in 1936, that the steering gear wasn't necessarily at fault and the problem probably lay elsewhere – human error or simply the severity of sea or weather conditions.

More appointments followed, three of particular note. He was co-opted on to the General Council of the British Standards Institution, to act as an advisor on a broad range of engineering matters and then became a governor of Queen Mary's College, London. This was followed by membership of two Ministry of Transport committees set up to consider the question of rail electrification and the installation of automatic train control. The GWR introduced just such a system in the first decade of the twentieth century and extending its use to the other companies was seen as a way of tackling increasing accident rates. Undoubtedly, Gresley would have observed and learnt much from Churchward's work in this field and based recommendations on the GWR's design and operation. And these were just a few of the tasks that the CME took on in the 1930s. But there was one event which, according to Bert Spencer, gave him the greatest pleasure in the last decade of his life. On 20 May 1936, an honorary Doctorate of Science was conferred on him by the University of Manchester, with Professor J.L. Stokes making the presentation. His speech contained many warm and humorous words that summed

Gresley resplendent in his robes on 6 May with Sir Christopher Needham, Chairman of the University's Council and an LNER director, beside him.

Throughout his time as CME Gresley often welcomed members of the Royal Family on tours of the facilities he managed, and occasionally attended their departures from King's Cross to their properties in the North. He became a familiar face to them. The Duke of York, in particular, showed a keen interest in railway matters and was often photographed with Gresley, even during a very relaxed visit to the Romney, Hythe and Dymchurch Railway. Here the future King George VI and the CME admire models at an engineering exhibition shortly before the 'Abdication Crisis'.

Gresley up so well, and must have brought a smile to his face:

'I present to you a designing man – the man of the articulated bogie and funnel less railway engine…. The many technical improvements he has introduced have been no mere variations on traditional themes; they have a scientific foundation in fundamentals, spring from the close study of materials and of such central problems as air resistance, fuel consumption and the balance of moving parts.

'But in him science is paired with imagination and he also has something of the artist. When the engine driver has gone the way of the highwayman and the railway has become a romantic memory, the museums of the world will compete for his masterpieces, and the silver ghost of his Jubilee train will vie with Dick Turpin for pride of place in the storied memories of the road to York.'

While there were many other things to engage his mind, the LNER would never be far from his thoughts and still exerted a huge influence on his life. For people of great substance there will rarely be release from responsibility and stress. So as the end of the 1930s approached, Gresley continued to immerse himself in railway work and an ever growing list of extra-curricular activities but his time and energy had finite limits and his reliance on his team grew considerably. Yet in a brief period he would not only lose Thom, but Bulleid as well. Meanwhile, in the background, the international situation slowly and surely deteriorated. Germany invoked its four-year re-armament plan, re-occupied the demilitarised zone of the Rhineland, regained the Sudetenland, seized Austria and Czechoslovakia and looked to the East for further gains. While this happened many in Britain sought appeasement and others looked to the Royal Navy to protect her shores, the Empire and international trade routes from the beasts growing in Germany and Japan. Time would prove what a poor policy this was, but in the meantime, life went on pretty much as usual and this was nowhere more apparent than on the railways.

While the LNER's attention seemed firmly fixed on the A4s and the development of other high-speed

A4 No. 4497, *Golden Plover*, a second batch engine that appeared in October 1937, pulls away from King's Cross for Waverley with the recently formed 'Coronation' service.

services, new construction of other types went on and streamlining was extended to the W1, P2s and B17s. But in the shadow of the 'streaks', another locomotive of great importance was taking shape. In 1936 the 2-6-2 V2 mixed traffic engine began to appear from the works at Doncaster. This proved to be the second most numerous locomotive to be built under Gresley's management and, some would say, the most successful commercially. It was also the second locomotive to be designed by a drawing office team re-organised by Gresley in 1935, the first being the A4. A short note appeared in the LNER's *Journal* in early 1936 describing the changes made:

'The CME has arranged to concentrate the designing of new locomotives in a central Drawing Office at Doncaster. Mr T. Street has been appointed Chief Locomotive Draughtsman in Charge of the new office, with Mr E. Windle and Mr D.D. Gray as his Principal Assistants. It is interesting to hear that the whole of the drawings of the "Silver Link" were prepared under Mr Street's supervision.'

Gresley's aim seems to have been to achieve greater specialisation amongst his staff. This suggests that in the past his various drawing office teams had intermingled too much with lines of demarcation between engines, rolling stock and machinery becoming blurred. The future clearly lay in providing a central focus for each area of work, with Tom Street becoming the locomotive man, whether it be steam or electric. However, in practice it does seem as though the CD retained some management control of all areas of design work, even though his primary task was to produce locomotives. So it was within this new structure that the design of the V2 came together. However, it was a proposal that had a long gestation according to Spencer, who wrote in a draft for his 1947 presentation:

'For some time (since at least 1932) a need had been felt for an engine more suited than the 2-6-0 type K3 class for express goods and passenger services. In response, during 1936, a new series of 2-6-2 type class, three cylinder engines were put into service.'

At this point, he related the story of Gresley's attempt to fill this gap with an articulated design before agreeing that the V2 was a better option. The proposed 2-6-4-4 engine was largely condemned on the grounds that fitting the brake gear and ejectors presented a 'considerable complication'. With the way clear, the Locomotive and Traffic Committee formalised this plan by turning it into a provisional programme that would see fourteen V2s built in 1935; a number reduced shortly afterwards to five. Nevertheless, with revisions being made to the design, it took until late in that year for final approval to be given and construction to commence. Spencer continued:

'Much of the design work was completed by Clifford Cocks, a senior draughtsman in the Doncaster Drawing Office, who seemed to have had a particular liking for 2-6-2 engines. These engines have 6ft. 2in. diameter coupled wheels and 18 ½ in.

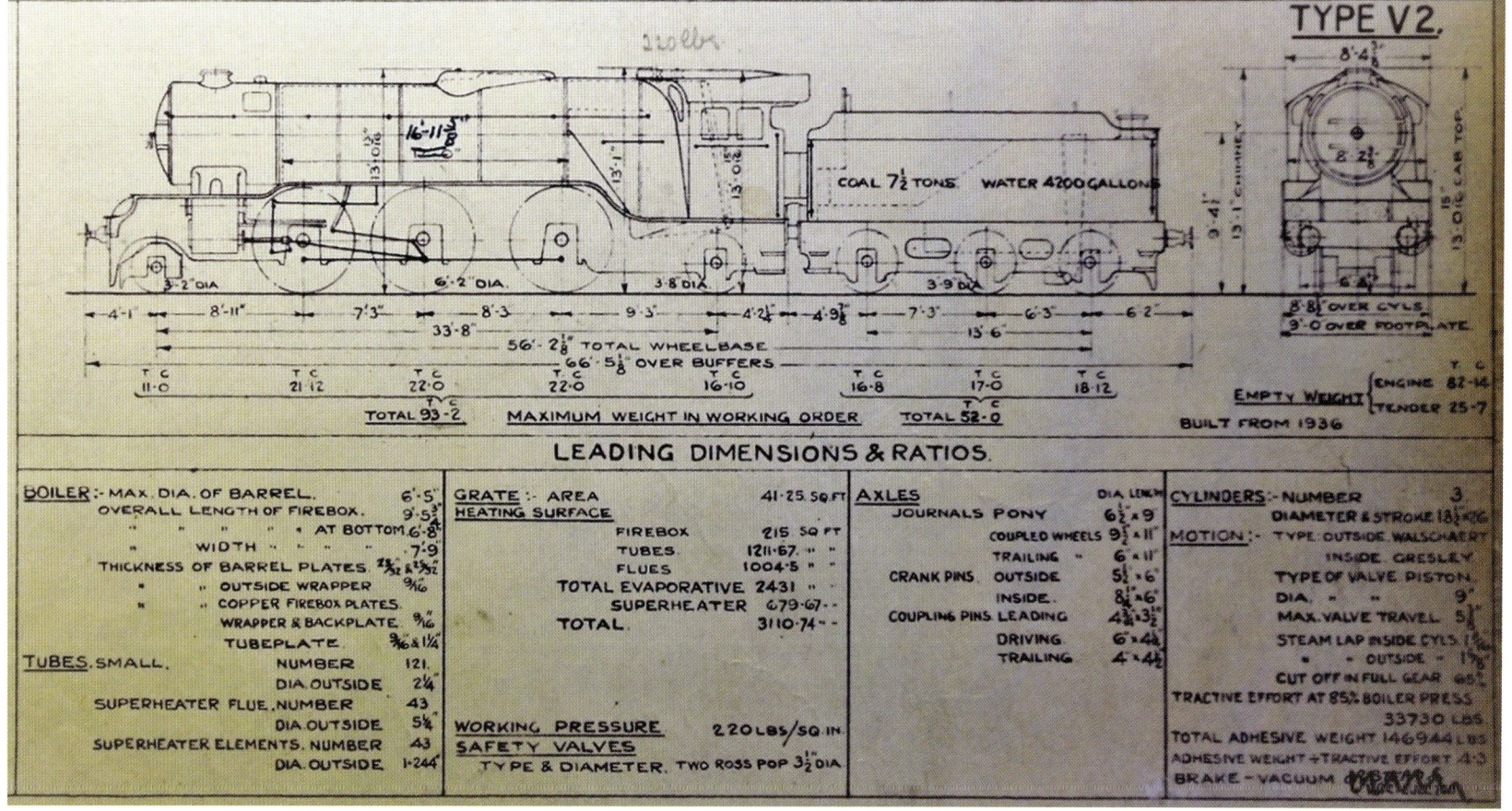

The V2 in outline.

by 26 in. cylinders, with 9in. diameter valves. The 6ft. 5in. diameter boiler carries a working pressure of 220lb/sq in., and follows the design of the A3 class boiler, with the distance between the tubeplates being reduced from 18ft. 11¾ in., to 17 ft (and a 'banjo' steam collector replacing the A3 type traditional dome). Gresley valve gear is arranged in front of the cylinders, which drive on the second coupled axle.

'When discussions were taking place regarding the maximum traffic availability of the V2 class there was some criticism because of the engine being too long for certain outlying turntables at that time used by the K3 class engines. The suggestion that the K3 should be retained as the highest powered engine on the routes affected was not acceptable as it was considered that they were not really suitable for the high speeds required.'

In the short time available for his paper to be read, Spencer was limited in what he could say about the design, but there was much more he could have added. At one stage, streamlining was considered, though in the event this idea doesn't seem to have been developed to a model testing stage, let alone to the final design. One can only wonder why this was so, especially with the A4s being produced in such numbers at that time and the P2s and two B17s to follow shortly. Perhaps it was simply a case of the Drawing Office lacking the time to design and test the casing or it may have been that Gresley was otherwise engaged in what was proving to be a very busy year.

Other design features included wider spacing of the coupled wheels, compared with the A3s, and a slightly longer wheelbase. The cylinders were contained in a Monobloc casting which incorporated the smokebox saddle, outside steam pipes and steam chest. There was a simple blastpipe arrangement and the large cab adopted a wedge shape from the A4,

The first of the class nearing completion at Doncaster. Although the initial batch of five were assembled here, plus twenty more later, the remaining 159 would be constructed at Darlington between 1937 and '44.

A new V2, No. 4774, the fourth of the class, appearing to make light of its load. Surprisingly, only eight of these engines were named. 4774 was part of the large mass that wasn't and remained anonymous, unusual for such large express locomotives.

having proven successful in lifting the exhaust away from the driver's line of sight. However, a standard 7½ ton, 4,200 gallon capacity six wheeled tender was used, which in service restricted their range for comparison with the Pacifics.

The 22 ton axle loading of these engines limited their use considerably as it did the A3s and A4s. With this restriction in mind, and with a perceived need for a more powerful mixed traffic engine to work over the rest of the network, the possibility of building a lighter version to achieve this wider route availability began to be explored. This did not happen immediately and even when the first two of the new V4 class appeared, in early 1941, it was a thought to be a speculative venture. But as the V2s began to roll out of the workshops, this was still far in the future and in the meantime there were more pressing matters to manage, two significant departures amongst them.

Bulleid had worked with Gresley on and off since 1905 and had risen to a senior position under the CME's guiding hand. It had been an important relationship for both men, but an ambitious assistant will always wish to lead and experience the freedom that such a promotion brings. With Gresley showing no signs of retiring in the foreseeable future, and with no guarantee that the job would be his if he did, Bulleid must have pondered his future and when he looked at each of the Big Four companies, they all seemed to have CMEs who showed no signs of departing. But this

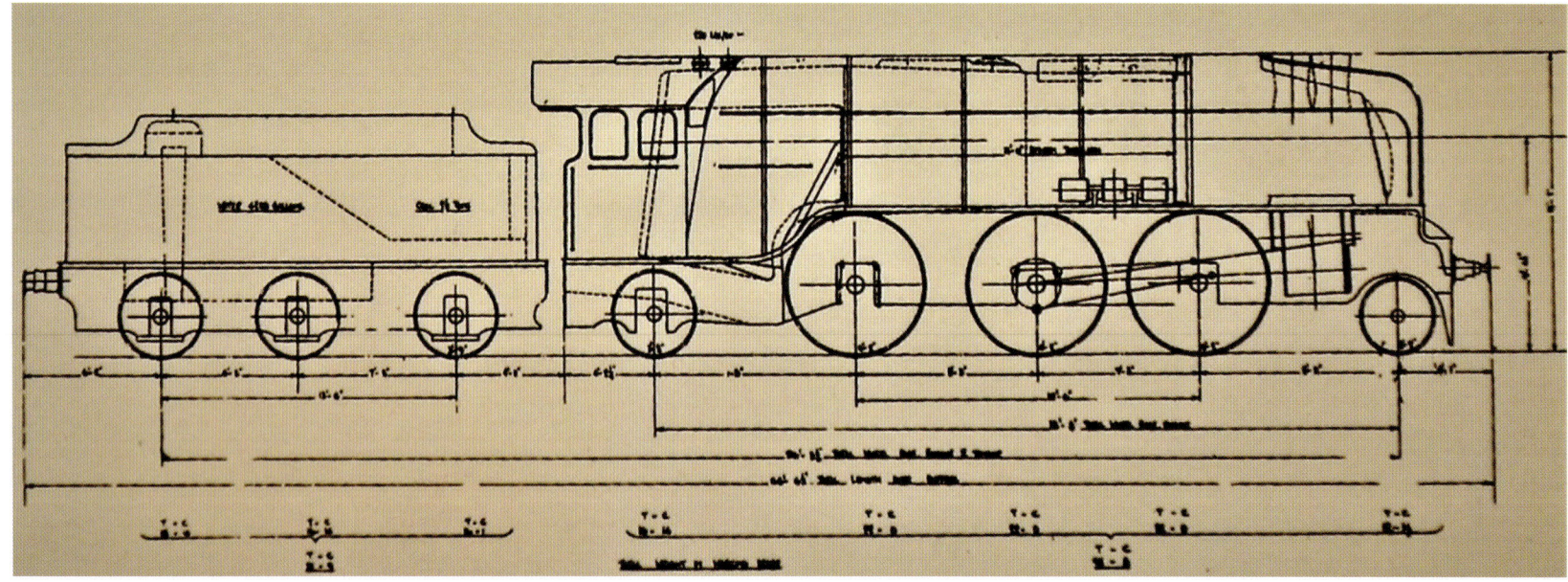

Two alternative proposals for a streamlined V2 showing a P2 or an A4 solution. A taller tender in both cases might have made these designs look less ungainly.

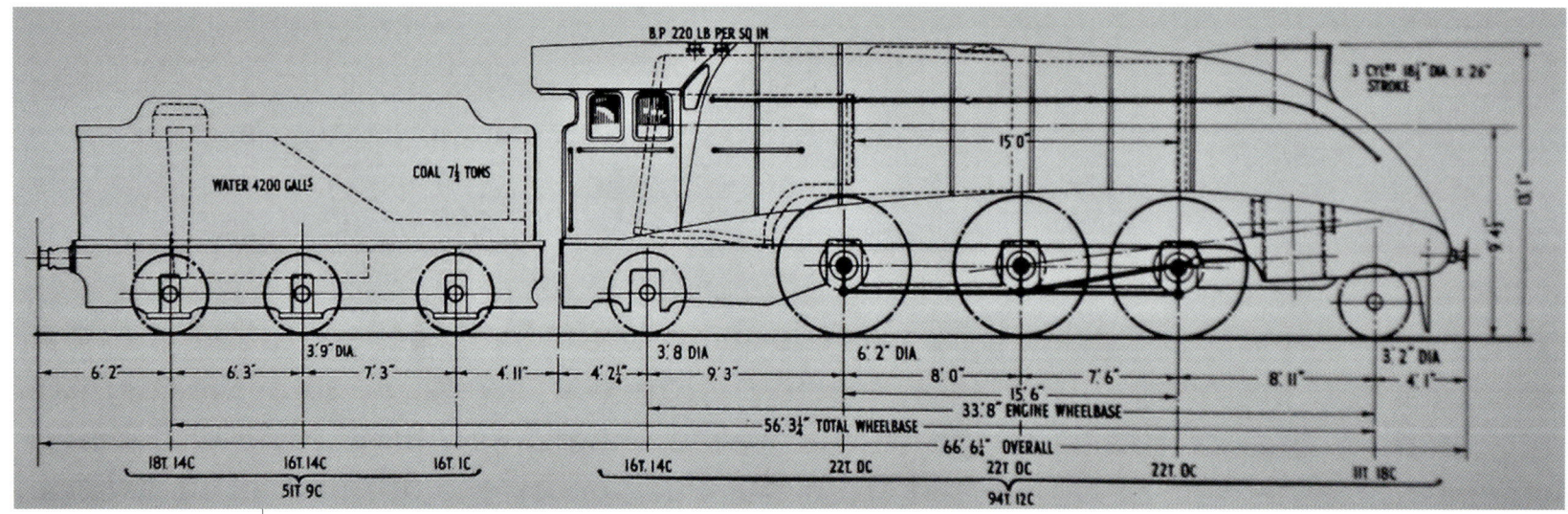

suddenly changed in 1937 when the 69-year-old Richard Maunsell decided to retire following a period of ill-health.

With electrification on the Southern in full swing, steam locomotion had been forced to take second place for many years. Although Maunsell had tried to re-invigorate the programme, the company had fallen behind the other main operators. Sir Herbert Walker, the Southern's General Manager, wished to correct this and when the CME announced his intention of retiring sought to bring in a more thrusting replacement. Bulleid was identified as just such a man and, encouraged by Walker and with Wedgwood and Gresley's approval, he applied for the post. An interview and acceptance soon followed and in September he began work.

Gresley it seems was undisturbed by his departure. Like any long relationship it must have had its ups and downs and he was aware of Bulleid's ambition to lead. But with no intention of retiring himself just yet, there would be no opening for him at King's Cross. However, the departure of such a lively lieutenant did leave a large gap in his ranks, but the man he chose to replace him, Douglas Ross Edge, could not have been more different in background or temperament.

The new Personal Assistant is something of an opaque figure, little being known about his family background. He was born on 19th April 1885 in Altringham, the third and youngest child of William, a railway clerk, and Marriane, who hailed from Exeter. During 1902 he became an apprentice fitter at the Gorton Works of the Great Central Railway. On qualifying, he rose quickly through the ranks, becoming a specialist in carriage and wagon work in the process. On amalgamation in 1923, he was the C&W Works Manager at Dukenfield, where he remained until 1934 when transferred by Gresley to Doncaster to take on a similar task there. Why the CME should choose him and not another locomotive man is unclear, but one can only think that he had impressed his leader with his performance and possibly his ideas. His appointment also suggests that Gresley was either tired of having such a challenging assistant as Bulleid or wished to have someone with a different outlook. Whatever the reasons might have been, it was certainly an interesting appointment and gave Bert Spencer a great deal more authority in the locomotive field than he had before.

Perhaps of greater importance to Gresley than the departure of Bulleid, and who would replace him, was the impending retirement of his stalwart ally and trusted deputy Robert Thom. It was in him that the CME had placed so much faith when embarking on his ambitious building programme and Thom had proved worthy of this trust, producing locomotives and rolling stock of high quality in the tightest timescales possible. It was a performance few, if any, could have equalled. But for his exceptional leadership and engineering skills, the Gresley legend might have been tarnished by the performance of a lesser man than Thom. Like Spencer and a few others, he provided shape, drive and support to all the CME attempted and all he achieved. But for their innate honesty, modesty and sense of honour they could, if they so wished, have claimed much of the credit that fell on Gresley's deserving shoulders.

Thom planned to leave in early 1938 just as he approached his 65th birthday. It was an auspicious moment, timed to coincide with the last of the A4s being constructed, a class in which his role had proved so crucial. Undoubtedly, Gresley would have cast around for a suitable replacement and might have found the field to choose from quite limited. Possible candidates from within his own team would have been sifted and some external candidates considered as well, but in the end, he selected the experienced Edward Thompson, who appeared happily ensconced at Darlington, to fill the vacancy. Like Edge, although a leader of some note, he wasn't considered to be a locomotive man and so the appointment was an interesting one.

Gresley didn't lose contact with Bulleid and remained a close friend

Edge in 1937 when replacing Bulleid.

Robert Thom's retirement photograph.

until the end of his life, often enjoying visits to the Bulleid home on Box Hill in Surrey, where he took a great pleasure in talking to his children and joining in their fun and games. It was, perhaps, an enjoyable echo of the time when his own children were young. But, as Bert Spencer recalled, it proved to be a double edged sword:

> 'Bulleid's young son Hugh was tragically killed in 1938, when his bike was hit by a car. Sir Nigel was profoundly saddened by his death and remained so for some considerable time.'

As the decade drew to a close, the pace of his life didn't change appreciably and the things that had fascinated him for so long remained in his thoughts. With design work on the A4 and V2 complete, he turned once again to the issue of streamlining, with the P2s being the first to experience the next stage in this evolution. Although approval to build six had been given, it took two years, from the launch of 2001 and 2002 in 1934, before construction of the last four of the class could begin. Reaction to the engines had been mixed and an extended period of testing was thought necessary to prove their worth. But for some these engines would never be right and debates would rumble on and eventually come to a head in the aftermath of Gresley's death.

Between June and September, one new engine left the works each month and to the casual observer they looked entirely different to their older sisters; such was the impact of the A4's streamlined shape being extended to the new engines, although side valances over the wheels and motion weren't included as part of the package. These were rejected at an early stage in favour of a straight running plate to make cleaning easier. However, it isn't clear why these changes were sanctioned at all, because the deflector systems applied to the first two engines had proved fairly effective. The simple answer may be that with such an avaricious coal burner, any improvement that greater streamlining might achieve was worthwhile. But there doesn't seem to be any evidence that this was the case, so the exercise might simply have been an aesthetic one that was extended to 2002 in 1936 and 2001 in 1938. Apart from this,

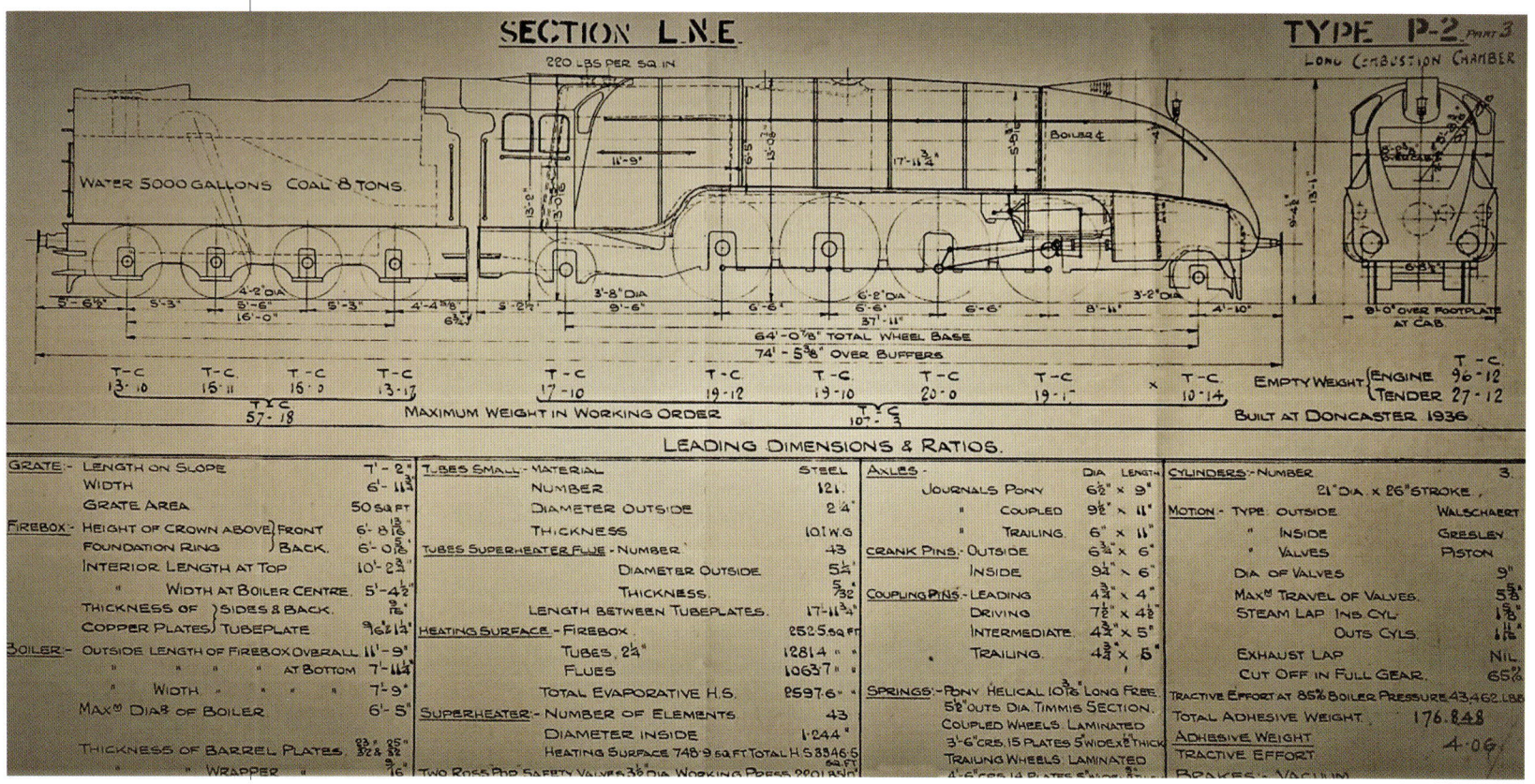

The diagram for Part 3 of the P2 programme. Part 1 covered 2001 and Part 2 engine No. 2002.

any other changes to the class were fairly slight and often only existed between the locos in the class. One of these involved 2004, *Mons Meg*, which was fitted with a by-pass valve to help divert some of the excessive amount of exhaust away from the blastpipe. It was hoped that this would cut the pull exerted on the fire by the blast and reduce the effects this phenomenon had on the engine's efficiency and economy.

Even after the arrival of the A4s, these new streamlined locomotives still caused a stir amongst railway journalists who were eager to see them and, perhaps, get on the footplate. *The Engineer* was widely read in the upper echelons of the railway industry and its journalists were actively encouraged to view work first hand. Several times they took advantage of this with the P2 and detailed reports appeared in their magazine, the most interesting by E.H. Livesay. In a long article, he succinctly summed up his impressions of the class and Gresley's work:

The elegant lines of the P2s captured to perfection. The shape adopted provides an interesting contrast to the A4s as built and to some it was a great improvement.

'With one exception, no. 2005, "Thane of Fife", all the P2s have Kylchap double exhaust pipes and chimneys, and No. 2006, "Wolf of Badenoch" has a longer combustion chamber than the others which reduces the tube length to 18 feet. After experimenting with several kinds of streamlining, the present standard type was adopted. As to whether it seriously reduces wind resistance I have my doubts, particularly as the P2s were never intended to travel at more than, say 70mph. Up to that speed streamlining is more ornamental than useful.

'The vee-shaped cab front makes larger windows possible, and certainly improves the look ahead. The boiler cladding comes right up to the limits of the loading gauge, so the steam collector projections can cause no air eddies. Attention may be drawn to the adhesion weight – 80 tons, far greater than is to be found on any other type of British express engine, the outcome of the four driving axles. The first run I made with an engine of this class was out of Edinburgh on the 4.15 am train, the "Aberdonian" which was hauled as far as Dundee by No. 2004, "Mons Meg", the load being 320 tons gross, with Driver McIntosh and Fireman Richardson in charge. The weather at the start was rainy, with a north-easterly head wind.

'I was beginning to note the riding, which I had been looking forward to passing judgement upon, on this, my first trip on an eight-coupled engine in this country. I had wondered how an engine with a long rigid wheel base – 19ft. 6in – would behave on this much curving route, and was pleased to find its action easy. It took the bends quite sympathetically, though I could only feel them as it was still dark… I noticed rear end sway, evidently due to the drawbar gear between engine and tender needing a little attention… Dundee was reached on time at 5.35 am in 80 minutes at an average speed of 44.25mph.

'It had been an interesting journey on a strange and outstanding class of locomotive. The run was non-stop, the load a little more than half of what it is capable of handling and the timing easy, but I was pleased with the action on a difficult track, which was so much better than I had anticipated, as, when all is said and done, a 19ft. 6in rigid wheel base is hardly likely to enjoy too much curvature, to which it certainly must accommodate between Edinburgh and Dundee.

'They undoubtedly have the best cabs of any engine I have ridden on in England. It is what a cab ought to be, comfortable and well arranged, with a view to the convenience of the crew. And the front end of the P2s is also very good, the easy curvature and ample area of the steam pipes being one of the chief features. "Mons Meg's" steam flow is evidently extraordinary free, so much so that after Leuchars with half-regulator and 23% cut-off, the steam chest pressure has been marked on record as 5lb. more

Lord President eases through Kirkcaldy in August 1936 with the 0900hrs Aberdeen to Waverly express. This picture shows the distinctive shaping applied to cover the cylinders and provide the forward section of the running plate.

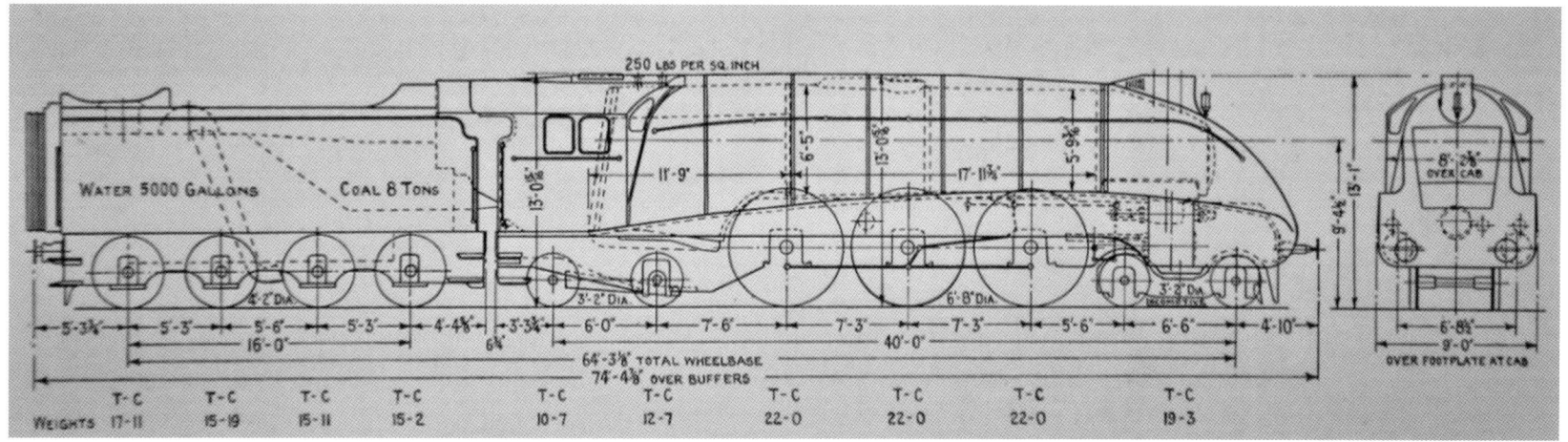

W1's conversion summarized and (below) how the finished product looked having completed a run to London and awaiting right of way to proceed to the sheds for servicing.

than the boiler pressure! This looks very much like a miracle to me, and it is a phenomenon worth noting.

'The conjugated lever gear for the valve of the inside cylinder is an interesting feature of LNER engines. It obviously works well, any little defects that may have existed when it was first adopted having been long eliminated. Heavier castings for the pivot supports and the use of roller bearings at the most important points ensure long periods of operation without adjustment, the valve action remaining correct. I noticed that on starting "Mons Meg's" exhaust was heavier on one beat than on the following two, but it was later made clear to me that this was probably not due to the valve gear, but to one of the valves developing a defect.'

Though not the ringing accolade Gresley might have wished to read, it was at least complimentary and impartial and makes no real mention of the criticisms that pursued the class.

With the P2s in this modified form earning their keep, it was the turn of W1 to become the focus of attention again. In August 1935, whilst waiting for a period of maintenance to begin, it was decided to take her out of service whilst her future was considered. As a test bed she had proved invaluable, but the results were not as good as expected and there comes a point in any experiment where a theory is proved sufficiently valid to warrant production or confirms to scientists that no appreciable gains can be made and is dropped. W1 had reached this point after six years of work and Gresley realised that now was the time to withdraw the engine from service and scrap or rebuild her. While he contemplated her future, the engine was stored in the Paint Shop at Darlington and here she remained until October 1936, while a new design slowly emerged.

As things turned out, the changes made proved fairly straightforward to implement. Apart from the boiler, the engine was of fairly traditional design. So the simple solution was to dispense with the boiler and its ancillary equipment and mould the rest into a more established LNER form, which in 1936 meant streamlining and three-cylinders. When she emerged from the workshops at Doncaster in November 1937, the changes were only too obvious and were quickly picked up by Cecil Allen who, after consulting his notes, wrote in a letter during 1956:

'The boiler is similar to those used on the P2 class, except that it carries a working pressure of 250 instead of 220lb. per sq in. As rebuilt, No. 10000, with a weight of 108 tons without and 172 tons with tender (in working order) is the heaviest express engine in Britain (other than the turbine driven LMSR, 4-6-2 No. 6202, which weighs 110 ½ tons without tender) and is exceeded in tractive effort only by the P2s,

A busy scene captured at King's Cross. 10000 pulls away with a rake of traditional LNER teak carriages, whilst A4 No. 4497. *Dominion of New Zealand*, reverses back to be coupled up to her train. Meanwhile a J52 saddle tank (ex-GNR J13) shuttles past on shunting duties.

No. 10000 would be based at three sheds for the remainder of her life – Doncaster, Haymarket and King's Cross but it was the London shed where she would become most familiar, as captured here while being turned.

which have driving wheels of 6 in. less diameter.

'Apart from the firebox, the boiler does not differ greatly from that of the A4s in the tube heating surface, and the superheating surface is identical. But the cylinders are enlarged in diameter from 18 ½ to 20 in., which is the secret of the increase in tractive effort, at 85% of the working pressure, from 35,450 to 41,440 lb. Each cylinder has its own 5 in. diameter steampipe, and is fed through 8in inside admission piston valves; the exhaust is passed to a double blast-pipe of the Kylchap type, with 5 ¼ in. diameter blast pipe tops and above there is a double chimney….The cab is considerably larger than that of the Pacifics. On my first run with the modified No. 10000 (the up Flying Scotsman) the train was made up to fourteen vehicles weighing 446 tons and I joined it at Darlington which we left three minutes late. From York we bettered even time, but the most impressive demonstration of power was given between Grantham and London with speeds of 85mph down past Little Bytham. However, from Huntingdon to Stevenage was an astonishing tour de force, which I fancy, must be an unprecedented outbound time with such a load as 470 tons behind the tender…. In all, therefore, No. 10000 by this impressive performance gained 13 ½ minutes on the Flying Scotsman from Darlington to King's Cross and the impression in the train throughout was that the engine was being held in rather than extended in achieving these times.'

W1 seems to have gained a reputation for fast running and for the rest of her life ran relatively trouble free and seems to have been a popular engine amongst the men who crewed her. Despite her weight and higher working pressure, coal consumption does not appear to have been excessive and compared favourably with the A4s and being a single member of a class doesn't seem to have disadvantaged her to any great extent. Sharing many parts with the Pacifics clearly allowed for interchangeability and some commonality of spares, so reducing maintenance costs.

The next streamlining proposal probably had more to do with form than function. Construction of the B17s had run on since 1928 and the final batch of eleven were turned out by Robert Stephenson and Co in 1937. These sturdy performers had wide route availability but tended to run mostly from Liverpool Street over the old Great Eastern lines. The fast expresses between London and Norwich proved particularly popular and was one of the region's premier services. To promote it even further as a high-speed service, a proposal to streamline two B17s was acceded to, although the physical benefits to arise from this work were at best debatable. So the work was commissioned and engines 2859, *Norwich City* and 2870, *Tottenham Hotspur*, were withdrawn from traffic in July 1937 and moved to Doncaster to begin a two-month conversion programme.

As a publicity stunt it had much to commend it. With the A4s, P2s and the W1 running along the East Coast route and attracting much press attention in the process, re-invigorating a lesser service by a simple conversion made sense. It wasn't a major programme of work that sought to push back design boundaries and test theories, as their bigger streamlined sisters had done. In this case, streamlining similar to the A4s was simply fitted over the existing boiler plates, so as not to damage the lagging. One report suggested this was like wearing two overcoats at once, or as another one put it 'placing a shroud over the coffin' and the streamlined look was completed by aerofoil valances over the wheels and motion and tenders fitted with side plating and curved tops to enhance the

One last streamlining exercise, though in this case it was most probably only a PR exercise.

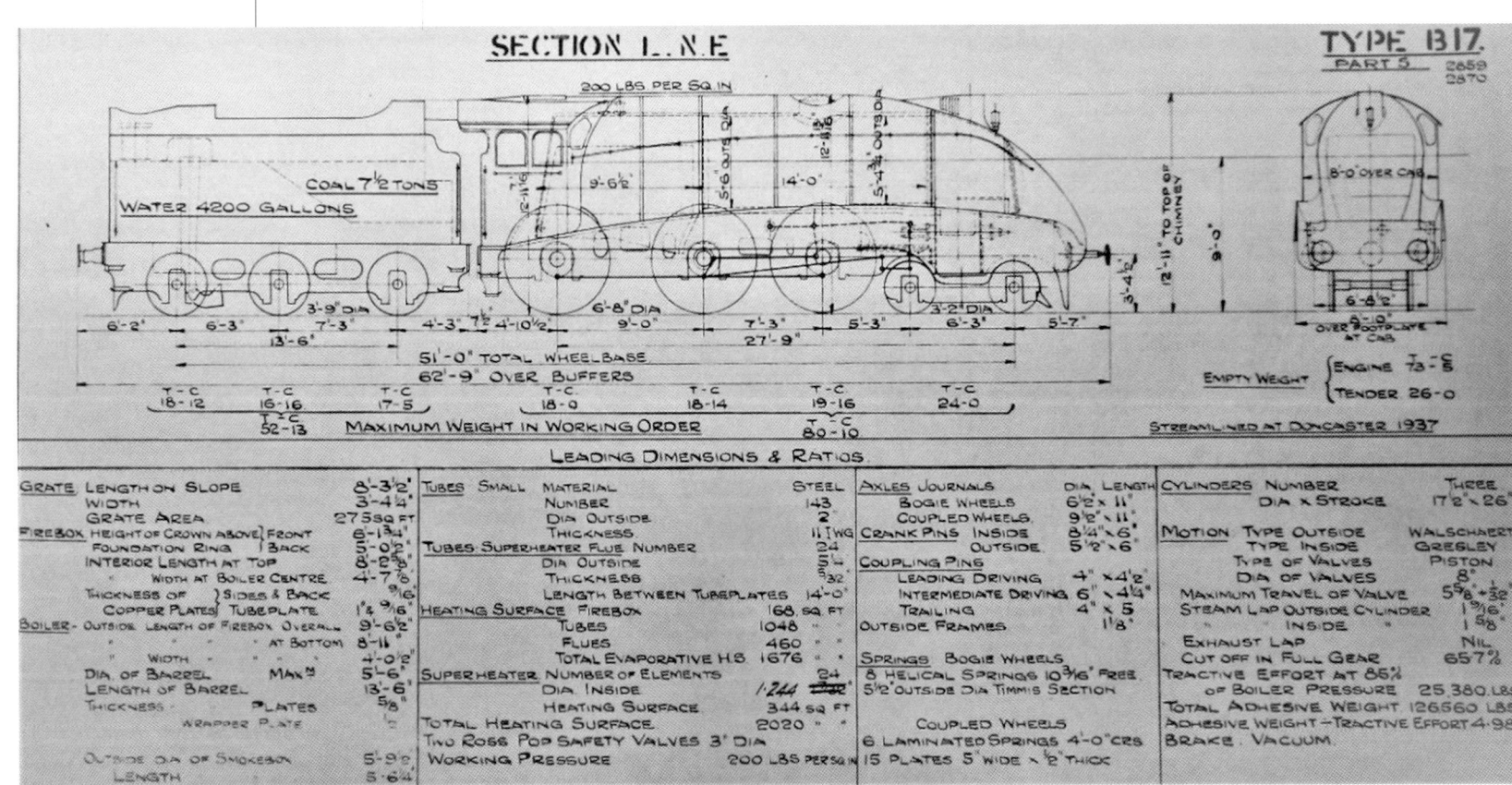

Fete and Fated (1936–41) • 253

2859 almost ready to be launched as *East Anglian*. (Below) Engine No. 2870 soon to be streamlined. Both locomotives would be based at Norwich Shed and both would run in this streamlined state until 1951.

Engine No. 2970 as she appeared in 1938. This engine was named Manchester City when first built, later becoming Tottenham Hotspur. When streamlined she became City of London in which guise she is seen here pulling the *East Anglian* in 1938, with a rather ungainly, cobbled together rake of coaches behind her. Not quite the image suggested by the glamorous 'Silver Jubilee' and 'Coronation' services which these two B17s sought to emulate.

sleek appearance. This look was spoiled, to a certain extent, by the absence of a new rake of carriages with a matching modern look. So to a mass of publicity the 'East Anglian' services began in late 1937, though it is hard to gauge from the limited material available whether these superficial changes improved profitability to any extent.

Since 1923, Gresley had re-populated the LNER with many new engines and modified a considerable number of those he had inherited. As war approached this programme continued with Darlington, Doncaster, Gorton or one of the company's contractors still gainfully employed building A4s, V1s, V2s, B17s, J39s, J50s and K3s, but there seemed to be a hiatus settling over the design teams. This may simply have been one of those things; a constant development programme is hard to sustain continuously. There will naturally be gaps and pauses but there may have been another reason for this. Gresley was now into his sixties and was beginning to suffer periods of ill-health.

His time was also thinly spread, with many other commitments crowding in on his life. So, age may not have been wearying him, but a full schedule might well have done so. Bulleid's departure, and with it the loss of his dynamism and sense of purpose, must also have affected the output of the design team on locomotive matters at least. His energetic, bustling personality, though possibly tiring at times was nevertheless an invigorating presence, which the more measured Spencer was unlikely to copy. So in the last few years of Gresley's reign, much had changed and the energy that had once been part of his regime seemed to be missing.

There were the new electric locomotives and multiple units to consider and a constant programme of modifications under way, but

Fete and Fated (1936–41) • 255

2859 seen here at speed presumably on the 'Anglian' service in the calm period just before the war.

The K4 as built.

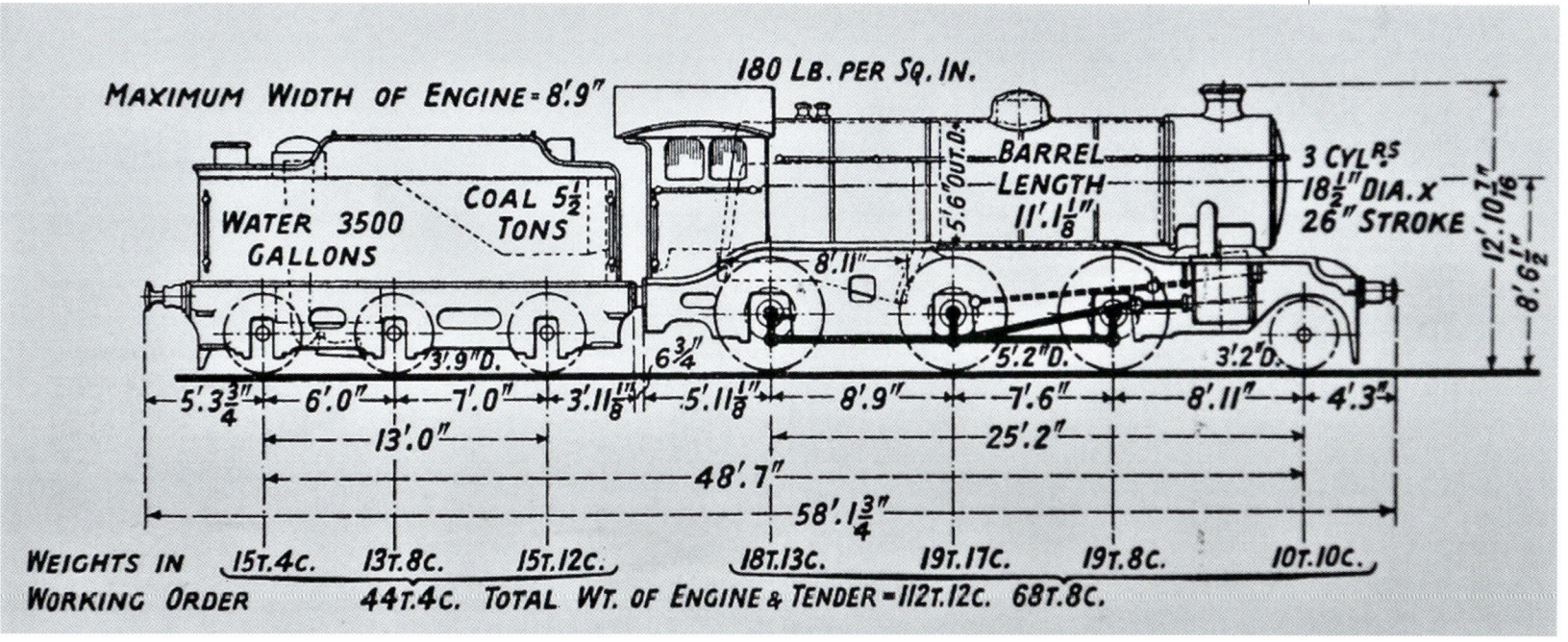

The K4s in operation. These locomotives were designed to operate over some of the most difficult and remote terrains in Britain, where weather conditions could be unpredictable and extremely difficult. The ability to keep to schedules and support all the needs of isolated communities all year round was all important. (Above) Engine No. 3443, *Cameron of Lochiel* pulling a freight train up a long drag and judging by the snow plough expecting bad weather. (Below) 3445, *MacCailin Mor* makes light work of her fairly short load. This engine was converted, during 1945, into the first of the two-cylinder K1s in which condition she ran until the early 1960s.

other new ideas, with the prospect of reaching fruition, seemed few and far between. So as the decade ended there were only two steam projects that could be thought to be new – the K4 class 2-6-0 and the V4 class 2-6-2 – but both were based on well-established and tried principles.

The K4 had its origins in a requirement for more powerful locomotives to operate over the very challenging West Highland Line from Glasgow to Fort William and Mallaig. To achieve this Gresley went back to basics to design a new engine, even though only six would be required. Here Bert Spencer takes up the story:

'Two proposals were considered to provide an engine having a tractive effort approximately 50% greater than that of the K2 and keep to the bridge loading limits imposed by the (civil) engineer. The first scheme was for a 2-8-0 type three-cylinder engine using O2 class cylinders, 5ft. 2in. diameter coupled wheels, and a 5ft. 6in. boiler tapering to a 5ft. diameter at the smokebox. The second scheme, which was adopted, was for a 2-6-0 type three-cylinder engine having 18½in. by 26in. cylinders and the K3 class valve gear, connecting and coupling rods with 5ft. 2in. diameter coupled wheels and a 5ft. 6in. diameter boiler based on the B17 class boiler. The tractive effort at 85% boiler pressure was 32,939 lb., an increase of 40% over that of the K2.

'The first engine, No. 3441, 'Loch Long', went into service in

March 1937, and proved to be capable of successfully handling 300 ton trains. In June 1937, it was decided to increase the boiler pressure from 180lb. to 200lb/sq in, for which the boiler was originally designed. The tractive effort thus increased from 32, 939 lb. to 36,598lb., an advance of 56% over that of the K2. '

With 3441 proving a success, five more of the class were commissioned and appeared from the works at Darlington between 1938 and '39. And for the next ten years they successfully worked the West Highland Line proving themselves to be good performers in the process. With the arrival of B1 class 4-6-0s in the mid-forties and ex-LMS Black Fives, after nationalisation, in 1948, the K4s gradually found themselves relegated to freight duties but, in the process, they did find a wider operating area in which to perform and appeared on other lines across Scotland.

While the K4s were being built, and making their appearance in Scotland, events elsewhere were moving at great pace. By 1938, few people could be unaware of the growing threat posed by Nazi Germany, even though appeasement still appeared to be the favoured option of some of Britain's leaders. A determination to avoid another Great War style bloodbath lay at the root of this, though undoubtedly there were those who greatly admired Hitler and wished to see him as an ally.

Despite the best efforts of Neville Chamberlain and Lord Halifax to side-step a war, by 1938 it seemed unavoidable. Despite this, a level of cordial relations still existed between engineers in Britain and Germany, although in Gresley's case this appears to have been tinged with suspicion, wariness and a strong sense of competition, stirred in part by events in Germany two years earlier.

On 1 May 1936, the DRG Class 05 locomotive, No. 002, in a highly tuned state and pulling the comparatively light load of 197 tons achieved a speed of 124.5mph on the Berlin-Hamburg line. It was a PR exercise that sought to glorify the Nazi State and photos of the engine under a swastika appeared world-wide.

Engine No 3442, *The Great Marquess*, just about to set off on another journey south. This locomotive survived into preservation when the class were withdrawn in 1961.

In October 1937 the 100th LNER Pacific made its appearance at Doncaster. To commemorate the event, and the huge contribution made by Gresley, it was decided to name the locomotive in his honour. Although born Herbert Nigel Gresley he seems to have preferred using his middle name. His father and brother had both been Nigel, but they were now long dead. So perhaps in dropping Herbert he was simply honouring and remembering them.

With only three locomotives in the class, there was little intention to provide the sort of long distance, high speed service the LNER planned and was probably timed to make their dominance plain on the eve of the A4's launch.

There was also a home-grown threat to the LNER's position of eminence in the form of the LMS's new streamlined Princess Coronation class, the first of which was launched on 1 June 1937. On a special press run four weeks later, 6220, *Coronation*, seized the British speed record when reaching 114mph on the run down to Crewe. There is some doubt about the authenticity of this accomplishment, but this did not seem to matter in the flush of headlines that followed. However, whilst breaking records had a clear PR benefit they could prove dangerous in execution. Engine No. 6220 was unable to slow down sufficiently, after its late burst of speed, hit the curve into the station far too quickly and was barely able to stay on the track let alone stop at the platform. So for a time, safer running and high average speeds became the norm. But there seems little doubt that Gresley, aware of the commercial imperative and the crowing of German propaganda, would, if an opportunity arose, show what an A4 could do. This moment came on 3 July 1938, when 4468, *Mallard*, achieved 126 mph on the downward slope of Stoke Bank, south of Grantham.

Fete and Fated (1936–41) • 259

The DRG Class 5 002 awaits departure. On 1 May 1936 this loco was scheduled for a brake test, but was in fact pulling a train containing leading Nazi figures. Clearly it was intended as a high profile record run and was promoted as such with all the fanfare that could be mustered.

Eric Bannister, who rode on the train that day, left a brief but revealing account of this record run:

'By this time, the tests for the quick acting brake valves were almost finished and Gresley told Norman Newsome that he could "have a go". In great secrecy, a speed run was arranged in conjunction with one of the Sunday brake tests. As I had assisted at some of the tests at Norman's request, I was present on the train when the Doncaster A4 headed out of King's Cross with the "Coronation" set of coaches and the LNER dynamometer car.

'We proceeded to Barkston, where we turned on the triangle. D.R. Edge, the senior representative, told the Westinghouse team what was proposed and offered them a taxi if they did not wish to return with us. They declined!

'At Barkston, Inspector Sam Jenkins asked me to help him go beneath the engine and douse the middle big-end with superheater oil as a precaution against possible overheating…. Then we got the signal to get away and Driver Duddington turned his hat back to front – he was that sort – and off we went.

'Approaching Grantham we slowed down as there was a permanent way check at

Just before the 'brake test run' began the engine was checked over at Barkston by the crew, Inspector Sam Jenkins and Eric Bannister, and given a clean bill of health.

24mph…Even so we passed the summit of Stoke Bank at 74½mph and our speed gradually increased down the bank… I asked Newsome what speed we were doing and he said "Over 120".'

At this point, Bannister moved into the vestibule next to the dynamometer car. Here he and his colleague, Bernard Atkinson, leant out of the windows to see if they could smell any signs of overheating. To help this process a 'stink bomb' was inserted in the hollow crank pin of the middle big end and this then bursts if the parts became too hot and in due course, this smell came drifting back:

'So Bernard immediately signalled to Inspector Jenkins to steady up. Back at our table, Norman, who had felt the touch of the brake, said that our speed then seemed to be 125mph. Coasting down to Tallington, we had a conference with Mr Edge and all the railway people to formulate a plan of action for our arrival at King's Cross because we knew that the Press would be waiting. At Peterborough, Mallard went to the slip points and on to New England Shed while the station stand-by took over. Mr Edge phoned Sir Nigel at Watton and gave him the news.

'On arrival at King's Cross I dropped off the train, ran over the central bridge to my office where I had a number of photographs of the A4 and returned to the platform. Meanwhile, Mr Edge had

Fete and Fated (1936–41) • 261

This photograph is reputed to show *Mallard* during her record run. If not, it does at least provide a view of the way she looked that day.

Fireman Tommy Bray and Driver Joe Duddington photographed after their record run.

The record has been set and all involved can relax. Those identified in the group facing the camera are (left to right) Bray, Duddington, Jenkins, train guard(?), Atkinson (?) and, half hidden behind him, Eric Bannister(?), A.G. Brackenbury, from Westinghouse, and D.R. Edge.

Mallard's record run was widely acknowledged and used for publicity purposes by the LNER and its suppliers. Here the manufacturers of the double Kylchap exhaust system get in on the act with a wonderfully stylised art deco image of the locomotive. However, 4468's record card (below) for the period strips the engine's glamorous history to the bone.

invited the Press into the dynamometer car to look at the record charts.

'Mr Robson extracted the charts and Bert Spencer told me to trace them for Gresley the following day. Sir Nigel told the daily newspapers of the record. When tracing the charts, I found they showed a peak of 126mph but the Chief declined to mention this as the duration was less than a mile.'

There is little doubt that this was a very special day, which still echoes loudly with us today. Rightly or wrongly, it has come to define the whole of Gresley's career. Would he have minded? As a pragmatist who knew the power of the press, probably not, but may have laughed all the same at the fuss this one event created. In reality, genuine achievement is realised by hard work, a clever mind, a gradual development of ideas and success measured by more than speed achieved over a short length of track on one day. Nevertheless, it's *Mallard* that sits as a prime exhibit in the national collection, whilst you have to search through rarely read books or learned papers to discover the true extent of his achievements. And even then it is only the engineering aspects of his career that are clearly perceived, not his wider talents as a leader and statesman, for that is what he was. Simply being an engineer would probably not have taken him so high or so far.

He was blessed with a very rare combination of skills that only few are lucky to possess – scientist, engineer, diplomat, financier, publicist, politician, academic and leader of people. Some might say he was lucky to have been in the right place at the right time, as good fortune will always play a part in any life. But my experience is that those with great skill often create their own opportunities and good luck. To think otherwise is to demean or belittle their achievements. Gresley was, by any standards, a man of unparalleled skill who achieved all he did by grit, determination and a steady application of intellect. And as his life moved towards an end, these qualities didn't leave him, but age and illness certainly affected his ability to respond.

From 1938 he is reported to have suffered from bronchial problems, not helped by pipe smoking. He was overweight and lived a busy and stressed existence, where high blood pressure was a likely result. His death certificate reveals that he suffered from arteriosclerosis, which is a condition that grows more severe over the years if left untreated. As plaque forms, leading arteries harden and thicken, so restricting blood flow. This tends to lead to angina, mental confusion and difficulty moving in its primary stage, then blood clots, heart attacks or strokes when reaching the tertiary stage. Nowadays we have a whole range of treatments to combat these conditions but in the 1930s, diet and rest were all that could be suggested. Gresley doesn't seem to have taken these precautions and, as a consequence, he was diagnosed as having a 'failing heart'. Most of those working around him seem to have been unaware of these problems developing, presumably because such a strong, larger than life character would have seemed indestructible. Nevertheless, the symptoms were there to see and several accounts record that his behaviour at times was giving cause for concern. Dr Ransome-Wallis for one reported that, 'The most pathetic picture of the end of his life was the sight of him walking down the departure platform at King's Cross insisting on all drivers of all Pacific locomotives blow their whistles for him.'

In many ways we see someone in sharp decline, but whose sense

The ILocoE maintained close links with railway engineers in Germany up to the beginning of th Second World War. In many cases this became even closer in 1936 when members of the Institution, led by William Stanier, toured Germany and viewed many aspects of their railways and society, meeting a number of leading Nazis in the process. They also rode on and behind Class 05 No. 002. The poor quality photo above shows some of the party, including Stanier (third from the right), looking at and discussing the engine. The picture on the right captures Harold Holcroft on the same day.

of duty and purpose were so strong that he couldn't be stopped merely by the body and mind failing. I'm told that clever and resourceful people have the capacity to adjust to failing mental health and disguise its effects, a response most noticeable in sufferers of dementia, and this seems to have been the case with the CME. A determination to carry on to the end sustained him and gave him strength no matter what he would soon face. He was without doubt a courageous man and one who wouldn't be defeated, except by death itself.

In many ways, his work and life in professional institutions had always sustained him at difficult times in his life and did so again now. But there was one particular event in 1938 that drew him into a controversy that seemed to encapsulate the British government's policy towards Germany in the 1930s. Was it appeasement or was it simply turning a blind eye to the obvious? Either way, it was playing a dangerous game that appears naïve with hindsight but in 1938, the ILocoE fell into the same trap.

A number of British engineers continued to maintain close links with their opposite numbers in Germany, despite the worsening international situation and Nazi involvement in the Spanish Civil War. In 1936, senior members of ILocoE, led by William Stanier, but not including Gresley, had toured Germany and, amongst other things, travelled behind Class 05 002 shortly after she attained the world speed record and witnessed first-hand the spread of Nazism. So a visit to Britain two years later returned the compliment the compliment with William Stanier acting as host throughout their tour. After a fast run to Scotland from Euston, behind 6225, *Duchess of Gloucester*, a formal dinner was held in Glasgow attended by the Minister of Transport, Edward Bruce the 10th Earl of Elgin; Sir James Lithgow, the Scottish shipbuilding and steel magnate. Gresley also attended, escorted by his son Roger, but, according to contemporary records, sat apart from the German guests.

Later in the tour they visited the LMS works at St Rollox, the Forth Bridge and the LNER sheds

June 1938 and the ILocoE plays host to a party of German engineers eager to see all new developments in Britain. (Above left) When looking at pictures of Nazis visiting Britain in the late 1930s, they seem to have adopted a pseudo English gentleman look which grates slightly. For that reason, it isn't difficult to pick out members of the German party as they admire the latest streamlined product of the LMS works at Crewe, shortly after arriving in Glasgow. As President that year William Stanier played a key part in arranging and hosting the visit and is seen clearly in both pictures. (Above right) The visit ended with a tour of the Forth Bridge overlooking the Royal Navy's key base at Rosyth. This was all rather bizarre because in a little over a year German aircraft were creeping in over the North Sea to bomb this key target, using the bridge as a reference point to guide them. Photos taken by the visitors must have added something to the work of German intelligence agencies eager for any information about 'enemy' installations.

in Edinburgh and other industrial facilities. Gresley, although included in the programme, chose to limit his presence to a minimum essential for politeness. He attended the dinner on the 9th, having travelled north the day before on the 'Coronation' service from London in the company of General-Direktor Dr Julius Dorpmuller, General Manager of the DRG and also by then Reich Minister of Transport. No record of their conversation has survived, but it is likely to have been cordial and non-committal. Both were too old and experienced for it to be otherwise, but they were forthright men, unafraid of expressing themselves, so the conversation might have had a challenging edge to it. In any event, Gresley carefully avoided any other contact and doesn't appear in the photographs that have survived.

By this stage, Dorpmuller had voluntarily decided to exercise German law concerning the employment of non-Aryan races and rid the railways of anyone not fitting this narrow and horribly racist vision of the future. And throughout the war he bore responsibility for keeping the railway system going across Occupied Europe, which meant transporting soldiers and armaments in vast quantities, but also taking millions of innocent people to the death camps. An inconvenient truth, perhaps, but a truth nonetheless. If Britain had been invaded in 1940, he would have run this system in the same way and probably helped dispose of Gresley, Stanier and thousands of others along the way. He was culpable in all of this and probably much more, yet in May 1945, the British considered him fit to run the peace time German railway system again, having been cleared for this duty by General Eisenhower himself. Luckily, this Nazi leader died of cancer in July 1945 before he could take office, or more appropriately be brought to justice at the Nuremburg Trials. As a man he could not have been further from Gresley and the high moral standards by which he lived.

So Europe slowly slipped towards another conflict. The foolishness of appeasement eventually seen for what it was and Britain finally began to re-arm. For the moment though, Gresley could enjoy his success and consider the next generation of locomotives and continue with a series of dynamometer car tests using the A4s pulling different size loads over different routes. Judging by the forty or so Flamman indicator rolls that have survived, from the period 1937 to 1939, *Mallard*'s run was one of this series, which suggests the record set on 3 July wasn't an impromptu affair at all, but one long planned. These tests began in December 1937 with engine No 4496, '*Golden Shuttle* hitting 104mph on the 'Coronation' service and ended on 19 June 1939 with 4486 *Merlin* doing something similar. Around mid-1938 there were a spate of tests each recording high speeds, but only one involved an engine with the double Kylchap exhaust system; this was *Mallard*.

Apart from the Flamman rolls, no other report describing these tests appears to have survived, so one is left to ponder their purpose. Other than measuring speeds attained over different routes and the engines' general performance, there seems to have been few benefits to be derived from this work. But in terms of preparing for a new National Test Centre, their purpose makes more sense. In early 1939, all that Gresley had worked long and hard to achieve seemed to be reaching fruition. Approval to proceed had finally been given, Heenan and Froude Ltd of Worcester were selected to undertake all design and construction work and a site in Rugby had been selected. Work began, it seems, in late 1938 and was well advanced by the summer of 1939, but the situation in Europe became so dire that work was temporarily put on hold in August, shortly after the LNER had run its last test with an A4. Consequently, construction was suspended completely in early 1940 as invasion became a real possibility. But as Bert Spencer recalled much later, 'Gresley still lobbied the powers that be to complete this test facility as soon as possible seeing great

Dr Julius Dorpmuller, General Manager and Chairman of the German State Railway. He was a prime mover in the pursuit of speed records as a means of championing the Nazi cause of which he was a strong advocate. Gresley and 'Mallard' upheld British prestige at a time of appeasement by its political masters.

Despite failing health there were still moments to enjoy. On 20 May 1939, Gresley attended the naming of V2 No. 4843 at Doncaster (The King's Own Yorkshire Light Infantry) and enjoyed this moment of humour with Lady Eve, wife of the regiment's Colonel, General Sir Charles Deedes.

value to the war effort in its work.' Sadly, it wasn't to be, and work would only resume in 1944 with the end of the war in sight.

The last few months of peace saw Gresley's health continue to decline and he spent more time at home at Watton-at-Stone, unable to enjoy the pursuits that had been part of his life for so long – fishing, golf and membership of institutions and clubs. It was at Watton that he set up a small office to work alongside the ever faithful Spencer, who frequently visited on days when Gresley was too ill to travel to London. Occasionally he was accompanied by Eric Bannister and Harper, the CME's Chief Clerk. These visits grew more frequent as the CME's cardio-vascular problems began to multiply, made worse by occasional bouts of bronchitis. But even when the pace of decline grew more rapid, he doesn't seem to have considered retirement and appears to have had no encouragement to do so from Charles Newton, who succeeded Wedgwood in 1939, or Ronald Matthews, who had replaced William Whitelaw a year earlier. However, both men would have been deeply respectful of such a prominent figure as Gresley and so were less likely to go against his wishes.

Even though spending more time confined to his home, this didn't stop him considering future projects with Spencer. Bannister later recalled what it was like to sit alongside his CME and noted the way that Spencer understood his way of working and the best means of supporting him:

> 'HNG was a pleasant man to work for. He did not like interruptions to his train of thought, so BS and I waited until he asked us – with the well-known twinkle – for our opinions. We presented the facts as we found them, knowing HNG would make some comment which would automatically cause a re-assessment of opinion and so lead to further conversation. He would always consider carefully before reaching a decision and we were never kept in suspense because of the 'third copy' procedure. When I first went to King's Cross, BS warned me that HNG did not appreciate criticism of his marine big-end nor of his conjugated valve motion, but otherwise he encouraged original thought.'

In the last two years of his life, as war descended and chaos reigned, he and Spencer would quietly map out new schemes or developments of old ones as this once robust man slowly succumbed to illness. Perhaps when facing death, he found some comfort in thinking about the future. If so, their work seems to have focussed on a 4-8-2 express locomotive, which the CME predicted would be needed to pull even longer, faster trains in

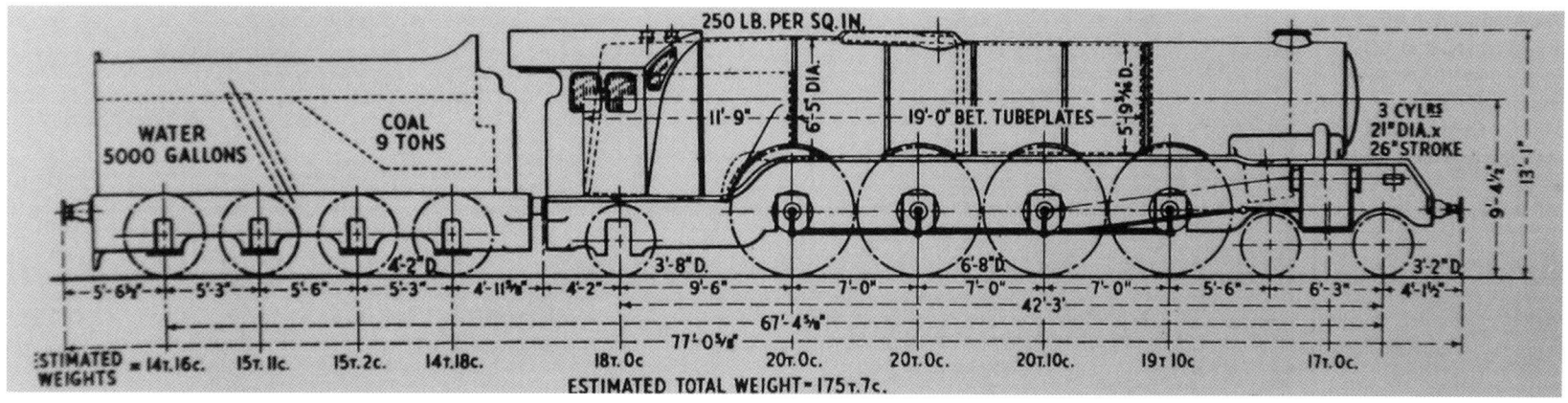

Gresley and Spencer's ideas for the next generation express locomotive, one traditional in shape, the other with a degree of streamlining

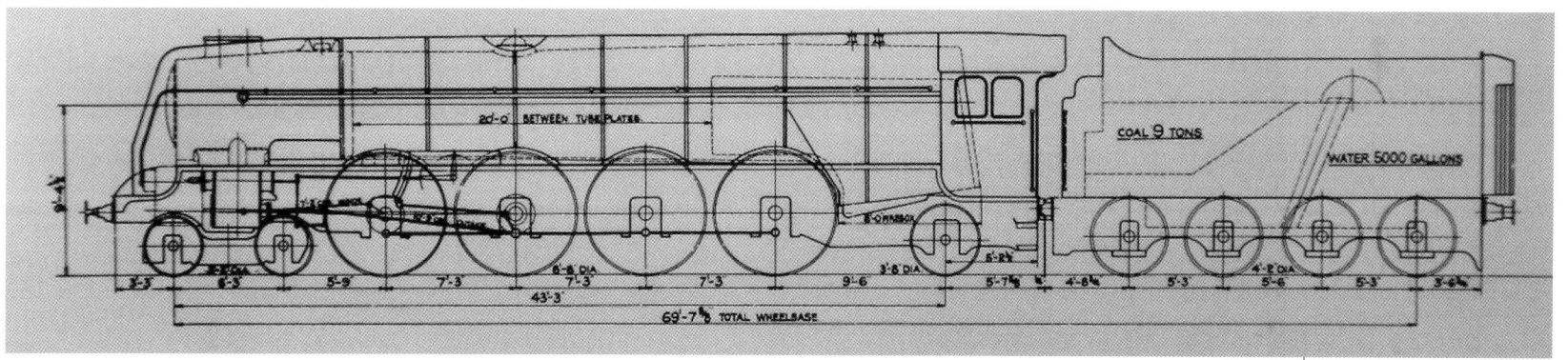

due course. Spencer spoke of this work in 1947:

'Any appreciable increase in the average speed of the heavy express trains, averaging 50-55mph., could only be secured by faster uphill running, and, to effect this improvement in timing, designs for a three-cylinder 4-8-2 type engine were considered. The proposed engine had 21in. by 26in. cylinders and 6ft. 8in. diameter coupled wheels, the tractive effort at 85% boiler pressure being 45,700lb. and a grate area of 50 sq. ft. There was every prospect of this engine and the modified A4 [with a boiler pressure raised from 250 to 275 lb per sq. in] being proceeded with when the war intervened.'

He added that these designs remained with him during the war and in spare moments he continued working on them, as well as a streamlined 4-8-4 engine, another of Gresley's ideas. Here the CME may have been following development work in America where ALCO produced a prototype engine during 1926. The concept was taken up by companies around the world, but there was one example, more than any other, which may have caught Gresley's eye.

The Krupp Works in Germany produced two Class 06 4-8-4 engines in 1939 each capable of pulling 650 tons. Considering the level of competition that existed this may have acted as a spur to Gresley. If so, it was a thought that occurred to Chapelon as well. In both cases, the war intervened before any proposals could be considered in detail. For Gresley it all came too late, but Chapelon, unable to build a new engine, proposed converting a notoriously poor 'Mountain' Class 241 engine into a 4-8-4 type, finally gaining approval to do so in 1942. With wartime restrictions in place little happened before Germany's surrender in 1945 and the 'new' engine, designated 242 A1, finally appeared a year later. There were no examples built in Britain, but

The Krupp's D06 001, one of two built in 1939. Such a powerful engine found ready use in wartime Germany and both survived until 1951.

out of respect for his former CME Spencer carried on with some broad planning. In the immediate aftermath of war, when the LNER was seeking to re-establish itself again, a diagram of a streamlined 4-8-4 was circulated for discussion, according to Spencer. But times had changed, the future was uncertain and such an exotic beast could no longer find a place in the locomotive inventory.

During 1940, Gresley and Spencer also considered other designs including a new 2-6-4 tank engine with only two cylinders. Production of the V1 was coming to an end and it was decided that the final batch would have their tractive effort increased from 180 to 200 psi. These were designated V3s and became the sole new design tank engine built 'during the Gresley regime' as Spencer described it. But there were many others he sought to build without success and the two-cylinder engine was the last of these. His aim with this design was to produce a locomotive capable of greater acceleration than the V3s on suburban services. For this reason, it would have been fitted with 5ft. 8in coupled wheels, a wide firebox capable of supporting a working pressure of 250 psi, and a boiler that tapered from 5ft. 4in to 5ft. at the smokebox.

It's hard to say why Gresley contemplated a two-cylinder design when so obviously favouring three cylinders throughout his career. The only reason given for this was put forward by Spencer when he wrote:

'To compensate for the loss of water capacity owing to the restricted tank dimensions adjacent to the wide firebox, a two-cylinder design was considered incorporating an additional rectangular tank fitted across the frames between the driving and trailing coupled wheels.'

Fete and Fated (1936–41) • 269

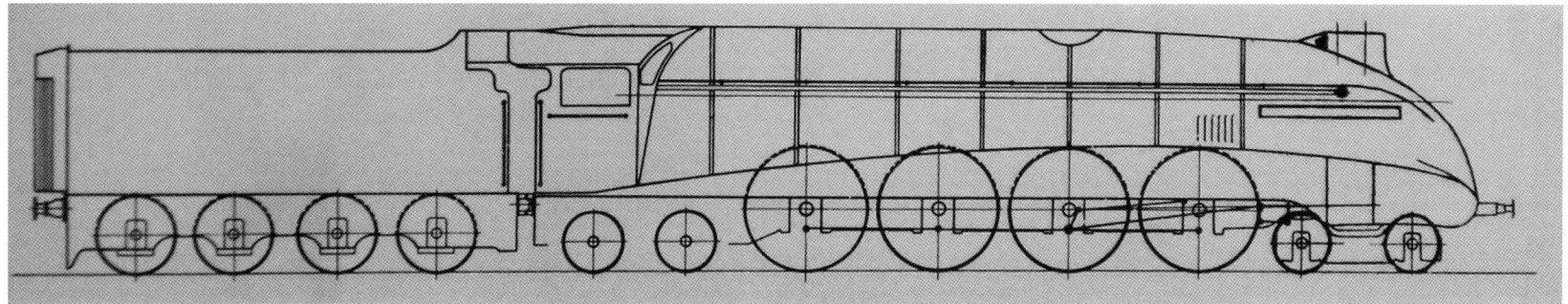

How an LNER 4-8-4 might have looked if Gresley's preference for streamlining had been allowed to continue into the 1940s and '50s, The drawing suggests Spencer's influence and, perhaps, a desire to honour his late and much-lamented leader.

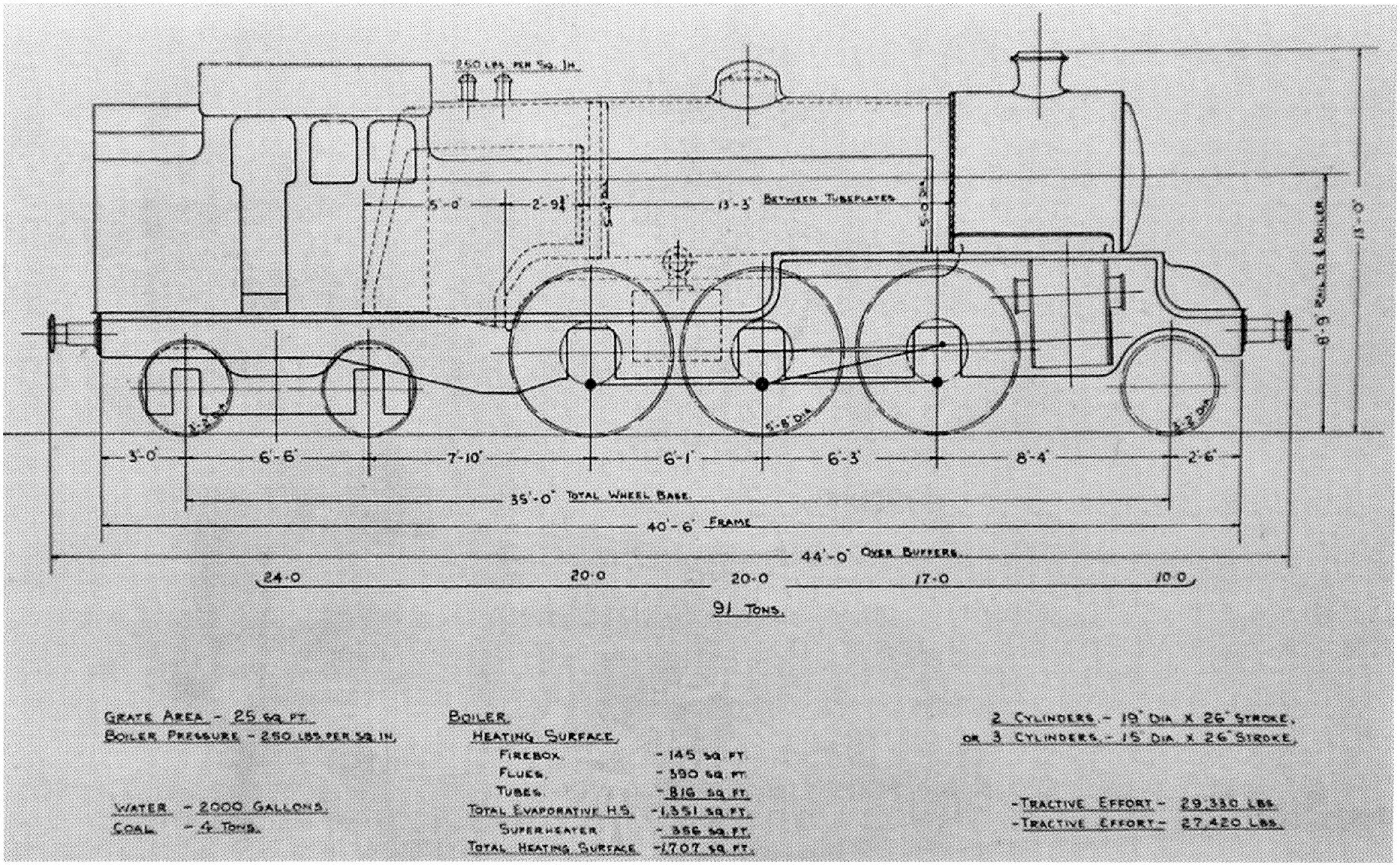

Gresley's final tank engine design which bore a strong resemblance to the two cylinder 2-6-4 tank locomotive introduced by the LMS in 1935, which remained in production until 1943. The LNER design proposed using the type of outside cylinders fitted to the A4 but increased to a 19in diameter.

It was an interesting concept, but surprising in so far as Gresley was prepared to consider dropping his strongly held belief in the use of three-cylinder designs. Or was it a case of a greatly trusted assistant using his skills to produce a practical solution when his leader was unable, through advancing illness, to do more than look on? Ransome-Wallis, for one, had observed with great concern how the CME's mental capacity appeared to be slipping, and this is likely to have affected many other aspects of his life, to his family's great and growing concern. This may be why his son Roger accompanied him on his trip to Scotland in 1938 and then seems to have escorted him fairly regularly after that as well. Vascular dementia, with its distressing side effects, can be a disturbing by-product of arteriosclerosis and seems to have afflicted the ailing Gresley. And so, in the last year of his life, we have a picture of this great man fighting his last battle against a ruthless and unforgiving enemy with great bravery and as much composure as he could muster in the circumstances.

As his end approached, there was the appearance of one last steam locomotive for him to savour. The V4 had been some years in development, following the successful introduction of their big sister, the V2s. But with their axle loading of 22 tons, these engines were restricted in use over parts of the network. By 1939, a view had gradually formed that a stronger, more modern engine, combining the virtues of the V2s with wider route availability, was necessary. Such a locomotive would be able to achieve greater economies over secondary lines, where older, less efficient engines, tended to congregate. Spencer described how this was achieved:

'In order to conform to the limitations imposed on these lines by the Civil Engineer, various methods were adopted to reduce weight, such as the use of 2% nickel steel for the

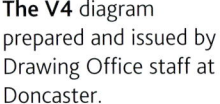

The V4 diagram prepared and issued by Drawing Office staff at Doncaster.

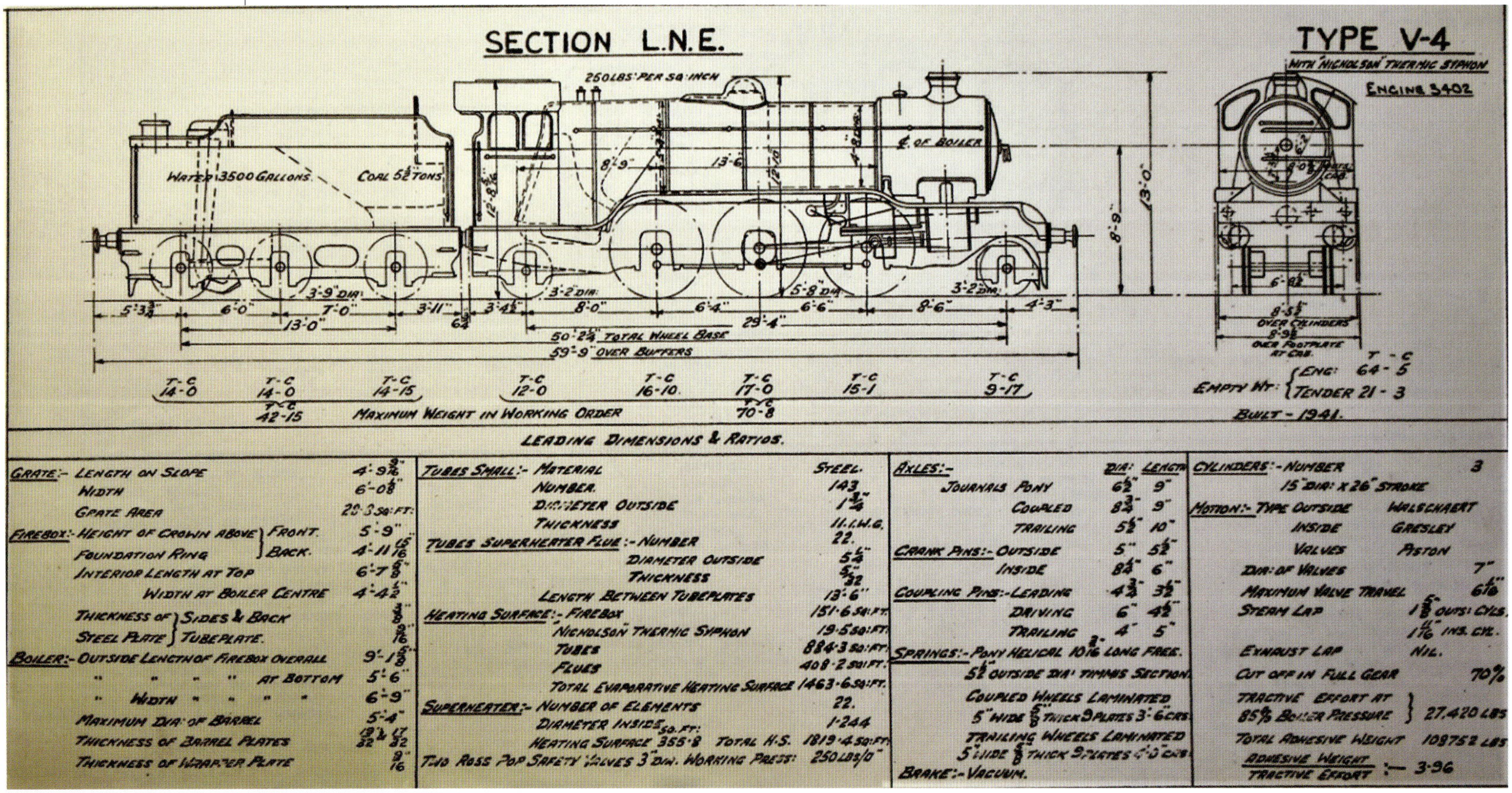

boiler barrel and the extensive substitution of fabricated construction in place of steel castings. The boiler, which carries a working pressure of 250 lb., followed the same general design as those fitted to the Pacific and V2 class engines, but is of smaller proportions, the maximum diameter of the barrel tapering from 5ft. 4in. to 4ft. 8in. The three 15in. by 26in. cylinders had 7in. piston valves and drive on to the second pair of 5ft. 8in. diameter coupled wheels.

'The V4 has a maximum axle loading of 17 tons so has wide route availability (5,000 miles out of a total of 6,414). The second engine differed from the first in having an all steel welded firebox with a single Nicholson thermic syphon [the first LNER locomotive to do so], but this was replaced by a copper firebox in 1945 [the absence of suitable water treatment system proving a disadvantage].'

It is interesting to speculate whether the use of a welded steel firebox with thermic syphon was influenced by Oliver Bulleid in any way. At the time, he was using this solution in designing and building his Merchant Navy Class

MONOBLOC CYLINDER CASTING.

FRAMES FROM BACK END.

BOILER MOUNTED IN FRAME.

ENGINE AFTER WHEELING.

Throughout its construction the first V4 was regularly photographed and this montage was circulated amongst a number of journals. The *Locomotive* magazine picked it up and included a detailed assessment of the new engine which appeared just before Gresley died.

locomotives. If so, one can assume that both men remained very close and were eager to share and absorb each other's ideas. With Gresley so poorly, there would a been a degree of poignancy in their contact – the apprentice becoming the sorcerer can be a difficult and sad process. Having known each other for so long there must have been a familiar ease and understanding in their relationship that allowed their minds to meet.

Only two V4s were built, insufficient to prove the concept sound, but 3401 and 3402 were later described as 'running like a Rolls-Royce' by one driver. There is a suggestion that ten more were planned, but with Gresley's death his successor, Edward Thompson, quietly dropped this proposal, eventually substituting his B1 4-6-0 design in its place.

For the moment though the prospects for these new engines appeared good and the first, named *Bantam Cock*', rolled from the works at Doncaster in February 1941, the second appearing a month later. By this time, Gresley was finding it increasingly difficult to walk and his failing heart made each day an increasing struggle but he managed a short holiday in Devon with Violet and her family and in early 1941 made the long journey from Watton to Doncaster.

With 3401 and his first electric locomotive being unveiled it was an occasion he did not want to miss. Accompanied by Roger, he was able to stand and view the last products of his great mind and great team but was too ill to climb on to the footplates.

The effort expended in this long arduous journey must have seriously weakened him, but a man of his determination was unlikely to be deterred by such things, despite any concerns his children may have had. Home had become his refuge and to Hertfordshire he returned where Violet continued to care for him. There were still simple pleasures to be had and his

3401's elegant and balanced lines captured on 19 February 1941 at Doncaster. In many ways this engine summed up so much about its designer in chief. It may not have been one of his 'big engines' but it was functional, effective and espoused all he stood for, so was a fitting tribute. Sadly, neither engine survived into preservation, both being scrapped – 3401 in 1957 and 3402 the following year.

daughter recalled, in a letter written to Tom Turner shortly after her father's death, an evening ritual that they followed. After dinner, he would suggest they go out and watch the night express go by. A short journey to an open stretch of line near Hatfield followed and there they would sit listening for the distant sounds of the train. Watching intently, he observed it fly by, checking the time on his pocket watch. As its echoes receded into the distance, they drove home.

Moments of such peace were few and far between in a country continuously under attack by German bombers by then. Any thought of invasion had been deterred for the time being by all the young pilots who had fought so gallantly and died most bravely in the Battle of Britain, but the threat remained and across Europe the blackest cloud continued to spread and the innocent suffered unimaginable horrors. Gresley was spared all this, but died not knowing the outcome of the war, undoubtedly fearing for his nation and his family. Yet all he had worked to achieve would serve his country in its darkest hours.

Looking very old and ill, despite being only 64, Gresley stands looking up at the new V4 in the last official photograph taken of him on duty. Although the picture is of poor quality it has been included for its obvious historic importance.

Arguably Gresley's most famous locomotive, *Mallard*. Even though the World Record Holder for speed she had to 'earn her keep' and would often be rostered to very mundane duties and not simply be reserved for the glamorous express services. Here she is captured with a mixed bag of carriages and wagons slipping into King's Cross just before the War.

The A4s didn't quite make it to the end of steam in 1968 but even before withdrawal they could still look what they were – thoroughbreds. Sadly, *Silver Fox* didn't make it into preservation, being cut up at Doncaster Works in December 1963.

On 5 April 1941, a long threatened cerebral thrombosis finally occurred. A blood clot formed in his dural venous sinuses, cutting the blood supply to his brain. He died a little later with Roger at his side, as he had been 12 years earlier when Ethel passed away. Four days later, he was laid to rest in the cemetery at Netherseal, beside his wife, with his mother, father and brother Arthur close by. Above them all, the oak tree planted by the Reverend Gresley, seven years before Herbert was born, gave them shade. A little later that day, his friends and colleagues gathered at Chelsea Old Church, in London, to which the CME had been a regular visitor over the years, for a memorial service. A week later, it was badly damaged by German bombs, another sign of the old order passing.

EPILOGUE

It was a damp Saturday morning when I pulled off the M42 and drove along country roads to Netherseal. I parked in front of St Peter's Church, only a few yards from the Old Vicarage where Gresley had lived and walked the short distance to the cemetery where he is buried. It is a peaceful spot with only the murmur of cars occasionally passing to break the silence. Just inside the entrance gate is a large sign which describes the life of the village's most famous son and on his memorial cross someone had placed a model of *Mallard* pulling a teak carriage.

A gentleman in the local shop told me that I was one of a number of visitors who made a pilgrimage to the village each month and left mementoes on his grave. These were periodically removed when the grass was cut, but usually involved an A4 locomotive and occasionally a duck. For someone who died so long ago, this is quite remarkable. He wasn't royalty or a prime minister of note or a war hero or someone whose work had changed the world or our lives and yet his memory still resonates and means a great deal to many people. To reinforce this we have two iconic locomotives – *Mallard* and *Flying Scotsman* – that

Netherseal Cemetery. Gresley's grave is graced by a model of Mallard and is within sight and sound of the places where he played and worshipped as a young boy. Ethel lies to his right.

continue to transcend time and act as reminders of all he and his team achieved. But does the myth outweigh the reality of his life and accomplishments? Over the years, some have questioned his successes, none more so than Robert Riddles, a leading light in the LMS, who rose to become British Railway's first Chief Mechanical Engineer. In an authorised biography, by H.C.B. Rogers, he allowed the following words to remain, suggesting they were his:

> 'On the LNER Gresley, great engineer though he was, embarked on a policy which was the very antithesis of the Churchward school. Though he was forced to follow Churchward's ideas to obtain the best results from his own locomotives, he never attempted any standardisation. His engines were frequently "tailor-made" to meet local conditions; and he designed a range of engine classes which were mostly fitted with three-cylinders and a valve gear that was difficult to maintain. There was on the LNER no general purpose mixed traffic engine, such as Stanier's Class 5, until Edward Thompson, who succeeded Gresley, produced his excellent B1 class 4-6-0.'

And later he added two more comments:

> 'If Vincent Raven had become CME of the LNER instead of Gresley the whole main line between King's Cross and Edinburgh might have been electrified before the War.'

> 'Gresley's Pacifics required considerable modification before they were really good.'

'Is that the best you can do, surely the man deserved a greater accolade than that?' was my initial thought on reading Riddles-Rogers' book. But he wasn't alone in thinking or expressing

Gresley's K4, *The Great Marquess*, which rolled out of Darlington Works in July 1938 and survived into preservation.

A sight very familiar to the LNER's many followers in the four years before war came. A near pristine *Silver Fox*, her tender apparently near empty, inspection panels open, is turned at King's Cross ready to be serviced and returned to duty.

similar thoughts. In his book *Speaking of Steam*, Ernest Cox, another locomotive engineer of note, reviewed Gresley's work and found barely anything praiseworthy to note, other than his advocacy of the national test centre. His words are littered with such things as:

> 'All who are interested in locomotives have their own pet hobby horses, the inmates of railway design offices as much as any other….Gresley was no exception, and his addiction to the use of three cylinders for everything was an abiding obsession. Similarly, he thought nothing of the Belpaire firebox. Not only would he not use it on any of his own creations, but he aimed to get rid of it as replacement boilers were required on engines which he inherited.'

> 'It would seem abundantly clear from the evidence which remains that the conjugated valve gear was wholly Holcroft's….Whether Gresley thought he had made a new and personal deviation by placing the 2 in 1 levers in front of the cylinders, instead of behind as Holcroft advocated cannot be known, but the fact is equally clear that Gresley came to think of this gear as his own.'

> 'Gresley, like many other innovators, found that his own work had been forestalled by a previous patent.'

> 'Gresley was so imbued with the blood, sweat and tears which had been expended in bringing his machine (in this case W1) to a viable outcome, that for him, it was desirable that a full description of the engine with the nature of initial difficulties overcome was made public as soon as possible. This was not what the engineering world was really waiting for

Gresley knew the value of a good headline and encouraged wide circulation of photographs such as this one involving 4472, *Flying Scotsman*. Although the locomotive was a noteworthy development and made records, a steady flow of publicity probably promoted its status to a level far above its accomplishments. The picture also captures Gresley's joy of being on the footplate and the ease of his relationship with crew and VIPs alike.

and some disappointment was expressed during the subsequent discussions.'

There were other engineers who expressed similar views, but these were not, or so it seems, shared by his own team. But are these fair assessments or simply opinions that fail to take account of the conditions and problems Gresley faced at the time? Or could they be the product of professional jealousy, given credence by the application of beneficial hindsight? In Riddles' and Cox's case this might well be so. In the aftermath of war, when nationalisation took hold of Britain's railways, these two men were chiefly responsible for continuing a policy of building

A regular part of W1's life – static testing.

steam locomotives in huge numbers and ignoring other solutions. In so doing, they set back the cause of diesel and electric locomotives by a decade or more. It was an action that led to the ludicrous situation of locomotives being built then scrapped in only a few years. Each in their own way deflected criticism of their work by pointing the finger at Gresley, forgetting that conditions in the 1920s and '30 were hardly conducive to such a huge investment. Yet to prove he was a moderniser, one only has to look at his continuous support of electrification from early in the 1920s. And when conditions changed, and Government sponsorship seemed likely, he was the first to encourage and initiate a substantial electrification programme, only to see it forestalled by the war. As Bert Spencer wryly observed, Gresley might have been a far better man to lead BR into the future than Riddles.

The criticisms of his locomotives also seem disingenuous. Amalgamation created significant problems for the LMS and LNER as both inherited a huge mixture of types and classes with little or no commonality. Each constituent company also attempted to perpetuate the principles that had served them so well. Tribal loyalties remained and continued to distort locomotive development, making a single cohesive policy very difficult to achieve. By force of personality, Gresley managed to bring some order to this muddle, but he was limited in what he could do by the parlous state of the railways and lack of funds. For the LMS, it would take until the mid-1930s to achieve some harmony. Gresley, to his great credit, did it much more quickly and in the process set in train a development programme that succeeded in producing some of the finest locomotives ever to run in this country. He may have demonstrated a stubborn attachment to three cylinders or pursued streamlining too far, but, as Bert Spencer observed:

'They did their jobs very well and proved economical and effective in practice. Three cylinders had many advantages over two (greater hauling power and an increase in mean tractive effort) and these outweighed

A3 No 2501, *Colombo*, shortly after entering traffic in July 1934. She was withdrawn from service 30 years later and scrapped in January 1965.

the complication introduced…. Streamlining was seen by many as a meaningless fashion and condemned it for that reason. Yet it was a science still in its infancy, with future applications then barely glimpsed. Gresley saw its potential, as he did many things, and began the process of experimentation with the A4s proving its worth.'

To the end of his life Spencer didn't waiver in his views, and he was no sycophant, and held to the assessment he produced in 1947, particularly on the benefits of three-cylinders and streamlining.

Some of the criticisms may not simply be explained by the restrictions he faced or Spencer's strong advocacy of his work. He was, without doubt, an ambitious and possibly a ruthless man; no one who reaches the top does so without displaying these characteristics. This may have been why he claimed credit for work that was rightfully Holcroft's, or, for that matter, any design that his team may have produced under his direction. However, this is a very difficult issue to consider or judge, because of the damning issues they contain of plagiarism and unearned credit. Perhaps the simplest way of judging this issue is to assume that a leader takes responsibility for all that happens when in charge, so a penalty for failure is theirs, but so is the credit for success. It is a tough regime but no one who worked for him took the opportunity to broach this issue publicly when he was alive or dead and this suggests it wasn't of concern to them. And each man who recorded his thoughts, enshrined their deep respect and admiration for him in their words.

On the moral question of 'adopting' other people's ideas, altering them then taking credit, the issue is clouded by the nature of science and invention itself. Engineering contains many examples of seemingly unrelated discoveries being brought together to create new, probably unguessed outcomes. The Wright Brothers didn't invent each part of the first powered aircraft, but they did absorb lessons learnt and discoveries made in a number of fields. Their skill lay in spotting the potential of different inventions and combining them successfully to achieve manned flight at Kitty Hawk in 1903. Likewise, neither Holcroft or Gresley invented the steam locomotive, or their many parts, they simply developed ideas, from many sources, then attempted to take them to a new level. So where does the credit really lie and who can rightfully claim ownership of an idea, especially in a highly competitive world, where incremental advances can barely be measured at times? It is a grey area, but I don't think sufficient 'evidence' exists to allow Gresley's reputation to be tarnished by such an accusation. In any case, his accomplishments were far wider than this one issue. So it is important to view the totality of what he achieved, often in the most trying circumstances, to fully understand his greatness, for that is what it was; and engineering was only one part of this.

When writing about someone so famous, who has been the subject of many books and articles, but who wrote so little himself, it is difficult to see that person clearly. When standing by his grave, I hoped to find a way through all these words, the descriptions conveyed and opinions expressed. It was no easy task. To some he was a sociable, warm and generous man, whilst to others he could appear distant and autocratic. This was only the tip of the iceberg of often mingled, conflicting thoughts. To a certain extent, each of us has myriad roles to play in our lives, so being all things to all people is a basic human condition. For a leader, this is even more so and this might explain many of the contradictions contained in peoples' memories of him.

Having carefully read most things that Gresley wrote, or which have been written about him, the descriptions I think most closely seem to reflect this exceptional man tend to fall into a number of categories. You have the family man, who was loving and considerate. Then there is the scientist and engineer displaying an enquiring and analytical mind, with a willingness to seek and explore new solutions and not be hidebound by tradition or bias. He was also a pragmatist who balanced all factors before reaching the best possible solution in the circumstances, even though his scientific mind craved more exploration. Pragmatism is an essential part of being a business man, who has to move and shape an organisation to produce a profit as well as plan for the future. Not for him the comfort of state sponsorship or the weakness of

political masters, but a much harder, colder world. Yet, it was an environment that seemed to suit him.

In a later age, he would be called a 'mover and shaker', or someone of substance who initiates events and has a major influence on all developments. And for this you need immense self-confidence and assurance, superb personal skills, an ability to communicate and debate successfully, possess a keen grasp of politics and economics and much, much more. Few have these skills and even fewer exercise them as effectively as Gresley did throughout his career and this ensured that even in decline, few could challenge his decisions. As Bert Spencer again observed, the CME had an openness to new ideas if presented in a clear and reasoned way and it was in fulfilling this role that his long-time assistant excelled.

Spencer more than anyone else seems to have been able to gauge Gresley's moods and needs correctly. He used his considerable

A3 No. 2565/60066, *Merry Hampton*, still draws a group of admirers in the early 1960s. She was condemned in September 1963 and cut up a few days later at Doncaster.

1930s glamour comes to Scarborough.

to think and develop new ideas without disturbance. But he was also a very clever engineer who could contribute much to Gresley's designs. Being respected, he could diplomatically discuss alternatives and be listened to very intently. The length of lap gear debate, shortly after the A1s were introduced, was just such an occasion and Spencer's suggestion, which Gresley eventually accepted, made a good locomotive even better. The lesson once learnt went on to influence designs that followed and contributed greatly to their success. His quiet manner and able assistance contributed to Gresley's immense success in a largely unrecognised way.

Spencer wasn't alone in this, because the CME had managed to surround himself with many other men of great skill. This was in itself a rare ability and says something more about the man himself. He was an astute leader, supporting, cajoling, advising and admonishing in a balanced way and this helped guarantee a smooth transition in 1923 and effective performances through the 1930s and '40s. William Stanier, who inherited a 'dog's dinner of a mess' with the LMS, as he described it, when becoming CME in 1932, could only look on with envy.

With Gresley's death, the old order came to an end as a new regime took hold, though some of his most trusted associates had already left the scene. Thom, who for so long had played a pivotal role as Mechanical Engineer at Doncaster, enjoyed a long retirement at his home in North Yorkshire and died there in 1955. Harry Broughton was not so lucky.

engineering and management skills to support his greatly admired leader by constant and educated support. Spencer without Gresley is unthinkable, but so, I believe, is Gresley without Spencer. It may not have been a partnership of equals, but Spencer provided an essential filter that worked in a number of ways. On one level, it gave the CME protection from the minutiae of daily life, allowing him

It seems that he was ill when ceasing to be Chief Draughtsman in 1935 and survived only a few short years. His replacement, Tom Street, only remained in post until 1941. When Thompson was appointed CME, the General Manager decided to create a new Chief Electrical Engineer, with Richards in charge, and Street became CD in this new group. He retired in the late 1940s, as BR formed, and died in June 1952 at home in Doncaster without fanfare. The leading part he played in the A4's design was largely forgotten. His successor, Edward Windle, remained in post until the last days of the LNER and then transferred to British Railways where he became part of the design team for BR's Standard class locomotives. He died in November 1960 at his home in Sprotborough.

Bulleid went on to greater glory with the Southern Railway, where his Pacifics caused much controversy and, as some would say, his behaviour became more eccentric. A slow political eviction by Riddles and Co when BR was formed took place and Bulleid resigned to become CME of Coras Iompar Eireann in Ireland. In retirement he lived in Devon but then moved to Malta where he died suddenly on 25 April 1970, having seen most of his Pacifics rebuilt then scrapped.

Bert Spencer never quite recovered from Gresley's death. He would serve both Thompson and Peppercorn when they became CME, in 1941 and 1946 respectively, conscientiously. However, he didn't retain the privileged position he enjoyed with Gresley. When BR was formed he managed the 1948 locomotive

'**They also** serve'. Although most attention fell on the likes of *Mallard* and *Flying Scotsman*, the main work of the railways was undertaken by engines such as this N2. No. 2674/69580 was built, under contract, by Hawthorn Leslie in 1929 and worked commuter services into King's Cross for most of her life. In 1960, she transferred to Grantham and was scrapped, at Doncaster, in September 1961.

P2 No. 2001 well into her stride. At the time of writing, the seventh of the class is being constructed and will, in due course, re-enact this 1930s scene.

exchange trials in which engines from each of the four regions were tested and compared. The aim was to establish best practice before building BR's new Standard range of locomotives. At the same time, he played a leading role in designing Peppercorn's A1 and A2 engines, which made their first appearance in 1948.

When Peppercorn retired in 1949, Spencer remained with the Eastern Region of BR. Until the mid-1950s, he continued in an advisory role using his considerable skills and experience to assist in the design of 'the Standards' but also the new generation of diesel and electric locomotives. He and his wife retired to Shaldon in Devon and he lived there until 20 July 1968 when he suffered a cardiac arrest and died. Oliver Bulleid's house was only a few miles away on the other side of the Exe Estuary, but it seems they weren't close and didn't meet or keep in contact, though they shared the same offices for 15 years or more. A comment Eric Bannister recorded may explain why this was so:

> 'A very clever man, Bulleid was rather eccentric and he had some strange ideas. Indeed, he seemed to have a new one every week and of these, one in a year would be brilliant….BS used to say, "What other mad idea has he got?".… His ideas, many of which wouldn't work, are typical of some of his Southern engines. Some of these were good in many ways but, like him, a bit eccentric.'

Spencer and Bulleid were both good engineers but cut from different cloth and approached their work very differently. They seem to have supported Gresley in isolation of each other with the CME providing the linkage. While Spencer provided close support, the more ebullient Bulleid – though some thought him a 'loose cannon' – moved around a great deal dabbling in particular projects. Two such men are unlikely to have found common ground and this seems to have been the case.

With the war raging, Gresley's team disbanded and found new masters to serve and mountains

Gresley's legacy still running effectively in BR's colours.

184 of Gresley's V2 Class were built and have been described as being essential to Britain's war effort, such was their pulling power. Here No. 60885 awaits another turn of duty in the early 1960s, the rain giving her a polished look despite the grime. She was scrapped in October 1965.

to climb. But one thing seems certain; the golden age they had experienced with him wouldn't be repeated and would forever remain the high spot of their careers. So to end this book, and summarise Gresley's life and work, it is fitting to quote the words of the three men who sat beside him at King's Cross and lived each of his triumphs and each of the low spots in his life:

'The effect of that first interview remained with me until the end of my working life. By his patience and willingness to listen to a raw recruit he won my loyalty and respect. He made me want to give him all the help I could – and that unsparingly.'
Eric Bannister.

'He was a great man, scientist and leader. But like all great men he was a pragmatist and told us "when you run out of ideas then copy the best"; very good advice.'
Oliver Bulleid (as told to John Click when the SR's CME).

'I admired Sir Nigel tremendously and never found him inconsiderate or too busy to listen and discuss my ideas. He had the ability to think broadly and absorb a great deal of information before reaching conclusions. He sought the advice of those he respected and would always consider other possibilities, modifying his own plans accordingly if the arguments put forward held value. But once a decision was made he pursued a course of action with great determination,

Some of Gresley's achievements as summarized by Spencer. Locomotives were, of course, only one part of his work as CME.

taking stock and reviewing progress all the time.

'When a job was complete he insisted on a programme of testing to make sure the locomotive was as good as it could be and used whatever information he collected to modify the design. It was a constant frustration to him that the authorities were so tardy in building a test centre where better solutions might have been developed. He believed that Churchward achieved greater success because the GWR invested in such a facility and the LNER struggled to match their achievements because we had none.

'He inspired confidence and led us all with a sure touch, often in very difficult circumstances. He was a great man and it was a privilege to work for him. At the end of my presentation in 1947 I summarised all his new locomotive designs for the GNR and LNER in a single table. Although not everything he did was included, I felt that this would speak for itself in describing his greatest achievements. I don't think there was another designer except, perhaps, Churchward, who accomplished so much.

'I was lucky enough to see the CME's ideas on electrification finally come to fruition after the war and see his influence continue to spread. Whilst his steam locomotives clearly pleased him I have no doubt that he would have been proud to have witnessed the Shenfield line open and the electric locomotives he planned come in to service and move Britain's railways into the future.'

Bert Spencer.

LEADING DIMENSIONS OF G.N.R. AND L.N.E.R. LOCOMOTIVES.

	Date built	Cylinders. Dia. × stroke. in. in.	Coupled wheel dia. ft. in.	Boiler pressure, lbs. per sq. in.	Heating surfaces, sq. ft. Tubes.	Firebox.	Total.	Supr.	Grate area, sq. ft.	T.E. at 85% B.P. lb.	Weight in working order. Engine T. C. Q.	Engine and Tender. T. C. Q.
G.N.R.												
Class O.2, 2-8-0 tender (No. 461)	1918	3 18 × 26	4 8	180	1868.5	163.5	2032	430.5	27.5	34523	76 8 0	119 10 0
,, K.3, 2-6-0 ,, (No. 1000)	1920	3 18½ × 26	5 8	180	1719	182	1901	407	28	30031	71 14 0	114 16 0
,, O.2, 2-8-0 ,, (No. 477)	1921	3 18½ × 26	4 8	180	1868.5	163.5	2032	430.5	27.5	36470	75 16 0	118 18 0
,, A.1, 4-6-2 ,, (No. 1470)	1922	3 20 × 26	6 8	180	2715	215	2930	525	41.25	29835	92 9 0	148 15 0
L.N.E.R.												
Class P.1, 2-8-2 tender	1925	3 20 × 26	5 2	180	2715	215	2930	525	41.25	38500	100 0 0	151 8 0
,, U.1, 2-8-8-2 "Garratt"	1925	6 18½ × 26	4 8	180	2504	223.5	2727.5	650	56.5	72940	178 0 3	- - -
,, J.38, 0-6-0 tender	1926	2 20 × 26	4 8	180	1283.25	171.5	1454.75	289.6	26	28414	58 19 0	103 3 0
,, J.39, 0-6-0 ,,	1926	2 20 × 26	5 2	180	1226.28	171.5	1397.78	271.8	26	25664	57 17 0	102 1 0
,, D.49, 4-4-0 ,, piston valves	1927	3 17 × 26	6 8	180	1226.28	171.5	1397.78	271.8	26	21556	66 0 0	118 0 0
,, D.49, 4-4-0 ,, O.C. poppet valves	1928	3 17 × 26	6 8	180	1226.28	171.5	1397.78	271.8	26	21556	65 14 0	117 14 0
,, D.49, 4-4-0 ,, R.C. ,, ,,	1929	3 17 × 26	6 8	180	1226.28	171.5	1397.78	271.8	26	21556	64 10 0	116 10 0
,, A.3, 4-6-2 ,,	1928	3 19 × 26	6 8	220	2477	215	2692	706	41.25	32909	96 5 0	152 11 0
,, B.17, 4-6-0 ,,	1928	3 17½ × 26	6 8	200	1508	168	1676	344	27.5	25380	77 5 0	116 13 0
,, W.1, 4-6-4 ,,	1929 {	4 HP(2)10 × 26 LP(2)20 × 26	6 8	450	1067	919	1986	140	34.95	32000	103 12 0	166 0 0
,, W.1, 4-6-4 ,, (rebuilt)	1937	3 20 × 26	6 8	250	2345.1	252.5	2597.6	748.9	50	41437	107 17 0	172 16 0
,, V.1, 2-6-2 tank	1930	3 16 × 26	5 8	180	1198	127	1325	284	22.08	22464	86 16 0	- - -
,, P.2, 2-8-2 tender, R.C. poppet valves	1934	3 21 × 26	6 2	220	2477	237	2714	776.5	50	43462	110 5 0	165 11 0
,, P.2, 2-8-2 ,, piston valves	1934	3 21 × 26	6 2	220	2477	237	2714	776.5	50	43462	107 3 0	167 10 0
,, A.4, 4-6-2 ,,	1935	3 18½ × 26	6 8	250	2345.1	231.2	2576.3	748.9	41.25	35455	102 19 0	167 18 0
,, V.2, 2-6-2 ,,	1936	3 18½ × 26	6 2	220	2216	215	2431	679.7	41.25	33730	93 2 0	145 2 0
,, K.4, 2-6-0 ,,	1937	3 18½ × 26	5 2	200	1253.6	168	1421.6	310.0	27.5	36599	68 8 0	112 12 0
,, V.3, 2-6-2 tank	1939	3 16 × 26	5 8	200	1198	127	1325	284	22.08	24960	86 16 0	- - -
,, V.4, 2-6-2 tender	1941	3 15 × 26	5 8	250	1292.5	151.6	1444.1	355.8	28.5	27420	70 8 0	113 3 0

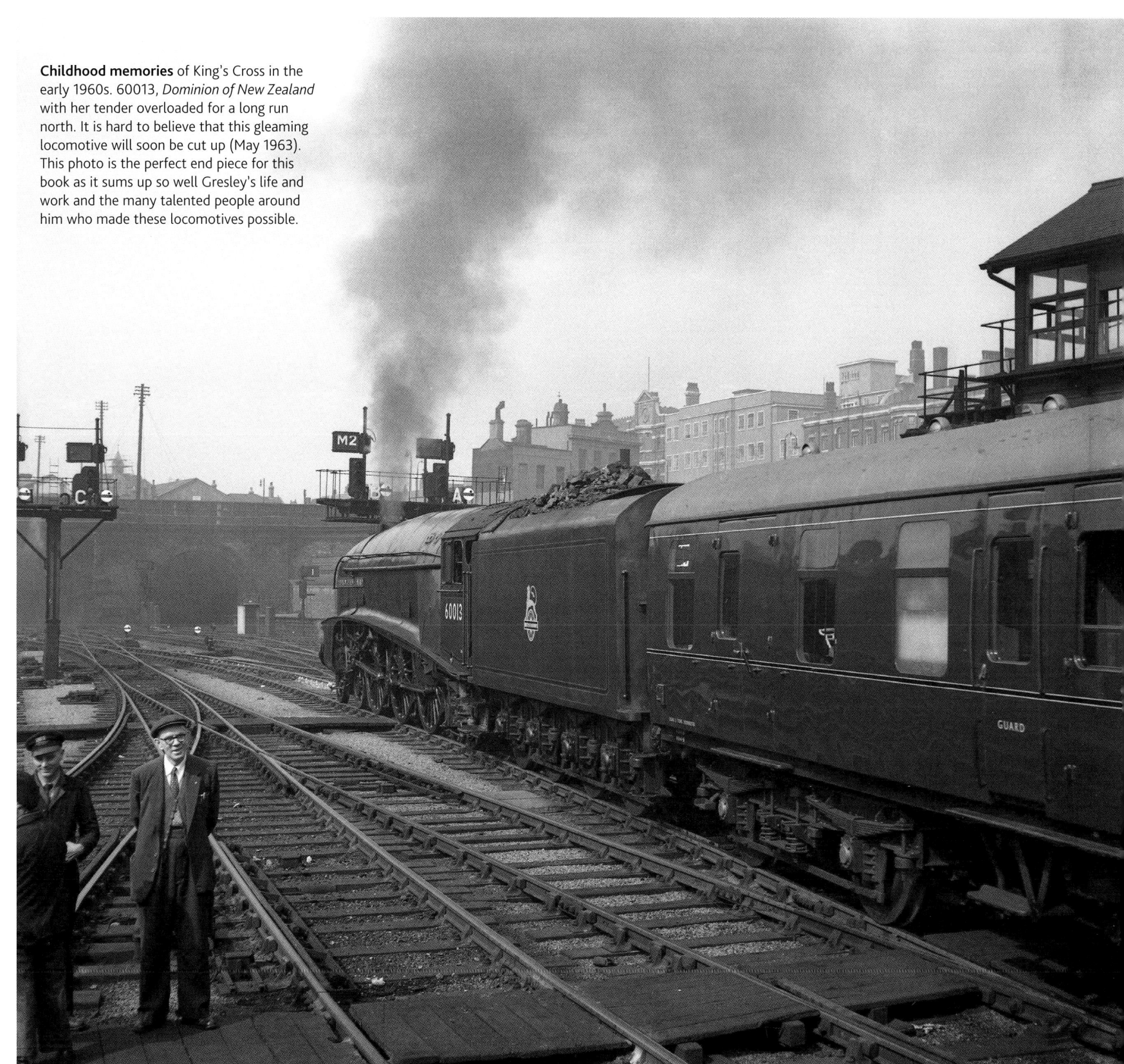

Childhood memories of King's Cross in the early 1960s. 60013, *Dominion of New Zealand* with her tender overloaded for a long run north. It is hard to believe that this gleaming locomotive will soon be cut up (May 1963). This photo is the perfect end piece for this book as it sums up so well Gresley's life and work and the many talented people around him who made these locomotives possible.

Perhaps Gresley's true legacy – the beginnings of a modern transport system for the twenty-first century.

SOURCES

The National Railway Museum (Search Engine)
Records Consulted
Corr/LNER/1 to 6.
Calc/LNER/1
Loco/LNER/1 to 9.
Spec/Don/7
Spec/LNER/1 to 7.
Test/LNER/1 to 10.

The E.S. Cox Collection.
The R. Riddles Collection.
The Immingham Collection. } Donated to Search Engine by the author

The National Archives (On line 'Discovery' Programme)
Various files relating to Frederick Johansen's research work.

Other Collections
R A Hillier.
A R Ewer.
T F Coleman/M Lemon.
B Spencer.
J Click.
H A V Bulleid.
R A Thom.
N Newsome.
H Holcroft.
T H Turner.
F A S Brown.
Dr P Ransome-Wallis.
David Neal

Newspapers and Journals
IMechE/ILocoE Journals
The Engineer
The Gazette
Meccano Magazine
Backtrack

Books
ALLEN and Bursley, Heat Engines, Macgraw-Hill, 1941.
BANNISTER, Eric, *Trained By Sir Nigel Gresley,* Dalesman Publishing, 1984.
BOND, Roland, *A Lifetime With Locomotives*, Goose and Son, 1975.
BROWN, F.A.S., *Nigel Gresley. Locomotive Engineer*, Ian Allan, 1961.

BULLEID, H.A.V., *Bulleid of the Southern,* Littlehampton Book Services, 1977.
BULLEID, H.A.V., *Master Builders of Steam,* Ian Allan, 1963.
BULLEID, H.A.V., *The Aspinall Era,* Ian Allan, 1967.
BUSH, Donald J., *The Streamlined Decade,* George Brazillier, 1975.
COSTER, Peter, *Book of the A3 Pacifics,* Irwell Press, 2003.
COSTER, Peter, *Book of the A4 Pacifics,* Irwell Press, 2005.
COSTER, Peter, *Book of the V2 2-6-2s,* Irwell Press, 2008.
COX, E.S., *Chronicles of Locomotives,* Ian Allan, 1967.
COX, E.S., *Locomotive Panorama Vols 1 and 2,* Ian Allan, 1965/66.
COX, E.S., *Speaking of Steam,* Littlehampton Book Services, 1971.
DALBY, William Ernest, *The Balancing of Engines (reprint),* Forgotten Books, 2012.
HARESNAPE, Brian, *Gresley's Locomotives,* Ian Allan, 1981.
HOLCROFT, H., *Locomotive Adventure Vols 1 and 2,* Ian Allan, 1962.
HUGHES, Geoffrey, *Sir Nigel Gresley: the engineer and his family,* Oakwood Press, 2001.
JOHANSEN, Frederick, Handbook of Aeronautics, Pitmans, 1934.
NOCK, O.S., *Locomotives of Sir Nigel Gresley,* Railway Publishing Co., 1945.
POPE A, Wind Tunnel Testing, Wiley, 1947.
SIMMONS, Jack, *The Victorian Railway,* Thames and Hudson, 1995.
ROGERS, H.C.B., *The Last Steam Locomotive Engineer,* Allen and Unwin, 1970.
TOWNEND, P.N., *East Coast Pacifics at Work,* Littlehampton Book Services, 1982.
W B YEADON, Registers Nos 1, 2, 3, 4, 5, 8, 9, 10 and 25, BLR, various dates.

Photographic Sources/Credits

B Spencer (BS), R Hillier (RH), T Colman/Mike Lemon, (TC/ML), Author (THG), H A V Bulleid (HB), F Johansen (FJ), H Holcroft (HH), LNER Journal (LJ), LNER PR (PR), A Ewer (AE), J Click (JC), R Thom (RT), N Newsome (NN), BR PR (BR), and David Neal (DN).

Copyright is a complex issue and often difficult to establish, especially when a photograph or document exists in a number of public and private collections. Strenuous efforts have been made to ensure each item is correctly attributed, but no process is flawless, especially when many of these items are more than 70 years old with photographers or authors long gone. If an error has been made, it was unintentional. If any reader wishes to affirm copyright, please contact the publishers and an acknowledgement will be included in any future edition of this book, should a claim be proven. We apologise in advance for any mistakes.

PHOTO CREDITS

BS – 9, 20, 32, 77, 83, 86, 120, 121, 124, 125, 133, 134, 135, 136, 150, 152, 154, 156, 159, 161, 176, 177, 178, 180, 195, 210, 216, 217, 225, 226, 227 and 244.

RH – 7, 8, 11, 14, 46, 48, 49, 50, 51, 52, 56, 61, 62, 63, 69, 70, 71, 73, 74, 78, 81, 82, 83, 84, 88, 89, 94, 98, 102, 109, 111, 112, 114, 115, 116, 119, 120, 122, 128, 129, 132, 143, 144145, 151, 158, 159, 160, 162, 163, 164, 166, 168, 169, 170, 171, 172, 174, 179, 181, 182, 184, 185, 186, 188, 191, 192, 196, 198, 201, 202, 206, 207, 208, 214, 218, 230, 231, 233, 234, 237, 238, 242, 243, 250, 251, 253, 254, 255, 256, 257, 259, 261, 268, 272, 273, 277, 278, 283 and 288.

TC/ML – 12, 44, 45, 54, 187, 189, 190, 213 and 229.

THG – 16, 17, 18, 22, 23, 26, 27, 35, 36, 37.39, 40, 41, 42, 43, 53, 55, 60, 61, 64, 65, 67, 71, 92, 95, 97, 100, 101, 104, 106, 116, 117, 121, 130, 131, 138, 140, 142, 147, 153, 167, 173, 175, 183, 197, 198, 204, 205, 212, 223, 235, 241, 245, 246, 249, 252, 255, 262, 264, 265, 270, 274, 275, 276, 278, 279, 281, 283, 284, 285 and 287.

HB – 19, 20, 193 and 194.

FJ – 155 and 199.

HH – 85 and 267.

LJ – 12, 13, 23, 57, 105, 131, 141, 146, 211, 212, 238, 239 and 273.

PR – 7, 8, 11, 12, 13, 28, 32, 34, 61, 79, 80, 82, 83, 88, 89, 91, 96, 99, 109, 111, 112, 114, 115, 117, 119, 122, 128, 129, 141, 143, 144, 158, 159, 160, 162, 168, 169, 170, 179, 180, 181, 182, 184, 185, 186, 188, 191, 192, 201, 207, 208, 214, 218, 225, 226, 230, 231, 237, 242, 243, 253, 258, 260, 261 and 266.

AE – 232.

JC – 233.

RT – 113, 118, 123, 127, 133, 140, 142, 149, 157, 165, 203, 219, 221, 222 and 219.

NN – 258.

BR – 288.

DN – 15, 24, 25, 30, 58, 59, 66, 93, 103, 107, 110, 224, 236, 240, 247, 248, 249, 267 and 271.

INDEX

ACFI – 130-133, 176, 182.
Accrington Municipal Technical School – 19.
Adams, Frederick – 204, 206.
Adams, William – 151.
ALCO – 121, 123, 267.
Allen, Cecil – 151, 250.
Altoona Test Centre – 95, 152.
Ardsley – 29, 59, 64.
ARLE – 70, 138, 238.
Armstrong, J – 38.
Art Deco – 170, 173, 174, 197, 203, 204, 224, 262.
Articulation – 65, 66, 165, 166, 222.
Aspinall, J – 21, 51-56, 70, 151, 169.

Baker, P.S – 13, 30.
Baldwin Locomotive Works – 59, 80, 92.
Bannister, Eric – 198, 215, 216, 259-261, 266, 284, 285.
Barham House Prep School – 36, 38.
Barrington-Ward, Victor (Sir) – 182.
Barton Wright, W – 54.
Beames, Hewitt – 10, 44, 52, 138.
Bell, G (Rev) – 40, 41.
Bell, Robert – 104.
Belpaire – 53-55, 75.
Beyer Peacock – 24, 28, 52, 90, 124, 127, 207.
Bel Geddes, Norman – 204.
Billington, J – 21, 52.
Bond, Roland – 33, 108.
Breda, Ernesto – 173, 174.
British Empire Exhibition – 115, 116.
Brown, W – 13.
Broughton, Harry – 13, 18, 96, 175, 176, 178, 189, 282.
Brunel, I K – 38.

Budd Company Zephyr – 174, 175.
Bugatti, Etorre – 171, 172, 173, 202.
Bugatti Factory – 171.
Bugatti Railcar – 171, 173.
Bulleid, Henry – 6, 105, 108, 194.
Bulleid, O V S – 6, 8, 12, 13, 19-24, 29, 47, 90, 105-108, 118, 129, 138, 154, 156, 168, 170, 174-178, 187, 189, 192, 194, 195, 202, 216, 220, 222, 239, 244, 245, 271, 282, 284.
Bury, Oliver – 67, 71.

Cambridge University – 28, 29, 36, 72, 151.
Camlet House – 104, 106, 147.
Cassidy, M (Sir) – 144, 145.
Canadian Pacific (2-10-4 Class 'Selkirk') 145-147.
Chalmers, Walter – 104.
Chapelon, Andre – 118-120, 129, 139, 147, 176, 183, 201, 202, 267.
Churchward, George – 8, 17, 38, 39, 71, 80, 81, 82, 92-94, 238, 286.
Clayton, John – 8, 87.
Click, John – 192, 285.
Clifton College – 38.
Cocks, Clifford – 241.
Colman, Tom Francis – 6, 8, 18, 54, 93, 190, 199, 200, 229.
Colwick Loco Depot – 29, 64.
Cook, A F – 120.
Cowlairs – 33, 202.
Cox, E S – 6, 33, 277, 278.
Crewe Mechanics Institute – 44.
Crewe Works – 10, 43-47.

Dalby, W E (Prof) – 151, 152, 154.
Darlington Works – 25-28, 33, 104, 123, 127, 135, 144, 152, 153, 157, 202, 235, 242, 250.

Davey, Paxman & Co – 120.
Day, Frank – 108, 220.
Dean, William – 38, 80.
Delaware & Hudson Railway – 123, 148.
Doncaster Works – 21, 23, 28, 29, 56, 86, 87, 90, 95, 96, 102, 104, 106, 108, 111, 118, 126, 135-137, 175, 178, 185, 187, 188, 202, 207, 215, 218-221, 240-242, 250, 274.
Doncaster Technical College – 20, 29, 33.
Dorpmuller, Julius (Dr) – 264, 265.
Douglas, Emily – 38.
Dreyfus, Henry – 204, 205.
DRG Class 05 – 171, 204, 226, 257, 258, 263.
DRG Class 06 – 267, 268.
Drummond, Dugald – 71.
Duncan, William – 139.

Edge, Douglas R – 13, 245, 259, 260-262.
Eggleshaw, F – 13.
Electrification (GNR & LNER) – 25, 26, 209-211, 230-237, 244.
Ells, Sam – 8.
Elwess, William – 18.
Engineer Magazine – 22, 40, 95, 247.
Ewer, Alfred – 219.

Fiennes, Gerald – 209, 210.
First of the Few (Film) – 13.
'Flying Hamburger' (SVT 877) – 171, 173, 200, 205-207, 215.
'Flying Scotsman' – 32, 115, 141, 160, 211, 212, 251, 275, 278.
Fowler, Henry – 52, 71, 138, 152.
'Fury' No.6399 – 152.

Gateshead – 28, 149.
Geddes, Eric (Sir) – 97, 101.
General Strike (1926) – 127.
Germany (and Nazism) – 147, 148, 170, 202, 215, 239, 257, 258, 263.
Glaze, Charles – 104.
Glazebrook, R – 72.
Gooch, Daniel – 39, 245.
Gorton – 23, 122.
Gough, H J (Dr) – 195.
Gray, D D – 240.
Great Central Railway (GCR) – 23, 59, 80, 98.
Great Eastern Railway (GER) – 44, 96, 98, 123, 130, 137.
Great Southern and Western Railway (GSWR) – 21, 56, 57.
Great Western Railway (GWR) – 38, 39, 80, 82, 92, 97, 115, 116, 124-126, 139, 196, 238.
Gresley, Arthur – 37.
Gresley, Beatrice – 37, 238.
Gresley (nee Fullager), Ethel – 52, 144, 145, 274, 275.
Gresley, George – 37.
Gresley, Joanna – 34, 51.
Gresley, Marjorie – 67, 159.
Gresley, Nigel (Rev) – 36, 40-42, 144, 274.
Gresley, Nigel (Brother) – 37.
Gresley, Nigel (Son) – 67.
Gresley, Roger – 67, 233, 272, 274.
Gresley, Violet – 67, 145, 146, 159, 238, 272.
Gutteridge, H – 213.

Harper, H – 13, 266.
Hartley, Harold (Sir) – 195, 200, 201, 219.
Hawker – 155, 219, 220.
Heen & Froude Ltd – 265.
Helmholtz Truck – 193.
Henschel and Sohn AG – 172.
Herbert, Thomas – 72, 201.
Heywood, Tom – 104.
Hibberling – 216.
Hill, Alfred – 46, 97, 100, 123, 130.
Hockley, Alexander – 233.

Holcroft, Harold – 82, 85-87, 263, 277, 280.
Hopkins, Alfred – 233.
Hoy, H – 52.
Hughes, George – 21, 52, 54.

Institution of Civil Engineers (ICE) - 40, 55, 70.
Institution of Electrical Engineers (IEE) – 40, 41, 238.
Institution of Mechanical Engineers (IMechE) – 6, 24, 27, 29, 41, 44, 52, 55, 70, 73, 82, 83, 109, 135, 147, 148, 151, 169, 172, 196, 198, 205, 238.
Institution of Locomotive Engineers (ILocoE) – 22, 27, 38, 73, 78, 85, 105, 139, 147, 198, 210, 216, 238, 264.
Ivatt, Henry – 8, 19, 20, 29, 33, 56-61, 64, 67, 68, 75, 175.

Jackson, William (Baron Allerton) – 67, 69, 71.
Johansen, Frederick (Dr) – 6, 72, 139, 140, 155, 156, 168-172, 191, 199, 200, 204.
Joy, David (Joy Valves) – 54, 55, 82, 85.

King's Cross – 7, 33, 56, 62, 64, 85, 102, 103, 106, 108, 126, 136, 137, 141, 154, 174, 176, 181, 187, 205, 207, 213, 216, 224, 230, 238, 251, 263, 273, 285.
Kitson-Clark (Colonel) – 77.
Kuhler, Otto – 204.
Kylchap Exhaust System – 119, 176, 247, 262.
Kylala, Kyosti – 119.

Lancashire, Derbyshire and East Coast Railway – 23.
Lancashire and Yorkshire Railway (LYR) – 21, 51, 56.
Langridge, Eric – 33.
Lehigh Valley Railroad – 91.
Lemon, F A – 44.
Lentz – 120, 134, 176.
Liverpool University – 21, 52.

Livesay, E H – 247-249.
Loewy, R – 204.
Locomotive Classes –
  GER – N7 – 123.
  GNR - A1 – 7, 27, 91-98, 102, 106, 108-110, 114-118, 124-126, 129, 137-143, 150-152, 161, 200, 212.
  Atlantics – 58-62, 66, 72, 75, 94.
  Class 461 – 83.
  H1/H2/H3/H4 – 59, 79-81, 87-89, 93, 111, 112, 118, 126, 164.
  J13 – 89, 250.
  J21/J22/J23 (later LNER JI, J5, J51) – 62, 64, 89, 91.
  J2 – 79.
  K1 – 59, 60.
  N1/N2 – 18, 62, 63, 79, 84, 90, 91, 112, 162.
  O1/O2 – 80-84, 112, 168, 256.
  Steam Railmotor – 65.
  GWR – Castle Class – 115, 116, 124-126.
  Class 2600 – 80.
  Class 2800 – 80, 81.
  Class 4300 – 80.
  Pacific (The Great Bear) – 92-94.
  LNWR – Experiment Class – 48.
  Jubilee Class – 48, 50.
  Precedent Class – 47.
  2-2-2-2 Greater Britain – 47.
  LMS – Princess Royal – 199, 200, 224.
  Princess Coronation – 200, 201, 258.
  LNER – A3 – 7, 132, 140, 148, 161, 170, 192, 200, 201, 216, 220, 220, 229, 242, 243, 279.
  A4 – 11, 32, 33, 140, 148, 161, 170, 173, 194, 196, 199—201, 210, 215-230, 240-247, 252, 258-260.
  B1 – 136, 276.
  B17 – 8, 27, 28, 142, 143, 148, 168, 240, 242, 252-255.
  D49 – 27, 133-135, 142, 143.
  J38 – 27, 64, 127, 128.

J39 – 27, 28, 64, 127-129, 133, 148, 168.
J50/J51 – 89, 112.
KI/K2/K3K4 – 27, 89, 118, 142, 148, 164, 168, 241, 255 257, 276.
P1 – 116-120, 129, 174.
P2 – 9, 21, 33, 107, 118, 132, 174, 176-196, 199, 216, 230, 240, 244, 246-252.
U1 – 122, 124.
V1/V3 – 29, 162-164, 168, 268.
V2 – 28, 29, 192, 241-246, 266, 270, 285.
V4 – 243, 256, 270-272.
W1 – 21, 27, 107, 123, 136, 140, 143, 148, 152-162, 164, 167, 183, 230, 240, 249- 252, 277, 278.
LYR – Class 5 – 54.
  Class 7 – 53.
  Class 30 – 55.
NER - Pacific (under LNER became A2) - 26, 27, 107-112, 148, 149.
London, Brighton and South Coast Railway – 38, 233.
London Midland and Scottish Railway (LMS) – 44, 52, 97, 108, 169, 199-202, 219, 257, 258, 264, 269, 279.
London and North Western Railway (LNWR) – 43-47.
London University – 19, 139, 151.

Mallard – 148, 228, 258, 259-261, 265, 273, 275.
Manning, Wardle and Co – 56.
Maunsell, Richard – 8, 10, 56, 66, 87.
Marlborough College – 28, 36, 40, 41, 72.
Massey, W – 13.
Matthews, Ronald (Sir) – 266.
Maybach – 215.
McKillop, N – 185, 186, 192.
Metropolitan Railway – 23.

Metropolitan-Vickers – 108, 202, 232, 233.
Midland Railway – 28, 38, 59.
Ministry of Transport – 97, 182, 238.
Musgrave, G – 13.

National Physical Laboratory (NSP Teddington) – 72, 140, 154, 155, 172, 195, 200, 218, 238.
Netherseal – 36, 144, 274, 275.
Newsome, Norman – 220.
Newton, Charles (Sir) – 266.
Newton Heath – 55, 56.
North British Railway Company – 23, 114, 130, 142, 152, 164.
North Eastern Railway – 24-26, 98.

Paris-Orleans Line – 176, 187, 188.
Place, Pierre – 183, 196.
Pennsylvania Railroad (L1 and K4 Classes) – 94, 95, 116, 117.
Peppercorn, A H – 8, 10, 13, 29, 93, 229, 282, 284.
Petravel, J – 72.

Railways Act 1921 – 97.
Ransome-Wallis, P (Dr) -263, 270.
Raven, Vincent (Sir) – 25-28, 71, 97, 100, 108-110, 112, 115, 204, 276.
Richards, Henry – 233, 282.
Richardson (Side valves) – 55.
Riddles, Robert – 8, 11, 194, 275, 278, 282.
Robert Gordons College – 23.
Robinson, J – 23, 71, 80, 81, 97, 100, 101.
Robson, R J – 26, 152.
Rossall School – 36.
Royal Engineers – 28, 29.

Salisbury Hall – 198.
Schmidt, W – 54.
Schobelt, C – 24.
Schwarzkopf- Lofter Locomotive – 148.
Sentinel Shunting Locomotives – 148.

South Eastern & Chatham Railway – 85.
South Africa – 52, 233, 234.
Southern Railway – 78, 97, 196, 209, 210, 232, 233, 244, 282.
Sparshatt, William – 211-214.
Spencer, B – 8-10, 13, 17, 20-24, 29, 83, 87, 92, 93, 95, 102, 106, 108, 112, 118, 120, 123, 125-127, 129, 134-136, 139-144, 146, 149, 152, 154, 160-163, 166, 168, 175-178, 180, 187, 190, 191, 194, 195, 198, 202, 206, 211, 215, 216, 220, 227-230, 233, 238, 246, 254, 262, 265-271, 279-282, 284, 286.
Stamer, Arthur – 8, 13, 24-28, 52, 77, 104, 108, 136, 138, 144, 149, 152, 154, 158.
Stanier, William (Sir) – 8, 17, 47, 71, 93, 138, 190, 195, 201, 263-265, 282.
Stanton, Thomas (Sir) – 139, 155, 156.
Stirling, Patrick – 32, 42, 57, 58, 70.
Stokes, J L (Prof) – 238, 239.
Stratford Works – 28, 151, 180, 202.
Street, T – 8, 13, 18, 189, 194, 233, 240, 241, 282.
Supermarine – 72, 155, 200, 219, 220.
Swift, Harry – 233.
Symes, Sandham – 152.

Teague, D – 204.
Thom, R A – 8, 23, 24, 29, 104, 113, 127, 129, 131, 136, 137, 140, 147, 149, 157, 175, 176, 179, 189, 194, 200, 202, 203, 215, 219-221, 235, 236, 239, 245, 282.
Thompson E – 8, 10, 13, 27-30, 41, 90, 104, 235, 245, 272, 276, 282.
Thompson, F – 28, 29, 41.
Thurston, G – 118.
Turner T H – 202, 227, 273.
Turner T (Prof) – 202.

Uniflow Engine – 134, 135, 151.
Union Pacific M-10000 – 174, 175.

Vitry Test Centre – 182, 183, 187, 188, 195.

Wagner, R P (Dr) – 147, 148, 202, 204.
Walschaert – 57, 61, 80, 03.
Watton at Stone – 266.
Webb, F W – 43-52, 54, 56, 57, 151.
Webster, F W – 19.
Webster, Robert – 211-213.
Wedgwood, Ralph (Sir) – 12, 100-102, 108, 125, 210, 212, 226, 231, 266.
Westinghouse – 18.
Whitelaw, William – 23, 100, 101, 125, 136, 210, 211, 215, 266.
Wightman, W – 213.
Winder, O – 55.
Windle, W – 18, 30, 215, 240, 282.
Wintour, Francis – 13, 17, 19, 23, 24, 56, 90, 104, 111, 125, 129.
Woolwich (Royal Ordnance Factory) – 28.

Yarrows – 123, 136, 140, 149, 154, 157, 158.
York – 24, 28, 149, 251.